Poverty
and Society

Poverty and Society

The Growth of the American Welfare State in International Comparison

DANIEL LEVINE

Rutgers University Press
New Brunswick and London

Library of Congress Cataloging-in-Publication Data

Levine, Daniel, 1934–
Poverty and society.

    Bibliography: p.
    Includes index.
    1. Public welfare—United States—History.
2. Public welfare—Great Britain—History. 3. Public
welfare—Germany—History. 4. Public welfare—
Denmark—History. 5. Welfare state—Case studies. I. Title.
HV91.L39   1988   361.6'0973   88-4695
ISBN 0-8135-1337-5
ISBN 0-8135-1353-7 (pbk.)

British Cataloging-in-Publication information available

For SRL

Contents

Acknowledgments

I am grateful to the John S. Guggenheim Memorial Foundation, the Fulbright-Hays Program of the United States, and the Bowdoin College Faculty Research Fund for support of this research.

Clarke Chambers (University of Minnesota), Niels Finn Christiansen (University of Copenhagen), Peter Coleman (University of Illinois, Chicago Circle), Roger Howell (Bowdoin College), Gaston Rimlinger (Rice University), Pat Thane (University of London), Christoph Sachsse (University at Kassel), Florian Tennstedt (University at Kassel), and Robert Wiebe (Northwestern University) have read parts or all of this manuscript to my great advantage, but they are not therefore implicated. I have been fortunate in my research assistants: Virginia Laursen in Denmark, Pia Bungarten in Germany, and Andrew Lightman in the United States. They have all made my research in the periodical literature much more efficient than it otherwise would have been.

Parts of this book, sometimes in different form, have appeared in *Albion, Amerikastudien/American Studies, Comparative Social Research,* and *Comparative Studies in Society and History* (reprinted with the permission of Cambridge University Press) and as a chapter in Florian Tennstedt and Christoph Sachsse (eds.), *Soziale Sicherheit und soziale Disziplinierung,* (Frankfurt am Main: Suhrkamp, 1985). I am grateful for permission to reprint.

Poverty
and Society

Introduction

The central questions of this book are comparative questions in intellectual history. How were developments toward a welfare state in Germany, Denmark, Great Britain, and the United States shaped by the basic social perceptions that people in those countries had about poverty, the poor, industrial workers, society, government, and the like? How did the perceptions of people in European countries differ from those of Americans, and even more, how did perceptions in each country differ from the perceptions in all the other countries? Conversely, what does the shape of the developments toward a welfare state in the four countries reveal about basic social assumptions in those countries? What do the social perceptions of people in one country reveal about the perceptions of people in another country, and what comparisons can be made among the four?

The "welfare state" is a complex, interrelated system of subsidies, tax laws, protective legislation, and income maintenance. It involves political relationships, economic functioning, and ideological factors. Yet central to the welfare state are the ways income that is normally generated from wages and salaries is maintained when earnings are diminished or stopped. This study is concerned with the development of government income-maintenance systems in the urban and industrial sectors of Germany, Denmark, Great Britain, and the United States and with the perceptions, assumptions, and ideologies that were the bases for those systems.

All statements about an individual or a group are usually at least implicitly comparative. When we say a person is tall, we mean he is taller than most people his age. When we say a society is hierarchical, we mean that it is more hierarchical than many other societies. To understand what the term "United States" (or any other collective expression) means is to see the United States in some sort of comparison with something that is not the "United States." That is what this book does. It looks at the United States in comparison with a group of other nations.

The purpose of this study is to bring about a greater understanding of heterogeneity and variation. The goal here is to explicate the world view, or at least the social view, of the people who made policy. This understanding constitutes my definition of what "explanation" means in history. For example, a poor person may react to his poverty with fury at a system that treats him unjustly, or he may take his poverty as proof of his own inadequacy, or he may assume that he, his ancestors, and his progeny are inherently people who are poor. How a person sees his own poverty—or that of others—will affect how that person behaves. Thus, a person's actions are "explained" not by the measure of his annual income, but by understanding of his world view. This understanding does not lead in the direction of what social scientists call "theory"—that is, examining the particular in order to illustrate a general concept. I am less interested in the United States as an illustration of how a federal system functions and more interested in understanding the world view of the New York Charity Organization Society or of Harry Hopkins and others who took part in the controversies and struggles over welfare legislation. History in this sense is situated in the humanities rather than in the social sciences. The focus in this book is on the unique instead of the general, and on understanding rather than explanation—better stated, the focus is on understanding *as* explanation.[1] This focus on the unique means that differentiations will be made between words, institutions, and conceptions that seem similar. For example, consider the sentence "In Denmark and Germany, more than in Great Britain and the United States, it was regarded as the duty of the state to guarantee

2

the welfare of the individual." On one level this sentence makes a true statement and may help us see patterns, but if a central concept, such as "state," is understood differently in Germany and Denmark (which is the case here), such a sentence may mislead more than illuminate.[2]

This book is also intellectual history, a particular type of intellectual history. Its basic assumption is that people act not in relation to reality but according to how they perceive reality. As G. P. Chesterton wrote a century ago, "There are some people—and I am one of them—who think that the most practical and important thing to know about a man is still his view of the universe. . . . The question is not whether the theory of the cosmos affects matters, but whether in the long run anything else affects them." R. G. Collingwood said that all history is the history of thought. I acknowledge that other forces and factors may affect history, but to have any understanding of the welfare state we need to know not so much the theory of the cosmos of the men and women who shaped legislation, but how they viewed the social cosmos around them. So in this study I am interested less in formal philosophical systems than in assumptions and perceptions.

Some examples may help to illustrate this. Is industrialism understood as an intruder in a pastoral idyll, as in George Innis' painting *The Lackawanna Valley,* or is industrialism seen as providing a new kind of beauty, as in many of the paintings of Charles Sheeler or in Feininger's *Brooklyn Bridge?*[3] Are class lines clear so that there is no doubt, for example, who is *Arbeiter* (worker) and who is *Angestellte* (salaried employee), or are class lines so fuzzy that generations of sociologists produce dozens of theories about where the lines should be drawn? Workers in all countries might organize and express dissatisfaction, but what determines policy are the ways various political leaders, businessmen, and the workers themselves see these actions. To come still closer to the welfare state, are the poor perceived as victims, as in Hauptmann's *Die Weber* and Dickens' *Oliver Twist,* or as people in need of moral instruction (in the case of the charity organization societies) or of religious instruction (in the case of General William Booth)? These are the kinds of perceptual questions that the people who struggled with one another over the making of the welfare state were asking and that shaped policy, and it is such questions that are the subject of this book.

No investigator can ask people who were not philosophers to produce essays on their theory of the cosmos. The question must instead be broken down into smaller questions for which there might be answers (or implied answers) in the historical record. To get at the answers, I ask the historical record how and what the shapers of the welfare state thought about the poor and poverty, and how the poor should be treated, and how and what the shapers thought about workers and social class, about the structure of society, about the relationship between society on the one hand and government on the other, about the nature of the historical process, and of course what the shapers of the welfare state thought about social welfare legislation. Not all these questions could be answered by all groups in all the countries studied, but many of them were answered, at least implicitly, by many groups and individuals in all or several of the countries. In sum, answers to these questions help us see how the people who made the welfare state viewed the social cosmos.

Comparative history of this sort makes visible through comparison what might go unnoticed otherwise. We can see more clearly what Americans mean when they talk about "class" if we see how it contrasts with the way the Germans use the term, and we understand the American charity organization societies better if we see them in relation to British charity organization societies. This purpose for comparative history seems too obvious to defend, but because a number of political scientists and economists seem to be uncomfortable with it I make it explicit here: comparison makes it possible to see what one might not see without comparison.[4]

The central thread and motivating force in this study is an interest in the United States. What conceptions of class, of government, and of poverty animated the men and women concerned with poverty in the United States? Those questions are answered here with a deeper and more complex understanding than before through comparison of the answers Americans gave with those that Germans, Danes, and the British gave. One could well ask, why not France or New Zealand or Canada or Sweden? There is no good answer, except to say that one has to stop somewhere. There is, however, some logic in the choice of the four countries for this book. The United States is where my training and previous research has been; it is my intellectual starting point. The New World is indeed different from the Old

World, but both are a part of the Western world and should at least occasionally be treated together. As the notes for this introduction indicate, an increasing number of books now deal with both Europe and the United States, a trend that this study continues. Germany is where it all began in the modern industrial world. Denmark is the source of the Scandinavian version of the welfare state. Since World War II the Scandinavian system has often been spoken of as the "Swedish System," but this is correct only for the years after the 1930s; Denmark was the pioneer. In some instances, other countries, notably Great Britain, looked to the Danish example. England is the source for much of American thinking about the poor. It is the conduit through which Americans often interpret developments on the European continent. It is the starting place for industrialization, and it confronted the costs of industrialization influenced by that primacy. Thus, the four chosen countries make sense individually, but they also make sense as a unit. They are four differing species in the same genus, perhaps with different ancestors but with a degree of external resemblance.

The time period covered is also limited. I want to deal with questions of urban industrial poverty, and this coincides roughly with the formation of a unified parliamentary system for Germany and Denmark and with the post–Civil War years in the United States. For Great Britain there is no way to avoid beginning in Chapter 1 with the 1834 Poor Law Report, which dominated British thinking about and dealing with poverty for the next seventy-five years and was the starting point for American thinking as well. The termination date for this study is around World War II, or events close to it.

A problem peculiar to the United States is that while the other countries studied here have a single core of legislative history—in London, Berlin and Copenhagen—the United States in most of this period had forty-nine jurisdictions. What took place in Springfield, Illinois, might or might not have anything to do with what happened in Sacramento, California, or Washington, D.C. I chose to concentrate not on a "typical" state but on states that were atypical in that they were particularly concerned with welfare in the industrial sector: the state that had the largest number of industrial workers (New York) and the state that had the longest history of government concern with social problems (Massachusetts), and of course on the federal government. Where relevant, I also looked at Illinois, Wisconsin, Ohio, and other states, and I summarized laws of all the states.

A terminological problem peculiar to Great Britain is that the poor laws of Ireland and Scotland were slightly different from the poor laws of England and Wales. With regard to the poor laws of England and Wales, the term "England" will be used. All other laws discussed here applied, with only slight modifications in wording, to England, Wales, Scotland, and Ireland (after 1922, Northern Ireland). For these laws, "Great Britain" or "the United Kingdom" will be used.

The last quarter-century has produced a good deal of scholarship—or writing, at least—on the welfare state. People who call themselves historians have generally confined themselves to one country, or at most to a couple, but social scientists—particularly political scientists, sociologists, and economists—have tried to look at the development of the "welfare state" phenomenon in a more general or multinational way, in some cases considering scores of countries. Two central questions emerge from much of this scholarship. One is the attempt to explain why welfare states were founded when and where they were. The focus is on finding or asserting some factor or combination of factors that are causal and concluding that this explanation has some general validity. The second central question has to do with coming up with some general explanation for the expansion of welfare measures once they came into being.

In previous work on the founding of welfare states, two major tendencies, each of which can be further subdivided, can be discerned. The first broad tendency might be described as the "developmental" school, although terms like "pluralist" or "logic of industrialism" or "modernization" have also been used. For scholars in the developmental school, modern welfare measures are a necessary and more or less natural (but not necessarily conflict-free) consequence of the development of a modern democratic (the term used is often "mass democracy") industrial state.

The other major tendency is what has been called the "neo-Marxist" or "social democratic" school. The emphasis here is on the mobilization of the industrial workers and the growth of unions, on national labor organizations, on political parties with a dominant labor membership, and on the influence labor organizations have on policy, either through pressure groups or by forming the government. For these scholars the welfare state can be understood only as a product, either direct or indirect, of pressure from "below." While this approach is not necessarily in logical contradiction to that of the developmental school, the focus tends to be different and the emphasis on conflict greater.

On its broadest level, the developmental school sees such measures as a national poor law, accident or sickness insurance, and old-age pensions as part of the process of state-building that occurred at different times in different places but had its beginnings in the sixteenth century. The concept of state-building appears again and again in various studies, but it is discussed particularly by Stein Rokkan. Peter Flora and Jens Alber relate the idea specifically to the founding of welfare states.[5]

Within the developmental school there are many different emphases. Some scholars focus on economics—for instance, Harold Wilensky writes, "Over the long pull, economic level is the root cause of the welfare state." For Christoph Sachsse and Florian Tennstedt, industrialism produced a new kind of poverty that had to be met with new types of institutions, and in Germany at least, "workers insurance" (as it was called) was the logical step. Gaston Rimlinger, an economic historian, writes: "The social relations represented by the old system were in conflict with the economic and social requirements of industrialism." We cannot say that any of these people were simply economic determinists. Rimlinger in particular wrote a complex nuanced study that takes into account a wide variety of factors, from ideology to political systems, and that recognizes and even emphasizes national differences. More recently he has put increasing emphasis on the political fears of those who already held power, people "whose primary concern in protecting workers was protecting the state." Gerhardt Ritter implies the same thing when he singles out the fears of elites in reaction to the Paris Commune of 1871 as an important formative factor.[6]

Another group within the developmental school recognizes the importance of economics but puts more emphasis on political factors, particularly the democratization of the polity. As Peter Flora and Arnold Heidenheimer state, "The real beginning of the modern welfare state . . . had to await the transformation of the absolutist state into mass democracy." Phillips Cutwright's conclusion is that, as between economic systems at roughly equal levels of economic development, "more representative governments introduce programs earlier than less representative governments," a conclusion that is at variance with some other research. In dealing with Denmark, Kjeld Philip seems to assume that an increasingly sensitive government naturally inaugurated and expanded welfare programs. Hans Achinger sees both economic and political development as important and perceives what in Germany is called "social policy" moving from a relatively peripheral problem to, by the end of World War II, dominating at least domestic policy in Germany. Hugh Heclo and Ann Shola Orloff and Theda Skocpol emphasize administrative interest in and capacity for welfare measures. Samuel Mencher also writes of increasing democracy, but he traces the source of this movement back to the major social philosophies, like changing ideas about what "liberalism" really implied. Peter Flora tries to integrate these various threads in the developmental school by proposing an analytical schema in which industrialization and urbanization produce problems. Depending on where they occurred, these problems are dealt with by such institutions as the church, cooperative groups like "friendly societies," or private charities. The problems put varying degrees of pressure on the regime, but eventually the mobilization of various helping groups and the desire of the government to maintain order will produce welfare legislation.[7]

The second major tendency discernible in writing about the founding and growth of welfare states, called the "neo-Marxist" or "social-democratic" school, is not in some versions incompatible with the more political analysts of the developmental school. The developmentalists, however, generally emphasize the democratization of the political system, while the neo-Marxists emphasize the mobilization of labor, either as unions or as political parties or both. Val Lorwin writes about the political mobilization of what was "in most ways, a new class," and John Stephens argues the welfare state is "a product of the growing strength of labor in civil society." After examining eighteen industrialized countries in the post–World War II period, David Cameron concludes that countries heavily involved in international trade have had more generous welfare policies, but further asserts that this is because export industries tend to be concentrated and to produce a labor force that is organized and politically effective. Walter Korpi, writing about Sweden, and Francis Castles, considering all of Scandinavia, both find the influence of organized labor and the Social Democratic Party to be crucial. Ivar Hornemann Møller finds that, in Denmark at least, social welfare expenditures became larger or smaller as the labor movement was stronger or weaker. Gösta Esping-Andersen analyzed the differences between the Danish and the Swedish Social Democratic parties and found that the Danish party, not made up exclusively of the proletariat but also including shopkeepers, artisans, and agricultural workers, had more-limited aims than the Swedish party, which was formed predominately from workers in the iron-mining or timber industries. For Ian Gough, everything is a product of the working class, either through direct pressure or through fear on the part of the capitalists. He argues that workers have actually contributed to the survival of the system that oppresses them. Similarly, Frances Fox Piven and Richard Cloward argue that social welfare is functional for capitalism, that it dampens lower-class protests and provides incentives for workers to work.[8]

Many scholars who emphasize the importance of the Social Democratic parties, not for the founding but in the growth of social welfare programs, concentrate on the post-1930 period. In this period, and even more after World War II, programs grew faster under Social Democratic governments than under nonsocialist governments. But this is almost a historical tautology, because, as I show elsewhere,[9] a party that wanted to increase welfare measures is almost a definition of a Social Democratic party. Thus we can say only that when a party that wanted to broaden and deepen welfare coverage was elected, welfare coverage grew. This is perhaps significant, but it is not the same thing as saying that socialism leads to social welfare, or welfare to socialism.

Historians who consider themselves Marxists or neo-Marxists or "radicals" have found it difficult to deal with the welfare state. Capitalism has not acted as it was supposed to. States that call themselves socialist have not acted as they were supposed to. Above all, the "proletariat" has not acted as it was supposed to. These historians have frequently written about "the crisis of capitalism." Capitalism has certainly had its crisis, but the syllogism "Capitalism is in crisis, therefore socialism" is flawed in logic and has been rejected historically. Capitalism has shown itself to be capable of modification. When a crisis comes, capitalists have been forced, willingly or unwillingly, to look for the causes of the crisis and to fix them, at least partially, by welfare legislation, among other things. A socialism that does not become tyranny might be possible, but the Soviet Union, Eastern Europe, China, and Cuba have disappointed their hopeful supporters. In most Western nations, workers seem to have found the middle class attractive. They have shown their support for a "social democracy," which has very little relation to socialism. Indeed, some workers have been and are quite conservative in a number of dimensions. If the whole welfare story has been a fraud, the people on whom the fraud was presumably perpetrated seem pleased with it, and in fact want more. Either they are dupes to fiendishly clever manipulators or they are on to something.

At the grossest level of analysis, both the developmental and the social democratic approaches are plausible. During the past one hundred to one hundred fifty years, most nations, at least in the West, have become more industrialized, more capitalist, more democratic, and administratively more capable and have had increasingly mobilized labor movements. Yet as we try to be more precise about the timing of social welfare legislation, we find that each theory has implications that tend to exclude the others. Analysts who emphasize development expect social welfare to appear at similar stages of development in different countries, perhaps modified by the fact that people in one country would know what had already been done in other countries. Scholars who emphasize economics would find economic development to be crucial; for others the major factor might be the degree of democratization or of political mobilization. For neo-Marxists the decisive issue would be the development of capitalism to the point where large industrial firms created a large proletariat, or perhaps social welfare might be expected to occur when the workers were organized to a large degree or when a socialist or labor party became politically significant.

The most recent scholarship on these issues throws doubt on all the expected correlations. A group of scholars at the European University in Florence, the HIWED (Historische Indikatoren der westeuropäischen Demokratien), collected statistics on twelve European countries between 1815 and 1875. They concluded that the degree of industrial development or of mass democracy or of labor union or labor party strength has not been a consistent influence on the establishment of welfare measures.[10] Even if an invariant or nearly invariant relationship between some factor or combination of factors and the founding of the welfare state could be determined, it would only show what David Hume long ago called "constant conjunction." The relationship might be coincidental, or some other factor might give rise to both phenomena. To establish a causal relationship—and quite apart from the philosophical problems of "cause" in history—would require detailed investigation of each situation.

Even if some causal relationship could be found in nearly all cases, that would not obviate the usefulness of nation-specific or culture-specific investigation. In physical science, one of the principles is the "principle of parsimony," where the simplest possible explanation that takes into account all observed data is preferred to more complex explanations. The discipline of history has the reverse principle, what might be called the "principle of profligacy." Like other humanistic disciplines, history always wants to know more. If slavery was an exploitive labor system, historians want to know more than the economics of exploitation. Was there also a paternalistic element? a religious atmosphere? a built-in incentive system? a sexual penumbra? and so on and on. With each layer of complexity we get a richer, more nuanced picture of our collective past. Thus, if welfare legislation had always been enacted in countries at a certain level of industrialization (which it was not), it would still be useful to ask about the ways in which the English system and ideas differed from the German, or how Danish social perceptions contrasted with those of Americans. This study is a step toward a more complete understanding of differences in social perceptions among the four countries. Alexander von Humboldt stated the overall conclusion more than a century ago: "Whenever we offer philosophical or political reasons for political institutions, we will in actuality always find historical explanations."[11] Nations perceive reality in their own ways and act according to those perceptions' relation to their own history. It is to this history that we now turn.

This book begins where American thinking began: with the 1834 Poor Law Report in England and the organizations that supported the philosophy of that report. Part Two will outline the alternative views and mechanisms in Germany and Denmark—what was there in the history of those countries that impelled them to apply solutions different from the solutions the British and the Americans came up with? Then, in Part Three, we see how Great Britain and the United States, starting from similar positions, went in different directions. The British moved toward the solutions applied on the European continent, for British reasons and in British ways. The United States, with some exceptions, rejected the continental solutions and pursued different aims up until World War I. In Part Four, we shall see how after World War I, socialists in both Germany and Denmark found themselves abandoning socialism and instead supporting extensions of the welfare state within capitalism. Until World War II, the British seemed incapable of going beyond the formulations of the pre–World War I decade. The United States, in a remarkable demonstration of its flexibility, of its willingness almost to forget history and tradition, moved sharply toward its own version of welfare state solutions in the 1930s. In a sense, this story supports versions of "convergence theory" because by about World War II all four countries, even the United States, had fairly similar government mechanisms in place. By the time we get to the end of the story, however, it will be clear that similar mechanisms do not imply similar social perceptions.

The concluding chapter puts the whole story together in an explicitly comparative way. Here I go beyond the comparisons made in each preceding chapter to talk about the four countries together, or at least next to one another. The differences—sometimes clear contrasts, sometimes nuances—will help us understand better what is meant when we say "Germany" or "Denmark" or "Great Britain," or "the United States." The evidence in this study comes only from questions relating to social welfare. It may be that in other spheres (e.g., economics, war, high culture) the social assumptions are different, but I doubt it. In the sphere of social welfare there is evidence of broad perceptual assumptions that transcend the sphere in which the evidence is gathered here. Unless someone can show that in some other sphere the perceptions were different, I can say that I have found some aspects of what the words "Germany," "Denmark," "Great Britain," and "the United States" mean.

PART ONE

Beginnings

1

England's Poor-Law Report and the United States

The most important factor in the shaping of the American national character has been *plenty,* according to David Potter, who entitled one of his books about the United States *People of Plenty.* The United States was indeed a land of great abundance and seemingly boundless wealth. This factor of abundance has been mentioned by others, but its centrality, particularly in relation to thinking about welfare, has not been emphasized enough. For instance, workers in Germany argued that American workers did not need social insurance, that because their wages were higher they could afford to save or to buy private insurance.[1] But the abundance is less important than the perception of abundance. The context of prosperity, of plenty, is the background against which all welfare efforts in the United States must be seen. "There is no poverty in America," claimed Alexis de Tocqueville, that complimentary French visitor to the United States in 1835, and Martin Anderson, President Ronald Reagan's first adviser on domestic policy, begins his book *Welfare* with the same assumption.[2]

This background assumption that there is no real poverty in the United States has many implications for welfare policy. First and most obvious, it makes poverty among the able-bodied ipso facto a character fault but, more important, it makes American reformers revert to an argument that was almost unnecessary in Europe. They had to argue that there *was* poverty—yes, there was, just look at it! Jacob Riis's *How the Other Half Lives* (1890) and Robert Hunter's *Poverty* (1904) may make other arguments, but the existence of poverty is their central point. England in the nineteenth century also believed that it was a prosperous country. One can find constant references in England to being the most prosperous country in Europe. However, prosperity in that country did not imply an absence of poverty. In the United States it did.

Another implication of the assumption that there was no real poverty in the United States was the belief that poverty could be cured. The Danish, German, and twentieth-century British assumption was that in a wage economy there were predictable and inevitable causes for the loss of earnings—sickness, old age, accident, and disability—and that these should be dealt with. The American assumption about wealth was that poverty would be eliminated if just the right steps were taken—for example, put fences around dangerous machinery, require children to go to school until the fifth grade, and eliminate corruption, watered stock, collusion, inhumane working hours and working conditions—and poverty would disappear. From the earliest industrial depressions to President Lyndon Johnson's War on Poverty, including most of the measures of the New Deal, the assumption was that poverty was unnatural and unnecessary in prosperous America and could be eliminated.

The best insights into what mainstream charity workers believed in the last two decades of the nineteenth century come from the annual reports of the National Conference of Charities and Corrections (NCCC), after World War I called the National Council of Social Work. In those reports the assumption of prosperity was prominent again and again. There is almost a refrain, a constant incantation: "There was work in this country for every man, if he could only be put in touch with it"—for example. "The only able-bodied poor who are entitled to relief are of course those who cannot find remunerative employment. Such difficulty of finding employment may easily occur in an old and crowded country like England, but is not apt to occur in the United States."[3] If there was such prosperity, why was there poverty? In 1881–82 the NCCC sent questionnaires to charity workers all over the United States, asking what they considered the most important causes of "pauperism and crime" (which were considered nearly identical). While the answer they got overwhelmingly was that "intemperance" was the most important cause, a second frequently cited cause was "almsgiving." Again and again, speeches at the NCCC meetings condemn "almsgiving" or, more often, "indiscriminate almsgiving." These charity workers were convinced that Americans were far too generous and that to give a drunk a dollar would enable him to get drunk for a day, but they were sure that if he were made to learn a trade and get a job his poverty would be cured. The idea was that there were always jobs for people who did not try to avoid them. Those who used this argument really believed that charity caused poverty, not the other way around.[4] Some people deserved relief, but any "outdoor relief" (that is, relief outside a poorhouse or other institution) should be private, not public.

Throughout the 1880s the emphasis was on the perniciousness of public relief and the virtues of well-controlled private relief. In support of this position, the conclusions and recommendations of the report of the Royal Commission investigating the operation and administration of the poor laws in England, published in 1834, were constantly referred to both within the National Conference of Charities and Corrections and outside it. Josephine Shaw Lowell, who had a great influence on the whole charity establishment in the United States in the 1880s and 1890s, set out the most vigorous argument in a little book she published in 1884 titled *Public Relief and Private Charity*. She quoted page after page of the 1834 Poor Law Report and concluded: "There was not only a constant failure of all the efforts to check pauperism and crime, but . . . the very efforts intended to check them merely served to increase them.[5]

In 1832 the British government had appointed a Royal Commission to make "inquiry into the practical operation of the laws for the relief of the poor in England and Wales" and to recommend improvements. The occasion for the new investigation was the perception that, during the first decades of the nineteenth century, expenses for supporting the poor were increasing at a shocking rate. The results of the inquiries were published as the Report of 1834, and on the basis of that report a new poor law for England and Wales was passed that same year. The law was a complex document that technically was an amendment to earlier laws that forbade relief, with certain exceptions, outside a workhouse or poorhouse ("outdoor relief"). The actual law concentrated on establishing administrative machinery, consisting of a system of "inspectors" for its own enforcement. What influenced later thinking was not the law, but the report that led up to it.

Historians are now convinced that the Royal Commission did not accurately report how the "old" (pre-1834) poor law functioned, and in fact did not even accurately represent the results of their own inquiries.[6] Whether accurate or inaccurate, the impact of the 1834 Poor Law Report was great. Its moral judgments and its system of values permeated all discussion of poor-law policy for the next seventy-five years or so. Indeed, many of the English men and women who in 1911 favored national health insurance went to extraordinary lengths to argue that they still subscribed to "the principles of 1834."

Although the major attitudes reflected in the Poor Law Report had been widespread in parliamentary commissions and articles in the press before 1834, the report did more than sum up previously stated views. It provided a moral universe, a *weltanschauung,* into which bits and pieces of social attitude could be fitted, so that people representing a variety of points of view could seize on it and say, "That's what I thought all along." It also fit with the interests of various groups: those who wanted a status society superseded by a contract society; those who, through the establishment of a centrally controlled inspectorate system, wanted central power to be more dominant and local power to be less dominant; those who wanted to save money under the new system; and those who wanted to increase their power. The same *weltanschauung* influenced practice in the United States.

The Poor Law Report of 1834 was simply another in the long line of reports on the subject that extended back over centuries. With the dissolution of the monastaries, the state had been left with the problem of dealing with the poor. The results of more than a century of struggling with the problem were summed up in the "old" poor law, or the "Elizabethan" poor law of 1601 summing up previous legislation. The old law made it clear that the able-bodied poor had a claim against the landholders of their home parish. These landholders were required to pay a special tax, or "rate," to support poor people who had a "settlement," or legal residence, in the parish. Thus it was clear as early as the sixteenth century that society, acting through the locality but under compulsion from the central government, was in charge of what neither village, monastary, guild, nor family could manage any longer. This Elizabethan law remained essentially un-changed until 1834.

The members of the Royal Commission saw the world as popu-lated by vast numbers of weak-willed and temptable people who would be able to resist temptation only if they did hard physical labor for a great many hours a week. Their work would increase the national wealth, but as far as policy toward the poor was concerned, the product of their work was not very important. It was not what was produced that saved a man, woman, or child from sliding into "degradation," it was the process of work itself. Anything in society that tempted a person away from hard work was pernicious and should be eliminated.

The "allowance system" was such a factor. According to the 1834 report, the system was widespread (except in northern England) and should be done away with. Under this system (often called the Speenhamland System, after the parish in Berkshire where it was thought to have originated in 1795), a minimum family income would be established by the local parish according to family size. If the family income did not reach that minimum, it would be supple-mented by the parish, but a person who received such aid automati-cally became a "pauper" instead of an "honest labourer." Even only passing contact with parish relief was degrading. The authors of the report believed that the "disease" of poverty was hereditary and that therefore once a family was on relief it would never get off unless driven off by public policy.

The purpose of the new poor law passed in 1834 in response to the report was to "depauperize" England. The process of "degradation" could be reversed if the proper steps were taken with sufficient rigor. In the United States there was no "allowance system," but the moral danger in receiving such aid was seen to be the same, no matter what the source of the aid. If a person knew he could live without working, he would not work and would be "pauperized." The word "pauper" implied far more than just a person who was receiving money. According to the 1834 report, a pauper was a different kind of human being—not only someone who admitted being unable to support himself and his family, a person who had managed his affairs badly, but also a "degraded" being in a broad moral and ethical sense.

These degraded creatures were as visibly different from other people as if they had been wearing prisoners' stripes. "The independent labourer is comparatively clean in his person, his wife and children are clean, and the children go to school; the house is in better order and more clean. Those who depend on parish relief or on benefaction, on the contrary, are dirty in their person and slothful in their habits."[7] Cleanliness was, however, only the externally visible sign of a more thorough moral degradation. Because paupers get their income without working, they squander it on drink or other "immoralities," not specified. The most serious effect of the corrupting influence is that it destroys natural family affection and duty. Mothers will not care for their own children unless they are paid for it; children will not care for their aged parents, nor will working children living at home put their wages into a common fund. The pauper and his family become perpetrators of fraud—feigning sickness or disability or many children or lack of work in order to stay on parochial relief.

So the Poor Law Report of 1834 deemed the fundamental fault with the system of "poor relief" to be a moral one. The character of stout, honest English laborers was a weak vessel that could be destroyed by the temptation that poor-law support offered, but it could be strengthened if government policy were different. We shall see again and again, in Great Britain and the United States, the argument that poverty is produced by charity, whether public or private. Denial of aid would induce people to be self-reliant, and by this means their character would be strengthened and their self-respect reestablished, and they would be reclaimed for virtue.

Although London had a population of more than 1.5 million in 1834, all the examples and strictures in the Poor Law Report applied to agricultural areas. However, the judgments of the commissioners and the morality set out in the report were applied later in the century and on both sides of the Atlantic to urban poverty as well as to rural poverty. Similarly, even though the report dealt with only the able-bodied, its views were expanded later to include other categories. There are only four paragraphs that deal with the "impotent"—which meant mostly small children, the sick, and the aged. The commissioners expressed satisfaction with the development of medical dispensaries for the poor and hoped that the system would be extended. Theoretically, then, one could argue in accord with the principles of the 1834 report that there could be certain forms of public relief for the non-able-bodied, such as the sick, the aged, or accident victims. In fact, social insurance was possible in England only when a number of people became convinced that such arrangements were compatible with the report. It was the belief that there was abundance and plenty in the United States that prevented the same rethinking from taking place in that country.

The Poor Law Report noted that a number of parishes had already been applying the remedy the commissioners proposed to make national: they had eliminated all forms of public relief except workhouses or poorhouses. Those parishes had been "depauperized" not by the needy fleeing to other parishes but by their being transformed again, from "paupers" into "independent labourers." The transformation was remarkable, affecting not only their material well-being but also their cleanliness and their behavior as parents and citizens. Crime diminished, wages rose, and even health improved. The report recommended that the allowance system be done away with by imposing a simple self-acting "workhouse test":

> Except as to medical attendance and subject to the exception respecting apprenticeship herein after stated, all relief whatever to able-bodied persons or to their families, otherwise than in well-regulated workhouses (i.e., places where they may be set to work according to the spirit and intention of the 43 Elizabeth) shall be declared unlawful, and shall cease.

By this means "the line between those who do and those who do not need relief is drawn and drawn perfectly. If the claimant does not comply with the terms on which relief is given to the destitute, he gets nothing; and if he does comply, the compliance proves the truth of his claim—namely, his destitution." In essence, then, the Poor Law Report of 1834 was not primarily an investigation of conditions, a proposal for legislation, or an administrative innovation. It was a morality tale or fable. To paraphrase Alexander Pope, the commission said:

> The Universe was wrapt in darkest night,
> Just change the law, and there'll be light.

Not all Englishmen accepted the "principles of 1834." There was opposition in the periodical press and practical opposition in many northern and industrial districts. Some areas simply refused to obey the new law that was to implement the report's recommendations. Where the principles were implemented, they were never implemented fully, as intended. "Outdoor relief" continued, particularly in times of trade depression. Many places did not have adequate workhouse space, so the "workhouse test" could not be applied. A "task of work" (often on the roads), which was made a substitute for the workhouse test, was difficult to apply and required supervision from skilled foremen. Above all, it was cheaper to provide a few shillings of relief to augment too meager wages—the allowance system—than to maintain a person, and possibly his whole family, in the workhouse.[8] In a realistic political sense, then, the Poor Law Report of 1834 was a failure. It did not achieve its own objectives, and where it did the objectives did not have the predicted consequences. Yet in an ideological sense it was a success. It had an enormous influence on the terms—the very language—in which "the poor" were discussed, and as much so in the United States as in Great Britain.

Although the 1834 report was quoted as widely in the United States as in Great Britain, it was quoted by a different group of people and in a different context, so it took on a different meaning and had less staying power. In Great Britain, the report was cited in official documents, by public figures, and by quasi-public bodies, such as charity organization societies, but in the United States it was most on the lips of private charity workers, who had little and wanted even less to do with government. Any poor law that existed in America was of local and small moment. Family, neighbors, or church were supposed to be adequate for meeting most needs. In the larger cities there were often organizations with a broader base, such as the New York Association for Improving the Condition of the Poor, or the Children's Aid Society. Although some of these organizations received public money, public authority was concerned mostly with the "defective or the dependent." Even in the relatively well organized states of New York and New Jersey, poverty among the able-bodied was hardly an issue. Massachusetts established a State Board of Charities in 1863, and New York did the same in 1867, but these had virtually no powers beyond that of inspection. In New York after 1874, state monies were limited to institutions for the blind, deaf, and juvenile delinquents. New Jersey first created the position of Commissioner of Charities and Corrections in 1905, but the commissions had almost no powers.[9]

This is not to say that "outdoor relief" did not exist in the United States. In many states, particularly those on the East Coast, local authorities contributed public funds to such causes as hospitals or child-saving organizations. Indeed, the barrier between public and private spheres, otherwise almost impermeable, seemed easily pierced so long as the public side of the barrier meant the local, rather than state or federal, public authority. In fact, it appears that "private" and "local" were often nearly synonymous. In addition, many states required that local poor-relief officers aid all legal residents.[10]

So the principles of the 1834 Poor Law Reports were not implemented any more strictly in the United States than they were in Great Britain, but they were respected as principles to guide public action. In the United States the report was quoted in a context in which there was no landed gentry, no magistrates, and no permanent class of farm laborers, but it was quoted. Most important, it was quoted in a context of abundance, in a context that saw no reason for people to be poor and therefore no reason for any but the most minimal, mostly private, charity.

2

The Charity Organization Societies in Great Britain and the United States

Private relief was not free from dangers. Josephine Shaw Lowell, while condemning the old poor law, also condemned "almsgiving and dole giving" as harmful. Through such practices "false hopes are excited, the unhappy recipients of alms become dependent, lose their energy, are rendered incapable of self-support, and what they receive in return for their lost character is quite inadequate to supply their need."[1] The aim of the "charity organization societies"—called "associated charities" in some cities—was to control private charity so that it would not be "almsgiving and dole giving." The charity organization society (COS) like so many American institutions from the bicameral legislature to the settlement house, had its origin in England and emigrated to the United States. The London Charity Organisation Society, along with many other charity organization societies on both sides of the Atlantic, is now a private social work organization called the Family Welfare Association.

Charity organization societies in major British cities and in almost all the major northern cities in the United States took the London Charity Organisation Society as their model. Organized in 1869, the London Charity Organisation Society soon had district committees in most of the poor-law districts of London, and parallel organizations were established in other major cities. It grew rapidly in numbers and prominence. The many noble names on its letterhead included, by the end of the century, the Queen herself as patron. Men were prominent at the leadership level, but most of the day-to-day work in the districts and in the field was done by women, who because it was all volunteer work were women of the leisure class.[2] The London COS was superb at self-advertisement, which may lead a later age to overestimate its importance. Yet its influence spread well beyond London, and its members were on important committees and were witnesses before parliamentary commissions. It may have had less influence on day-to-day philanthropy than it claimed, but its influence on ideas about charity can hardly be overestimated.[3]

Charity itself was as old as recorded history. In nineteenth-century England the novels of Charles Dickens and Disraeli, the cries of the Christian Socialists, and the writings of John Ruskin and William Morris all made the question of "the poor" and of charity an almost constant aspect of Victorian society.[4] But the charity organization society was something different. Its purpose was, first, to put resolution and backbone into those who administered the 1834 poor law and to make sure they neither shirked their responsibilities nor became lax in their adherence to the law and its philosophy, and second, to be the conscience of private charity, to make sure that private generosity did not undermine the virtues of public strictness. Its third purpose was to suppress begging, to which the other two purposes would contribute. The importance of the charity organization society for a history of the welfare state in England is that it thought of itself, was thought of, and in fact became almost a public body. It was involved, in a way that even trade unions or "friendly societies" were not, at the policy-making level of national and local government. The American charity organization societies had the same three goals as their London ancestor, but the circumstances and therefore the developments of the American version turned out to be different from the model.

In the same year the London Charity Organisation Society was organized—1869—the mood, the attitudes, and to a considerable degree the practices of the London organization were illustrated in an article written by one of its guiding forces, Octavia Hill. In 1865 John Ruskin, from whom Hill had been taking painting lessons, asked the twenty-seven-year-old woman to manage three working-class tenements he owned in Marylebone, and it was there that Hill developed her ideas. "I feel most deeply," she wrote four years later, "that the disciplining of our immense poor population must be effected by individual influence; and that this power can change it from a mob of paupers and semi-paupers into a body of self-dependent workers." It is almost unnecessary to say anything else about the COS philosophy, for Hill here revealed such straightforward and undisguised attitudes that the ideas of the charity society were mere glosses on her words. In telling the poor how to live, she said, "I would not set my conviction, however strong it might be, against your judgement of right; but when you are doing what I know your own conscience condemns, I, now that I have the power, will enforce right." Hill prided herself on knowing each family that was her responsibility in great detail, and thus she is often considered the founder of social casework in England, but her leadership, however benevolent in intent or even effect, was still clearly dictatorship. She was sure she knew what the poor needed, and she saw that they got it and were prevented from getting anything else.[5] This severe but in its own view benevolent dictatorship provided the spirit in which the London Charity Organisation Society functioned for the next fifty years.

Because the sacred text of the London Charity Organisation Society was the Poor Law Report of 1834, it is unnecessary to detail the organization's fundamental philosophy.[6] Consistently and with tireless regularity, the fundamental belief that "outdoor relief" pauperized people, deprived them of their self-respect, tempted them to sloth, and destroyed their character was asserted. One could take a speech of Charles S. Loch, longtime guiding spirit of the London Charity Organisation Society, or Octavia Hill and interleave it with the 1834 report without producing any ideological inconsistency, and in many cases not even a stylistic one. Octavia Hill wrote in 1889:

> I am quite awed when I think what our impatient charity is doing to the poor of London: men, who should hold up their heads as self-respecting fathers of families, learning to sing like beggars in the streets—all because we give pennies; those who might have a little fund in the savings banks discouraged because the spendthrift is at least as abundantly helped when time of need comes; women stand-

ing gossiping or quarreling, dirty and draggled, about the door-steps, while we are cooking at school for their children the dinner they should be preparing each in the tidy home; others going out to work because we are providing the *creche* instead of leaving the care of the baby to its mother. Is family life forgotten . . .? There is hardly a single necessity of life we do not now half take upon ourselves the duty of providing?[7]

This belief that private charity could be as pernicious as public relief was the greatest influence on the American branch of the COS movement.

In addition to careful organization of all charitable giving to avoid "indiscriminate alms," another method the charity organization society used was "friendly visiting" to the poor by the well-to-do. "Friendly visiting" was supposed to provide counsel in thrifty, orderly, sanitary household management, and advice on personal problems. It was not a new invention, having been practiced for decades in different versions by the religious, quasi-secular, and secular segments of society.[8] It is difficult to say how effective the "friendly visiting" was, but its publicity and public relations efforts were certainly a resounding success. Articles by leading members of the London Charity Organisation appeared in many journals, and its leaders were witnesses before or members of parliamentary committees and commissions. Prominent members, especially Charles Loch, were considered experts on matters having to do with the poor and poverty. COS members often ran for and were elected to positions on the local Board of Guardian, and the COS district committees were often in close communication with board members.[9] One can be critical of the fundamental social philosophy and overall political influence of the London Charity Organisation Society and yet not be blind to its social contributions. The organization insisted that cases of individual distress should be investigated and analyzed carefully on a case-by-case basis by trained investigators.[10]

Around the turn of the century, the American version of the charity organization society found its ideas challenged, and in fact changed in response to some of these challenges. The English charity organization society was far more consistent, or more rigid. In opposing all state aid, specifically for unemployment relief, Charles Loch said in letters to the *London Times* that since 1886 England had been slipping back into a situation like that before 1834: "The maintenance of the individual should as a rule be left to the individual. We want no social experiment." He argued that the poor law should receive the trust it deserved. The London Charity Organisation Society vigorously opposed old-age pensions when they were discussed in the 1890s. In its annual report for 1899 the organization sneered at the idea that a new era in poor relief was coming; the tried and true was best. By 1904 the society was afraid that legislative changes were leading to socialism.[11]

In 1877, eight years after the founding of the London Charity Organisation Society, the first American charity organization society was founded—in Buffalo, New York. During its transatlantic migration, the COS idea both lost something in the move and added new elements. For example, the kind of aristocrat that had been prominent in the movement in England was difficult to find in the United States. In addition, although churches were important in the American version, American ministers and priests had different relationships to their congregations and to society than ministers of the Church of England or the dissenting ministers. England did not have America's ethnic diversity. These different circumstances led to a different history for charity organization societies on each side of the Atlantic, but the starting point was the same.[12]

At least initially, the purpose and the methods of the American COS were also the same as its model in England: charity should be more organized, more "scientific." The words "science" or "scientific" were constantly on the lips of COS founders, and "scientific charity" and "organized charity" were often used synonymously. Although the Darwinian analogy would have been useful to their argument, it does not seem to have been used. Instead, COS people frequently compared themselves to medical doctors. Doctors were specialists in administering medicine; COS people were specialists in another sort of medicine, that of charity.[13] The methods of the American version followed the English model too. Applicants for aid would be visited by paid agents of the COS and where possible by "friendly visitors," almost all of whom were women. The purpose of the agent's visit was to determine whether applicants were worthy of aid—for example, whether they were telling the truth about their need, whether they could support themselves if they used their money more wisely, whether they were wasting their resources and strength in drink. These paid agents were a major source for what was later to be called "social work." In 1897 the New York Charity Organization Society began the first formal training in the eight-week Summer School of Philanthropy (now the Columbia University School of Social Work). Except in a very few cases, the COS itself did not provide relief. The person was referred to an appropriate charitable society or to a potential employer, or both.

The purpose of the "friendly visitor" in the American charity society movement was quite different from that of the paid agent. "Not alms, but a Friend" was the motto of the London Charity Organisation Society and of the COS movement in general. The theory, but not the practice, was that much more would be given through the "friend" than through the paid agent, and the theory was maintained with increasing defensiveness as the friendly visitors became fewer and fewer in the pre–World War I period. The annual reports of the charity organization societies were constantly calling for more people who would be willing to be visitors. By 1902, however, in Baltimore, only about one-quarter of COS visits were by friendly visitors.[14]

The theory of "friendly visiting" was the topic about which COS leaders wrote most and on which they expended the most thought and enthusiasm. In 1883 the New York Charity Organization Society published a *Handbook for Friendly Visitors among the Poor.* This handbook instructed visitors on how to distinguish between cases that were worthy of relief (e.g., aged people, people with a protracted illness or disability, widows with small children), "shiftless cases needing counsel, stimulus and work," and cases not needing relief at all. The methods recommended included visits on Sundays to see the working men of the household, and what can only be called spying: "You will sometimes have to seek further information from friends and neighbors." It should be recalled that these people were self-appointed volunteer visitors.[15]

Thus, the attitudes exhibited by the American version of the charity organization society differed little from the attitudes in London, exemplified by the writings of Octavia Hill. There is the same self-righteousness—the calm confidence that a distinction could be made between who is worthy of assistance and who is not, that COS people knew how to determine worthiness, that they knew best how to bring up children, that standards of thrift and cleanliness from the "better" classes could be inculcated into the habits of the poor, that financial independence should be the goal of every person. This way of thinking is a clear case of "social control," although one must be careful how that term is used. In its extreme form, social control means controlling the poor so that they do not become disruptive and so that they are docile workers for the direct or indirect benefit of those who are doing the controlling. Certainly the "Best People" of the charity organization society wanted to socialize the poor, but many of the poor wanted to be socialized. They wanted to learn English and to acquire marketable skills, and many of the second generation of immigrants wanted to learn American customs and leave the confines of any ethnic or linguistic ghetto.

Although COS leaders insisted that public charity was evil, they clearly thought of themselves as fulfilling some of the functions of a government, a government superior in quality to the municipal administration. Josephine Shaw Lowell actually said that those who administer private charity "have assumed a quasi-public trust."[16] This meant not only that private institutions must be subject to public supervision, but also that the charity organization society was exercising a function of "society." In some intellectual worlds, if "society" exercised a function it would be through government, but this was not the case in the United States. The English charity organization societies were proud that they worked closely with government, but among American COS leaders there was a good deal of contempt for government—municipal, state, or federal. Government was seen as corrupt, amateurish, and inefficient—a judgment that was not entirely undeserved.[17]

In any study of poverty in the United States one must ask "What about black people?" All American charity organization societies were urban, and most were in the North, so the black population, which was largely rural and in the South, did not constitute a large part of COS work. The question does exist, though, and the treatment of blacks varied. It was perhaps a little more benign than, though not wholly out of line with more general attitudes in the United States on race. In Boston, blacks seem to have been treated more or less like any other ethnic group. The tenth annual report

(1889) of the Associated Charities stated matter-of-factly: "A large proportion of the families under our charge are of African descent, and seem especially liable to pulmonary disease. . . . Much of the need arises from the temporary or permanent disability of the bread-winner from sickness."[18] The tone of the Rev. J. W. Backman of the Associated Charities of Chattanooga, Tennessee, was different:

> We have to deal down there with a class that you do not. I speak of the negro. It may astonish you when I say that a negro don't make a good pauper, and you cannot make a good orphan of him at all. A negro from six to eight years old is generally a self supporting institution in his way.
>
> We object to his way, but still he is self-supporting. Negroes are not paupers generally, I have lived among them all my life. I was raised with them. A negro down south just goes to his white people and says he wants fifty cents and he generally gets it.[19]

A detailed examination of Chicago around the turn of the century concludes that blacks had to form their own charitable organizations because they had been systematically excluded from mainstream charities.[20] Charity organization societies were certainly not in the forefront of asking Americans to change their ways when it came to race relations.

The COS movement in England firmly retained its principles well into the twentieth century, but the fundamental approach of the American version began to be challenged much earlier. The detailed data gathered by charity organization societies actually revealed a flaw in the organizations' own assumptions, a flaw that they themselves slowly acknowledged. Over and over again it appeared that the primary causes of poverty were not shiftlessness or drunkenness on the part of the poor, but circumstances beyond their control. For example, of the 1,154 applicants for relief dealt with in the annual report of the Buffalo Charity Organization Society for the year 1881, only 175 (or 15 percent) were reported to be needy because of drunkenness, and 166 (14 percent) were cases that "could be self supporting if they worked harder and were provident." Some 210 cases of need were due to old age, 218 to sickness, 198 (54 percent in all) to lack of male support, and most of the other causes, including lack of work in 56 cases, were due to "misfortune" rather than "misconduct."[21] Similar figures are given in COS reports from Cincinnati, New York, and Baltimore.

This stage in the history of the charity organization society was summarized in Amos Warner's influential *American Charities,* published in 1894. Warner was professor of economics at Stanford University and had been superintendent of charities for the District of Columbia. Although not a member of a charity organization society, he was close to the movement and dedicated his book to John Glenn, chairman of the executive committee of the Baltimore Charity Organization Society. Warner gathered information from about two hundred charity organization societies on what they deemed to be the causes of distress of the applicants for relief. His results showed that about 75 percent of the poverty was due to "misfortune" and only about 25 percent was due to "misconduct." The two largest categories, each almost one-quarter of the total number of requests for aid, were "lack of employment" and "sickness." And in even the misconduct category he looked for social causes: "We found that disease produces poverty, and we now find that poverty produces disease; that poverty comes from degeneration and incapacity, and now that degeneration and incapacity come from poverty. . . . But in tracing the long circle about which we have traveled, there have been many contributing forces . . . which are distinctly preventable." Warner did not depart completely from widespread views. He believed that heredity played a large part in pauperism, that public "outdoor relief" was pernicious, and that gross figures for unemployment in times of depression were probably greatly exaggerated, but he did not emphasize personal character weakness as a cause for poverty. Social reform was more important than character reform.[22]

Warner's high figure for unemployment as a cause of poverty reflected conditions in the midst of the major depression of 1893–96. The effects of the depression on the attitudes of charity workers has not been sufficiently emphasized.[23] On some economic measures, the depression was not as sharp as the depression of 1873, but in twenty years the nation had become far more urbanized, and several million new immigrants had arrived, mostly in the cities and mostly poor. In some ways, the charity organization societies were established as a reaction to the inadequacy of relief and administrative failures during the earlier depression. The organizations, in turn, found their own ideas and methods inadequate in the 1893–96 depression.[24] Debates over outdoor versus indoor relief or public versus private relief were simply abandoned under the pressure of the emergency, and virtually every city had some form of outdoor relief, usually with some government participation, if only providing plans and tools for jobs.[25] This may not have been "public outdoor relief for the able-bodied" but it was certainly "outdoor relief for the able-bodied with public participation."

Increasingly after the 1893–96 depression the American charity organization societies began pressing for measures that they believed would prevent poverty, in addition to their traditional functions of dealing with individual cases. The Cincinnati Charity Organization Society recognized in its annual report for 1895–96 that "honest, able-bodied men and women are sometimes driven by necessity to ask for relief. They do not want alms, they do want work." The Buffalo Charity Organization Society worked for municipal playgrounds and gymnasiums, for "vacant lot cultivation" of gardens, for a tenement law, for municipal baths, and for an employment bureau. The Associated Charities of Boston reported in 1895: "The public spirited citizen is no longer satisfied by simply alleviating the immediate suffering of poor people. He is beginning to think, what are we doing in regard to this problem of poverty as a whole?" By the next year, 1896, P. W. Ayres, who in previous reports had talked confidently of the power of "moral force" from "friendly visitors" to the poor, now said in a report of the NCCC Committee on Charity Organization:

> By improving the conditions of labor, we may remove cases and causes of poverty. Thus, if there is better education among children, more intelligent self-support becomes possible. Shorter hours of labor fosters home life. Larger wages make larger savings possible. It is essential that we look at our problem occasionally from the industrial point of view.[26]

One can see this increasing emphasis on reform being added to COS goals most clearly in the work of one of the largest and most influential charity organization societies—that of the City of New York. In 1896 the motto on the title page of the New York COS annual report read:

33

> The argument for Charity Organization is not that it saves money, or detects imposture, or that it suppresses vagrancy. Whatever of good it accomplishes in those directions is subordinate to its principal work in the cultivation of wholesome relations between the charitable and the destitute, and in the permanent improvement of the conditions of those under its care.

In fact, the arguments in favor of the charity organization society had been precisely that it saved money, detected imposture, and suppressed vagrancy. That these arguments were now scorned is a measure of the change that had taken place. The annual report for 1897 described the major problems facing people concerned with charity and poverty. No longer was there mention of suppression of begging or of indiscriminate alms-giving. Instead, "the problem of providing or securing work for the worthy, able bodied heads of families on any adequate scale, is as yet unsolved. The provisions for the care of the convalescent and of respectable aged persons whose children are unable to provide for them are inadequate." The report went on to urge strict enforcement of sanitary laws, regulations against exorbitant charges by insurance companies, inspection of food supplies, and all regulations "that have been passed for the protection and benefit of those who are least able to protect and help themselves."[27]

The areas needing and responding most to government regulation were tenement house reform and prevention of tuberculosis. The work of the New York organization toward prevention of tuberculosis was a springboard for many kinds of social reforms. In 1903 the New York Charity Organization Society published a *Handbook on the Prevention of Tuberculosis,* which began with the statement that no one should regard tuberculosis as a hopeless cause, something that is in the hands of fate. Things can be done to prevent it and cure it. Statistics showed that while certain occupations and ethnic groups were particularly susceptible, "density of population . . . is one of the most important factors." The report maintained: "Tuberculosis is a social disease, not only in the sense that its prevalence and persistence depends on social factors, but also because it is itself a factor of primary influence in other social problems." It continued, "There are no figures to indicate the amount of poverty that is due to consumption, [but] the experiences of charitable societies in every city furnish examples of families who became dependent from this cause." The handbook called for a type of social reform that would have been wide-ranging coming from any source during the Progressive period:

> Everything that can be done to make men healthier and happier is germane to this purpose of preventing tuberculosis. The improvement of the housing of the working classes; and the sanitary conditions of theatres and churches; as well as factories and shops; the multiplications of parks and playgrounds, gymnasiums and baths; the widening of streets and the enforcement of a standard of healthful conditions in all occupations; the reduction of the working day; the raising of wages; the education . . . in the art of housekeeping and the science of food preparation; . . . scientific instruction about the effects of alcohol in the public schools [*sic:* presumably what was meant was instruction in the schools about the dangers of alcohol].[28]

The emphasis was no longer on repression or on worthiness.

Thus, within a few years of the 1893–96 depression the charity organization societies in the United States, without abandoning their treatment of individual need, adopted most of the reforms that are thought of as characteristic of the "social justice" aspect of progressivism. They did not rethink their entire social philosophy. Work with individual cases continued, and schools of social work were set up to train people for casework. There was increasing emphasis on the reform of conditions and on government involvement, but moral preachment and opposition to indiscriminate giving continued, as did the belief that poverty was evidence of character fault. The tone of Mary Richmond's *Friendly Visiting among the Poor* (1897) was not very different from that of the New York COS *Handbook for Friendly Visitors among the Poor,* published fourteen years earlier. Richmond condemned "reckless giving," urged visitors to teach thrift and cleanliness, and referred to the great debt she owed the London Charity Organisation Society and to Josephine Shaw Lowell.[29]

Along with change, then, there were strong elements of continuity. By the second decade of the twentieth century, leaders in English charity organization societies were seriously considering social insurance. In the United States, the charity organization societies moved not to social insurance or similar ideas for social security, but toward reform and various ideas of social justice.[30] Each emphasis was a child of the context in which it arose. American COS spokesmen became convinced that if tenements could be made healthier, if wages could be raised, if people could be required to stay in school longer, then poverty would diminish to the point where private benevolence could take care of the few remaining cases. Social justice would provide access, abundance would provide the security.

During the same years, some charity workers, often with settlement house connections, would move toward social security through social insurance, but then they found themselves talking to a diminishing audience. It was far more popular to be in favor of social justice. In 1912 the Committee of Living and Labor of the National Conference of Charities and Corrections endorsed social insurance for accidents, for industrial disease, in old age, and for the unemployed. The committee, strangely enough, did not include general health insurance, although John B. Andrews of the American Association for Labor Legislation was a member. Owen R. Lovejoy, of the National Child Labor Committee, was chairman of the NCCC committee, which also included such people as Edward T. Devine of the New York COS and Alice Hamilton and Florence Kelley, both of whom had started their careers in social service at Hull House.[31] In general, social insurance was considered a foreign import, unsuited and unnecessary for the United States.

PART TWO

Different Imperatives: Germany and Denmark

3

The Poor Law as a Unifying Force in Germany

It was indeed foreign, but some things foreign—the charity organization society for instance—were adopted and adapted, and some were rejected, as was the case with social insurance. It all began in Germany in 1883. The beginnings of social insurance, the seeds of the idea and practice, could be found in other places and in other times, but modern social insurance as a way of dealing with the cost of industrialization was first introduced in Germany. All Western industrializing nations adopted some version of social insurance, but of these nations the United States was affected the least.

The imperatives that drove each country in the direction of the welfare state—and in particular, social insurance—were different. For Germany the dominating imperative was an effort to create a national state. Unification dominated German politics for the half-century before 1871, when it occurred, and it dominated German and in some ways European politics for the half-century after it occurred. Unifying Germany meant tying together eighteen states, each with its own traditions, rulers, and political systems and many of which were not enthralled by the idea of a dominant Prussia. Education, police, and public health were left to the states, and Bavaria was allowed to keep its own ruling family and War Ministry. Southern Germany was largely Catholic; northern Germany was mostly Protestant. There was an industrializing and urbanizing area in the Ruhr valley, yet the area of Prussia east of the Elbe, from which Bismarck came, was a region of huge landholdings and peasant agricultural labor. Unification of this heterogeneous group of states was the starting point, the context in which revisions of the poor law and new aspects of social welfare were to take place. In Germany, unification provided the pressure for revising poor relief, and an increasingly industrializing society provided the pressure for revising and centralizing already existing local or state arrangements for dealing with accidents, old age, sickness, and disability.

Any account of the development of the welfare state must begin with poor relief. Some historians regard poor relief and social insurance as separate subjects—one having to do with protection for workers, the other having to do with "the poor." Yet in the Germany of the first half of the nineteenth century, the words "poor" and "worker" were nearly synonyms. The literature on pauperism was a major genre. Throughout the nineteenth century, pauperism loomed large in people's consciousness, the same way the absence of pauperism loomed large in the American consciousness. Neither represented a true picture of society, but the picture of pauperism or absence of pauperism dominated consciousness.

Well before unification, however, poverty was a problem that people in the higher classes were aware of and that government actions could legitimately provide solutions for. A great outpouring of pamphlet literature on pauperism occurred in the 1840s. Most of the writers at that time clearly favored some kind of *staatlich* (state) intervention. Not only did the "state," whatever form that might take, have the duty to relieve poverty, but unrelieved poverty was a danger to the existence of the society that it was the state's duty to preserve. The state's duties included not merely ensuring the survival of the poor, but also taking measures that would lessen poverty in general. This would be done partly by providing work for those who were willing to work and partly through police action and prisons for those unwilling to work.[1]

Traditionally, poor relief in Germany, as in other nations, was a matter for local communities. A person acquired or was born to "right of residence," or legal residence (or, as it was called in England, a settlement). That meant a person was an official resident of a community and that if he were in need that community was responsible for providing aid. The laws of the various German states said that the community must provide the minimum necessary for existence (*unentbehrlich*), which each community determined for itself. One cannot say that at the time of unification in 1870 the system worked well. If it had been, the literature on pauperism would not have been so extensive. Unification, however, put new strains on the system. If a person moved from one German state to another—as all citizens of the new nation had a right to do—he might well lose his right to relief in one place and not acquire that right somewhere else.

The unification of Germany took place in steps. The most important step prior to the creation of the German Reich in January 1871 was the constitution of the North German Confederation in May 1867. The legislature of the confederation passed the new poor law on June 6, 1870 (Unterstützungswohnsitzgesetz), but the law continued to apply in the new Reich and was actually superseded only by a law of the Weimar Republic passed in 1924. For more than half a century this law of 1870 provided the basis for poor relief in Germany.

The poor law of 1870 was similar to the Prussian poor law of 1855, but it extended its coverage over the entire North German Confederation and then, in 1871–73, over the whole Reich, except Bavaria and Alsace-Lorraine (until 1910 and 1916, respectively). The basic idea was twofold. First, in the entire area in which the law applied, there should be no place where there was no public body responsible for the poor (*Armenverbänd*). Many areas were very rural and did not have such public bodies, but this law required them to establish such a body immediately. Second, a standard period of residence for acquiring the right to relief—two years, and after 1908 one year—would apply throughout the whole confederation (later the Reich). A two-year period of absence would mean loss of that right. In most cases it was assumed that a period of absence in one place meant that the right in some other place would be acquired, but this would clearly not be so if one moved around a good deal. In discussing whether a needy person (*Hülfsbedürftig*) should be sent back to his legal residence if he became needy somewhere else, Representative Rudolph Friedenthal, a large landholder from eastern Prussia, indicated that there was little desire to make receipt of public aid humiliating or to assume that most people were poor simply because they did not want to work. Making poor-law aid unattractive and forcing people to work were the bases of the English law but not of the German law. Friedenthal said: "We are humane enough to understand that situations can occur in life where a person, through no fault of his own, needs help, and we want to make this sad necessity as mild as possible. We do not want to make these people into vagabonds."[2] The law, then, was fairly centralized in its requirement and administrative machinery, but not in content. Each German state had the power to decide the type and amount of help a person was to receive. Yet poor relief was accepted as a duty of the political authorities.[3]

The law's silence about the type and amount of aid was a recognition of a firm principle in German poor-law administration: individualization. There was no national set of benefits to be received when a person met certain requirements—for example, so much money for a family of four. Instead, poor-law administrators for the district, most often unpaid workers from the upper layers of society, would decide what was needed. One implication of individualization was that neither grantor nor recipient was bound by rules and regulations, that needs could be met as they occurred. Another implication, however, was that poor people had no legal right to demand relief, much less to demand a certain type or amount of relief. In this sense, the principles behind the German poor law were similar to the ideas of the English and American charity organization societies. Decisions about the poor were to be made on a case-by-case basis and by the "best people." In Germany, however, the "best people" were government officials, the *Beamtenschaft;* in England and the United States, private groups made those decisions.

Germany in 1870 was overwhelmingly agrarian. A few cities were sizable, and the indemnity from France helped accelerate the move toward an industrial economy, and with it the population movement from rural to urban areas. The rural poor were a problem, but problems of poverty were most obvious in the growing cities, and it was for the urban poor that the German welfare state was gradually developed. The example the large cities of Germany used was the so-called Elberfeld System. The system had been developed before the 1870 poor law, but its spread throughout the urban areas of Germany took place during the first three decades of the Reich's existence. In the 1850s the city of Elberfeld, near Wuppertal in the Ruhr valley, tried to systemetize the administration of poor relief by dividing the city into districts and appointing unpaid workers for each district to find out who was in need and to administer relief according to individual need. Those appointed were required to serve for at least one three-year term. Although what happened in Elberfeld was not all that different from what other cities were doing, the name "Elberfeld System" has come to be identified with the theory and practice.[4]

The chief points of interest in the Elberfeld system are (1) the attempt by a town government to organize the relief in a logical way, (2) the use of great numbers of unpaid workers, (3) individualization, (4) decentralization. It should be emphasized that the system included aid to people who were employed but whose wages were judged to be inadequate to maintain a minimum standard of living. This was known as "relief in aid of wages," which in England was called the Speenhamland System, the presumed awful effects of which prompted the English Poor Law Report of 1834. In Germany, however, there was not a murmur of protest against the policy. The collective had a duty to see that every person had a minimum standard of living, whether sinner or saint. If wages did not provide the minimum, the collective must do so. Without really understanding it, the charity organization societies in England and later in the United States aspired to something as systematic and logical as the Elberfeld System, but neither country was very successful.

We have some idea of how extensive and how adequate poor relief was in Germany. The Deutsche Verein für Armenpflege und Wohltätigkeit (German Association for Poor Relief and Charity) was an organization of people, both public officials and private citizens, who were more or less professionally concerned with poverty.[5] It is roughly comparable to the National Conference of Charities and Corrections in the United States, though the context is totally different. Two studies by the Deutsche Verein give at least a partial picture of the way poor relief worked in Germany. In 1892—after the social insurance laws were in place, during rapid industrialization, but before the worldwide depression of the mid-1890s—the Deutsche Verein made a survey of the cities and larger rural districts of the Reich to find out how the poor-law authorities determined the type and amount of support. Local officials in each area had determined a minimum wage per day for an unskilled laborer, set so that a man with a small family could presumably just barely maintain them with six days work at this rate. A few towns made sharp distinctions between the worthy poor and the unworthy poor, but it is noteworthy that the great majority of towns did not.

In several German cities the average aid given to the head of the family, *per week,* was 125 to 150 percent of the *daily* minimum wage. The wife received between 80 and 100 percent of the daily minimum wage, *per week,* and children not working were given between 33 and 80 percent of the daily minimum wage *per week.* Thus, a fairly large family might get as much income per week as three or four days worth of the minimum daily wage. In many towns, because there was no limit on income from relief, a particularly large family might actually get more than a worker would earn for six days of work at the minimum wage. Many officials in the area of poor relief regarded this as only natural for "child rich" families. Support amounts were low, but an attempt was made to calculate them at a level that would maintain life. Some German towns tried to keep relief below the minimum wage, but most did not. In no town were the poor any more than objects of relief; they had no rights or claims, and in all towns need was judged solely by the authorities. Workhouses and poorhouses were not common—though they did exist—and they were certainly not required, as in England.

Supervision of the poor seems to have been relatively mild, compared with Great Britain or Denmark, judging by the answers given the Deutsche Verein in their surveys. Not everyone in the Verein was happy with this relative leniency. In discussing the need for more disciplining of the poor or the likely-to-become-poor, one member of the Verein complained impatiently that this subject had been discussed for a decade, that the 1870 poor law had no teeth, and that the Verein had done nothing. However, his proposal that anyone who was able-bodied and did not support his wife and children should be forced to work, inside a workhouse or outside, was not adopted. In fact, many voiced the opinion that the English system might be all right for England, but not for Germany. The complaint itself may well indicate that the poor were not being "disciplined" very strictly. Another survey by the Verein at about the same time gives us some idea of the number of people receiving public relief inside or outside of institutions—that is relief based only on poverty, not on membership in any church or other organization, or on the fulfilling of any duties, like paying insurance premiums. A rough calculation shows that in some cities—for instance, Berlin—6 or 7 percent of the population might be receiving relief; in other cities the figure was perhaps around 2 percent.[6] The figures must remain only indications of the situation, however, because there is often no way to tell how many were long-term recipients and how many were short-term. In most cases, there are no statistics on how many of the recipients were able-bodied, how many were single mothers with dependent children, and so on. The figures for a few cities are given in Table 1. In England, the figures were gathered by simply counting the number of recipients on a particular day, but such a method does not give precise figures on how many people received relief in the course of a year or other period. The result for England and Wales is that, over the years, somewhere between 2.0 percent and 2.5 percent of the population was receiving aid at any one time. The numbers are very rough, not very comparable, and only suggestive. They do show, however, that the German poor-law authorities might have been willing to be more generous with relief than the English Boards of Guardians. This is certainly consistent with the rhetoric

Table 1. **Relief Recipients in Selected German Cities, 1892**

City	Total population	No. recipients	Percent of population
Aachen	105,000	3,973	3.70
Berlin	1,564,000	100,000[a]	6.70
Bochum	47,618	1,375	3.00
Cologne	280,400	10,710	3.80
Düsseldorf	145,954	4,873	3.30
Elberfeld	125,899	4,978	4.05[b]
Frankfurt am Main	180,000	10,683	6.00
Halle	100,348	2,066	2.00
Kassel	74,000	1,325	1.80
Munich	349,024	4,257	1.20
Stuttgart	139,817	8,570	6.50

SOURCE: Data from DV, "Die Fürsorge für Obdachlos," *Schriften* 16 (1892).
[a]My estimate. Figures are given for families, and I have judged about four times as many individuals.
[b]Elberfeld was the only city to give the figure in their reply.

in the two countries: the English were very restrictive; the Germans were a little less so.[7]

All the large German cities and many smaller ones reported the existence of private charities, and in some places a great many organizations, whose influence was sometimes described in the answers the Deutsche Verein received simply as "an important reduction on the load on the public poor law authorities." Many cities stated explicitly that private charity did not significantly affect the public poor law, and the official who answered the questionnaire for Düsseldorf said contemptuously that most of the private charities worked "more with their heart than with their head. There is, therefore, no significant reduction in the burden on public poor law administration." Many of the private organizations were church-related, and most cities had both Catholic and Protestant (Lutheran) groups. The largest private group, certainly the one that appears in the survey responses most often, was Vaterländischer Frauenverein (the Women's Club of the Fatherland). We can conclude that private charity had some, but overall rather small, significance.[8]

In general, support from poor laws was perhaps a little better in Germany than in England, Denmark, or the United States. There was some attempt in Germany to meet minimum physical needs, and there was less desire to humiliate or punish the recipients. Being destitute in Germany was certainly terrible, but it was worse in other places. This, then, must be seen as part of the context in which the Bismarckean social insurance laws were enacted. Long before the legislation against the socialists—in fact, before the Reich came into existence, and one could easily go back before the writing of the *Communist Manifesto*—there was a tradition and bureaucratic machinery for dealing with poverty. In Germany, poverty was regarded not as extraordinary but as routine, and it was clearly accepted as part of the government's responsibility to meet the needs of citizens at least in a minimal way. Nor was poverty regarded as clear evidence of irresponsibility on the part of the poor person. Before, during, and after the social insurance laws, care of the poor was a government—that is, local, provincial, state, and national—responsibility. The social insurance laws were in part simply a new way of fulfilling that responsibility under changing circumstances.

Social Insurance in Germany in the Context of Conflict

Unification in Germany after 1871 meant not only welding together a group of heterogeneous political units, but also holding together a new nation rent by a long list of other conflicts. As with the German poor law of 1870, one way unification of these centrifugal forces was cemented was through social insurance. Although there was widespread acceptance of state action in aid to the needy, there was considerable opposition to government social insurance. When Chancellor Otto von Bismarck began talking about taking steps to improve the lot of industrial workers, he found himself confronted and temporarily blocked by a bureaucracy fervently devoted to free trade and "liberalism"—that is, against state intervention in the domestic economy. Yet in the realms of ideas and politics there were several tendencies working against this type of liberalism. In fact, it was only during the roughly thirty-year period from the defeat of the revolutions of 1848 to the late 1870s that the ideas of liberalism, in the antistate sense, were dominant. By tradition and ancient practice, the Prussian government had not felt itself debarred from any aspect of the life of its subjects.[1]

As workers moved from rural areas to city and town, as manufacturing and industrialization increased their influence in the economy, as the "worker question" (*Arbeiterfrage*) or (*soziale Frage*) became increasingly insistent, there was an official climate of laissez-faire, but the memories of state intervention were not too far in the background. Liberalism as an economic doctrine had never been as deeply rooted in Germany as it had been in England or the United States. Even during the period of liberal dominance there were currents of opinion working toward a reassertion of government intervention: in intellectual circles, in Catholic and Protestant churches, among industrial leaders, among nationalists who wanted to strengthen the state against alternative centers of power—and also currents of what might best be called *noblesse oblige* on the part of the "best people" and currents of charitableness.

In the realm of changing ideas, the most important role was probably played by what was then and is now again known as "political economy." In the 1860s, Gustav Schmoller and Bruno Hildebrand, among other economists, developed the "historical school" of political economy. They rejected the idea that Adam Smith and his followers had found universal laws of political economy, and held instead that "liberals" had developed rules that worked in the particular historical circumstances in which England found itself at the end of the eighteenth century and the beginning of the nineteenth, but that in the different historical circumstances of Germany in the 1860s, different rules might apply. So in 1872, under the leadership of Schmoller, the Verein für Sozialpolitik (Association for Social Policy) was founded. Its goal was to combine political activity with theoretical studies and thereby bring about an amelioration of social tensions and conflicts.[2] During the last decades of the nineteenth century, a number of American economists studied in Germany with leading members of the German historical school. They returned to the United States and founded the American Economic Association (AEA), which in its first years was devoted to spreading the new German approach. The AEA soon became simply a professional organization, but the German historical school and its ideas became a basis for asserting, in the United States as in Germany, that not all forms of government intervention were pernicious.

Most of the intellectual effort of the Verein für Sozialpolitik was devoted to questions of the relationship between the state and the economy—relations with industry, monopolies, the tariff, and foreign trade. As far as social policy went, the emphasis was on protective legislation—as with the unions and the Social Democrats—and not as much on social-welfare legislation. By emphasizing the "worker question" and arguing for state intervention in a variety of spheres, however, the Verein also was strengthening the arguments for welfare laws. Occasionally the Verein dealt directly with welfare. Only a little more than a year after its founding, the Verein organized a conference an old-age and disability pensions. The speakers agreed that the workers were *ungebildet* meaning not simply uneducated but also uncultured, almost primitive. Such people could not be depended on to spend their savings—even forced savings—wisely, so that for them a pension of a few marks a month was necessary. Thus, the movement of ideas was in the direction of state intervention for workers' welfare.[3]

Industry, particularly large firms in heavy industry, also recognized the problem and supported state action as a solution. In fact, much of the driving force for social insurance came from Freiherr von Stumm, called by his enemies "King of the Saar." Stumm owned one of the largest iron and steel works in the country. He was also a member of the Reichstag and a founder of the organization of German industrialists as a political pressure group—the Central Verband Deutscher Industriellen—the dominating sectors of which were the iron and steel industry and the textile industry. Bismarck was in close touch with these sectors even before the group's founding in 1876.[4]

The industrialists and the more academically oriented Verein für Socialpolitik were not antagonistic or separate groups. For example, another founding member of the organization of industrialists, H. A. Bueck, was also a member of the Verein and shared its views on the misery of the workers. Reminiscing about the 1870s many years later, Bueck scornfully rejected laissez-faire, saying that the doctrine had had some good effects but also many bad ones, most important its effects on and reactions to the "worker question." He believed that many of the new bourgeoisie in both England and Germany "lacked the general largeness of spirit and heart to understand their workers rather than exploit them." He was convinced that state action was necessary.[5] The organization of industrialists therefore supported—indeed, it was a leading force in the creation of—the social insurance plans of the 1880s.

There were many methods other than insurance plans that the

industrialists could have favored for dealing with the worker question, among them simply higher wages for their workers. From the point of view of firms that already had some kind of social insurance, state insurance actually might be less of a burden than company insurance, and it would certainly improve their relative position because all firms would share the burden. For industries like smelting, where there was considerable danger of accidents, insurance could spread out the risk and perhaps decrease costs; at least, costs would be more predictable. Pure economic self-interest clearly contributed to the position of the industrialists, but it was not the only factor. Of course, there was also bitter opposition to state social insurance from business and industry, particularly from the smaller and middle-sized firms and firms heavily involved in export. The burden of such insurance might put exporting firms at a disadvantage with foreign competitors. These firms, however, had less influence over Bismarck than the organization of industrialists.

There is considerable question whether the word "paternalism" applies to the attitudes of the German industrialists, because the word is used more frequently among non-German scholars than among Germans themselves. It was originally used mainly with regard to the large landholdings of the East Elbe region, not for the industrializing areas of Germany, and its use for that region referred to a complex arrangement of close psychological, social, and personal relationships combined with an enormous social distance—not merely to provision for members of the work force in times of sickness and old age. In the Saar region, however, there was both social and economic distance, but no personal closeness, and there was little evidence that the workers in any of the three types of labor unions regarded themselves as part of what could be called a paternalistic system.[6]

The Roman Catholic and Protestant churches also recognized the problem, but even more they were opposed to state action. Looming largest on the Catholic side was certainly the bishop of Mainz, Wilhelm Emmanuel von Ketteler. From his sermons in 1848 ("On the Largest Social Questions of the Present") to his death in 1877, he continually pointed to the misery of the lower classes. The cause of it, he maintained, was the descent from the Christian spirit, which he thought could be recaptured by production cooperatives and by workers associations that did not have the class-conflict aspects of socialist-dominated labor unions. Von Ketteler's programmatic recommendations were ignored by legislators, however. Instead, he was important in that from 1848 he kept the social question always on the Catholic agenda.[7] Protestants too were divided on the issue of state intervention and were perhaps even more skeptical than Catholics. Many Protestant spokesmen believed that private Christian charity should take care of the "social question" and that if it did not the solution was greater effort on the part of people of means to help those without means. The "Inner Mission" movement was partly an attempt to revive and rejuvenate the Christian impulse in its spiritual and charitable aspects both.[8]

So there were many whirlpools of contradictions and tensions that characterized the German response to the "worker question": Localism mixed with centralism, Christian charity mixed with economic theory, political control mixed with some idea of cooperative groups (*Genossenschaften*), recognition of class conflict mixed with a denial of its necessity, and a combination of scorn, pity, fear, and respect for the workers, an attraction for the new industrialism, and at the same time a nostalgia for a preindustrial society or rather for a vision of that preindustrial society. Bismarck too was pushed, pulled, and shoved by these whirlpools and contradictions. As Hans Rothfels said as long ago as 1927, we must think of Bismarck as more than just a manipulator—though he was certainly that—and as more than the genius, evil or otherwise, who made history go where he wanted. Like all statesmen, he was influenced by the people around him and by the circumstances in which he found himself. Obviously a man of extraordinary strength and effectiveness, Bismarck was also a man of his society, not apart from it. His heritage as an estate owner, a *Gutsbesitzer,* and his desire as a politician to win votes, must be taken into account.

For Bismarck the state stood above all. He had devoted his life to the creation of the state—the State of Germany, under Prussian leadership and the Hohenzollern dynasty. Twentieth-century non-German concepts of Germany as a centralized entity—and during the Third Reich as a totalitarian entity—should not lead us to think of Bismarck's Reich in the same way. The forces of *Partikularismus* (localism) were strong, and Bismarck's devotion to what he had created made any local threat even more dangerous in his mind. All his domestic policies, definitely including *Sozialpolitik,* were directed toward turning this sense of loyalty to a local political entity in the direction of loyalty to the nation, the Fatherland.[9]

The United States too was a federation with local rights firmly embedded in law. Most of the time states' rights led to frustration for both private and public welfare activities. In Germany, in an inverse way, federalism led to welfare legislation, for welfare legislation was seen as a way of combating localism and creating a nation. Creating a nation through welfare legislation did not seem relevant in the American context. Employers in the United States played a large part in formulating workmen's compensation laws, if not other forms of social insurance. In both Germany and the United States, large firms were in the forefront, but smaller firms eventually joined the campaign.

The new German nation was threatened not only by localism but also by two, perhaps three, international movements, although the third was stronger in other minds than Bismarck's. One of these movements was Roman Catholicism. To say that Bismarck was not motivated by his own Protestantism would be to go too far. The war against France could be seen in part as a war against a drive by Catholics to regain European hegemony. Partly the *Kulturkampf,* the label Bismarck gave to his measures against Catholicism, could be seen as a Protestant reaction to visions of a conspiracy stemming from Rome. Yet with Bismarck the political motive probably should never be given second place. Catholicism was a potential alternate center of loyalty, and Bavaria, the most Catholic part of the new Reich, was also the most independent. In a complex way, this too had a bearing on social insurance. There was the possibility that the Social Democrats and the Catholic Center Party would find a common interest in opposing the laws that suppressed them—the socialist laws and the *Kulturkampf.* As Bismarck turned from free trade to tariffs, he lost some support among the National Liberals. He would need to find support in the Reichstag somewhere else. The Center Party would and did support the chancellor on social insurance in return for his ending the *Kulturkampf.* From Bismarck's point of view, this had the added advantage of increasing the distance between the Social Democrats and the Center Party. On the one hand, the Social Democrats opposed the insurance, and on the other hand, the reasons for the alliance of Social Democrats and the Center Party would no longer exist.[10]

The second international threat to the new German nation was socialism, which could be a threat both to Bismarck and to the state on many levels, including its focus on loyalty to an international movement instead of to Germany and, its opposition to religion. Socialism could be depicted as a threat to the family, to social stability, to the position and power of those who by right should have them, and to the right of private property. Particularly after the Paris Commune of 1871, socialism seemed a threat not only to all that promoted stability in society but also to all that promoted patriotism. Bismarck feared—mistakenly as it turned out—that the German worker might come to see himself first as a member of a class and only second as a German. The urban and increasingly industrial worker might be led in that direction if the German state did not deal with the "worker question." While the "worker question" and socialism were not identical, the Social Democrats and the unions were the loudest voices emphasizing the conditions under which their members had to work and live. Yet as we have seen, others were aware of and trying to do something about it. The "worker question" existed apart from socialism, and to some extent socialism could be said to exist apart from the "worker question." One of Bismarck's aims was to increase the distance between two.

The third international threat to the German nation was seen to be the Jewish conspiracy. Bismarck himself probably did not share the anti-Semitism that had age-old roots in all of Europe. However, some of his supporters, like Court Minister Adolf Stöcker, tied social insurance, the suppression of socialism, and anti-Semitism into parts of a single effort—made more logical by the fact that many socialists, particularly those in Berlin, were Jewish.[11]

Bismarck was also a politician. As chancellor of a state with some democratic elements, a Reichstag with almost universal male suffrage, he would have to think about electoral advantage, or finding a coalition to make a parliamentary majority. This politician had to function within a context that included both a strong liberalism and deep interventionist strains, a context that included a well-developed poor-law system, mutual insurance institutions like private "sickness funds," some workers insurance in large firms, and strong pressures asking that these beginnings be further developed—by the state. As in Great Britain, and the United States, then, the German social insurance laws were completely within the institutional and ideological framework into which they were born.

Bismarck's introduction of the socialist laws in 1878 was accompanied by the statement that socialism could not be combated merely with repression, that there must also be positive steps to meet the legitimate complaints the Social Democrats had, which Bismarck thought of as only excuses for their agitation. Three years later, the "Speech from the Throne" on February 15, 1881, marked the inauguration of social insurance as a policy of Bismarck's government. In support of a bill insuring workers in the case of industrial accidents— what would now be called workmen's compensation—the speech (of course expressing Bismarck's views) said:

> His Majesty the Kaiser, at the opening of the Reichstag in February 1879, expressed his confidence that in relation to the law of 21 October 1878, the Reichstag would no longer fail to provide cooperation for the healing of social wounds through legislation. This healing is not to be sought exclusively through the repression of socialistic excesses, but also through positive furthering of the welfare of the workers.[12]

The bill was thus presented both as a way to combat socialism and as a way to heal social wounds. It was recognized that there was a "social question," not merely extremists' agitation, and that the government and the monarch had a responsibility to try to do something about it. Bismarck supported the bill with a written argument in its favor that had a significantly different, or perhaps additional, tone from that of the Speech from the Throne.

> That the state must interest itself more than previously in those of its members who are needy is not merely a duty of humanity and Christianity, by which all public institutions should be characterized, but also a policy which strengthens the state because it has as its consequences the furthering of the view, also in the propertyless classes of the population, which are at the same time the most numerous and the least educated, that the state is not only a necessary institution, but also a beneficent one. To that end, they have to

perceive through recognizable direct advantage, that the state is not merely for the protection of the better situated classes, but one which also serves their interests.

Here Bismarck emphasized that social insurance generally—and at the moment accident insurance—had as its aim binding workers and other groups to the state, not only through bonds of loyalty but also through common self-interest. He was herewith invoking patriotism (*Reichsfreundlichkeit*). He then took aim directly at those whom he correctly perceived as his chief parliamentary opposition— the National Liberals. The Social Democrats, having only a dozen members, were of no importance in the parliament. Bismarck appealed to ancient tradition rather than to innovation:

> The worry that a socialistic element will hereby find its way into legislation ought not to be a hindrance. To the extent that this is really the case it is not a matter of anything really new, but only a further development of the modern idea of the state. The state, beside the defensive duties of protecting existing rights, also has the duty, through the erecting of useful institutions and through the utilization of the means at the disposal of the commonality, to provide for the welfare of all its members, particularly the weak and the needy. In this sense, there is indeed a limited socialistic element in the regulation of poor relief by law, a duty which the modern state recognizes, in contrast to the state of ancient or medieval times. In reality it is, so far as dealing with the propertyless classes goes, merely a matter of further developing the idea at the basis of poor relief.[13]

Bismarck could appeal to tradition in a way that was impossible for an American leader. In the United States there was no tradition of central government responsibility for welfare, so there was no tradition for American reformers to invoke.

Bismarck's leading mouthpiece in this "state socialism" was the extremely conservative newspaper *Neue Preussische [Kreuz] Zeitung,* the voice of the landed aristocracy, with a concentration in East Prussia. In January 1882 the newspaper ran a lengthy, almost scholarly, series of editorials titled "Our Position in Relation to Socialism" in which it made clear that its position was not entirely negative. There were basic differences, but much of what the Conservatives wanted had a socialistic aftertaste. The series began: "The Conservative Party is in its inner being, as important as its political and religious aspects are, a social party. It has become conscious of this basic social aspect since it has begun to feel its opposition to the growing of an over-powerful capitalism."[14] This anticapitalism and communalism from an *ancien régime* viewpoint also existed in Denmark, though with less of a religious penumbra. It was almost wholly absent in British deliberations over social insurance, and totally absent in the United States. It is worth emphasizing that the German newspaper saw the solution as coming through the state.

The first proposal for accident insurance in Germany was defeated in 1881, essentially because it required more centralization than the existing "states'-righters" were willing to endure. In fact, it took three years to find an acceptable solution, for while what was being discussed was accident insurance, what was at stake was the locus of political and economic power. The second form of the accident insurance law was introduced in May 1882, but what aroused most interest was the medical insurance bill introduced at the same time. This bill, which became law on June 15, 1883, can be regarded as the beginning of national social insurance legislation. The accident insurance bill had been presented as simply an extension of the poor law, which was only partly true. The medical insurance bill was presented as a necessary part of accident insurance, which was also only partly true. The relatively easy passage of that bill, in contrast with the difficulties the accident insurance bill, told the government something crucial about the constellation of political power in Germany of the 1880s.

There were already roughly 6,000 "sickness funds" (*Krankenkassen*) in existence, of varying size and quality, and Bavaria had a kind of sickness insurance system. There was also existing national legislation that actually preceded nationhood, foreshadowing the insurance of 1883. Through measures that became law on April 7 and 8, 1876, communities throughout the Reich were empowered to establish compulsory sickness funds, but very few had done so because there was no incentive. The new law was an attempt to provide both an incentive and compulsion from the central government. As the *National-Zeitung* said, "It is merely a matter of broadening what already by law exists."[15] In fact, as adamant as the National

Liberals had become in opposition to accident insurance, many of them were enthusiastic about the medical insurance bill. Opposition to medical insurance still came from the "consistent liberals" of the Progressive Party. Their leader, Eugen Richter, whose arguments were frequently interrupted by applause from the Social Democrats (the other major source of opposition), said that compulsion by the state was never good, that there was too much variation among different parts of Germany for one law to cover all, that the voluntary funds were working well, and that this law was only the first floor of what would turn out to be an elaborate structure.[16]

The Social Democratic opposition was outspoken on the medical insurance issue, but there was a little less fervor than on the subject of accident insurance. The socialists and the labor unions saw the inadequacies of the existing "aid funds" (*hilfskassen*) and "sickness funds," but these funds had one clear virtue: they could be established by groups of workers and, because they were voluntary, could be administered exclusively by workers. The "sickness funds" envisioned in the law provided for one-third membership in the administration from employers. The SPD newspaper *Vorwärts* ridiculed the proposed law as providing for "meddling" (*Einmischung*) by employers and argued that "the emancipation of the working classes must be accomplished by the working classes themselves," but this phrase was probably not reaction to the particular law, but rather an automatic reaction to any product of the government.[17]

Aside from the opposition liberals of the Progressive Party (the "consistent liberals," who had 60 seats) and the Social Democrats (12 seats), many people of various opinions were enthusiastic about medical insurance law. The Conservatives were in favor of it, but for the benefit of doubters they emphasized how much the law took regional variation into account. Support came from the Catholic Center Party, which argued that sickness could easily ruin a factory worker, most of whom lived at a minimum existence level anyway, and that insurance would mean that the society, through the *Armenverbände,* would be relieved of the burden. There was also support from the National Liberals on the grounds that the law preserved as much local autonomy as practical, but within a national framework.[18]

Although one might find precedents for the medical insurance law of June 15, 1883, in various German states, that law was in many ways the beginning of social insurance for an industrializing nation. Its title designated it as being "for workers," and in fact the whole complex of insurance laws of the 1880s was listed in the Reichstag index as "workers insurance." It required that all workers, representing a broad variety of undertakings—including mining, smelting, privately owned railroads, and inland shipping—or in any trade or business where machinery was used, be insured, and it also required insurance for tradesmen who worked for others. Communities could extend this list to include, among others, agricultural workers, workers in the "putting-out" system, and apprentices. Household servants were not explicitly excluded, but if their employer was obligated to care for them for at least thirteen weeks they could be exempted from required insurance (secs. 1–3).[19]

The medical insurance law did not envision a national health insurance system. Instead, it established a wide variety of "funds." People who were required to be insured could meet the requirement by being a member of any fund that met the minimum requirements established by the law. These included medical benefits and a "sickness benefit," which was a cash payment calculated to amount to roughly half the average wage for that type of work. At the local level there could be community funds administered by community officials. There could also be regional funds (*ortskrankenkassen*) (sometimes called "local funds" in English, but "regional" is preferred here, to avoid confusion with the "community funds"). These regional funds became both the most common form of insurance and the most politically controversial, because they were "captured" by the Social Democratic trade unions and the Social Democratic Party. They were essentially self-governing in that they could write their own bylaws within the framework of the national legislation, but these bylaws had to be approved by the "Higher Administrative Authorities." Even more important, elected representatives of the members and their employers were to administrate the funds. Insured employees were to pay two-thirds of the premiums and have two-thirds representation on the central governing body (*Vorstand*). This method of governance, as well as the bookkeeping for the funds, was to be supervised by the "Higher Administrative Authorities," who had the power to compel records to be produced and to bring criminal charges against administrators.[20] The medical insurance law of 1883 also established "factory funds," run by the employers, and also funds in various types of construction work, such as the building of canals, where employment might be for an extended period but was essentially temporary, unlike work in a factory (secs. 59–68). The law allowed establishment or continued existence of funds run by guilds for journeymen and apprentices. Funds in the miners society (*Knappschaften*) and various funds already established or to be established outside the framework of the law were permitted to continue, provided they met the minimum terms of the law by the end of 1886.

So the medical insurance law contained a good deal of individual freedom within a basically authoritarian system. There was supervision by at least two levels of authority ("Supervising Officials" and "Higher Administrative Authorities") and in some cases by a third level (community officials). The German idea of freedom was traditionally not the image of a person alone in the woods of Kentucky. Such a person was not free from the worry of injury or illness and did not have the freedom to choose a way of making a living, a church or religion, or whether to enjoy the cultural artifacts of other human beings. A person achieved freedom within human society, and that meant within the rules of society. The "sickness funds" created an empirical reality corresponding to this theory.

While the medical insurance bill passed the Reichstag easily, the more centralized accident insurance bill did not. The government drew the obvious conclusions and in March 1884 submitted a far less centralized version that was quickly passed. The accident insurance bill did not contain public subsidies, and an organ of government would not be the insurer. A National Insurance Office was to be limited to supervisory functions and to be a court of final appeal in cases of differences of opinion about compensation or about safety regulations. Instead of a centralized insurance agency, the firms were to form "employer cooperatives" (*Berufsgenossenschaften*) that were to act as mutual insurance companies and supervisory bodies both to persuade and to pressure their members to institute safety measures. These employer cooperatives could be national and regional. Such provisions eliminated most of the centralizing features that caused the defeat of earlier versions of the bill.

Speaking in support of the bill, Bismarck sneered at private insurance companies—to cheers from the Conservatives—saying that accidents and misfortune should not be in the hands of stockholders who have a greater interest in private profit than in social necessities. One can imagine that phrases like "stockholders" and "private profit" were spoken with contempt, appropriate both for a landholder assured of income and for a socialist.[21]

An old-age and disability insurance law was widely regarded as the next and, by most people, the final stone in the edifice of social insurance. Such insurance had been talked about for years—Bismarck made no secret that it was on the agenda—and it had served as a threat and a promise throughout the debates on the other insurance laws, yet there was as much doubt about this type of insurance as about the other insurance laws. In fact, this law was fundamentally a new direction for social insurance and involved different considerations. Because it covered only industrial accidents, accident insurance could be a means of spreading the costs of industrializing to keep them from falling entirely on the shoulders of the individual worker who was injured in an accident and on the employer who might have to pay compensation, instead being shared by the entire industrial sector—employee and employer. The sickness insurance law was tied to the accident insurance law, for under the latter, accidents resulting in less than thirteen weeks of inability to work would be covered by the "sickness funds."

Old-age and disability insurance was different. It is significant, in the first place, that disability insurance and old-age insurance were always considered together; one type of long-term disability was indeed old age. Thus, the law of 1889 covered permanent loss of ability to earn a living from causes other than industrial accidents. It was not a generalizing of the direct costs of industrialization, although it might be thought of as dealing with indirect costs coming from the social changes—for instance, a new form of family pattern—that were the result of industrializing. This law was a far more generalized sharing of social burdens, in a sense symbolized by the public subsidies the insurance received. For this reason the law was opposed with added fervor by the liberals, who argued that it added a function for the state that was qualitatively different from even the previous social insurance laws—the function of caring for the poor rather than organizing insurance against catastrophe.

The objections of the Social Democrats to disability and old-age insurance also differed from their reactions to the other insurance laws. Whereas much of the reaction earlier had been essentially that nothing good could come from a government dominated by the possessing classes, they added at this time a more specific indictment of the law. In a long editorial, "Social Reform—Beggars Reform," in their newspaper (named *Der Socialdemokrat* for a brief period), they sneered at the whole program of what the government called social reform, for which this law was supposed to be the finale. "Hocus-pocus," they wrote, "one-two-three, the social question is solved." But aside from general sarcasm, the newspaper analyzed the law in detail. It used the phrase that has since become a cliché, that the pensions were "too large to die on, too small to live on" (*zum Sterben zu viel und zum Leben zu wenig*), and in fact the pensions were terribly low. The old-age pension applied to people over seventy who had contributed for at least forty-seven weeks a year for thirty years. Those provisions would keep most people from receiving a pension at all and might well also tend to keep people from striking. Overall, said *Der Socialdemokrat,* the insurance law was merely a reorganization of the poor law.[22]

The "Justification" (*Bergründung*) that accompanied the disability and old-age insurance bill had a lengthy statistical appendix with a complex analysis of life expectancy, rates of invalidity, expected pension expenditures, and the like. Thus, when the government argued that the proposed pensions would require a premium equal to 4 percent of the wages paid, but that reducing the pension age from seventy to sixty-five would require a 13 percent premium, no one was in a position to argue. In fact, all sides seemed to accept the statistical appendix without question. It was, after all, "scientific." Like all statistical conclusions, it was based on assumptions that could have been questioned but were not. Because it was prepared systematically by experts and presented by officials, it did not occur to anyone, even the Social Democrats, to challenge it.

The Conservatives supported the bill, and their position was well summed up by Otto von Hellsdorf, whose father had also been in parliament. The old relationship between worker and employer does not exist anymore, he said; we now have a relationship based purely on money. "We have to pay the price of the changed times" by giving wage labor a certain security. "The duty of society is to step in on behalf of the weaker parts of society," von Hellsdorf said. That was not socialism, merely the duty of the state.[23]

The disability and old-age bill became law, but doubts from the Right and clear opposition from the Left meant that the government could only muster a majority of twenty. These initial German social insurance laws were all based on an assumption by both sides that social conflict, mostly class conflict, was a fact. The socialists saw the conflict as inevitable; the upper classes saw it as regrettable and something to be lessened. The state was believed to have a particularly central role in such conflict. The state was not seen as society; the two words "state" and "society" were used as two distinct entities (in Denmark this was less so, but in Great Britain and the United States it was more so). "Society" was that series of groups—religious, class, city dwellers, country folk, noble, nonnoble, owners, workers— that sometimes might work in concert but that were more often in conflict with one another. Above them all was the state, trying to force them into an organic relationship for the good of all. Social conflict threatened that organic unity and should be lessened, both by negative acts like the socialist laws and by positive steps like social insurance.[24]

5

Changes in German Social Insurance

In Germany a major goal of social insurance was dampening of social conflict. The social insurance legislation may have been partly successful in achieving that goal, but the conflicts inherent in German society were also manifested in the insurance laws themselves. The bitterness of the social conflicts is revealed in the debates about altering the laws in 1911.

Although the Social Democrats, and to a lesser degree the unions, opposed social insurance on a theoretical level, they made use of it in their daily lives. The unions established a series of "Workers Information Offices" (*Arbeitersekretariate*) to keep workers informed about all kinds of laws and regulations. By the early years of the century, by far the largest category of questions concerned social insurance. When the laws were all coming up for review in 1909, the *Sozialistische Monatshefte* devoted article after article to the proposed revisions. The Social Democrats had voted against the original laws and would vote against the 1911 revision, but they did not by any means dismiss such legislation as irrelevant. Opposed they might be, but Robert Schmidt could write in 1909: "The great misery which used to commence when the family bread-winner had a long-lasting illness or disability, is now to a certain degree ameliorated."[1]

The Bismarckean social insurance was political as much as it was economic. Social insurance did not cease to be political when the laws were passed. Of all the programs, the "sickness funds" were the most important economically, but they were also the most significant politically. The Social Democratic Party, only partly because it had been forbidden to organize for a decade, developed a whole network of clubs—social, athletic, and educational. These clubs might have developed even in the absence of such repressive legislation, for they seem to have developed among working-class members in England and were a symptom of both a social and political sense of unity among industrial workers. To the surprise of all political sides, among these clubs were the regional sickness funds. As the workers lost an old institution, the *freie Hilfskassen,* they gained this new one—which was not quite as independent as the old institution, but still subject to being dominated by the workers through their control of two-thirds of the leadership.[2]

After 1883 the Social Democrats organized through the regional sickness funds, and after 1889 they could openly organize their party. The industrialists who had supported sickness insurance were surprised and alarmed; the Social Democrats were surprised and overjoyed. Soon positions within the sickness fund administration became means for workers to rise from the factory floor without being declassed. By the turn of the century, Social Democrats were agitating for eliminating all other kinds of sickness funds and allowing only regional sickness funds to continue.[3]

The first of the reforms in 1911 in the German social insurance law was a proposed revision of how the sickness funds were goverened. Instead of a two-thirds majority in the leadership of the regional sickness funds, the workers were to have half representation. In fact, the political uses of the insurance system produced the greatest amount of anger in the lengthy and detailed debates. There were a great many issues other than this one. The debates on the proposed revision were the longest of any in that session, and the resulting law had 1,805 paragraphs and was printed as a separate book of 485 pages. The "Justification" that accompanied the bill was a relatively technical document arguing why this or that provision should be changed, but for about 10 of its 755 pages it became anything but technical. Over the years, it claimed, many complaints had come into the government "that in many regional sickness funds, the insured have misused and exploited their predominance for partisan political purposes."

> The sickness funds are quasi-governmental (*öffentlichrechtliche*) institutions created exclusively for the public welfare and are exclusively to serve that end. They must provide their benefits to the insured without consideration of his political, economic, or religious positions. Under all circumstances, it must be ensured that the funds not be used in any way as a source for struggles against employers. No one can dispute that.
>
> In contrast to this assumption, it cannot be denied that in a great majority of cases in the larger cities and in industrial regions, candidates for the leadership and committees of the regional sickness funds are put forth by political or labor union organizations, and they are elected on that basis. It is normal, then, to speak of the victory of one or another political party or type of labor union represented among workers. . . .
>
> Even more of a problem is that the law provides no satisfactory way of preventing or meeting partisan encroachments into the area of the administration of the sickness funds.[4]

Over and over the "Justification" used the word "misuse" and said that existing laws were inadequate to deal with the problem.

The Social Democrats, who in the previous election in 1907 had received more votes than any other party but did not have a proportionate position in the Reichstag, could not be expected to allow those words to go unchallenged. All the political parties were aware that there would be an election in January 1912, and in the debates in May 1911 each side accused the other of simply wanting to build a record to run on seven months later. The nonsocialists wanted to be sure that Social Democratic Party would not be able to use its position in the sickness funds to support an increase in their strength in the Reichstag. "The Social Democrats have three centers of power," said Count Kuno von Westarp for the Conservative Party, "the party, the trade unions, and the sickness funds." No one could deny the legitimacy of the first two, but the third was used for purposes other than those intended in 1883.

Von Westarp's speech was continually interrupted by shouts from the floor, and several times he had to stop while the Reichstag president tried to restore order. When he claimed that in many places the leader of the sickness funds had to promise to join the Social Democratic Party, the party on the left broke out in fury. "You are barking like a dog!" shouted one member, provoking sharp reprimands from the chair.[5] Social Democrat Robert Eichhorn was so furious that in his response to von Westarp he spoke faster than the stenographer could write and several times had to be reprimanded for insulting other members. "You are talking about taking away the rights of the workers," he claimed. "It is a matter here of a step against the equality of the working classes." What it amounts to, he said, is another socialist law "against the workers, against the Social Democrats."[6]

The Social Democrats lost this political battle temporarily; they were reduced to half the sickness fund leadership until the two-thirds was restored in 1919.[7] For many years they regarded this as a major defeat, but they may have won the larger war because in the 1912 election their seats in Reichstag increased two-and-a-half times (from 43 to 110), and they were the largest party, with about one-third more votes than the next largest political party, the Center Party, which had proposed the law in the first place. This whole battle illustrated once again the degree to which social insurance was seen by all sides as, among other things, one more weapon in the class war.

The political uses of social insurance were also clear when in the fall of 1911 a law establishing a special insurance for white-collar workers earning up to 5,000 marks a year was introduced by the government. All sides were clear about what this meant and were open about their intent. The "Justification" accompanying the law had elaborate statistical data showing that the "dependent white-collar workers" (*unselbständige Angestellte*) were an increasingly large proportion of the work force. In some cases, the "Justification" went on, these people do not come under social insurance at all, but when they do the size of the pensions are only at the "minimum for existence, which only offers the possibility for a modest existence in areas of low living costs." When public funds are involved, nothing more than an *Existenzminimum* is justified. However, the "education, lifestyle, and social position of the majority of white-collar workers require additional benefits." This law gives them "a higher degree of public care than the workers insurance" can offer them.[8]

The purpose, then, was to put an economic lid on the category of "worker," to appeal to the new middle class, and to make sure the middle class would not identify with workers and join the Social Democratic Party.

The reasoning here is fairly complex: Even well-paid people of higher social status deserve some publicly organized welfare services, but payments from public funds should not be anything more than what is absolutely necessary. However, people at certain educational and social levels should not be asked to live at the same level as "workers." What kind of system could show public concern and provide higher pensions, but not involve public funds? The solution was to set up a system of insurance for all "dependent white-collar workers" that was self-financing. The coercive powers of government would be used to require membership, and the administrative apparatus of civil servants would run the system. Both the printed "Justification" and the speech of the interior minister when he introduced the bill on October 19 explicitly recognized that the law broke with the idea of workers'—that is, poor people's—insurance.[9]

The Center Party was enthusiastic about a law that recognized the *neuaufkommenden Mittelstand* (new middle class) and that would extend benefits to 2 million members of that class. The term "new middle class" needs explanation here. The traditional *Mittelstand* consisted primarily of independent small shopkeepers and skilled artisans. These people were conscious of themselves as a group, as a *Stand,* in society and were proud of their skills and independence. In income and education, the "dependent white-collar workers" were often the economic equal or superior of the traditional *Mittelstand,* but they were not independent. Would they identify with the traditional *Mittelstand* or with the workers, with whom they shared the status of employees? In retrospect we know that there should have been no doubt, but the conservative forces in Germany wanted to use this new law to increase the distance between "workers" and "white collar employees." The Conservative Party cheered at the idea that "at last we have found a way to carry on a *Mittelstandpolitik*."

The Social Democrats were caught in an unfamiliar dilemma. They saw that rather than increasing proletarianization, as Marx had predicted, they might be faced with an increasing *embourgeoisement* of the work force. They would want this new group to think of themselves not as a "new middle class" but as a new kind of proletariat, because the Social Democrats would want them as allies and, after all, they stood in the same relation to the means of production and were just as much dependent on the wage system as "workers." Robert Schmidt, a union official as well as a Social Democrat member of the Reichstag, tried to show that the traditional *Mittelstand* wanted nothing to do with this "new middle class" and did not support the proposed insurance. The Social Democrats said that the white-collar workers should simply be included in the workers insurance. On the other hand, the party did not feel it could vote against something that the people they hoped to have as allies wanted, so they ended up joining in the unanimous vote by which the law was passed. Ironically, the first social insurance law for which the Social Democrats voted was thus insurance not for the proletariat but for the middle class.[10]

The law revising the governance of the sickness funds and the law insuring white-collar workers both had overwhelmingly political motives. The primary purpose was to limit the influence of the Social Democrats in the regional sickness funds and to emphasize the differences, rather than the similarities, between "workers" and "salaried employees" (as the English often translate *Angestellte*). Thus it is clear that class conflict was a central factor in shaping German social insurance. We now shift the focus to Denmark, a society where the central factor was consensus and an attempt to preserve consensus.

Denmark and the Poor Law
in the Context of Consensus

To Americans, all versions of social insurance could look alike, and various systems might indeed be alike in their external characteristics. But social insurance was perceived in different ways in different countries. Since Marquis Child's book *The Middle Way* was published in 1936, Americans have thought of the Scandinavian approach as the "Swedish System," but in fact Denmark was the pioneer of what is now thought of as the Swedish System (although this does not imply that the two systems are identical in fact or in ideology). It is in Denmark that we find the genesis of a mechanism that shared some features with Germany but was built on different social assumptions.

In Germany social welfare policy was seen by all sides as a weapon in a system of conflicting powers, but in Denmark it emerged as a means for lessening conflict. Social welfare legislation in Germany became the battleground between the great industrialists and smaller businesses, between local control and centralization, between workers and employers; in Denmark it was the bridge across which all groups could communicate with one another. The entire mood in the two countries was different. In Germany the various groups were battling with one another, as it were, at long range. In Denmark too there is conflict, but it was a conflict across a smaller gulf, with boxing gloves instead of long-range artillery. The two antagonists are closer together and the damage is much less. After the match, the two opponents might actually have a beer together.

The modern phase of social legislation in Denmark is a product of the 1890s, of course influenced by Germany but stemming essentially from Danish assumptions, Danish conditions, and Danish antecedents. To a large degree, the fact that important legislation was passed during the 1890s is a product of politics rather than economics. There was no huge indemnity, like the French indemnity to Germany, to encourage rapid industrialization. Denmark's industrialization was far more gradual than Germany's, and the country's chief export products were agricultural during the entire pre–World War I period. The sharp economic decline of the 1890s did not come until after a start on welfare legislation had been made. Instead, by the 1890s political conflict in Denmark had reached a stage that seemed to threaten long-held assumptions about the way society worked. Passing social welfare legislation seemed to be a useful strategy for maintaining those assumptions. The assumptions were in such contrast to Americans' assumptions that it is not surprising that different institutions emerged.

In the history of social change in Denmark, stresses that resulted in violent revolutions in other countries were in Denmark accommodated with perhaps disruptions in the body politic but without violent revolution and without permanently ripping apart the social structure. For example, the transition from feudal decentralization to absolute monarchy in the middle of the seventeenth century was nonviolent, and in contrast to the French Revolution the agricultural reforms at the end of the eighteenth century were also nonviolent. In addition, the transition from absolute monarchy to a democratic constitution in 1848–49 was made without violence. This tradition of nonviolent social change could have been broken at any time, but by the 1890s it was nearly two-and-a-half centuries old and carried a good deal of weight. Most Danes seemed to view their country as a place where violence was avoided and where overt social conflict was the ultimate horror to be avoided at all costs. Yet by the 1880s there were signs that political strains were becoming unbearable and that violent revolution might result. To understand how this came to be, one must look at Danish constitutional and political history since 1848.

The Constitutional Convention of 1848 was a product of monarchical vacillation, agitation on the part of the democratic elements in the farmers organizations and among liberal intellectuals, and the serious clashes over democracy in Germany, France, Belgium, and elsewhere. Revolution seemed to be exploding all over Europe, and King Christian VIII, wanting to avoid an outbreak of either a nationalist or democratic revolution in Denmark, ordered that a democratic constitution be written. His death in 1848, before the new constitution was completed, put the project in doubt, but after some hesitation his son, Frederick VII, promulgated the results of the constituent assembly's deliberation.

The Constitution of 1849 was a remarkably democratic document. It provided universal suffrage, except for household servants and recipients of poor-law relief, and it appeared to give the lower house a veto over government policy through the power of the purse. The unexpected subversion of this apparent power turned out to be a major reason that the first batch of social legislation half a century later was passed.

In the aftermath of the losing war with Prussia in 1864, the Danish democratic Constitution of June 1849 (always called the June Constitution) was rewritten in a less democratic direction. In this 1866 constitution the lower house (*Folketing*) was left untouched—that is, democratic—but the upper house (*Landsting*) was elected by indirect voting, and seven of the sixty-six members were appointed by the king, thus assuring large landholders a majority. The result was a government that could be said to have checks and balances but that also contained the potential for its own destruction.[1] The two major political groups in Denmark each regarded the other as the enemy: the Left felt they had been cheated out of the Constitution of 1849, and its restoration became their rallying cry and the basis for their cooperation with the Social Democrats in the 1890s. The Right felt that they had a duty to God and the king to maintain order and stability in society. (One must always remember that, in Denmark, "Left" was the name of the party dominated by well-to-do farmers, not great landholders, and is not "left" in any socialist sense.)

71

The gulf between the two groups became ever wider during the 1870s, when the Left kept winning majorities in election but the Right, with support from the king, formed the government. The Right could also count on a permanent majority, and thus a legislative veto, in the upper house. They constantly quoted the clause of the constitution that said: "The King shall appoint and dismiss his ministers. He decides their number and the division of responsibility among them." Thus, with the support of the king, the Right could and did form the government for thirty-five years after 1866.

In 1875, J.S.B. Estrup first headed the government as prime minister. Estrup was a large landholder who believed that democracy was one of the most dangerous inventions of the nineteenth century and that those who owned large amounts of land were all that stood between Denmark and chaos. Almost his first political act was to lose the election held the following year. Nevertheless he remained prime minister, named by the king. It was his stubbornness, cleverness, opposition to democracy, and conviction that he was the person to save Denmark from chaos that meant he in effect ruled Denmark for the next fifteen years in what at least one historian has called a dictatorship.[2] Proclaiming an "after me the deluge" philosophy, he decided to use the paragraph of the constitution that gave the government the right to decree "provisional" laws if parliament (the Rigsdag) were not in session and an emergency demanded it. These provisional laws could not violate the constitution, but they did not need parliamentary approval, although they had to be introduced in the next session of parliament. This procedure was clearly meant to meet an emergency situation, which only a mind like Estrup's could perceive in 1876. For years Estrup made a practice of sending parliament home, then proclaiming "provisional" laws.

Even though there was doubt about the legality of the way Estrup governed, he was determined to continue it. For the Left, the only two alternatives seemed to be revolution or submission and totally abandoning their hopes for a restoration of the June Constitution. But revolution was not in the Danish tradition. The two parties faced each other at the end of the 1880s—one with popular support, the other with the powers of government: the army and the king. The potential for violence was inherent in the situation. Many members of both parties wanted to stand firm, to insist on their position, and not to talk to the opposition. There were also those who believed that if a subject on which moderate members of the two parties would agree or at least about which they could talk, could be found the crisis could be averted and something might turn up.

The compromisers found a leader in Frede Bojsen, from the Left, a man whose whole being was moderate, who was nonthreatening, not stubborn, almost colorless—but he was perfect for the task. He had been an army officer, but only a lieutenant. He came from a large family made up mostly of parish priests, and he had married Bishop N. F. S. Grundtvig's daughter. Grundtvig, the most influential religious leader of the day, had a strong social sense and the respect of virtually all Danes, with the possible exception of Søren Kierkegaard.

In 1890 Bojsen became the most influential figure in the Left party. On the other side, many members of Estrup's party were also friendly toward the idea of negotiations, if for no other reasons than that an appropriation for new fortifications by the parliament would be necessary. The leading figure on the Right was probably Hans Peter Ingerslev, a large landowner, a member of the upper house, and interior minister. The more flexible members of the Right signaled their readiness to compromise in a speech by Justice Minister Johannes Nelleman on Constitution Day, June 9, 1890. Nelleman said there should be cooperation among all "who saw the danger of European nihilism and socialism." At about the same time, Bojsen wrote a series of newspaper articles that declared there was no possibility of compromise on large constitutional issues and that revolution was unthinkable, but that efforts should be directed toward solving day-to-day problems.[3]

What provided the arena for compromise was the poor law and related social welfare legislation. In spite of Nelleman's reference to "nihilism and socialism," welfare was not approached primarily as a way to avoid radicalism or to break with Danish traditions, nor was it a response to economic crisis. It was instead an area in which all sides believed there was a reasonable chance for consensus. The poor law, and the social legislation that can be said to have grown from the poor law, was a natural subject for compromise in Denmark. Section 84 of the June Constitution stated: "Anyone who cannot support himself or his dependents, and is not himself the dependent of someone else, has a right to help from the public, though he must submit to applicable laws in such cases." That assertion was nothing new it merely summed up existing rules and customs. Virtually everything else in the constitution was new, but this provision was not. No matter what was changed in subsequent versions of the constitution, this provision remained constant. The right was certainly vaguely stated, containing nothing about whether it was enforceable by law, and if so against whom. Yet it was there and it was implemented.

The traditional policy was simply that no Dane would be permitted to starve in Denmark, that the community should take care of its own. Until the Protestant Reformation (1536 in Denmark), the church had fulfilled its traditional role of dispensing charity. After the Reformation, however, the traditional system collapsed and nothing replaced it. The poor were left to beg. Even begging met with restrictions—for instance, the poor were allowed to beg only in their own locality (*sogne*). Throughout the seventeenth century, the number of beggers increased to the point that the influential members of society became alarmed. Under the law of September 24, 1708, the first national poor law in Denmark, inspectors were established, and therewith a public poor-law authority under national jurisdiction. Under this law begging was forbidden. The inspectors were to weed out those who had contributed to their own poverty (the chief way to do that seems to have been too much drinking) and to divide the others into classes (widows, children, lunatics, etc.) who could receive aid from the public. "The public" in this case meant the locality rather than the nation.[4] As early as 1708, then, the distinction between "worthy" and "unworthy" entered Danish law, a distinction that would remain until after World War II.

By the end of the eighteenth century it was clear that begging had continued to increase, and decrees were issued concerning the poor—in Copenhagen in 1799 and in the rest of the country in 1803. These decrees ensured support for those who could not support themselves. They forbade the sending of the poor from parish to parish, and they did not require that support be given only in poorhouses, as the law of 1834 in England would do. They also made the minister in each parish a permanent member of the board of poor-law commissioners. Because ministers were both civil servants and churchmen, this in a sense provided for public administration of relief and at the same time reasserted the role of the church—but now a national church rather than international church. The decrees reasserted the concept that no one should starve in Denmark. Thus, by the beginning of the nineteenth century the central Danish government saw itself as ultimately responsible for the poor, even to the extent of legislating support for them.[5]

In addition to the clause giving the poor the right to relief, the constitution of 1849 contained what might be considered an expression of the restrictive aspects of poor-law support. All males over the age of thirty could vote—except servants, people who had been deprived of their civil rights, and those who had received poor-law support. It might be argued that this clause created a judicial line through Danish society where there had been none before—between first-class citizens, who had not received help from the poor-law authorities, and second-class citizens, who had received help. But one could also point to the vast number of adults not receiving help under the poor law who did not have the franchise—namely, women and servants. It would seem more historical to argue that the constitution had created a new class of citizen—the voter. It did exclude some people, but not from anything they had before. Moreover, one central theme in the creation of the Danish welfare state ever since has been that the excluded group has grown ever smaller, until it ceased to exist altogether.

The constitution was strict in its exclusions, but the legislature or administration quickly made exceptions to that strictness. Exceptions were made for families of men in the army and for periods of exceptionally hard times. According to these laws, people could receive help under the poor law "without the effects of the poor law" (*uden fattiglovens virkninger*)—that is, without incurring any legal disabilities. The phrase "without the effects of the poor law" appears again and again in Danish welfare history, and the category of aid that did have those effects became smaller and smaller. Thus, some kind of support for the poor was a tradition that those on the Right could support.

At the end of the 1880s and the beginning of the 1890s, the whole issue of the "workers"—that is, urban industrial labor—was widely discussed in Denmark, even in circles where one might not normally expect it. A *husmand* was a special type of small landholder, farming a tiny farm created by the state to keep the poor on the land and to have the poor available for labor on larger holdings. These small farmers were proud of their efficient farming techniques and had developed a sense of group identity. In 1889 their journal, *Husmands-vennen,* published a series of articles about how bad conditions in cities were and how society had a responsibility to do something about them. The journal of the *højskole* movement, a highly Christian group concerned with improving adult education in the countryside, had a long debate in its 1892 issues about whether it was possible to discuss external salvation with urban workers, whose needs were so pressing in *this* world.[6]

Although there was no group of political economists quite equivalent to the Verein für Sozialpolitik in Germany, the professors who taught political economy at the University of Copenhagen in the 1880s and 1890s were by no means pure liberals. They were far more influenced by John Stuart Mill than by his father, James Mill. Both the political economists and the small-landholder movement were heavily influenced by Henry George. George and John Stuart Mill argued that in some circumstances government intervention could ameliorate misallocation of goods and even increase freedom.

In Germany, the debates over social policy always took place in the shadow of the "socialist" threat and against the background of the socialist laws. In Denmark there were repressions of a smaller sort, and the man who founded the party in 1871, Louis Pio, was jailed from 1873 to 1876. Though a firebrand, Pio was not a steadfast leader. In 1877 he allowed the police to bribe him to emigrate to America, where he failed in an attempt to found a utopian community in Kansas and died in 1894. After 1870, leadership passed to leaders of the trade union movement, who were more interested in practical results than in socialist theories. Many members of the Social Democratic Party were actually not factory workers at all, but small proprietors and farmers. Although two Social Democrat representatives were elected to the lower house in 1884, they were content to work with the Left for parliamentary democracy and did not have a direct part in the negotiations between Left and Right in the 1890s that led to welfare legislation. Thus Social Democrats in Denmark were neither perceived nor perceived themselves as being in the same kind of adversarial relation to the rest of society that existed in Germany. Their position was much more comparable to that of the Labour Party in England, although the English party was more proletarian than the Danish.[7] In the United States, which had neither a Labour Party nor a Social Democratic Party, the labor movement had explicitly bread-and-butter goals, not the overthrowing of society or establishing a new social order.

In Denmark the labor movement and the Social Democratic Party, which were almost synonymous, were less Marxist and more revisionist than in Germany. The party argued that their ultimate goal, the reorganization of society, could not be achieved until they had a majority of the people on their side. In the meantime, because they believed they had a responsibility not only to future generations but also to those on earth at this time, they had a series of reform demands: "We demand, for example, that society assume the cost of children's education, of curing the sick, of a humane poor law, that the sick, within certain limits, shall not suffer economic harm from their sickness, and that the unemployed be supported."[8]

In general, the position of the Social Democrats on welfare legislation was subtly different in Germany and in Denmark. In both countries the Social Democrats opposed the laws. In Germany the opposition was based on the assumption that the government was the enemy and that the whole attempt at social legislation was simply a swindle. In Denmark the Social Democrats discussed the details of the laws and pointed out their shortcomings. The laws were inadequate, the Social Democrats were saying, but the fundamental idea of welfare legislation might have something to it. For German Social Democrats the laws were simply more evidence of the perfidy of the capitalists. In a typically Danish way, both the labor movement and academic economists scorned the kind of ideological conflict they saw in Germany. The leading professor of political economy sneered at the southern neighbor, "where out of every idea, no matter how uncertain, a theory is immediately created, and out of every theory comes a thick book."[9] No one, inside or outside of the Rigsdag, wanted the political debate to become as heated as it was in Germany.

The time for compromise seemed ripe when one of the more moderate members from the Right, Interior Minister Ingerslev, introduced a bill in 1889 to reform the poor law. The bill provided for rudimentary old-age pensions "without the effects of the poor law" (that is, without a person's having to place himself or herself under the supervision of the poor-law authorities or losing the vote) and for public money to be given to the previously entirely private "mutual-aid sickness societies" (*sygekasser*). Because moderate members of the Left and the Right had worked out the arrangements together outside the Rigsdag, the debate on the floor can be considered play-acting. Yet the direction of future legislation was indicated by the debates, especially by dissenters from the compromise who wanted the law to be less harsh.

The most thoroughgoing critic of the law was undoubtedly Peter Holm of the Social Democrats. He admitted that because he was in a tiny minority in the Rigsdag he could not even hope to gather enough information to introduce meaningful amendments to the bill, but many of his views eventually became those of the country as a whole. His basic point was that poverty should be regarded as a consequence of a misconstructed society and that poverty "is an unhappy accident that rests as a punishment on some people and brings suffering to many more who have not earned it at all." He recognized that the bill being proposed was an improvement over what existed, but he wanted a greater improvement, greater humanitarian feeling. He, and the Social Democrats generally, argued that the national state should take over all support of the poor. As far as I can determine, Holm alone argued that this would lead to greater "equality." The concept of equality was not a major element in Danish social thought, and the word is rarely mentioned, even by the Social Democrats, up to and including the 1930s. Perhaps there was a good deal of sentiment for Bishop Grundtvig's goal—a society in which "few have too much, and fewer still have too little"—but notions of rank and "estate" and position in society were too strongly rooted for "equality" to have much meaning. Even Holm, had he stopped to analyze the word, perhaps meant only that the law would be administered more uniformly if administration were national.[10] Holm was one of the few people to deal with the power of the poor over their own fate. He referred sarcastically to the right of the poor to complain and asked rhetorically to whom they could complain. The answer was that they could complain only to the same authorities against which they had complained.[11]

The law itself, as finally passed in April 1891, did not contain any great departures from past practice. What pointed toward the future was what the law did not say, particularly about the elderly and the sick. People from these two categories were the most numerous in various poorhouses, and both were later covered in laws dealing with their particular cases. Holm must be judged correct when he said about the poor law itself, explaining why he would not vote for the law, "If one reads through the bill now under consideration and becomes familiar with the rules it undertakes to assemble, one can say that the burdens of poverty—force, hunger, beatings, shutting in, and the loss of civil rights—it is these which the poor-law authorities, in most instances, offer to those who more or less through no fault of their own come in under it."[12]

The law was harsh by modern standards. In its fundamental ideas and in its details, it was harsher than the German law, which, for example, made no distinction between "worthy" and "unworthy." Under the law, the poor could be required to work without pay, though not rented out against their will, and could be required to stay in a workhouse or poorhouse, with police help if necessary (sec. 39).[13] Again, there was no recourse to the courts. The poor were required to bring up their children "responsibly" (*forsvarligt*), and that word was defined as sending them to school, not teaching them to beg, and however else the authorities might define it. Where children were not brought up "responsibly," they could be taken from their parents (sec. 40), again without court action. For behavior "contrary to good order and morals, such as neglect of duties, contrariness toward authorities, drunkenness, incorrigibility, unwillingness to work, leaving assigned work or residence without permission, leaving an assigned workhouse or poorhouse without permission," the poor could be punished by up to six months in prison if the town police chief agreed. There was no recourse to the courts (sec. 41).

The law contained a phrase that made the relationship between the authorities and the poor clear: "Decisions made pursuant to this law by supervisory authorities cannot be brought to court" (sec. 59). It is true that all civil servants were governed by laws forbidding them from doing things that were not within their authority (sec. 60), but this was to control criminality, not differences in judgment. Moreover, it would have been a rare poverty-stricken individual who would bring the authorities to court. So this provision meant that decisions of the county administrator, the town police chiefs, and in the highest instance the justice minister—all people within the system of poor-law control—could not be appealed to anyone outside the system. This made the poor law authoritarian and didactic. The poor were simply objects to be dealt with and could not become subjects except by illegal means, such as burning down their poorhouses, which occasionally happened. Yet even this didactic and authoritarian law hinted at what was to come.

Section 6 of the law dealt with special circumstances, and it is worth noting that these included help from the national state and from the public that did not bring a loss of civil rights. Once this category existed, it was quite possible to enlarge it. As in the past, the blind, dumb, retarded, and mentally ill, if they were helped in national institutions, could get that help "without the effects of the poor law" as could Danish seamen who were shipwrecked on the Danish coast and families of men called to military service in time of war (secs. 64, 65). More significant, perhaps, was the provision that people who had not previously requested help from the poor laws, who were members of the private mutual aid sickness associations, and whose benefits had run out before they had recovered would receive continued support without the legal effects of the poor laws (sec. 63).

So the new poor law was no great departure from previous practice and represented very little change in previous attitudes toward the poor. It continued to see them as "others" and to give their supervisors greater power over them than authorities had over ordinary civilians. The law continued its attempt to scare the poor away from "help from the public" and to put a blot on the name of those who had received public aid. In all its provisions the law assumed that the size and nature of the help would be determined by local officials. This gave the officials enormous power and was further evidence that the poor were seen simply as things to be taken care of. The law does not mention the size of the payment. This issue of the power of local authorities to give help as they saw fit (*frit skøn*) was later opposed by those who wanted predetermined payment amounts (*faste takster*) and who wanted the poor to be able to predict what circumstances would bring what consequences. As it was, a poor person had to declare himself or herself impoverished and petition the well-to-do for just enough to hold body and soul together. The issue of whether to eliminate this power and this relationship between the poor and the well-off became one of the chief battles—and one of the chief victories of the next forty years. Because the responsibility for administering the poor law lay with individual localities and administration varied from place to place—unlike Germany, where there was no convenient nationwide organization—we cannot say with certainty how the poor law in Denmark was administered. However, tradition in Danish society has it that kindness was a rarity, that going to the poor-law authorities was a last resort, and that those who held the authority under the poor law made the poor feel the law's heavy hand.[14]

The only real victory that critics of the poor law won was in the area of old-age pensions. The Left wanted the pension system "freed from any feelings of humiliation." No one argued with the implication that other forms of poor relief did involve such feelings, but neither did anyone contradict the fundamental idea of a humiliation-free pension. Proposed clauses in the poor law relating to the aged were dropped and became a separate law, which established noncontributory old-age pensions for the poor.[15] While there were some disputes about the size and financing of such pensions, most Danes agreed that the aged poor should receive some kind of aid. The explanation for this belief may be the practical one of simply letting the burden be shared equitably instead of letting it depend on feelings of loyalty among the children of the aged or on humanitarian feelings toward the aged, who should not be deprived of human rights merely because they are old. But it is more likely that the reason was a conception of Danish society as an organic unit. Babies, children, young people, adults, and the elderly each had their functions and places in that society. Rich and poor, male and female, farmers and city dwellers—all had their places. Elderly people who had successfully fulfilled their productive function should not be abandoned to humiliation and left in institutions that were, at least partly, places of punishment. "These poorhouses . . . are a blot of shame over a middle-class society," said a Social Democrat member of the lower house, "and there could well be written over the door [of the poorhouse] 'Let all who enter here, abandon hope.' They stand as a threatening and almost unavoidable cloud on the horizon of most ordinary (*smaakaarsfolk*) people in this country, and the fear of ending up there embitters a whole lifetime." He believed that "honorable men and women who have exhausted themselves in the service of society have rights simply as human beings to ask more in their old age than that."[16]

The Danish old-age pension law, which took effect on April 15, 1891, is very different in tone from the Danish poor law. Occasionally a note of punishment or control comes through as the pension law reveals its origins in the earlier law. It is short, containing no sections or chapters and only eleven brief "articles." The tone of the whole is set by the first article: "Whoever, after his 60th year, is not able to furnish himself or his dependents the necessary support, or necessary medical treatment, shall, if he is a citizen, be entitled to old-age support according to the following rules."[17] The German law, based on actuarial principles, made the retirement age seventy, not sixty, in order to keep premiums down—a consideration that was absent from the debates in Denmark. The tone of the Danish old-age pension law is more generous, less punitive, and more conscious of the rights of the recipients than the poor law, but it was not the most generous bill introduced in the session of 1890–91. Viggo Hørup's and Sigurd Berg's wing of the Left proposed a broader law, partly because they favored it and partly because they opposed any negotiating with the Right and hoped to show that the Left was giving up too much. The more generous law never had a chance of passing, but Hørup's speech introducing the bill is significant nonetheless. "It is a principle," he said, "established in our constitution. It is recognized there that society has a responsibility for its helpless members."

> I think that the task of the future will be to increase more and more the feeling of solidarity between the various layers of society, so we will move away from the old feeling of atomism and individualism, because it no longer fulfills the stage of civilization which we have reached. If anyone says that is socialism, that it goes in a socialist direction, I answer, Yes, what proposal, not just in Denmark, but anywhere else in the world, does not go in a socialist direction if it is good for anything?

"They have their demands," he continued, speaking of the elderly, "and we have our duty to fulfill these demands"—a sentiment shared by the vast majority and brought to fruition in the final bill, which if it had more conditions than Hørup's was nevertheless similar in outline.[18]

The Danish old-age pension law was the first to involve the national treasury—to the amount of 2 million kroner a year in 1891. It was therefore in many ways of greater portent for the future than the poor law. Formally support was given by the locality, but up to half that support could be refunded by the national government. Thus, the surface of old forms was maintained, but the reality of new power structures would be assumed by the central government in one form or another.

To fund this pension, a small tax was put on beer, but even a moderate like Bojsen was willing to mention the term "income tax" if no better nuisance taxes could be found and so long as the income tax was "moderate."[19] Eventually income taxes and a value-added tax were the chief sources for welfare expenditures, and transfer payments thus became the basic thought behind them, instead of forced savings or insurance.

Although it was passed under the shadow of the German pension law of 1889, the Danish law was different from the German in two fundamental points. First, the assumption was that no special premiums for the pension were necessary. An elderly Dane had in effect paid his premiums with a lifetime of work, and not simply for himself but also for the society of which he was a member. Second, in contrast to the German law, which provided a pension for anyone who had paid premiums and who reached the retirement age of seventy, without any moral judgment, the Danish law was explicitly for the "worthy needy," and this worthiness and need were to be judged by others. The Danish old-age pension law was clearly a modification of the poor law and one strand in the development of the Danish welfare state. The other major strand was the sickness fund law, which grew out of a history quite different from that of the poor law.

7

Social Insurance in Denmark in the Context of Consensus

When Viggo Hørup introduced his bill on old-age pensions, he said that the task for the future would be to increase the "feeling of solidarity between the various layers of society, so we will move away from the old feeling of atomism." From a very different social stratum, a similar view was expressed by Baron Tage Reedtz-Thott in the upper house of the Rigsdag in 1888, during the debates on public subsidies for mutual-aid sickness societies. As one of the country's largest landowners, the baron is hardly the person one might expect to have the greatest insight into social-welfare problems, but his statement sums up much of the thought that dominated the direction of legislation from that time on. In the past, he said,

> there had gradually developed a chain of small societies with internal cohesion, where the individual received support in difficult times, but on the other hand, the individual did not have the freedom of movement he ought to have had. Through the legislation of the last forty years, we have changed all that. At the moment, the individual stands entirely free . . . . All the oppressive bonds which existed have now fallen away, but at the same time the individual floats free, unattached in society. He has no firm ground under his feet. I believe that the great duty which the future imposes on us is to rebuild a society such that the chain of sub-societies, which we have gotten rid of, and which were bound to each other historically,

come into existence again in a way which is as equally distant from the past's restrictive as from socialism's chaotic condition.[1]

By far the largest part of the political spectrum in Denmark, including those who might oppose particular pieces of legislation, believed that some kind of mutual aid was desirable and, more important, that the pattern for such help could be found in the Danish past, specifically the guilds, rather than in newly invented or imported institutions. Banding together for help in case of illness had been a practice for hundreds of years in Denmark, originally through the guilds. In 1857 the Left and the National Liberals had passed a law ending the monopoly power of the guilds over prices, production, and entry into a trade, but this law on "freedom to earn one's livelihood" (*næringsfriheden*) contained nothing that would discourage continuation of the mutual-aid associations within the craft guilds. These funds were continued by the now weaker guilds, often reconstituted as labor unions, and the feeling of common purpose was continued.

By the middle of the nineteenth century, "sickness funds" had grown beyond their guild origins and had become a movement in their own right, with regional organization and a belief that their value lay in having grown from the bottom levels of society—the guilds—rather than being imposed by the government.[2] Proponents of the sickness funds believed that the funds did their socially beneficial work mostly outside of government and that they should continue to do so. Actually, the sickness funds did not have their origins in the bottom levels of the working class. In fact, they excluded most of the rural proletariat and the increasing urban proletariat—the guilds had been made up of workers with skills. Workers without skills who became ill had only the poor-law authorities (*fattigvæsen*) as a refuge.

If sickness funds became social or drinking clubs or were used as strike funds, they encountered opposition from employers, the government, or doctors, but generally they were used to aid poor sick members and were supported and even encouraged by the people who held power in the society. Yet these same people were worried by the economic changes taking place all across Europe. In England and Germany the "worker question" was the important domestic issue in the latter third of the nineteenth century. In Denmark the "worker question" was never as acute as in Germany or England, but employers and landholders alike were frightened by the Paris Commune of 1871. A Danish governmental commission in 1861 had done little more than assert moral approval for workers' helping themselves through sickness funds, but a commission that began its work in 1875 asked the Danish government to go further in 1878.

Dominated by men of the Right and led by a titled nobleman, the commission was strong on moral uplift:

> If there is manly power in the people, together with true religion and morality, and hard times of the past return to find . . . honor for inherited institutions together with a willingness to give them the form which the future demands, and if a powerful government, which feels strong enough to hold revolutionary tendencies at bay takes the workers question in hand, then poverty will be diminished, and satisfaction will prevail.[3]

In addition to true morality and religion, the commission wanted inherited institutions honored and a strong government. It also recommended that the local community (rather than, as in 1892, the national government) support sickness funds that had used up their own means and that the national government free sickness funds from such requirements as having to stamp all their official papers. What was important was that the commission's very existence was proof of the government's concern for the condition of the workers in general and for the sickness funds in particular. Of course, that concern was not without its political motives. For both major parties the sickness fund was an existing institution that might be expanded without frightening anyone and that might leave the Social Democrats without an issue.

By the time of a study commission on sickness funds in 1887, laissez-faire liberalism had been explicitly abandoned. "No matter what theories one may have of the nation's duties," said the commission, "practice in this area, as in so many others, has not always followed theory." The Danish upper house went a step further by proposing that insurance against illness was only one part of "the larger duty of society . . . to make it possible for those without means to insure themselves against events and situations which, through no fault of their own, interfere or interrupt their earning ability."[4]

About the same time the Commission of 1887 was at work, P. Knudsen, foreman of the Social Democratic Party and chairman of the Frederiksberg Sickness Fund set up his own commission to study the subject. Knudsen examined in great detail what workers made and what they would have to spend on life's necessities in various parts of the country. He concluded: "The cause of most workers' not joining sickness funds is that they are not in a position where they can insure themselves medicine, doctor's treatment, and support in the case of sickness." If the statistics were at all correct, workers were on the edge of poverty and could not afford to insure themselves. Knudsen's estimate is that less than half the workers in Copenhagen and less than one-third of those outside Copenhagen were insured. Knudsen's commission was not official, was not established by the Interior Ministry, and had no legal standing. Yet the work was carefully done and the statistics were difficult to refute.[5]

So there was strong sentiment from both left and right of the political spectrum to support the sickness funds in some way. Interior Minister Ingerslev introduced a bill for that purpose in 1888, proposing subsidies to sickness funds to enable them to enroll members with lower incomes. If they chose to accept the subsidies, the funds would have to conform to certain rules established by the law, but no fund would have to accept subsidies and the controls attached to them. When this bill was debated in the Rigsdag, there was a good deal of agreement between the parties, although they talked more about their disagreements. Liberalism pure and simple was nearly dead. When it reared its head in the person of the conservative from the Left party, Johannes Hage, who objected that everything would soon be in the hands of the government and that people should be free to do as they wanted, the point of view was generally ridiculed. Both sides agreed on the words "help to self-help." While one side might emphasize one part of that phrase and the other might emphasize another, both sides agreed that society as a whole, acting through government, should support some form of health maintenance. Both sides also agreed on the wording "build on existing institutions" (*bygge paa den bestaaende*) which meant that public support would go to the already existing sickness fund instead of to newly created national institutions, as the still politically weak Social Democrats wanted.

Thomas Nielsen, one of the true pioneers in the sickness fund cause and one who took the lead in a variety of social questions, related sickness funds to the Middle Ages. He too sounded a bit like Baron Reedtz-Thott when he said: "The old society of the Middle Ages was in many ways a strong society. It was, if I may use the expression, a society of associations (*foreningssamfund*), where there were not really so many rootless individuals. There were cloisters, which were a help for many. Nobles were a help to many. And finally, there were the guilds in the large market towns." Nielsen saw a growing feeling that the state should do more, that complete individualism was not the solution to social problems. Some people thought the solution was socialism, he said (perhaps to scare his listeners), and others believed the state ought to intervene to strengthen existing institutions and make sure that they reached far enough to solve the problem they addressed. For example—and here he drew on the Knudsen Commission—the ordinary worker in Copenhagen was already at the subsistence level and could not afford to pay for sickness insurance in addition. The state or, as N. P. Madsen "of Mygdahl" (the father of the future prime minister of the Left) expressed it, a just society, had an obligation to meet that need. This argument of Nielsen's made it very difficult for conservatives to disagree with him. After all, he favored subsidizing only existing institutions, and those institutions had their roots in the Middle Ages. Only theoretical liberals can oppose that, and there are not many of those left.[6]

The bill did not pass in that session, and Ingerslev introduced it again in the next in virtually the same form, emphasizing that this was voluntary insurance, not forced, like the German social insurance bill. This time the bill passed and went into effect on April 12, 1892. The law itself came down on the side of voluntarism, but only a relative voluntarism, for if a person was a member of a sickness fund and that fund was "recognized," he or she might share in the benefits from a national subsidy. That person was perfectly free to be uninsured, as the sickness funds were free not to seek recognition (a number did not, at first), but people were actually bribed to be members. Eventually the voluntarism became more apparent than real.

Perhaps the most important provision in the law was section 14, which declared in a single sentence that benefits of the law that came from the public to an individual were not to be considered poor-law help. Together with old-age pensions, the sickness funds law opened the major hole in the provision of the constitution and the poor law that created two classes of Danes. The first paragraph of the law says that every sickness fund that is "an association of people who have come together to insure each other help in the case of sickness" has the right to public recognition and public support if it fulfills certain conditions. Thus the law clearly was to support the existing sickness fund movement and put its emphasis on private insurance rather than on charity or a centralized system. No set of permissible organizing principles was established, as in the German sickness fund law. The Danish law was even less centralized than the later British law, which was also built on existing institutions, the "friendly societies." In Great Britain in 1911, however, the existing institutions were incorporated into a system that limited their freedom of action far more than the Danish 1892 law did.

The law was clearly for poor people or "people of small means" (*smaakaarsfolk*). Recognized sickness funds could consist only of "workers without means, small farmers (*husmænd*), craftsmen and tradesmen, low-paid workers, and other men and women situated on a similar level" (sec. 6). Notice first that there were no clearly defined lines below which a fund could be established. It was a matter of understanding terms, which the Danish legislators knew they could count on, not a definition in kroner and øre. Notice too that small farmers, craftsmen, and tradesmen were included. The law was for both the urban and the rural *smaakaarsfolk*. The German and later the British and much later the American insurance laws were for "workers" or "employees." The definition of the object of the laws was related to their position in the scheme of production. The object of the Danish laws is defined much more by their status in society: they were *ubemidlede*, people without means, or *smaakaarsfolk*.

There was provision for members who had higher incomes, but they could not get any public funds, and there was no provision for people who might move out of the categories mentioned. Presumably they would move up and out of the sickness fund—but were they members for the rest of that year, or could they be required to go through the waiting period if they again became poor? The law is silent on these questions because social mobility was not perceived as an important question. The law assumed that most poorer people would remain poorer people. The sickness fund law of 1892 was one way that better-off people in society could help the more badly off through transfer payments. It was not yet a scheme for national health insurance to which anyone could (or even was required) to belong.

Through the sickness fund the national treasury would provide 500,000 kroner (par. 11),[7] to be divided among the individual sickness funds according to their size and members' contributions. In this way the public treasury would help support what had been private institutions, and there was no objection on the grounds that because the institutions were private they should not be touched. The wall between public and private was not a sacred object, as it usually was in the United States, but a permeable area.

The law treated women somewhat differently from men, but for 1892 it was relatively egalitarian. Where individual sickness funds permitted, or where sickness funds were for all who lived in a certain area, women could be members like anyone else. In some sickness funds, wives had membership through their husbands. They were eligible for help in lesser amounts—they were not the chief breadwinner in the family—but only if they were required to pay a lower premium. Women who gave birth could receive a specified lump sum instead of daily monetary help.

To run the sickness fund organization, the law of 1892 set up the position of Sickness Fund Inspector, The inspector, a highly paid functionary in the Interior Ministry, was responsible for supervising the accounts of the sickness funds and making suggestions (secs. 23, 27). There was little hesitation about mixing private and public functions. The inspector's job included being chairman of a representative committee of sickness fund members. Recommendations of this committee, if agreed to by the interior minister, had the force of law. So the system was thus very lightly administered. The inspector was the only new bureaucrat, and while he had considerable powers they were far less than those of the administrative authorities for sickness funds in Germany.

It was clear, however, that although the Danish government was now involved in health insurance both financially and administratively, the sickness funds were still to a large degree a nongovernment institution. There was much talk about the sickness fund movement—a movement in the general populace, a stream of thinking parallel to the cooperative movement or the labor movement (and overlapping with the first in rural areas, the second in urban areas). The committee (*nævn*) over which the sickness fund inspector presided was made up of nongovernment representatives of nongovernmental units, and there was nothing in the law that explicitly prevented these nongovernment institutions from being partisan. But they did not become partisan, as they did in Germany. The movement considered itself a popular people's movement, not a part of any political party or of the government.

The medical insurance law had originally been viewed as closely tied to a law relating to industrial accidents. The Commission of 1887 had been established to consider "the question of the organization of the sickness funds and the insurance of workers against the consequences of accidents during work." Because there was considerable disagreement over the accident insurance, the sickness fund law was passed separately, but industrial accidents remained a significant public issue. Of course, accidents could be considered a form of sickness, but the law on employer liability applied to accidents and not to other forms of sickness. As in all industrializing countries, the law of liability (more or less the same as the law in Germany) was satisfactory to neither employer nor employee. The Commission of 1887 knew about the German law, about the insurance through employers' cooperatives, and believed that the same system should be adopted in Denmark, with the added provision that a worker to be insured must be a member of the as-yet-private sickness funds. This clearly would have been tantamount to making health insurance a requirement for most employees. A bill to this effect, amounting to a broadened health insurance system but without any temptations for employers to join, was submitted. Moreover, it did not cover those most in need—people too poor to have health insurance.

The accident insurance bill did not pass at that time, but it did pass in altered form in 1898.[8]

The law defines dangerous occupations in a way that would be considered broad today, although agriculture was not included, which left out a great portion of the population. The Left—the farmers—would not have supported the bill if their employees had been covered. Occupations that were included were all factories, all places where machinery was used, and all types of mining and building jobs. The law applied to all workers and supervisors who earned no more than 2,400 kroner annually. Hence, like the earlier laws of the decade, it was meant to apply to poor workers who could not be expected to insure themselves. In this case, however, the boundary was set by level of income rather than according to the vague but socially understood term "people of modest means."

By the law, an injury that lasted more than thirteen weeks, that had not been declared permanent, and that deprived a person of earning power would qualify a worker to receive three-fifths of the daily wage from insurance. If earning ability was only partly reduced, the payment was to be proportional. If the injury was permanent, the worker was entitled to six times his annual wages. If the worker died, heirs would get four times the annual wages. In all cases, the sum could be taken either as a lump sum or as an annuity, though "women and minor children," not being considered reasonable human beings, were to take what the council (which the law established) thought best for them. Certain insurance companies— as it worked out, all the large ones—were certified as "recognized" and an employer could either buy accident insurance from one of them or self-insure. Only in Germany and in a few American states were private insurance companies excluded from the work-accidents field. The law did not deprive workers of the right to sue their employers, but they had to choose: Either they sued and took their chances with the case, or they accepted payment under the workmen's compensation law; they could not do both. Most accepted compensation under the law, but the law did not set any limits on the liability of an employer who might be convicted. There was an incentive not to sue, but no prohibition against it. Likewise, there was profit for the employer in not being careless about employee safety.

Characteristically, the accident insurance law went to great lengths to establish a council to determine doubtful cases—degree of injury, how monies should be divided among heirs, ensuring that employers' insurance companies would pay damages, and so forth. The king appointed the chairman and two members, one of whom had to be a doctor. There were two employers, appointed by the interior minister, and two "workers," elected by members of the sickness funds, which were not made up exclusively of workers. It was considered acceptable that the interior minister appointed the employers because the minister was assumed to be in that group, even if he himself was not an employer. But the workers, who would not accept the idea that the interior minister should appoint their representatives, were assumed to be antagonists of the government-employer faction (one can say "class" here, provided one does not assume a struggle over control of the government) and were given the right to elect their own representatives. Thus an inherent difference in interest between an employer class and a worker class was recognized. Workers were allowed to have some degree of power, although they were very much in the minority, whereas "the educated and the gifted" were given a majority, and it was assumed that the government was on the other side from the workers.

In many ways, the accident insurance law was unlike other Danish social welfare legislation in that it involved no subsidy from public funds, either local or national. It did directly state that public authority had responsibilities, but these responsibilities were carried out in a system that is much looser and gives more choices than the German system. In Denmark, responsibilities were defined by law, and a mechanism for dealing with questionable issues was established. Outside those basics, employers were free to meet the responsibilities any way they wanted to. They could form employer cooperatives, as in Germany; they could buy their insurance from private companies; or they could take their chances. Again, it was a less strict, less bureaucratic, and less clearly defined system than Germany's.

The Danish unemployment insurance law of 1907 also shows a significant difference between German and Danish societies. Germany had no unemployment insurance until 1927 partly because employers would not let the unions administer it and workers would not let the government—the enemy—administer it. In Denmark the unions ran the system under government supervision and neither side objected. The unemployment insurance law was really the beginning of a new attitude that recognized that under some circumstances the economic system would not support all worthy Danes. It is not surprising that the law was passed by the Left majority in the lower house. Passage came only after other laws of the Left, it involved a very small state subsidy, and it was clearly in the pattern of "help to self-help" so dear to the hearts of the Left. It was directly patterned on the sickness fund law, which all sides agreed had been highly successful. As with the sickness fund law, many Danes were already covered before the law was passed, and the law was seen as an extension of the funds for various purposes established by most large unions. Moreover, these unemployment funds had already received public support in Cologne, Basel, Bern, Ghent, and other cities. The Danish parliament did not have to break any new trail.[9]

The commission that proposed the law argued that society had made the poor law unpleasant in order to avoid laziness, but that it was unreasonable to have these conditions affect those "who have done everything in their power to earn their daily bread, but have been visited by some form or other of inability to work." So there was a strong tone of instruction in the commission's report. The poor law and other social laws were supposed to make the poorer classes work hard to avoid poverty, but also provide aid for those who had tried.[10] The commission and later the law met the goal through a subsidized "voluntary insurance plan"—"there is the advantage that this will only mean an extension of something that already exists." It was in this spirit that Thomas Larsen, floor leader (*ordfører*) for the bill, argued that unemployment insurance should be voluntary, like the sickness fund. Niels Neergaard—one of the chief authors of the old-age pension law, a member of the commission that proposed the law, and later prime minister—supported the bill in more general historical terms, which was appropriate because he was also a historian. He argued that for the last half-generation or so the Rigsdag had tried to undercut the poor law by providing support to which people are entitled without any legal effects. The old-age pension law was one such law, and this unemployment insurance law was another.[11]

So the unemployment insurance law, like so many others, passed with support from all sides. It followed the general pattern of the sickness fund law and actually mentioned the earlier law. This new law also mentioned class descriptions without any embarrassment, for it was intended only for "wage-earners" (*lønarbejdere*) whose economic situation gave them access to national help through recognized sickness funds (sec. 6).[12] And even there, people had to be morally upright, for the funds had the right (appealable to the interior minister) to refuse members on "moral or physical grounds" (clause 5). The law forbade insurance funds to give payments to members who neglected or left their work, who were drunk on the job or otherwise guilty of misconduct, or who refused to accept offered work that was in accordance with their abilities.

There was obviously fear that unemployment funds would be used in the class war. Because there was a state subsidy, the funds were to be held strictly apart from other funds and must not be used for anything else, either as a loan or a gift (clause 8). In addition, people who lost their jobs because of a strike or a lockout were to receive no support (clause 13). The unemployment insurance law was the first to deal specifically with social mobility. Of course, mobility might make a person ineligible or newly eligible for other types of help, but this was the first law to discuss the problem explicitly by creating the category "contributing members" (*bidragydende*) for people who were still members of the unemployment fund but not eligible for benefits. For a small fee, a member who had improved his economic situation could keep his membership in case he became eligible again (clause 5). The device was later incorporated into the sickness fund legislation and shows an increased awareness that the relative position of members in society might be fluid rather than static. There are no good studies to show whether mobility was actually increasing or not—it probably was—but certainly consciousness of the possibility was on the rise. Denmark was (and in many ways still is) a status society, but the thought was growing that one might move around within it.

In 1914 the unemployment insurance law, like the accident insurance law, was revised to define "worker" or "lower class" (*ubemidlede*) in financial terms: 5,000 kroner a year if single, 10,000 kroner if married. Anyone falling below this annual income line, whether traditionally considered "worker" or not, would be eligible for unemployment compensation, sickness fund benefits, and the like. To set such a boundary line was a significant change. No longer was status in society to be decisive, with the lower layers (as traditionally defined) eligible for benefits from the upper layers, and the upper layers receiving loyalty and labor from the lower. Objective conditions—such as annual salary—was now the crucial point. Ascribed status still remained important in society, but there were now some cracks in the wall.

PART THREE

Divergence:
Great Britain
and the United States

Perfecting the Perfect System: Social Welfare within the Poor Law of 1834

In the 1880s Germany dealt with the problems of industrial accidents, medical treatment for the "workers," and poverty in old age by constructing elaborate new social machinery: the national sickness fund system, the employers cooperatives for accident insurance, and the pension bureaucracy. During the 1890s Denmark dealt with the same problems (with the addition of unemployment in 1907) by trying to nudge already existing institutions—the sickness funds and the trade unions—into dealing adequately with the new society.

In the latter half of the nineteenth century, Great Britain too faced and dealt explicitly with these problems, but instead of inventing new social machinery or making major adaptations in existing systems, she did so by trying to stick closely to the mechanisms created under the poor law of 1834, and even more by insisting that the problems could be dealt with within the moral suppositions of the Poor Law Report of that year. In the last years of the nineteenth century, England took steps to solve each of the problems Germany and Denmark had dealt with. In the United States, however, there was considerable doubt that the problems even existed. In England the question was never whether the problems existed. Instead there was the attitude that the problems had already been responded to—without any fundamental change in their way of thinking.

By the 1880s, Englishmen could believe that illness in the lower classes was being faced and dealt with in Great Britain, in a British way, as it had been dealt with in Germany in a German way. The poor law of 1834 had made an explicit exception to the workhouse test in the case of medical aid (esp. sec. 54), and medical aid for the poor was clearly seen to fall within the category of "sudden and extreme emergency." Over the next decades, however, it became clear that medical care for the poor was unsatisfactory by the standards of nineteenth-century Great Britain. Investigations showed that medical attendance was bad, nurses were unqualified, sanitation was revolting. These studies clearly assume that the sick poor had a special claim on the Boards of Guardians. They were not the able-bodied, for whom the workhouse was to be a deterrent, but the "impotent," for whom care must be provided.[1]

When in 1867 poor-law medical dispensaries were established under the Metropolitan Poor Act, there was virtually no opposition. Many members invoked the 1834 report in support of the bill. The distinction between the sick poor and "paupers" was stated by Sir Harry Verney when he proposed that the sick poor be supported by a citywide fund, to be established by the law, and that "pauperism alone should be dealt with by the local rates." He clearly saw "pauperism" and "the sick poor" as mutually exclusive categories.[2] The distinction between "medical" relief and "pauper" relief meant that the former type of relief was not governed by the doctrine of "less eligibility"; it also raised the question whether someone in receipt of medical relief only would be disfranchised. That was not a serious problem as long as the franchise was as limited as it was before 1867, but after that year it was entirely possible for a recipient of medical relief to be qualified in other respects to vote.

One of the first actions of the new Conservative government in England in 1885 was the introduction of a bill titled "Medical Relief (Disqualification Removal)." Because both political parties were committed to removing the disfranchisement provision for medical relief recipients, the bill was assured of passage. Motions to kill it got support from only about twenty members of Parliament. In the debates, however, both sides tried to use the "principles of 1834" to support their respective arguments. The government did not have to say much because they had the votes. The opposition was vociferous in its weakness, arguing that there should be no distinction between medical relief and any other type of relief, and that Edwin Chadwick himself, the only surviving member of the 1834 commission, was opposed to the change. Arthur Balfour, president of the Local Government Board (which had succeeded the Poor Law Board as the central authority in supervising poor-law administration), supported the "principles of 1834," saying that the 1834 poor law had been passed "to teach lessons of thrift and self-dependence" but that a medical disqualification "instead teaches the poor not to call the doctor." He went on to say, "The maintenance of health and the giving of education are both primary duties, and the means of doing both are supplied by the State in cases of destitution"[3] In other words, he simply assumed a degree of state responsibility.

After a brief debate in the House of Lords, the bill passed both houses easily. The tone of the debate, however, shows that theories of the state or of pauperization were only one factor in the bill's passage. The Liberals and the Conservatives were both competing for the newly enfranchised voter, each saying that their party was the true friend of the poor and that their opponents wanted to take away with the left hand (disqualification) what had been given with the right (enfranchisement under the reform acts of 1867 and 1884). The pressures of "mass politics" were having their effects on legislation.

Poor-law aid for the unemployed was also affected by mass politics. Like the question of medical relief, the solutions found at the end of the nineteenth century and during the first years of the twentieth century had antecedents in the mid-1800s. And again with the issue of medical relief, all sides in the debate felt that they had to make their solutions fit with that "law of nature"—the 1834 report. The whole basis of that 1834 report was that there was adequate employment for those who really wanted to work; if this were not true, their whole case would fall apart. At various times and places during the decades after 1834, there simply had to be "outdoor relief" and abandonment of the principle of "less eligibility" (from the 1834 report, meaning that poor-law aid should always be lower than the pay of the lowest-paid independent laborer), or the "work test" in the industrial towns of the Midlands. In many places the new law had not yet been applied, and "outdoor relief" or "relief in aid of wages" continued as under the "old" law. The central authority in

London was cautious about insisting that the law be followed. Actually, London had very little power for enforcement, and local authorities simply ignored edicts from London that they found difficult, impossible, or distasteful to comply with.

Probably the next stage in thinking about unemployment was the "cotton famine" in Lancashire during the American Civil War. The Northern blockade and Southern embargo on the export of cotton meant that the raw materials for English mills were almost cut off. As a result, the industry was thrown into depression and many thousands of workers were suddenly unemployed. This case presented a better example than other depressions. The causes were clearly and explicitly external—war in a foreign country. By no stretch of the imagination could the workers be held responsible, nor could their savings last the length of the famine. There was no question but that they were willing and able to work; they were not "wastrels" or "loafers." In the debates in Parliament, in fact even in the Speech from the Throne, there were many references to the workers' industry, loyalty, and good behavior.

As with medical relief, the relief for the unemployed during the "cotton famine" was dealt with in the conceptual framework of the 1834 Poor Law Report. Although the law made exceptions for "sudden and extreme emergencies," the phrase was undefined, and local Boards of Guardians were left to define it as they saw fit. Some board members in Lancashire defined the cotton famine as such an emergency. As in previous crises they frequently relaxed the "work test" and, at the same time, private relief committees were formed in the affected cities.[4] By 1863, with the Civil War in America continuing, it became clear that local resources were no longer adequate. The government introduced a bill authorizing £1.2 million in loans to towns in the "distressed districts" for public works on which the unemployed would be engaged. The word "unemployed" was used without embarrassment, explanation, or quotation marks; the existence of this category was taken for granted.

It is significant that the loan bill was introduced by C. P. Villiers, president of the Poor Law Board, whose normal sphere of responsibility was not public works. This bill, like the Medical Relief (Disqualification Removal) Act, was justified by references to the moral values of the 1834 report. The few speeches that opposed the loan bill also referred to that report, but the argument of the winning side was that the public works would precisely prevent the "pauperization" of decent, hardworking citizens and save them from the poor law and the demoralization that came with it. Members of the House of Commons pointed out that this was an exceptional bill to deal with exceptional circumstances, but there was no significant opposition and the bill passed its second reading "without a division"—that is, without a recorded vote. Eventually some £1.85 million was authorized.[5]

Response among the major journals and reviews was as positive as the response had been in Parliament. Most articles on the cotton famine acknowledged the extent of the distress, the inadequacy of charitable efforts, and the need for something like the Public Works (Manufacturing Districts) Act. What criticism there was focused on the small amount of money appropriated in the act, the length of time it would take to put the program into operation, and the fact that the government or the manufacturers should have anticipated a possible disruption of the American supply. No one argued that such a public rescue effort might weaken the self-reliance of the workers.[6]

The Civil War in America was clearly an exceptional case, but a chronic and widespread unemployment began to percolate up to government consciousness in the late 1880s and 1890s. Once again the 1834 Poor Law Report was invoked as recommending a satisfactory system. Public works had always been a part of national activity, and the scheduling of such works had occasionally been related to the need for employment in a particular area. When the issue of a more systematic planning of public works in order to give relief to the unemployed arose in Parliament, the 1834 report was invoked by both sides to justify their respective positions. Would public works beyond what was normal paralyze private enterprise and pauperize individual workers? Would public works prevent the pauperization of workers? On March 15, 1886, Joseph Chamberlain, now president of the Local Government Board but previously mayor of Birmingham, where he had seen urban unemployment first-hand, issued what was later known as the "Unemployed Circular." The circular argued that there should be no general relaxation of the "labour test" or prohibition of outdoor relief, but that there was "exceptional distress . . . especially in centres of population." Working people deserve credit for trying to avoid pauperism. "It is not desirable that the working classes should be familiarized with poor relief and if once the honourable sentiments which leads them to avoid it is broken down, it is probable that recourse will be had to this provision at the slightest occasion." The circular went on to urge local authorities and Boards of Guardians to work together to find work that "will avoid the stigma of pauperism," that all could perform, and that would not interfere with others. The Local Government Board would "look with favour" on applications from local authorities for loans to provide such work. The circular was reissued several times by Local Government Boards of various political flavor.[7]

In the House of Commons, Chamberlain made harsh remarks about the unemployed and clearly believed that the "Unemployed Circular" was in keeping with traditional poor-law ideals. These ideals, however, were now seen as including not simply an act of God, like the American Civil War, but also a trade depression in "centres of population." Moreover, many people regarded the action of the central government to combat the effects of unemployment as legitimate. A phrase like the "worthy unemployed" was not seen as an oxymoron, as the phrase "worthy pauper" would have been.[8]

At the same time, there was some improvement in the institutions of care under the poor law. The Poor Law Report of 1834 had recommended an end to the "general mixed work house" and urged classification of inmates (aged, children, insane) and a special institution for people in each category. The 1909 reports (see Chapter 10) would recommend the same, so clearly the "general mixed work house" had not disappeared in the interim. Nevertheless, some improvements had been made. In some places there were experiments with the "cottage home" system of small, more homelike dwellings for children or the aged. In other places a special building or a section of the poorhouse was specifically designated for the aged. The building of infirmaries was a particularly widespread and popular form of institutional improvement.

In the 1890s it was not unemployment, but workmen's compensation, that was the pressing issue in Great Britain. Before 1897 the aspect of employer liability that caused the most outrage among British workers was the doctrine of "common employment," usually called the doctrine of the "fellow servant" in the United States. According to this doctrine, if the injury was caused by the negligence of a fellow employee, even of a foreman or supervisor, the employer was not liable. Perhaps the fellow employee might be liable, but usually he would not have much money. Therefore the doctrine in fact meant that in a great many cases the injured worker received nothing. In 1880 a law that limited the use of the doctrine was passed, but it had little effect on the probability that the injured worker would obtain any sort of compensation. Long before the act, well-paid workers in the skilled trades (almost always male) had begun mutual insurance societies against the economic consequences of injury, illness, and other disruptions of earnings. These were known as friendly societies. By 1878 more than 5.3 million were members in these societies. The members were almost entirely male, though a few societies admitted women late in the century, and almost all members were from the elite of the labor movement. There were a great number of tiny friendly societies, but many of them were huge—for example, the "Independent Order of Odd Fellows, Manchester Unity," founded in 1812, with some 750,000 adult members in 1896; the Ancient Order of Foresters, founded in 1834, with more than 725,000 adult members by 1895; and the Hearts of Oak Benefit Society, founded in 1842, with some 200,000 adult members by 1895.

Under the 1880 act, employers began contributing to the "friendly societies" in return for a worker agreeing not to bring action under the Employer Liability Act. This "contracting out" became an additional source of irritation for workers, in addition to the doctrine of "common employment"; workers claimed that frequently one had to agree to contract out in order to get the job. Thus the cure was worse than the disease. Bills to limit or eliminate "contracting out" or to otherwise alter the law on employer liability were introduced throughout the 1880s. At one time or other, both parties indicated that they favored alteration, but other considerations—such as Irish home rule and shifting party alignments—led to the frustration of all attempts at change. The nearest approach to success was the Liberals' bill of 1893, introduced by Home Secretary Herbert Asquith. The bill actually passed both houses of Parliament, but in different forms. Party politics between Liberals in the House of Commons and Conservatives in the House of Lords prevented agreement and final passage. Because it was clear that Asquith's bill bore the imprint of the Trades

Union Congress (TUC), a major issue was how strong a voice the labor movement had in British politics. At this point, with Liberal support, labor could get a bill introduced but could not prevail against Conservative opposition.[9]

When the issue was raised again, it was in the form of Joseph Chamberlain's proposal on workmen's compensation. Chamberlain had first proposed compensation in a famous article in the November 1892 issue of *Nineteenth Century* titled "The Labour Question." He had put the question on the parliamentary agenda with an amendment to the 1893 bill, and he was in effect in charge of the bill to make his proposals a reality in 1897. In the article, like Reedtz-Thott in Denmark, he wrote that the Liberal thrust of the first part of the nineteenth century was a "necessary labour of destruction." That task having been accomplished, a period of construction was necessary. He heaped scorn on his enemies to the right—the absolutist individualists—and to his left, the various versions of what he was already calling the Labour Party, probably meaning the Independent Labour Party. Most of his heat was applied to those on his left, presumably to convince his new allies that he would not be a dangerous companion in spite of his social program. Yet as a former mayor he had cautious praise for a category he called "state or municipal socialism." In a brief paragraph he outlined a variety of policies—factory legislation, sanitary inspection, old-age pensions— that could be termed "state socialism" and indicated that each should be examined in relation to the goal of making life less miserable and more fair for the worker. "Nous sommes tous socialistes," he concluded, if the word "socialist" meant simply amelioration.

An argument that was of central importance in the United States for those arguing for workmen's compensation was that a compensation law would reduce conflict between employer and employee. After all, what led to litigation and bitterness was determination of who was at fault, and with workmen's compensation, fault did not have to be determined. But in England, Chamberlain did not even mention the issue of conflict. In the United States, class conflict contradicted some aspects of the national self-image, and diminishing such conflict would be important, but the English seemed to assume no conflict, but rather that employers and workers would quite naturally have differing interests. Machinery should be constructed to deal with these differences in an equitable way, but no one wasted thought or breath trying to wish them away.

It was essentially Chamberlain's proposal, modeled in concept but not in administrative machinery on the German plan, which the Unionist government introduced in Parliament in 1897.[10] The labor representatives spoke in favor of the bill—although they could have been more enthusiastic—and many members identified themselves as employers in favor of the bill. Liberals, Unionists, and Conservatives favored it, and it passed without a division. It went through the House of Lords with only a short debate.[11]

The Workmen's Compensation Act as passed applied quite widely within the industrial sector of the economy. It included any railroad, factory, mine, quarry, engineering work, or construction over thirty feet high. In the case of injury, a person (the masculine pronoun was used throughout, but the law defined the "workman" as "any person") would receive half his wages for as long as the incapacity lasted, but what he could earn after the injury would be taken into account. In the case of death, the dependents would get three years wages up to a limit of £300. In the case of "personal negligence or wilful act of the employer" or his agent, the employee might choose to sue under the preexisting Employer Liability Act or claim compensation, but not both. An ambiguously worded clause said that no compensation would be paid if the accident was attributable to the "serious and wilful misconduct of the workman," and these words caused considerable litigation.

The act was not a social insurance act, and the word "insurance" was not used. Firms could insure if they wanted to, and most did. In the course of the debates it was assumed that the result of the act would be insurance, but it was neither required nor suggested. In contrast to the German and American debates on employer liability, there was in England no organized pressure group of employers in either 1893 or 1897. In both years a number of employers spoke in each house, and many individual employers wrote to Asquith.[12]

It is necessary to keep in mind that the Workmen's Compensation Act in Great Britain was not viewed as a major step, either toward social insurance or toward concern for the "condition of the people" question, or any other broad social issue. The 1880 Employer Liability Act had proven inadequate in certain ways, and this act was an attempt to fill the gaps. Joseph Chamberlain announced it as a revolutionary step, and in some theoretical sense it was, but Chamberlain tended to assume that anything he was associated with was of great moment. There was very little comment in the general periodical press. Historians should regard it as significant, but in a minor way.[13]

The "condition of the people" became a subject for widespread discussion in newspapers, magazines, and books during the last decade or so of the nineteenth century. Unemployment was only part of the broader "condition of the people" question. There were the issues of housing, "sweated labor," and the aged, but chronic, long-term, or frequent unemployment was recognized by people both in and out of government as a serious part of the problem.[14] A report drawn up in 1892 by Samuel Barnett of Toynbee Hall and Sidney Webb is interesting because of its authors. In that year Barnett and Webb found some local distress, but nothing very general or exceptional. They proposed establishment of a committee in each locality to provide a "work test" during the winter. Such work would be "a test of fitness for further help" and would help identify people "who have been sifted from the demoralized residuum." Barnett and Webb had nothing but scorn for "irresponsible charitable agencies" that appealed to the benevolent. Thus even the man who might be regarded as the founder of the whole settlement house movement in England and the United States, working with the future guiding spirit of the Fabian Socialists, feared generous charity and unfit relief claimants.[15]

Over the next several years, the government carried out various investigations of the unemployment situation, but no policy resulted.[16] Worry about chronic unemployment increased again in the first years of the twentieth century. There were demonstrations by the unemployed in major cities during 1903, and the problem grew worse over the next year or so. Suggestions to alleviate the unemployment included labor colonies and emigration, but there was the seemingly intractable problem of uniting a worker seeking work with an employer seeking workers.

The bill that became the Unemployed Workmen Act was introduced by the Conservative government in April 1905, to a greater degree of opposition on their own side of the house than from the opposition. Sir George Bartley denounced the bill in classic 1834 terms, quoting liberally from the 1834 Poor Law Report and from Charles Loch of the London Charity Organisation Society, whom he called "a man who has done more for the poor than almost any one else." The people, Bartley said, spend too much on liquor and amusements. Charles Cripps from Lancashire said the bill would create a new class of paupers, "free from the stigma of pauperism." The bill was actually extremely cautious. It established "distress committees" in London and other towns and boroughs that were made up not of volunteers, as had been traditional, but of members of the Boards of Guardians and the governing authority. Originally the bill had empowered these local bodies to provide work in the case of distress, with wages paid out of the poor rates (taxes assessed for poor relief). This provision aroused such hostility that the final version made a clear distinction between wages, which had to be paid out of voluntary contributions, and the expenses of the worker moving to a new location, or "labour exchanges," which could be paid for out of the rates. The bill aroused fervent but limited opposition, and it passed its second reading with only eleven negative votes. It is significant that Members of Parliament on both sides of the question sneered at "wastrels and tramps" and people similarly labeled. Everyone seemed to agree that there were some people worthy of support only under the poor law. In any case, the moral principles of 1834 were certainly unchallenged by the Unemployed Workmen Act of 1905. People in Great Britain could now feel that something had been done about medical aid for the poor, workmen's compensation, and unemployment—all within the moral philosophy of 1834.[17]

In Germany and Denmark a major issue was what to do about poverty in old age. The British government considered the issue during the 1890s and came to the ultimate conclusion that arrangements under the 1834 poor law were satisfactory. As with workmen's compensation, the issue first became a matter for government concern with Joseph Chamberlain's plan, announced in the *National Review* in February 1892. Chamberlain's idea was that "the industrious poor" would contribute £5 before they were twenty-five years old, the state would add £15, and the worker would pay £1 a year until he reached the age of 65. Then, considering how much the fund would have grown through compounded interest, the worker would be entitled to five shillings a week for life. A voluntary parliamentary committee worked on the plan for a year, and while the idea was clearly unrealistic from several points of view, it raised the issue at the level of policy-makers. The industrious poor, wrote Chamberlain, have "some claims on the Society they have served, and on the State as its representative."[18]

Few felt that the aged poor had no claim. The question was rather whether that claim was now being met and, if it was not, how it should be. At the extreme end of those who favored pensions was Charles Booth's proposal for a universal noncontributory system. Booth's views in general were that the poor should be thrifty enough to provide for most contingencies, but his investigations had convinced him that much poverty was caused by old age and that it was unrealistic to expect people whose wages were low and often irregular to think about an age that, for many people, would not be reached anyway. Booth had no government position, but his prestige as an expert on poverty meant that his views would be discussed, even if they were generally rejected as impossibly expensive.[19]

In 1894 a private bill had been introduced for noncontributory old-age pensions based explicitly on the Danish model, but that bill got nowhere. It was dismissed partly with the argument that a Royal Commission was at that moment considering the issue. The commission, known as the Abardare Commission, after its chairman, reported a year later. The majority concluded that "no fundamental alterations are needed in the existing system of poor law relief as it affects the aged." The argument of the majority was that most Guardians were already kindly in giving "outdoor relief" to the aged and that the increase in private savings and membership in friendly societies proved that thrift was growing. Because the number of aged paupers was decreasing, they said, the problem was decreasing too. A strong minority opinion was submitted by Henry Broadhurst, a blacksmith and stonemason, member of the Parliamentary Committee of the Trade Union Congress, and a longtime member of Parliament, eventually as a member of the Labour Party. Relying heavily on the testimony of Charles Booth before the commission, Broadhurst insisted that the treatment of the aged poor was scandalous and that the nation should "recognize the maintenance of the aged as a public charge, to be born by the whole community." Alfred Marshall had said to the commission, "Whenever I read the Poor Law literature of today, I am taken back to the beginning of the century; everything that is said about economics has the flavour of that old time." He was right.[20]

By the late 1890s, bills on old-age pensions were introduced in every session of Parliament, and some years there were several bills. Partly in response to continuing pressure from backbenchers and agitation outside Parliament, and partly following the suggestion of the Abardare Commission, the government established a Committee of the Treasury on old-age pensions in 1896. If anything, this Rothschild Committee (as it was known) was less sympathetic to pensions than its predecessor. It argued that it was the "duty of every man to make provisions for his old age" and found that "the industrial classes show an increasing disposition to appreciate and discharge this duty." Any system of state pensions would destroy this disposition.[21]

The self-interest of the friendly societies dominated the Rothschild Committee. The friendly societies provided mutual benefits, but they were also lodges, fraternal societies, social centers. They had a mystique and tradition of pride, good fellowship, and independence. By "independence," these societies generally meant independence from government. The members prided themselves on being able to take care of themselves and one another and believed that they were upholding the best qualities of Englishmen. In many respects, the friendly societies in England were like the sickness funds in Denmark. Both were examples of the kinds of virtues the culture wanted to uphold and encourage. With regard to old-age pensions, nothing was accomplished until at least some elements within the friendly society movement were in favor. The chief monetary benefit provided by the friendly societies was a sickness payment. A few had "superannuation" plans in return for additional premiums, but these were not very successful. Toward the end of the nineteenth century, increased longevity, an increase in the number of industrial accidents, and high rates of industrial illness put many of even the larger societies in financial trouble.[22]

In the early 1890s the Manchester Unity recognized that a problem existed. A review of Charles Booth's *The Condition of the Aged Poor* in their journal, *Odd Fellows Magazine,* said that old age was a problem the Manchester Unity must deal with, but that the friendly society was strongly opposed to state-aided pensions, which they believed would be "inevitably followed by state inspection and interference." By 1896, however, the annual meeting (called the Annual Movable Committee, or A.M.C.) passed a resolution favoring state aid, and the following year several lodges sent letters to the Rothschild Committee urging state aid. By 1900 the Grand Master could refer to the great division that the question of state-aided pensions had occasioned among members of the friendly society, but made it clear that he was in favor of the pensions. Other friendly societies followed approximately the same course, with the Druids passing a pro-pension resolution in 1897.[23]

In Germany, and until the 1930s in the United States, organized labor was hostile to state welfare actions, and Denmark passed its most important welfare legislation before labor became a powerful political force. In Great Britain, however, labor pressed for modifications in the Workmen's Compensation Act, and labor leaders supported old-age pensions, though the rank-and-file seemed less impressed.[24] Labor was increasingly vocal in its support for pensions. The Trades Union Congress had passed resolutions in favor of pensions at its annual conference in 1899 and in subsequent years. The Fabian Society was already on record in favor.[25]

The greatest extraparliamentary agitation for pensions came from a group offically named "The National Committee of Organized Labour (Trade Unions, Trade Councils, Federations of these Bodies, Friendly Societies, and Co-operative Societies) on Old Age Pensions, based on the Principle that every old person on attaining a given age should be entitled to a free Pension from the State; and charged with the Instruction to promote the legal enactment of this Principle"— often known as the National Pensions Committee, or NPC.[26] Organized in May 1899, the NPC included many of the most influential people in the labor movement, plus the single most important writer on poverty and old age—Charles Booth. Organized primarily to promote Booth's idea of a universal noncontributory pension, the committee issued a stream of pamphlets, instructed volunteer workers on how to press parliamentary candidates on the issue, and held mass meetings.[27]

The Rothschild Committee looking into old-age pensions was from the Treasury, but it was Parliament that would have to deal with the policy. Less than one year later, a select committee of the House of Commons, chaired by Henry Chaplin, president of the Local Government Board, came to conclusions that were precisely the opposite of those of the Rothschild Committee. The pension proposals of the Chaplin Committee were based directly on the Danish plan, and except for a few details amounted almost to an English translation of the Danish law.[28] The Chaplin proposals got nowhere in the cabinet. Only Balfour and Chamberlain had anything good to say about them. The Chancellor of the Exchequer heaped scorn on them as "an inducement not to thrift but to fraud." As in Denmark, the pensions would undoubtedly be increasingly expensive in a "Parliament depending on a working class electorate, who have already been told by many that any sum required should be obtained not in any degree from those who benefit, but from a graduated income tax, increased death duties or taxes on ground value." He would be willing to contemplate some Treasury contribution to more generous "outdoor relief" for the aged who were "proper subjects for relief," but certainly not any "eleemosynary grant" mistitled pensions. When Prime Minister Lord Salisbury supported his Chancellor, the issue was dead.[29]

The government would not consider pensions, but would undertake alterations in administration of the poor law. Even before the Cabinet considered the Chaplin proposals, Walter H. Long, soon to succeed Chaplin as president of the Local Government Board recommended that "the honest industrious pauper" should not have to spend the declining years of his life with "the drunkard and the wastrel." In August 1900 the Local Government Board issued a circular saying:

> Persons who have habitually led decent and deserving lives should in their old age, receive different treatment from those whose previous habits and character have been unsatisfactory.... [A]ged deserving persons should not be urged to enter the workhouse at all unless there is some cause which renders such a course necessary, such as infirmity of mind or body ... but ... they should be relieved by having adequate out-door relief granted to them. The Board are happy to think that it is commonly the practice of boards of guardians to grant outdoor relief in such cases, but they are afraid that too frequently such relief is not adequate in amount.

The circular went on to detail what kinds of better accommodations should be provided for the deserving aged within the workhouse, such as separate rooms and flexible schedules.[30]

By 1900, then, all the subjects on which Germany had legislated had also been dealt with in England, but within the bounds of the 1834 poor law: medical attention for the poor, accidents, disability, old age. Great Britain had even dealt with unemployment, whereas Germany had not. The British system had been perfected, perhaps, but it was the same system as before.

Voices for Change in Great Britain and the United States

In spite of a certain feeling of self-satisfaction within the British government—that the system established in 1834 could accommodate to the new reality—and a feeling in the United States that there was no real need to accommodate, various nongovernment studies and reformers made the point again and again: all was not well. By the last decades of the nineteenth century, both in Great Britain and in the United States, these voices found an increasing audience.

In a political sense, Charles Booth was for many years a major opponent of the London Charity Organization Society. After all, he was one of the chief proponents of old-age pensions. Yet he actually agreed with much of the philosophy of the charity society. In 1889 he published the first volume of his multivolume investigation of the poor of London, *Life and Labour of the People in London,* and was almost instantly considered the outstanding authority on the subject. This was at least partly because he did not challenge accepted ideas. "The only sure cure . . . for the evil of irregularity of work," he said in 1895, "is personal prudence." In fact, his goals were precisely to oppose "socialistic theories, passionate suggestions of ignorance, setting at naught the nature of men and neglecting all the fundamental facts of human existence." This made him a more acceptable figure, even to those who opposed his ideas, than if his ideas had been more radical.[1]

The section of his volumes that was most referred to both inside and outside Parliament was in the first volume, where almost as a beginning point for his study Booth classified the population of East End London into eight classes, designated A–H. Although he tried to maintain his neutral attitude, a good deal of moral judgment crept into this classification scheme. Class A is "the lowest class, which consists of some occasional labourers, street-sellers, loafers, criminals, and semi-criminals. . . . Their life is the life of savages, with vicissitudes of extreme hardship and occasional excess" (pp. 37–38). Class B was "Casual earnings—very poor." Booth was sympathetic to the widows or deserted women who made up a large portion of this class, but he was doubtful whether the men "would work full time for long . . . if they had the opportunity. . . . Many of them . . . from shiftlessness, helplessness, idleness, or drink, are inevitably poor" (p. 43). Together these two classes made up 12.5 percent of the population of the East End, with only 1.25 percent in Class A. For Class C, "Intermittent earnings," Booth showed considerable sympathy. "On them falls with particular severity the weight of recurrent depressions of trade." Even for those in this class who drank most of their earnings away, he showed some understanding, because their high earnings were "at the cost of great exhaustion." Many in this class, however, "have a very bad character . . . and are wanting in ordinary prudence" (p. 46). Class D was still poor and had "small regular earnings." Classes E through H were not classified as "poor" or "very poor" with Class H being defined as the "servant-keeping class." Together, the poor and very poor constituted about 35 percent of the population of the East End. To the dismay of most Englishmen, Booth's figure for all of London was just under 31 percent. Yet a careful reader would come away with the conclusion that Booth felt that more prudence, thrift, and hard work would keep most people from want. This classification scheme was referred to frequently over the twenty years after Booth's first volume (1889). It was taken not so much as a hypothesis or proposal, but as an established basis from which one could proceed to discuss implications and policy proposals.

To a degree, Charles Booth's study was like the slightly later study, *Poverty* by Robert Hunter, in the United States, or the work of the Deutsche Verein in Germany. Hunter, however, aside from the fact that he considered himself a socialist, was trying to convince a skeptical readership that there was poverty in their country. That point did not have to be made in England. If nothing else, the annual reports of the Local Government Board made it clear that the existence of poverty was routinely recognized. Booth's point was simply to measure and analyze poverty in London with greater precision, and perhaps to imply that more needed to be done about it. The investigations in Germany were much more a checking-up on a system already in place, as one might check whether drainage ditches were being cleared as they should. There was no implication that new systems had to be devised or new ways of thinking adopted. Hunter was a cry of protest; the German studies were checks on a satisfactory system.

A great number of reviews of *Life and Labour of the People in London* appeared in the 1890s on both sides of the Atlantic. Most summarized Booth and praised him uncritically for his industry, accuracy, and opposition to ill-supported sympathy toward the poor. For example, an anonymous reviewer in the *Spectator* wrote that Booth emphasized the importance of individual effort and the tendency of English laborers and artisans to drink and to be lazy. Only in the United States was the work reviewed critically. In the reviews by William J. Ashley one can see the confluence of German historical economics, the growing rejection of laissez-faire among American economists, and British social reform. Ashley was a Harvard economist who had been born and educated in England, had spent time in Germany, and was much influenced by the German historical school of political economy. He was the translator of Gustav Schmoller, one of the pioneers of the historical school. Ashley recognized the virtues of Booth's work, but he argued that Booth gave unwarranted ammunition to those who would blame the poor for their poverty by not recognizing that "the faults of this class as a whole are certainly in part the result of the character of modern industry."[2] Ashley's review showed up a clear difference between British reform and American reform. Americans recognized that the changes they sought would mean abandoning long-established ways of thinking. Americans, even an American of British origins, had no difficulty assuming and accepting that point without trying to justify it, but the British, even those who supported a change in the poor laws, went to considerable effort to show that no change in thinking was necessary.

In 1902 Benjamin Seebohm Rowntree published a detailed study of York.[3] Rowntree learned much from Charles Booth and was in constant communication with him. The study is perhaps methodologically superior to Booth's, but it delivered the same results. Basing his definition of poverty primarily on a detailed study of the caloric needs in a worker's diet, Rowntree concluded that about 30 percent of the population fell below the "poverty line." Rowntree was explicitly reformist, repeatedly making the point that the conditions under which the poor were forced to live were intolerable in "this land of abounding wealth" (p. 304). Booth is far less explicit and more neutral in tone. Several parts of Booth's work were given as papers before the Royal Statistical Society, and his tone is much more that of an investigator gathering information who is aware of problems in his data than of a polemicist arguing for a particular program. Yet when it comes to evaluating impact on British society, Booth's study is without equal.[4]

More critical studies of British society were those of religious spokesmen, whose purpose was not so much to affect public policy as to affect public morality or church policy. They certainly affected the consciences and consciousness of Englishmen, however, so they can be said to have influenced the development of the welfare state indirectly, but for a long time their efforts were in directions quite other than an expansion of state activities in welfare directions. In 1883 the Rev. Andrew Mearns, secretary of the London Congregational Union, published his *Bitter Cry of Outcast London*. Mearns' description of the horrible living conditions of the very poor caused a sensation and was very influential in the development of public policy toward working-class housing. His aim, however, was to change church policy, not public policy. He argued vigorously for better lower-class housing, but like William Booth, founder of the Salvation Army, his purpose was to alleviate the misery of the poor enough that they could accept the Gospel, for, Mearns wrote, "Little match makers are heard singing at their toil, 'One more day's work for Jesus.' " He quoted one urchin as saying, "If only my mother was a Christian we should all be happy." One can hardly deny that *The Bitter Cry* aroused great interest, but is difficult to document any effect it may have had on the income-maintenance policy of government.[5]

William Booth, founding "General" of the Salvation Army and no relation to Charles Booth, had a goal more similar to that of Mearns, but in his *In Darkest England and the Way Out* (1890) he sounded more like Charles Booth. His title was modeled on Henry Stanley's *In Darkest Africa,* which had caused a sensation in London. Stanley had told about cutting his way through an African forest so huge and so dense that dwellers within it were convinced it went on forever. But he knew and found a way out. Similarly, William Booth told about the poor of England, living in a dark jungle of poverty with seemingly no way out. But Booth knew and would show the poor the way to the light. He proposed establishing a series of "colonies" for those in need. The "city colony" would "inspire them with hope for the future and commence at once a course of regeneration by moral and religious influences" (p. 92). The "farm colony" would continue the process, reforming people partly by instruction and partly by the moral regeneration that comes from farmwork. Once they had learned agricultural skills, they would be encouraged to emigrate to "the overseas colonies" in the British colonial possessions. William Booth's goal was clear. "I must assert in the most unqualified way that it is primarily and mainly for the sake of saving the soul that I seek salvation of the body."[6] The primary impact of *In Darkest England,* in its turn a sensation, was its vivid writing on the poor as victims. A person who would hesitate to tackle Charles Booth's many dry volumes might tackle William Booth's single dramatic one.

Both Andrew Mearns in 1883 and William Booth in 1890 had taken it for granted that dealing with the poor was the responsibility of organized Christianity. Though neither argued explicitly that the state had no role to play, both put their emphases on either the already organized churches or on the "Army." In 1902 Charles Booth published the second part of his study. In the seven volumes of *Life and Labour* . . . devoted to "religious influences," he implicitly challenged the assumption of Mearns, William Booth, and the churches in general. His conclusion was that the various churches—the Church of England, the Roman Catholic Church, or the dissenting churches—in spite of what they may have thought of themselves, were not responding to the needs of the lower classes and that the lower classes were resolutely indifferent to their preaching. By 1902 he was perhaps implying that because there was nothing to hope for from the churches, other sources of improvement must be found.[7]

The English settlement house movement was the direct model for the American movement, but the English settlement house voices argued with a softer, less vigorous voice that did not always challenge traditional ways of thinking. In the United States, settlement houses—or at least a few prominent ones like Jane Addams' Hull House in Chicago or Lillian Wald's Henry Street Settlement in New York—were important voices urging an increased role for government. The English settlement houses were involved in questions of public policy—old-age pensions, for example—but compared with their American counterparts they were more interested in doing good than in affecting public policy, more interested in improving the character of both those who settled and the poor than in improving laws. They deplored the wasteful luxury of the rich and the deprivations of the poor, but their purpose seemed to be more to make the rich feel guilty than to propose programs that might accomplish something. Many settlement residents, such as William Beveridge and Clement Atlee, later became prominent in building the welfare state, but they did so as people who had once lived for a while in a settlement house, not as part of the settlement movement.

It may be significant that the British settlement house movement has been studied far less than the American movement, even though British historians are much interested in the origins of the welfare state. The settlements in England were simply not very important in that story. Almost the only settlement that has received scholarly attention is the first and the most prominent, Toynbee Hall, founded in 1884 in London's East End by Samuel and Henrietta Barnett. Samuel Barnett was the vicar of St. Jude's Church, so the settlement house was for him an extension of his Christianity. As with the "friendly visiting" of the London Charity Organisation Society, Toynbee Hall was to bring the higher life to the poor. Most of the residents of Toynbee Hall were recent graduates of Oxford or Cambridge. They ran classes to tutor the "neighbors" in the higher culture, and of course tutored only the higher end of "the working classes." Toynbee Hall itself was furnished so that the residents, not the "neighbors," would feel at home. The Barnetts' purpose was to break down barriers between classes, but they had much of the condescension of the charity organization society. "The only test of real progress," Samuel Barnett wrote, "is to be found in the development of character." He was originally a member of the London Charity Organisation Society, but he broke with them on the issue of state action. He was against "outdoor relief" and aid to the "unworthy," but was willing from the very beginning to contemplate some expansion of state responsibilities, even old-age pensions.[8]

In England, however, intellectuals and academics had more effect on public policy than they did in the United States. The Fabian Society, founded in 1884, was in some ways parallel to the Verein für Sozialpolitik in Germany. It regarded itself an idea factory for the Labour Party, of which it was an affiliate. Almost all important Labour figures in the building of the welfare state were members of the Fabian Society. Sidney and Beatrice Webb, its leading members, were influential in the formation of and pressure for old-age pensions, unemployment insurance, alterations in the poor law, and much else. Yet the Webbs were opposed to the National Insurance Act and to social insurance in general. Basically they felt that the kind of capitalist welfare state that had emerged in Great Britain, and also in Germany, Denmark, and the United States, was a betrayal of the real socialism they wanted.[9]

There were many other private charities, from "Dr." Barnardo's children's homes to the "bread funds" in almost every parish in the land, but aside from strengthening the arguments of those insisting that British care for the poor was adequate, these charities had little effect on public policy. Thus neither Charles Booth's social investigations nor settlement houses directly challenged the moral universe inherited from 1834. Yet in Great Britain during the 1890s there was a rumbling awareness that change might be needed. This awareness did not seriously affect government until the twentieth century, but there was evidence that the effect was growing.

The same can be said for the United States. Reformers in the United States could not hope to make their points on the basis of relatively casual investigation, like those in Denmark, but the tradition of small government meant that commissions like those in

England or investigations like those in Germany were rare. Settlement workers were one source of social investigation—not only the direct inquiries carried out by the settlement workers, but also investigations made by people (often women) who had their first experience with both poverty and social investigation as settlement house residents.

The impulses that led to the founding of settlement houses in the 1880s and 1890s were various and often ill-defined. The original American settlement houses—those founded during the first decade of the American movement—were influenced by Toynbee Hall. Often the founders had visited the London settlement, and some had spent considerable time there. However, as Jane Addams wrote her sister when she was looking for the home that would become Hull House, the best-known social settlement in the United States, "We still think we have a distinct idea of our own."[10] Addams and the other early settlement workers certainly had an idea of their own, but it was indistinct. Probably the most basic common denominator was an attempt to combat what they saw as a growing gap between the well-to-do and the poor. They tried to close this gap from both directions. On the one hand, they provided the services and education that might help integrate the poor into the mainstream of American life: citizenship classes, day-care for infants, after-school clubs for teenagers. On the other hand, they tried through journalistic articles and sociological investigations to tell the well-to-do about life in the poor districts of America's cities. This led them naturally into social reform, and the settlement workers became spearheads for the social justice aspect of progressivism.

The settlement workers were crucial for influencing the attitudes of Americans, and therefore what actions Americans would take to deal with poverty. As one writer put it, they were important for "rousing the new conscience," which they did through their actions and also through their writing. Looking back from 1911, Jane Addams said that originally young people became settlement workers prompted by the desire to "do something about the social disorder," but that after the turn of the century they were more apt to say "We want to investigate something."[11] These twin aspects of communication—giving the more-convincing details and providing data in

more organized form—were, for this book, the most important settlement house functions.

The first attempts at sociology done in the settlement houses were
tentative and crude, but the alternative was no sociology at all. For
example, *Hull House Maps and Papers* (1895) described the various
nationalities around Hull House and included a multicolor map
showing each dwelling, with an indication of whether it was occu-
pied by English, Irish, German, Dutch, Russian, Polish, Italian,
Swiss, French, French-Canadian, Bohemian, Scandanavian, Chi-
nese, or "Colored."[12] There was no mention or suggestion anywhere
in the volume about social insurance as in Germany, although Jane
Addams knew the German system well. As a matter of fact, there
was almost nothing about charity at all—but rather a demand for an
end to exploitation—yet it was clear to any reader that poverty
existed in the United States and would not simply disappear under
the influence of general wealth.

The settlement workers tried to "rouse the new conscience"
through a never-ending series, a flood, a mountain of articles about
their "neighbors." One marvels that the settlements could function
at all if the residents spent so much time at their writing desks.
During the first decade of the twentieth century, more than one
hundred articles on the nature of social settlements appeared in
magazines like *Chatauquan, The Nation, Review of Reviews,* and
Annals of the American Academy, and a greater number by settlement house residents on their neighbors. The dominant subjects
were chlidren, the labor movement, civic corruption, and immigrants. Poverty and its causes, the need for replacing income lost
through sickness or old age, programs of social insurance, and
methods for administering charity were all notable for their absence. Even accident insurance, though mentioned occasionally, did
not play a prominent part in settlement house thinking.

In sum, these articles argued that economic exploitation must be
ended by a labor movement that deemphasized conflict but insisted
on justice. The economic system should become more democratic,
and the political system should remain democratic. If these things
were done, or if there were movement in that direction, the natural
virtues of the poor would suffuse society, and abject poverty would

mostly disappear.[13] Yet while the settlement workers were naively optimistic, their writing, their lives, and the reception accorded them did affect American attitudes toward poverty. They, along with others like Jacob Riis, Upton Sinclair, and the muckrakers, showed a wealthier America what the underside of the United States was becoming.

The extent to which the views of settlement workers were accepted was surely partly affected by the "respectableness" of the settlement leaders. They were not bearded labor agitators or "walking delegates," as union organizers were called. They were not wild-eyed speakers on street corners or conspiratorial anarchists. They were instead ministers of mainstream faiths—mostly Protestant, some Catholic, some Jewish—or they might be women of good education and good families on what amounted to a secular mission. Jane Addams' ideas found favor at least partly because her listeners and readers did not realize the inherent radicalism of those ideas—after all, she was proposing that American individualism was no longer relevant—because it was hidden beneath a black dress of proper fashion for well-brought-up middle-class women.

The settlement house movement was different from the charity organization society movement. The most important difference was that the settlement people settled. Moreover, while the settlement workers continued to try to socialize their neighbors, the settlement workers allowed themselves to be at least a little socialized in return. They were more explicitly respectful of the traditions out of which the immigrant groups came. The English settlements were mostly among Englishmen, and there was no doubt about who was teaching whom. Learning, at least at the most famous American settlements, went both ways. The settlement workers were clearly less didactic than the charity society people. Mary McDowell, of the Chicago University Settlement but previously a "friendly visitor," reported: "Before I went to live so near these people, I must confess I sailed often into a house and told them to 'clean up' in a most righteous manner. I don't know whether I am demoralized because I live in smoke and dirt, but I find it very hard to ask them to clean up now. I look upon dirt now as a very small evil compared with other things."[14]

Yet we should not overstress the differences and ignore the continuities. Settlement houses spoke about "neighbors," whereas the charity organization societies spoke of "friends" or, after about 1905, "clients." Neither term expressed reality, and Jane Addams was more at home among the educated men and women who were residents of Hull House than she was reading a story to a group of neighborhood children. Although they seem not to have used the precise term "social gospel," more settlement houses than charity organization societies were explicitly religious.[15] Even those that were not were kinds of missions, not to exotic other continents but nonetheless to wild places.[16] Neither charity organization societies nor settlement house workers thought of themselves as almsgivers, yet both gave relief in spite of themselves. The settlements may have denied it, but they too wanted to make the poor like "us." Although Addams quickly realized that the Butler Art Gallery was not what the neighborhood needed, she was extremely proud of the Greeks performing *Aeschylus.* In an inverted sort of way, she was even condescending toward the poor. The America she saw around her was too materialistic, too self-seeking, and had confined its democracy to politics without including economic democracy. She thought she saw in the "neighbors" a greater sense of what she called a "social ethic," a giving even if they had less to give, a generosity and sympathy that she hoped would redeem the evils of the society of the upper classes—that is, she did not see the poor as like other people, but as more virtuous, more Christlike.

Settlement workers were sometimes referred to as "practical sociologists." Charity organization societies also developed systematic information, but there was a difference. Although the distinction was not clear-cut, the COS investigations were probably more directed internally—that is, at the charity workers, the incipient social workers, with the purpose of developing better ways to deal with the poor. The writings of the settlement workers were more directed at a wider public and more concerned with changing public opinion than with techniques of social work.

The charity organization societies, as they developed in the latter years of the nineteenth century, and the settlement houses shared similar assumptions about poverty and charity in the United States. The charity societies may have put slightly more stress on individual cases, and the settlements slightly more on reform and services other than relief, but both functioned within mainstream American perceptions. Both worked for social justice, not for social security.

For the settlement workers, sociology was an outgrowth of their efforts to change the society. Early American sociologists had very much the same set of values and wanted to use sociology directly to change society. This is clearly evident in the first issues of the *American Journal of Sociology*, edited and with many articles by Albion Small. Only a few of the fifty articles printed that first year were not explicitly concerned with social reform. Albion W. Small, born in 1854, was the son of a clergyman. Ethical or religious values were always at the center of his efforts. For him, like the settlement house residents, social science and moral goals were not even two aspects of the same effort, but were part and parcel of each other. He became head of the first department of sociology in the United States at the new University of Chicago in 1892.

Small was not at all shy about making clear the political, economic, and ultimately moral goals of his investigations. In summing up his philosophy in his Decennial Lecture ten years after his appointment at the University of Chicago, he made clear where his sympathies lay:

> The widening chasm between luxury and poverty, the security of the economically strong and the insecurity of the economically weak, the domination of politics by pecuniary interests, the growth of capitalistic world-politics, the absence of commanding moral authority . . . all these are making men wonder how long we can go on in a fashion that no one quite understands.

There is in this *cri de coeur* much that is conservative. Small believed that he was living in an age of moral decline. But for Small and other reformers, that consciousness was an argument for using new and powerful techniques for reasserting ethical rather than "pecuniary" values. "Ethics must consist of empty forms until sociology can indicate the substance to which the forms apply," he continued.[17]

The clearest attempt to do what Small advocated was Robert Hunter's *Poverty* (1904), which emphasized the inadequacy of available information but tried to arrive at some reasonable estimate of the extent of poverty in early twentieth-century America. Hunter tried to estimate the number of people who received public charity—

the number of people whom the charity organization societies considered poor—to get figures on eviction, which he took as an indirect measure of financial distress. He drew a sharp distinction between the "pauper," who allows himself to be permanently dependent, and the "poor person," who struggles to avoid dependency but finds the struggle overwhelming. He concluded that no less than 10 million out of a population of around 82 million fell below what he defined as the poverty line. He argued for many kinds of regulatory legislation: child labor laws, tenement reforms, and factory safety laws, and also for the inauguration, "on the lines of foreign experience, of measures to compensate labor for the enforced seasons of idleness due to sickness, old age, lack of work, or other causes beyond the control of the workman." He was a socialist, but in this volume his socialism was subordinated to his data.[18]

Reactions to Hunter's book varied according to the political persuasion of the reader, but his study was noticed. His use of statistics was criticized as "unsubstantial statistical sallies" flawed by "pseudopathos and literary falsetto," but most reaction was positive. Florence Kelley was most unstinting in her praise. Mary Richmond, one of the founding figures of social casework, criticized Hunter for emphasizing the social causes of poverty to the exclusion of the individual causes, but some reviewers even thought he was too gentle in his condemnation of capitalism.[19]

Hunter was acutely conscious of the shortcomings of his data. He had written the book largely to demonstrate the inadequacies of current knowledge. The most important detailed investigation of those early years of the twentieth century was the Pittsburgh Survey, financed by the Russell Sage Foundation and administered by Paul Kellogg.[20] Issued in six volumes between 1909 and 1914, the Pittsburgh Survey and its reception showed how much effort was required to gather meaningful information, and also how useful such information could be, once gathered. Kellogg and the researchers under his direction dug as deep as they could into the conditions of industrial workers, men and women, in Allegheny County—that is, Pittsburgh—in 1907–8. There was no attempt or desire to claim that the subject was approached in a detached way. The authors already knew that there was distress and oppression in the area. They wanted to show the world, in unanswerable detail, what they themselves already knew: conditions were terrible and could and should be improved.

In the strictest sense, only Crystal Eastman's volume in the Pittsburgh Survey, *Work Accidents and the Law,* is concerned with people who had lost their wage-earning ability. The other volumes dealt with working and living conditions and pay rates. The cumulative effect, however, was to emphasize again and again what Robert Hunter had used as his main theme: hard as they might work, much as they might struggle and plan, working men and women lived on the narrow edge of disaster. Writing about industrial accidents, Eastman had the most immediate policy impact in that she later used the same techniques for writing the report of the Employer Liability Commission in New York, the basis for workmen's compensation in that state. In her volume in the Pittsburgh Survey she provided detailed data on accidents in mines, steel-making, railroad work, construction, and the like. She had to compile much of the data herself from the coroner's office and from hospital and company records. There were no neat government compilations—and that was just the point. Industrial accidents were numerous and devastating in their economic impact—but now the facts were out for all to see. Eastman had statistics as well as telling anecdotes. She knew how many accident victims were compensated, what they received, and how many were not compensated. She had details about the effects of industrial accidents on the family. She had the details of how employer liability laws were in fact working, and she had recommendations for change.[21]

Eastman was one of that first generation of women who united professional training with a career as a reformer in a broadened version of the traditional woman's role. She could perhaps be described as a nurturer, but it was on a professional rather than individual and personal plane. Both her mother and her father were ministers. She herself was one of the early women lawyers in the United States, and after 1911 she was a leading organizer of the woman suffrage campaign in Wisconsin. One of the many activities of her younger brother Max was the editorship of the radical magazine *Masses.*

As a whole, the Pittsburgh Survey was a huge project, with more than 2,500 pages of details and many photographs—more detailed than any previous study in the United States. It changed the nature of social investigation, was the model for smaller surveys done in other cities, and provided ammunition for reformers for years. Louis D. Brandeis used that kind of data in making his case in *Muller v. Oregon* (1908), and Eastman used that kind of data as the basis for workmen's compensation laws in New York, which in turn became the foundation for legislation in other states. It had become clear that carefully compiled social data could produce results.

The data with regard to children were particularly compelling—children were innocent victims. Children became the focal point and lever for much social reform during the Progressive period. The settlement workers found that much of their time was being spent with children. Agitation for laws against child labor was widespread and eventually effective, at least temporarily. There was also a "child-saving movement" and a playground movement. In 1912, after years of vigorous agitation and the endorsement of two U.S. presidents, the Children's Bureau was created within the Department of Labor. Julia Lathrop of Hull House and the Illinois State Board of Charities was its head. The Children's Bureau did what it was supposed to do. It collected and disseminated the information needed to make such changes as milk inspection laws, school attendance laws, and child labor regulations, but its effect on income-maintenance systems was slight.

There were rumblings of criticism, then, both in Great Britain and in the United States. In Britain the rumblings simply were that there should be new applications of traditional principles. Americans tried to make the point that some bits of traditional ideas were just not in accord with reality.

10

Early Liberal Reforms:
Toward Continental Solutions
within British Assumptions

In the field of social welfare in Germany and Denmark, the first decades of the twentieth century were relatively tranquil, but in Great Britain and the United States they were full of activity and significance. In Britain there was no longer the sense that there was a complete and satisfactory system of social welfare, and without totally abandoning the social philosophy incorporated in the Poor Law Report of 1834, major steps were taken in the area of social insurance. This was the era in which the British welfare state, in its modern version, began. In the United States the active decades meant not a movement toward social insurance (except with regard to industrial accidents), but a movement toward social justice—and that difference is important.

Old-age pensions, begun in Great Britain in 1908, are normally thought of as the first giant step in the Liberal Party's reform program and really the beginning of the modern welfare state. Pensions were perhaps a beginning, but they were not a giant step. Their ties of continuity with traditional values and ways of thinking were very great. Pressure for old-age pensions came from a great variety of directions. Herbert Asquith and David Lloyd George moved on pensions only when this pressure, this consensus, was already formed. Violent as disagreement about the Irish question, or tariffs might

130

be, people of quite diverse political persuasions, from Conservatives to Fabians, were behind old-age pensions.

Pensions had no political viability in 1899 anyway, but the South African war (1899–1902) finished them. There was the war, its costs, and a change in reign from Victoria (who died in 1901) to Edward VII. Yet the idea, dead at any policy-making level, did not completely die outside or even inside Parliament. It was kept alive by the untiring efforts of the National Pensions Committee, by the annual resolutions of the Trades Union Congress and the new Labour Party, by a continual drift toward pensions by the friendly societies, and by an influential journalist, Edith Sellers, who was promoting the Danish example.

In 1903 a select committee of Parliament was appointed and heard a number of witnesses on old-age pensions, including Edith Sellers on Denmark. In fact, from the time of the Chaplin Committee to the passage of the Pensions Act in 1908, Sellers was the chief and very influential spokesperson for the Danish system, arguing that it provided a model for Great Britain. It was not so much the Danish system that was in the public consciousness in Great Britain, but the Danish system seen through the filter of a prolific journalist, Edith Sellers. Her testimony before the committee that was looking at old-age pensions in other countries set the tone of her influence and is a wonderful example of one country seeing what it wants in the example of another country. She praised the Danish system particularly because it differentiated sharply between "pauper" relief, which was for the "thriftless and worthless," and old-age pensions, which were for the self-respecting poor. For the British legislators this would be an important point. A major argument against old-age pensions, aside from their high cost, was that they were simply a disguised form of "outdoor" poor relief, without the deterrents and disqualifications that outdoor relief brought with it. Sellers was arguing here that old-age pensions could be sharply differentiated in the minds of the recipients from "pauper" relief—as they were in Denmark.

In Danish, however, there is no word that carries all the freight of the English usage of "pauper." *Fattiglem* is usually given in dictionaries, but that word is actually short for *fattighuslem* and means

"inmates of the poorhouse." The word certainly has a negative conno-
tation, and being a recipient of poor-law help was hardly a badge of
honor, but *fattiglem* did not imply all the judgment on a person's
strength of character, lifelong habits, and general moral worth that
"pauper" did in English. Moreover, the poor law in Denmark was of
far less central importance than it was in Great Britain. Yet In 1903
Sellers used the term and was understood in the full English meaning of "pauper," so even though Sellers' arguments were quoted and
paraphrased, including in the Cabinet, they were essentially based
on a misunderstanding that interpreted the Danish law in terms
that were important to Englishmen but not to Danes.[1]

When the Liberal Party came to power in 1906, it would need no
very bold leadership to introduce some kind of pension bill. Even if
there was sharp disagreement on means, a consensus was there to be
had. The election had given a large majority to the Liberals, and the
Liberals could have ignored the growing Labour Party, but they did
not. There was also considerable pressure from within the Liberal
Party. The recommendations of the Asquith government followed
the long-held Labour (and Fabian) position favoring noncontributory pensions—the idea that the German socialists would express
as *Fürsorge*.[2] But this program might also be less disturbing to
Conservatives who wanted simply to go a little beyond what was
now being done under the poor law. Social insurance would be new
in British law, but kind treatment for the "aged deserving poor"
would not. Moreover, contributory pensions smacked of social insurance and of Germany, and that was something few Englishmen
wanted in 1908.

When the decision to propose noncontributory pensions was made,
David Lloyd George, Chancellor of the Exchequer, introduced the
bill by arguing that there was no such thing as a noncontributory
pension because people had been paying taxes all their lives. The
idea had gone unchallenged in Denmark, but it did not in the British
Parliament. Lloyd George went on to reject a contributory plan because it would not include low-paid workers, many of them women,
and would not come into operation for years. The Germany system
made allowances for these problems, but Lloyd George ignored that.
He proposed simply that any "deserving" (and how that judgment
should be made provoked discussion) British subject over seventy

years old with an income of less than ten shillings a week could receive a pension of five shillings a week, to be administered by a local "Pension Committee," thus avoiding identification with the poor law, but to be paid for out of the "imperial" (i.e., the national) Treasury.[3]

In the House of Commons few argued that there should be no pension law at all. All differences assumed that there would be some kind of pension system. Henry Chaplin, the same man whose committee had proposed noncontributory pensions in 1899, was now the chief spokesman for a contributory system. Why he changed his mind is unclear. The Liberals answered by referring to Germany as a negative example. Asquith referred to "the two pillars of the German system," which he said were "inquisition and compulsion." You cannot, he claimed, have the "complicated and irritating machinery" in Great Britain that works in Germany. One member of Parliament said, "The German people could be sifted and regimented in a manner in which the people of this country could not possibly be treated."[4] These arguments were abandoned three years later. The Liberals were here clearly appealing to the British image of themselves as neither having nor wanting the bureaucratic machinery of Germany. The British cherished their freedom and thought of themselves as lightly governed. This self-image is almost exactly the same as the one the Americans had of themselves, except in that case it was the British who furnished the counterexample.

The opposite extreme from the proposals for compulsion and contribution was the Labour Party's desire for universal pensions beginning at age sixty-five. Labour was not very happy with the Asquith plan, but it was better than nothing.[5] Universal pensions were dismissed by the Liberals as being ridiculously expensive. Lloyd George said that only £7.5 million was available now, after "your" war (pointing to the Conservatives) had been at least partly paid for, and that was that.[6]

Only in the House of Lords was the basic idea of old-age pensions condemned. It was damned as reviving the "bad old days" before 1834, as being an indefinite extension of outdoor relief with no stigma or disqualification, as another step in destroying British individualism. The bill would lead the laborer to say, "Damn work! Blast work! Why should I work when I can get 10s per week from the rates for doing nothing?"[7] Some journals were still more shrill. *Black-woods Magazine* called it "the most ill-considered scheme" that had ever been placed before the country, in which nothing was allowed to injure the poor save thrift. It was a cheap pandering for votes that would be paid for by cutting the army and navy budget and imposing tariffs. The *Edinburgh Review* condemned pensions, along with school meals and the idea of unemployment insurance, as socialism born from a sycophantic effort to please the few Labour representatives. They were, said the *Review,* proposed by a temporary party with no future.[8]

There was, however, increasing support for the idea of old-age pensions from the friendly societies. For example, the Hearts of Oak Benefit Society was more and more distressed at the failing attempt to increase superannuation benefits and began to look to government pensions as a solution. At the National Conference of Friendly Societies in 1908, the presidential address by George Wilde of the Manchester Unity said that the bill then before the House of Commons was "extremely gratifying" and that although it might not be completely satisfactory to friendly society members, it was a welcome step.[9]

Old-age pensions in Great Britain did not become law until a broad consensus had been formed behind them. They were not devised by administrators or political leaders and pushed through by a party majority. They were the product of pressure groups of widely divergent political philosophies. Instead of being a victory for one side and defeat for another, they were an idea whose time had come. In the end, the vote on the second reading—and in effect on the bill—was 417 to 29. The bill passed the House of Lords 123 to 16.[10]

One could see the Pensions Act as simply a slight extension of the poor law, changing the designation "pauper" to "pensioner" with very little difference in substance. On the other hand, one could view the act as destroying the "principles of 1834" and setting the nation on a new road. Neither would be correct. Because the pensions carried no legal or social stigma, they were very popular and more expensive than planned. "Outdoor pauperism" among the aged declined to virtually nothing within a few years. On the other hand, the "principles of 1834" were still maintained and applied with the same force to the group for whom they were intended, the "able-bodied poor." In fact, those principles survived in the report of the Commission on the Poor Laws, which had been sitting since 1906 and would report in 1909. The moral philosophy from 1834 was still dominant, and in some ways would be until World War I.[11]

The Commission on the Poor Laws gathered an enormous amount of statistical and anecdotal evidence and heard hundreds of witnesses. There are striking continuities across the seventy-five years from 1834 to 1909. Where the 1834 Poor Law Report said that the parishes were too small and recommended that they combine to form poor-law "unions," the 1909 report said that the "unions" were too small and recommended that counties and boroughs be the units for poor law support. The 1834 report recommended that different categories of people in poorhouses should be treated differently. The 1909 report regretted that this had not been done and recommended such classification (pt. 9, p. 617). The 1909 Majority Report quoted great slabs of the 1834 report on almost every page and supported the conclusions and social attitudes of that now seventy-five-year-old document. Ths most important continuity is the judgmental one. In the course of the twentieth century, all four countries under study here, including Great Britain, have given up trying to differentiate between the "deserving" and "undeserving," but this distinction was absolutely unquestioned by the authors of the 1909 report and runs throughout their conclusions. In dealing with the aged, for instance, the report discusses the "respectable aged" without any further definition (pt. 9, p. 621).

The 1909 commission report (and the Webbs' *History* after it) seems to believe that the emphasis on the curative was a great departure from the 1834 Poor Law Report, but this is a misreading of the latter. The purpose of the 1834 report was also curative. Poor people were believed to be vulnerable to the disease of pauperism, which disease the then-current system conspired to spread. The reforms proposed in 1834 would not only arrest the spread of the disease, but also impel the sufferers to cure themselves and be well and self-respecting again. Within this similarity, however, there is an important difference. The 1834 report proposed a self-administering system with the "offer of the house" determining need. The 1909 report recommended detailed investigation of each case. Octavia Hill and Charles Loch, along with four other London Charity Organisation Society people, were members of the Commission on the Poor Laws, and this recommendation clearly reflects the experience of that organization, which had most rigidly upheld the "principles of 1834."[12]

One recommendation of the 1909 report was that there be a number of types of voluntary contributory insurance, all to cover temporary distress. They were to be financed with as little contribution from the state as possible because of the "heavy charge" imposed on the state by old-age pensions (pt. 9, p. 628). While praising the "old-fashioned virtue of thrift," the commission also recommended some form of unemployment insurance for unskilled and unorganized workers, with contributions from public funds. They recommended that such plans should make use of "trade organizations or of organizations of a similar character which may be brought into existence by a hope of participation in public contributions," by which they meant "friendly societies," trade unions, and what would in the 1911 National Insurance Act be called "approved societies."

The majority Report also suggested "invalidity insurance," but not health insurance for short illnesses. They argued that because industry made many people "old" in a wage-earning sense long before they reached the pension age, some form of national insurance was necessary for people in the unemployable but not pensionable period of their lives. The Minority Report was issued as a separate book, with Beatrice Webb as the principal author. What it proposed, in the words of its title, was *The Break-Up of the Poor Law* and the substitution not of social insurance but of what Eduard Bernstein called *Fürsorge,* or as the Minority Report put it, provision of "the reasonable necessaries of life, such as food, lodging, warmth, clothing and medical attendance, according to the normal standards of the times" and without any civic penalties—that is, a "social minimum."[13] Even though the Webbs undoubtedly had great influence in Labour Party circles, the policies that the party supported over the next few years were those of the Majority Report of 1909, not those of the minority, and when national insurance became law, Beatrice Webb greeted it with scorn.[14]

So the story of poor-law relief in Great Britain is not one of adherence to the "principles of 1834" until the Webbs came along and, destroying them, inaugurated a new system. It is an intellectual adherence to the "principles of 1834" right through at least 1909. The sacred text remained sacred—just somewhat reinterpreted. Even social insurance could be encompassed within that sacred text.

11

Liberal Reform in Great Britain: The Quest for Social Security

Prime Minister Herbert Asquith quickly rejected the idea of breaking up the poor law. "The principles which should guide legislation and eventually control the administration of Public Assistance," he wrote to the Cabinet in March 1909, "were adopted from the Majority Report." That Majority Report stated, "Under the present organization of industry there is a necessity for some form of insurance against the time when a man becomes entirely incapacitated from wage-earning." Exactly what form that insurance should take was worked out by David Lloyd George, Chancellor of the Exchequer, and Winston Churchill at the Board of Trade.[1]

Lloyd George had been just a little evasive when he discussed the financing of old-age pensions. He said the money was available but did not say from where. It would be surprising if in 1908 he had not given some thought to the budget he would have to introduce in 1909. The "People's Budget" might seem moderate to later eyes, but its raising of the income, land, and inheritance taxes produced shock. It would raise money for battleships, the increasing expenditures for old-age pensions, and other vaguely defined social reforms. The budget was passed by the House of Commons but rejected by the Lords. The battle between the two houses, which had been simmering for years, reached a climax over the next two years. Suffice it to say here that Asquith, Lloyd George, and the House of

Commons won. The powers of the Lords were strictly limited, and the government had the money available for its twin purposes: arms and welfare.

Old-age pensions in Great Britain had been a product of consensus. During the election of 1906, no candidate had opposed the principle, and everyone assumed that something would soon be done. This was not quite the case with health insurance and unemployment insurance, which together made up the National Insurance Act of 1911. This was a far larger step than pensions. There was a consensus on national health and unemployment insurance, but because it was hidden beneath a thicket of interest groups, it had to be brought to bear on the system by strong political leadership. Lloyd George, by extremely adroit maneuvering and by placating various pressure groups with seemingly significant but not actually crucial alterations in the original plan, managed to make an underlying consensus politically constructive. The question of why Lloyd George, who had so fervently defended noncontributory old-age pensions, just as fervently favored contributory health and unemployment insurance is easily answered: he needed the money. The question is why he or anyone else would see unemployment and health insurance as next on the agenda.[2]

Unemployment had been a nagging and growing problem since the mid-1880s. In 1908 and 1909 the Labour Party held special conventions on unemployment. The primary demand was for public works to guarantee employment for all except the "culpable unemployed," but the 1909 Labour Party convention, with Keir Hardie as chairman, cautiously endorsed the general idea of unemployment insurance as well.[3] Sidney and Beatrice Webb, young William Beveridge, and the wonderfully astute and influential Winston Churchill pressed the issue on Asquith and Lloyd George. Health insurance was also in the air. The Majority Report of 1909 had been willing to contemplate some form of what they called "invalidity" insurance, but the whole idea seems to be one that Lloyd George devised and pushed himself.[4]

Churchill was impressed with the way Germany organized its society, and that plus Lloyd George's famous trip to Germany in August 1908 brings up the question of how far the the British systems were modeled on the German systems. Certainly old-age pensions were not modeled on Germany's, because they were entirely different. Unemployment insurance could not have been either, because Germany had no unemployment insurance before 1927. That leaves health insurance, which was indeed to some degree influenced by Germany. More important than any specific program or mechanism, the idea that there could be insurance organized by the government against what might be regarded as personal misfortune, and that these misfortunes were calculable, was where Germany was influential. As Harold Spender, who accompanied Lloyd George to Germany, wrote, "The German example has taught us this great lesson—that the principle of insurance, which is used so freely in our own country to protect the prosperous, . . . may be even more successfully extended to protect the unprosperous." However vehemently Lloyd George might differentiate his proposals from the German, and however different they might in fact be, Germany was always in the back of everyone's mind.[5]

Other concerned factions also made trips to Germany. J. E. Gilchrist of the Manchester Unity Friendly Society, in his presidential address to the National Conference of Friendly Societies in 1909 describing his trip, was full of praise for the German system and explicitly endorsed the Chancellor's position that compulsory insurance would come. "It is a social necessity," he said.[6] In 1910 the Labour Party sent its own delegation to Germany, but the purpose was more to uphold free trade than to examine social insurance. The delegation reported, "It is brains, not tariffs, that account for Germany's progress in the world." In describing the results of "brains," the major emphasis was on social insurance. After outlining poor relief and sickness insurance, they wrote, "We cannot but think that measures of this character do more towards securing public health and industrial efficiency." So regardless of the details of the laws, Germany was on the mind of the Labour Party too.[7] As for Winston Churchill at the Board of Trade, there can be little doubt. In 1908 he wrote: "The main need of the English working classes is Security. In Germany . . . uniform & symmetrical arrangements exist for insurance of workmen against accidents & sickness, for provision for old age, and through Labour bureaux etc. for employment. No such State organization exists in England."[8] The health insurance side was more directly Lloyd George's creation. He had gone to Germany himself in 1908, and two years later he sent a young civil servant, William J. Braithwaite, specifically to look more closely at health insurance.[9]

There can be no doubt, then, about the influence of Germany, both specific and general, on national health and unemployment insurance in Great Britain. As always, though, influence works on something already there and is by no means simply a carbon copy of the situation somewhere else. There was in Great Britain no particular problem of national unity that a centralized insurance plan could counteract, and there was far less fear of a revolutionary workers movement than in Germany. In addition, the German tradition of a heavily interventionist state was absent in Great Britain; in its place was a preference for nongovernmental measures. Perhaps most important, the German measure had to satisfy only various relatively confined groups at the center of power—the National Liberals and the industrialists. The British Chancellor had to play mass politics far more than the German.

Historians tend to regard as humbug any statements of human sympathy, of humanitarian sentiments toward the poor and the exploited, on the part of politicians and see only self-interest or scheming as real motives. Considering the amount of humbug in politics, this is often a reasonable bet. Yet David Lloyd George, Winston Churchill, and William Beveridge—not to mention the Webbs, other Toynbee Hall residents, members of various factions of the Labour Party, and even members of the London Charity Organisation Society, were conscious of the misery that illness and unemployment produced. Even the more conservative members of the Majority Report endorsed some sort of health insurance. Motives were no doubt mixed, but the humanitarian motive was there.[10]

It was this humanitarian tone that Lloyd George struck when he introduced the bill on national health and unemployment insurance, titled "National Insurance," in a speech more than two hours long on May 4, 1911. He argued that there was a great mass of poverty that "is too proud to wear the badge of pauperism" and that ill health is responsible for much for it. The "working classes" are trying with all their might to insure themselves through the "friendly societies" and other forms of insurance, but often the benefits are too low to sustain life in time of need, and in any case, he said, insurance, even mutual insurance, does not reach the low-paid worker, many of whom are women.[11] The bill initially received a cordial reception in the House of Commons, with friendly speeches from Conservative and Labour members, so there was no considerable body of opinion opposed to the general idea of subsidized compulsory contributory insurance against sickness and unemployment. Even Claude Lowther, a Conservative and president of something called "The Anti-Socialist Union," spoke in its favor. Yet in its details the bill touched the interests of employers, the friendly societies, private for-profit insurance companies, doctors, various elements in the Labour Party (e.g., female workers), trade-union benefit societies, the Fabians, and the more radical socialists. As these groups looked closely at the plan the Liberals had devised, each found elements that threatened their own self-interest.

Perhaps there was most to be feared from the friendly societies. They had been willing to go along with the idea of pensions because they were unable to meet that need themselves and were glad to have state assistance. Aside from good fellowship, however, sickness benefits were their raison d'être. Would they regard state action in that area as a threat or an aid? Lloyd George had been dealing with the friendly societies for years, ever since he first contemplated old-age insurance. He had invited J. Lister Stead, from the Foresters, to work on the bill. In October 1909 the parliamentary agents of the friendly societies met with the Chancellor. Lloyd George was a master at making people feel that he agreed with them. He told the agents that he recognized the value of the friendly societies and would do nothing to injure them. His plan would subsidize them by providing premiums not only from the members but also from employers and in some cases from the state. By the time of the 1911 meeting of the National Conference of Friendly Societies on October 12 and 13, the bill had become law, and R. W. Moffrey of the Manchester Unity spoke enthusiastically about it, arguing only that doctors had too much power.[12] Lloyd George simply wrapped the friendly societies into the plan, by using them to administer the insurance. The friendly societies met the conditions of the act, became what were called approved societies, and provided health insurance on a better basis than before.

Some portions of the Labour Party presented no problems for

Lloyd George. Ramsay MacDonald was just one of the Labour members of the House of Commons to welcome the bill and praise the Chancellor. The Trades Union Congress (TUC) Parliamentary Committee met with Lloyd George in January, and in their report to the TUC annual conference wrote in favor of the bill in general and of the compulsory contributory idea in particular. The Trades Union Congress approved of the national health insurance bill and defeated by a margin of roughly 5 to 3 a motion urging that the whole plan be made noncontributory. Thus most of those who were involved in the realities of politics, plus a majority of the trade unions, were fairly moderate and supportive of the government.[13]

Lloyd George, and indeed the entire range of political opinion, was explicitly concerned with the position of women, particularly working women. Women in Great Britain, as in other countries, were mostly in the more poorly paid trades, yet in Britain they were better organized than in Germany, Denmark, or the United States—and more clearly organized as women, not simply as low-paid members of the working classes. In the United States energetic, devoted, and brilliant women attempted to organize female workers, but before the 1930s efforts to organize the unskilled in general were not very successful, and attempts to organize women, mostly in occupations that were considered unskilled, were even less successful. In Germany, even in the 1920s, the Social Democratic Party always felt ambivalent about whether to regard women as a special problem or simply part of the general problem of class oppression.[14] In Denmark no particular attention was paid to the working woman in the period before World War I.

In Great Britain, however, where the position of women was legally and economically no better than in the other countries, female workers were a recognized pressure group within the Labour Party. In June 1911 a delegation of "working women's societies" claiming to represent 20,000 women called on Lloyd George to assert that women were treated unfairly under the bill. They did not argue against the lower premiums and lower benefits that women would get—that feature of the bill was never attacked and therefore never defended—but they asserted instead that women would receive fewer benefits in relation to their premiums than men would, which was true. Mrs. Ramsay MacDonald, for the Woman's Labour League, asked that married women who had worked be allowed to continue as voluntary members, for a small premium. Lloyd George replied that would be impossible because there would be no employer's contribution. This was one issue on which he was forced to compromise.[15]

The divisiveness over the issue of whether the insurance plan should be contributory or noncontributory so split the Labour Party that it was not the effective pressure group it might otherwise have been. Ramsay MacDonald, Keir Hardie, and others either favored the idea of contributions, or acquiesced. What might be called the left wing of the party was scornful of what they regarded as a surrender of principle. Why, they asked, should the burden of what was a problem of capitalism be placed on those who were its victims? Philip Snowden said that MacDonald was no socialist, and a liar to boot. MacDonald indignantly replied that no one was going to tell him how to define socialism, and he accused Snowden of being ignorant of parlimentary procedures. The Fabians published a detailed analysis of the bill, criticizing many details and, more generally, the contributory idea.[16] Lloyd George, however, had most of the parliamentary Labour Party on his side, and they stayed on his side even after most of the amendments offered by the Labour Party failed in Parliament.

The most effective threat to the bill, even after it became law, was from the doctors. Many general practitioners had what was called a "club practice"—that is, they were employed by the friendly societies—but the leaders of the profession, who controlled the British Medical Association and were in charge of its *Journal,* were in private practice. These doctors were the more implacable enemies of health insurance. A special meeting of the British Medical Association was held on May 31 and June 1, 1911, with Lloyd George attending and answering questions on the second day. The doctors were concerned about four items. First, they wanted to be sure that doctors would not be managed by nondoctors; they wanted health committees made up entirely of doctors to administer the medical benefits. Second, they wanted patients to be able to choose their doctors freely. Third, they asked that only people below a certain income level be insured, and that the others pay as before. Fourth, they wanted "adequate remuneration," with some doctors wanting a fee-for-service system rather than payment per head. The special meeting passed a resolution saying that it "approved of the application of the insurance principle to the provision of the cost of medical attendance on persons who cannot otherwise meet it." This was the crucial point, of course. Once the British Medical Association had passed this kind of resolution, everything else was negotiable, and in fact was solved through negotiation.[17]

What is most striking in this list of issues from the doctors is what was *not* said. In the United States, doctors opposed health insurance on the grounds that there was no need or demand for it and that it would interfere with the free practice of medicine and with the sacred relationship between doctors and patients. Except for the last, which Lloyd George met to a considerable degree by establishing panels from which patients could freely choose a doctor, these arguments were not made in England. It was clear that there was need; investigation after investigation had shown that. During the Boer War, the army had rejected one-third of the enlistees as not physically fit, and the proportion was much higher for poor industrial districts. There was in England a clear acceptance of the idea that public health was a legitimate concern of the state. Doctors wanted more power in the system, and Lloyd George gave it to them. But they wanted more scope for private practice, and Lloyd George did not give in on that. The remaining issue was not principle but money. At four shillings a head the doctors rejected the plan; at eight shillings they accepted it. The American Association for Labor Legislation, the chief advocate of health insurance in the United States, would have been overjoyed to face such slight opposition from doctors. To be sure, there was a brief attempt at noncooperation in England after the bill became law, but it soon evaporated and doctors in general went along with the insurance.

Lloyd George also saw deputations of employers. The Employers Parliamentary Council wanted to eliminate the employer's contribution, a suggestion that no one took seriously. The Association of Chambers of Commerce said that they wanted a lower employer's contribution but that they were for the bill in general. Lloyd George pointed out that the employer's contribution in Germany, Great Britain's chief competitor, was higher still and that all kinds of costs were higher in the United States. He believed that British manufacturers could still compete.[18]

So support for the general principles of health and unemployment insurance came from the Labour Party, the Trades Union Congress, Conservatives, doctors, the friendly societies, and private insurers, when Lloyd George let them form approved societies, not to mention from the Majority Report in 1909. Each saw that their own interests would be served by the plan. Most had reservations about certain details, but most members of each group thought that, on balance, the national insurance bill was something they should support. In the United States, the analogue of all those groups (there was no analogue to the friendly societies) came to the opposite conclusion. They believed that any sort of social insurance threatened their interests, and so they opposed it until economic crisis overwhelmed them in the 1930s. Even if a strong leader like Lloyd George— Theodore Roosevelt comes to mind—had pressed for such insurance, he probably could not have overcome such united opposition. Lloyd George had a basis for consensus before he began and he skillfully built it stronger.

In a sense, then, the debates in the House of Commons were over details, no matter how fervent or lengthy the speeches. A look at two somewhat contradictory memorandums issued by Lloyd George as he introduced the bill showed the kinds of charges he feared. An "explanatory memorandum" spent a good deal of time showing how his plan was different from the German plan. The Germans were far more bureaucratic; the British plan would rely on already existing self-governing societies, which would find it in their own interests to guard against "malingering," a great fear in considerations of any sort of insurance in Great Britain. The German system was more expensive and provided lower benefits. It divided wage-earners into four classes, whereas, Lloyd George insisted, the British plan would not. At the same time, the Chancellor issued another report, which quoted insurance administrators and employers in Germany saying how well the German plan worked and how even those who were skeptical at first were now enthusiastic. There was no testimony from any labor leader, trade union activist or Social Democrat, and the memorandum was clearly aimed at British employers. No one pointed out that the first memorandum implied that the second was irrelevant, but the memorandums both indicate that Lloyd George feared being labeled pro-German and that he feared opposition from employers. The fear was unfounded, because although employers were better organized on this issue than on previous ones, they were only mildly active and not really in opposition.[19]

During the debates on the second reading of the bill, the various groups made the same arguments they had or would make in deputations to the Chancellor. A good deal of attention was devoted to women, particularly married women whose husbands were covered by the health insurance. Could not the wife and children also be insured? Lloyd George answered that it was simply too expensive, and the Labour amendment to insure them failed. The issue was again brought up in November, when the bill was being considered in detail. By this time Lloyd George had been persuaded, and he himself introduced a lengthy amendment to allow women who had been insured before marriage to continue, though no longer employed, at reduced premiums and benefits.[20] There was very little attempt to dismiss the bill with arguments from 1834. Insurance, after all, was for the thrifty and industrious, but more than that, members were now willing explicitly to reject the attitudes of seventy-five years earlier. "All the old theories have now been buried," said one member of Parliament. "With the advent of democracy to power, new views regarding the duty of the State toward its individual members have come into being." He was perhaps too sanguine.[21]

The bill passed its second reading by almost 4 to 1, and its third reading by better than 10 to 1, receiving the Royal Assent on December 16, 1911.[22] Health insurance and unemployment insurance were separate parts of the same act. The health insurance was compulsory for all employees in manual labor over sixteen years old, earning under £160 a year, except for those in the military, those "in employment under the Crown," and a few other small categories. People having an annual unearned income of £26 or more, which Lloyd George characterized as "a considerable income in the class for which we are providing," could petition to be exempted. Insured persons paid premiums at a rate of four pence a week for men and three pence a week for women, to which would be added in both cases three pence a week from the employer. For low-paid workers—those earning two shillings or less a day—the employer would pay more, the employee less, and some very low paid workers would pay nothing at all, the difference to be made up by the Treasury. In

Germany the whole insurance plan was to pay its own way, without any "imperial" contributions outside of administrative expenses. In Great Britain it was a small step on the way to transfer payments.

Germany and Denmark incorporated the existing "sickness funds" (*Krankenkassen* and *sygekasser*) into their scheme of national health insurance. Great Britain did the same with the friendly societies, trade union mutual insurance societies, and even the commercial collecting societies, which mainly offered burial insurance. Trade unions were required to keep health insurance funds strictly separate from their other funds—a provision to which they objected in vain—and collecting societies had to keep their profit-making function separate from their national health insurance funds. The device for incorporating these groups was the creation of approved societies. An approved society could not be profit-making and must be "under the absolute control of its members." These societies had to charge premiums, pay benefits, and accumulate reserves in accordance with the National Insurance Act, but beyond that they had the freedom to alter benefits, impose fines, and make rules (within certain limits) as they saw fit. Thus the appearance of autonomy and membership democracy was maintained, but in fact that autonomy was strictly limited, and to a considerable degree membership democracy was replaced by the kind of democracy that now operated through Parliament and the political parties.

Health insurance applied to virtually all low-paid manual employees, but unemployment insurance was far more limited. Only workers in trades considered to be subject to periodic fluctuations were included—for example, building and construction, shipbuilding, mechanical engineering, iron-founding, construction of vehicles, and sawmilling. Workers in these trades were to pay two-and-a-half pence a week, the employer paid the same amount into a central unemployment fund, and the Treasury would add one-third of the total amount. For this, workers could receive seven shillings a week for up to fifteen weeks a year, with certain limitations—for example, no unemployment benefits were to be paid to strikers, to workers fired for misconduct, or to workers receiving sick pay under the health insurance part of the act. Cases of dispute would go to a special court of referees made up of one representative of the workers, one from employers, and one from the Board of Trade. Decisions of the court of referees were final; they could not be taken to the ordinary courts. There were incentives for maintaining employment. For each worker continually employed for twelve months, the employer would receive back one-third of the premiums paid for that employee. A worker, however, would have to work ten years at a job before any refund of premiums, and then he received whatever excess he had paid in over what he had taken out, plus 2.5 percent interest. The fund could thus be a type of forced savings.

In Germany there was no unemployment insurance until 1927, partly because the workers wanted to control it and the state and employers would not construct such a system. In Great Britain there was virtually no opposition to the state running the system, and in Denmark no particular problem with the unions running it. In Great Britain, workers did not see the state as an enemy. There might be a huge social gulf between a high civil servant and a worker in an iron foundry; neither might want to share a pint with the other, yet neither would regard the other as a threat and probably neither would shoot at the other. There can be no doubt that national insurance constituted a considerable change in thinking. The state was now not only forcing people to be prudent, but also actually contributing to their maintenance—and without asking anything from them or applying any disqualifying factors. Yet elements of traditional thinking remained. Because unemployment insurance was so limited, the great mass of working people, even the skilled, were outside it. Moreover, one could support social insurance and still have nothing but contempt for "wastrels and loafers," and many supporters of the new law made it very clear that their solicitude did not extend to such people. Insurance was for the respectable, prudent, regular members of the working classes.

Contributory social insurance is in intent far less of a disciplining measure than poor-law aid or means-tested pensions for "the deserving." The poor law hoped to frighten people into working hard by the automatic test of offering the poorhouse or a "task of work," and the old-age pension law actually created a committee to judge whether the applicant was worthy. Under an insurance plan, a person who had paid premiums would get benefits regardless of whether he was a drunkard or beat his wife. Yet insurance also has its disciplining functions, as mid-twentieth-century critics of the welfare state point out. A worker must be regularly employed and must regularly pay premiums, and these things are compelled by law.[23] Insurance could be considered a counterpart in the modern administrative state of the poor law. Both function almost automatically to encourage virtue and punish vice, but the modern version is more humane, more subtle, more subject to democratic control, and available only when the bureaucratic machinery can handle it—as was not the case in 1834. Yet continuity was not absent. It would take the Great War to destroy that.

In the United States the years between the turn of the century and World War I were also years of reform, but the reform took directions quite different from those exhibited by the old-age pensions, unemployment insurance, and medical insurance of liberal England.

12

Progressive Reform
in the United States:
The Quest for Social Justice

The years of Liberal Reform in Great Britain coincided with the years of "progressive reform" in the United States, yet the direction of the reform in America, if not its ultimate end, was quite different. Progressivism had many strands: regulation of business, more direct democracy, increased strength for labor unions, and what has been called "the quest for social justice." The latter strand included things like a drive for child labor laws, more healthful urban housing, better playgrounds, and safer working conditions. It is significant that it is called a quest for social *justice*, not a quest for social security. Only in a few limited areas were more than a small minority of progressives concerned with income maintenance. Most progressives shared with conservatives the belief that they were living in an abundant society. All that was needed was to allow people to share in that abundance, to sweep aside barriers to opportunity, to provide justice. Once social justice provided access, abundance would provide the security.

In Germany, the first social insurance bill introduced by Bismarck provided for industrial accident insurance, although it was not the first bill to become law. It was seen in Germany as part of a general program of workers insurance, part of a response to the "social question" or "worker question." In the United States there was no such social question that accident insurance could be an answer to. Nor was there a general attempt by the government at any level to recreate a social fabric that was presumed to have been torn apart by industrialism and urbanization. While accident insurance was almost the only income-maintenance or social insurance program adopted in the United States during the progressive period, it should be seen as having different functions in the United States and in the European countries.

One strand of the progressive movement was that of limiting what were seen as excesses of business organizations. Many of those pushing for workmen's compensation laws seemed to see accidents at work as another area where corporate freedom had to be limited. But this desire to limit corporate excesses would not have been enough to account for the rapid spread of workmen's compensation laws between 1910 and 1920. The success of this reform came only after employers themselves urged workmen's compensation as economically desirable for employers.

As in other countries, compensation for American employees for accidents on the job was governed before workmen's compensation laws by the prevailing law of employer liability. A worker or a worker's surviving dependents could sue and in some cases collect. Employers had at least three lines of defense in court against such suits. They might assert that the employee was a free agent and had assumed the risk of his own free will; they might argue that if a "fellow servant" (i.e., another employee) had contributed to the accident the employer was not liable; or they might hold that if the employee himself had contributed to the accident the employer was not liable. These three doctrines of "assumed risk," "fellow servant," and "contributory negligence"—collectively known as the "common-law defenses"—meant that employees could collect compensation in only a few cases of injury, and then usually only after prolonged and expensive litigation.

Accident insurance and employer liability were not a live political issues in the United States before the twentieth century. Many of the early articles in periodicals had to use German accident figures because the information was simply not recorded in the United States,[1] but there was little reason to believe that there were fewer accidents in America than in Europe. Adna Weber, later one of the founding members of the American Association for

Labor Legislation, wrote in 1902 that on the contrary there were probably more accidents but that the issue did not seem so pressing because the injured workers became public charges less often in the United States.

> European workers, with their cramped position, their slender re-
> sources and the burden of militarism, have not been able to obtain
> an adequate reward for their toil, and hence are likely to be
> crushed by comparatively slight misfortune, and thereby thrown
> upon the public charities for maintenance. American workingmen,
> on the other hand, have earned and received high wages and have
> enjoyed what their European *confreres* would call financial indepen-
> dence; their savings or their insurance in fraternal orders would
> have enabled them to withstand the effects of all but the most
> serious physical injuries without becoming a burden on the public.[2]

Weber here was explicitly using American prosperity to explain why European workers were more fully covered by social insurance than their American counterparts.

Signs of employer interest in workmen's compensation began around 1905 and increased markedly after the 1906 Compensation Act became law in Great Britain. The full text of the law was printed by the U.S. Bureau of Labor Statistics, but these bulletins had a limited audience, and it was more significant that magazines for a broader public—such as *Outlook, North American Review, Every-body's,* and *American Magazine*—took up the obvious implication of the British law for the United States.[3] By 1906 many states had already broadened the liability of employers in intrastate commerce, sometimes only for railroads, sometimes for other hazardous work. So when President Theodore Roosevelt took up the issue, he was not building entirely without a foundation. However, most aspects of employee-employer relationships were within state jurisdiction, if indeed they were within any public jurisdiction at all. Injecting the federal government into the relationship was a step in a new direc-tion. The federal government had jurisdiction over workers in inter-state commerce (which meant railroads primarily) and over its own employees. Roosevelt tackled both types. He may have been influ-enced by British considerations of employer liability and workmen's compensation, but certainly more important was his conviction that only enlightened conservatism could fend off a more radical politics, and that enlightened conservatism involved some degree of social justice.

In the case of the railroads, the tactics Roosevelt chose were the essentially moderate ones of enlarging employer liability by eliminating the common-law defenses. The bill he proposed passed both houses of Congress easily during the spring of 1906 and became law on June 1.[4] In a rather tortured reading of the law, however, the U.S. Supreme Court in a 5-to-4 decision declared the act unconstitutional on the grounds that it might be read as including workers in intrastate commerce, where the federal government had no jurisdiction.[5] On April 22, 1908, the law was therefore repassed with specific wording to include only workers in interstate commerce and in the District of Columbia.

This extension of employer liability was very mild. It applied only to certain railroads and not to business as a whole, and the injured worker or his representative still had to sue and win the case. However, in the same message in which he recommended repassage of the Employer Liability Act for railroads, President Roosevelt argued for the far more radical principle of workmen's compensation for federal employees and urged compensation legislation on the states as well. Unlike most reforms of the progressive period, which began on the local level and then worked their way up to the state level and finally the federal level, workmen's compensation in the United States was pioneered from the top down. Only Maryland had previously passed a compensation law, in 1902, and that had been totally ineffective, was quickly declared unconstitutional, and had aroused no general public discussion. Roosevelt's pioneering was not done on the basis of restructuring employee-employer relationships, however, or as a general step to improve the lot of the workers. He made his appeal on the basis of one of his most popular acts: the building of the Panama Canal. He argued that the federal employees building the canal should have some form of compensation, and incidentally that other federal employees should have it too.[6]

A bill for workmen's compensation for federal employees was debated and passed in remarkably short order and became law substantially as submitted.[7] Of course, government was not in the same position as a private employer. It had virtually unlimited resources through the taxing power, and it was immune to lawsuits if it chose to be. That the government chose compensation over liability did not mean that private employers would do so, but it exerted some pressure in that direction.

Within the next few years, two books that placed two other important pressure groups on the side of compensation were published: Crystal Eastman's *Work Accidents and the Law,* part of the Pittsburgh Survey that appeared in 1910, and Ferdinand C. Schwedtman and James A. Emery's *Accident Prevention and Relief,* published by the National Association of Manufacturers in 1911. The first symbolizes support from what might be called the social progressives, the second put employers on the side of workmen's compensation through insurance. In the introduction to Eastman's volume, Paul Kellogg wrote that immigrants from Austria-Hungary, Germany, and Great Britain came from a region of law and order to a region of law-made anarchy and implied that the United States had a lot to learn from those countries.

Eastman proposed increased regulation for safety in the workplace, an enlargement of employer liability that eliminated the three common-law defenses, and the "radical departure" of abandoning altogether the idea of liability and substituting compensation. Her work was virtually impossible to argue with. She had collected data on accidents, their results, and compensation from coroners' offices, hospitals, company records, and court decisions. She had the data and no one else did.[8] Eastman pointed out the advantages that a workmen's compensation law would have for employers: predictable costs of insurance premiums, elimination of expensive and lengthy litigation, and perhaps most important, the elimination of one source of antagonism between worker and management. It was clear, however, that these words of advice came from someone outside the business community.

A year later, Schwedtman and Emery, without mentioning the Pittsburgh Survey, made the same point to the "busy man"—that is, the businessman—from businessmen speaking as a committee of the National Association of Manufacturers. Rather than basing their recommendations on a detailed study of accidents and their consequences, Schwedtman and Emery based their conclusions on the experiences of Germany and England. The National Association of

Manufacturers had sent the two to Europe, where they examined in detail the provisions, workings, and effect of accident insurance. They were explicitly not dealing with social insurance as a whole, but merely with this one aspect. Although their European trip included many countries, their report concentrated on Germany and England, with preference for the former.

Schwedtman and Emery recommended a system, voluntary or compulsory, that was in the form of insurance, with employee participation and for limited but predictable benefits. The compensation should not be considered an indemnity for injury, but a way of dealing with impaired earnings capacity. Because premiums, most of which they contemplated as being paid by the employer, would be related to safety records in the firm, there would be a built-in incentive to improving safety.[9]

In the United States, it must be emphasized, organized labor was not in the same position it was in Germany or Denmark. Only a small proportion of workers were organized, and those mostly in the skilled trades; most workers in the most hazardous trades were not organized. Perhaps even more important, because state legislation would be controlling for most workers, a national labor organization like the American Federation of Labor (AFL) was not as relevant as the national organizations of labor unions, or the Social Democratic or Labour parties of the European countries.

At the 1909 AFL convention, however, Samuel Gompers proposed and the convention endorsed broadening employer liability laws, compensation for federal employees in hazardous occupations, and compensation in all states for workers in hazardous occupations and all workers in interstate commerce. In a clear case of hyperbole, he claimed that compensation for federal employees in hazardous occupations had just been passed "wholly and solely" because of the activities of the AFL. Gompers was vigorously opposed to all other types of social insurance, but he made a clear distinction between accident insurance and health, old-age, and disability insurance. When the revised German insurance law was under consideration in the Reichstag in 1911, Gompers used the occasion to hammer once again at the growing "paternal" care of Germany for her workers. However, he said, "there is no 'paternalism' in compensation. . . .

Compensation is a totally different problem, necessarily a public concern, and not logically to be confused with state working-class insurance."[10]

In individual states, labor unions or state federations of labor played a significant role, and while many unions wanted both automatic compensation and the right to sue in cases of extreme employer culpability, they were in general willing to settle for compensation alone. By 1910, then, the federal government, humanitarian or social progressives, many employers, and, somewhat less clearly, organized labor favored some form of workmen's compensation, either in addition to or as a substitute for enlarged employer liability. In the course of political debates in many important states, the private insurance companies were added to this list. With this kind of political alliance, the idea of compensation looked like a good political bet, although nothing could be taken as a certainty. It was also significant that there was no organization behind a particular form of workmen's compensation and a particular form of administration. The precise nature of the laws would be worked out in accordance with the political pressures, preferences, and history in each state, and the various states could learn from one another, with regard to both political tactics and the contents of the laws.

The battle over compensation in New York actually began before the National Association of Manufacturers published its book. Governor Charles Evans Hughes appointed an Employer Liability Commission (ELC) to inquire into the subject. Although its members came from various parts of the state and represented various interests, Hughes chose members who would be in favor of compensation. Crystal Eastman was appointed secretary of the commission, which in her case meant far more than stenographer. The vice-chairman was Henry R. Seager, professor of political economy at Columbia University, student of Richard T. Ely, Simon N. Patton, and German historical economics, and founding member of the New York branch of the American Association for Labor Legislation. John Mitchell of the United Mine Workers and vice-president of the AFL represented labor. The business and employer members of the ELC were not blind opponents of all reforms. In fact, members of this and all other commissions emphasized repeatedly that the chief virtue of compensation laws was that they would remove one cause for antagonism between employers and employees. America's self-image would be restored.

As to what should be done, the Employer Liability Commission knew it was treading on dangerous ground in suggesting a compensation law "without consideration of negligence, but under which compensation shall be a limited amount," as they said in a questionnaire sent to employers and labor organizations. They quoted Theodore Roosevelt recommending compensation and even quoted the Kaiser's message to the Reichstag in 1881, adding, "With this message the German nation took up the social duty of providing for its disabled workers." In spite of the formidable political strength behind the idea of compensation, it was clear from answers to questionnaires and from testimony at hearings the ELC held in many cities that compensation would not be welcomed by everyone. A simple count of heads showed that employers opposed the idea by about 2 to 1, and labor organizations favored it by about the same proportion. The Employer Liability Commission concluded that three bills should be proposed: one to broaden employer liability by eliminating the common-law defenses; one to be a compulsory compensation law for a defined group of dangerous trades; and one to be a voluntary law that would give workers and employers in other trades the right to sign contracts that included workmen's compensation.[11]

The bills were introduced as recommended. As late as one month before their passage, the New York State Federation of Labor held a mass meeting denouncing them, but in the final struggle the union supported the bills. Important support came from the National Civic Federation (NCF), an organization that claimed to speak for all social classes but that was in fact dominated by large businesses, bankers, and settled older money.[12] Governor Hughes signed the Workmen's Compensation Act into law in June.[13] Firms in a defined group of "hazardous" occupations were required to provide compensation, and other firms could contract with their employees to do so. Clearly the law was a compromise, but it had garnered support from employers, organized labor, casualty companies, social reformers, Democrats, and Republicans. Although one might criticize the content of the act, as politics it was a triumph. However, the law was in existence less than a year. The New York Court of Appeals, the state's highest court, declared it unconstitutional on March 23, 1911, on the grounds that its compulsory section deprived employers in hazardous occupations of property rights.[14]

As the forces favoring compensation were regrouping, they received support from larger national politics. The 1912 Republican Party split created a four-party election: Republican, Bull Moose, Democrats, and Socialists. All four parties in New York endorsed compensation. Also, as the New York law was being redrafted, some fifteen other states passed compensation laws, so that by 1913 New York was no longer pioneering. An amendment to the state constitution had no trouble passing in October of that year; it said that nothing in the state constitution "shall be construed to limit the power of the legislature to enact laws . . . to pay compensation . . . without regard to fault, with or without trial."[15]

In principle now, workmen's compensation was accepted by all sides and all parties, as was the constitutionality of such a law. The hottest controversy in New York and several other states was whether private insurance companies would be allowed to sell the insurance or whether a state-sponsored mutual company should be established, either with a monopoly or in competition with private companies. In Berlin in 1884, Bismarck could sneer at private profit flowing from a public law and talk about the duties of a Christian state. In Albany in 1913, the insurance companies had more influence.

Two bills were introduced in the New York state legislature in early 1913, one with support from private casualty companies and the state insurance commissioner, and one supported by the New York State Federation of Labor. The insurance company bill required all employers to become members of the compensation system unless they explicitly opted out, in which case they would take their chances with a broadened legal definition of employer liability. Private companies would write the insurance, but the state would regulate premiums and set up an arbitration commission, whose decisions could be appealed to the courts. The labor federation bill was limited to hazardous occupations, had a higher schedule of payments than the insurance company bill, and established a state monopoly. Governor William Sulzer indicated that he favored the labor union bill, but after what the *New York Times* described as "very active lobbying" by the private companies, the legislature passed the insurance company bill and the governor signed it.[16]

Although in other states, the story differs in significant detail, several general points emerge from the New York case. Progressives saw workmen's compensation as a way of limiting excesses of corporations and of creating an incentive for factory safety. Employers hoped it would decrease antagonism between workers and employers, make costs more predictable, and spread the costs, both human and financial, of industrial accidents more equitably. A minimum amount of bureaucracy was established, but to an important extent the law was meant to be self-enforcing: payments were specified, there was no need to determine fault, and the courts were the ultimate judges in disputes.

Of the thirty-seven states that passed workmen's compensation laws before 1917—that is, the whole country except the Deep South, Oklahoma, and North Dakota—only six excluded private companies, and only one of those, Ohio, had a substantial number of industrial workers. Ohio had relatively well developed labor unions, a strong contingent of political leaders who thought of themselves as progressive, and, above all, an organization of manufacturers, the Ohio Manufacturers Association, which favored a state monopoly.[17]

The pressure to exclude private companies could be seen as at least a small rejection of capitalism and a slight trend toward "gas and water socialism," but this would be a misconception. From labor's point of view, the companies excluded were the same companies that had insured employers against liability judgments. Workers had had experience with these companies and knew they would try to get the minimum settlement possible. While employers were opposed to having the state go into any business at all, many sympathized with labor's position. Moreover, the employers frequently mentioned that private insurance companies would incur the cost of salesmen, advertising, and profits, which would mean lower benefits. Because a major purpose of compensation laws was to decrease waste (e.g., litigation) and animosity between worker and employer, a state monopoly had virtues from the employers' point of view. Both the Pittsburgh Survey and the New York Employer Liability Commission concluded that companies that insured against liability paid out less than half their premiums in benefits, and some employers and almost all labor unions believed that a state fund could do better than that. Some states chose state regulation to control private companies; some chose a state fund to act as a yardstick, but still allowed private companies; some excluded private companies altogether. All three were down-to-earth methods for dealing with specific administrative problems. None was a move toward a new society.

Of the laws adopted in thirty-one states by 1915; twenty-two were elective and nine were compulsory. "Elective" meant that employees and employers could agree by contract to enter a compensation system, but they were not required by law to do so. Many states included all industrial workers, although two excluded small establishments. Most, but not all, excluded agricultural and domestic workers, and some limited coverage to a defined class of hazardous industries. In most states the employee could choose to sue in cases of gross negligence on the part of the employer, but if he accepted compensation he was usually forbidden to sue; in the case of a lawsuit, however, the common-law defenses were not available to the employer. In all but three of the states the total cost was to be paid by the employer, and in only one state, Oregon, was there a state subsidy. The level of compensation varied widely. Death in one state might mean that surviving dependents would get the equivalent of half the decedent's pay for three years, in another state it might mean two-thirds. The loss of a leg might mean half pay for almost five years in Wisconsin, or 10 percent of wages for less than one year in Massachusetts. In about half the states a special commission or board of arbitration settled disputes, with the decisions appealable to the courts. In other states disputes were left to proceedings in equity.[18] The large number of states having elective rather than compulsory laws was due to doubts about constitutionality, but in 1917 the U.S. Supreme Court settled the issue by approving of three types of workmen's compensation laws: a compulsory New York State law that allowed private insurance companies, a compulsory law with a state monopoly in Washington state, and an elective law in Iowa. After this decision, most states made their workmen's compensation laws compulsory.[19]

By the time the United States entered World War I, then, one can say that the country had adopted workmen's compensation. This was partly an attempt to preserve the idea of a classless society in the face of increasingly undeniable class conflict, but on another level it can be seen as a part of the "search for order."[20] As the laws were being passed, no one could accurately predict that the costs of compensation would be less, but they would certainly be more predictable and they would not cost more than the insurance premiums. In no sense, however, was workmen's compensation seen, as it was in Germany, Denmark, and Great Britain, as part of a comprehensive plan to ensure a minimum standard of living for those who for various reasons suffered a permanent or temporary loss of income.

Before World War I, two other programs were instituted in the direction of income maintenance in the United States. Both were small in theory and in practice, but they were the basis for what would be significant portions of the Social Security Act of 1935. The first was the "mother's pensions" (sometimes called "widow's pensions"), the second was retirement pensions for public school teachers. Illinois was the first state to respond to the call for mother's pensions raised by the White House Conference on the Care of Dependent Children of 1909. Unfortunately, the committee report leading to the mother's pension law has not been preserved, but the law itself is quite clear about its intentions, and it provided a rough model for the laws of other states.

> If the parent or parents of such dependent or neglected child are poor and unable to properly care for such a child, but are otherwise proper guardians, and it is for the welfare of such a child to remain at home, the court may enter an order finding such facts and fixing the amount of money necessary to enable the parent or parents to care for such a child, and thereupon it shall be the duty of the country board . . . to pay . . . .[21]

In Cook County (Chicago) the law was administered by the Children's Court, an institution that in its origins was closely connected with Hull House; in other parts of the state the law was administered by the county court. There was thus an implication of judicial rather than administrative procedure.

This mother's pension law, unlike some others, allowed pensions even if both parents were present, but made it clear that the court had to determine that the parents or the single parent was both poor and worthy. No standards for either determination were given in the mere three pages of the law. Nor was there any guidance fixing the amount of pension. This could be an advantage, in that special circumstances could be taken into account, but it gave the court enormous power to give or withhold. Most important, the law was simply permissive. It did not say that the court or the county *must* give aid, only that it was allowed to. It gave the poor person, usually the mother, no legal right to "assistance."[22]

The committee reports in some states looking into mother's or widow's pension legislation do exist, and they give some insight into the thinking behind the laws. For example, the report of the Massachusetts committee repeatedly used the words "worthy" or "good family" or other synonyms to describe those who were eligible for what the report insisted should be called "subsidies." The Massachusetts commission report drew a parallel with workmen's compensation, arguing that widows in both cases were similarly situated—there had been a sudden loss of the breadwinner with no fault attaching to the widow and children. So what had been a controversial issue only a year or two earlier had become the basis for arguing a new controversial issue. The law as passed, however, left the determination of worthiness, the amount of subsidy, and the administration in the hands of the local overseers of the poor. Therefore, rather than being based on the conceptual foundation of the workmen's compensation law, where worthiness was not an issue and where the amount of settlement was written into the law, the widow's pension law in Massachusetts was in fact an extension of that state's poor law.[23]

The New York State commission report that led to the widow's pension law was unusually detailed, and the law that resulted was somewhat different from the laws in other states. It was in fact a law to require municipalities to establish boards of child welfare, although the granting of pensions was still merely permitted. The report made its arguments in the broadest possible terms and in terms that sounded very similar to those emanating from the White House Conference on the Care of Dependent Children in 1909. The basic principles of the report were that keeping children in the home was clearly to their advantage and that it was virtually impossible for even the most conscientious unskilled mother both to earn a living wage and take care of her children. The report took pains to describe the inadequacies of private charity. In fact, it can be read as almost a direct attack on the New York Charity Organization

Society: "The Commission finds that private charity has not the funds and cannot, in the future, raise the funds to give adequate relief in the home, nor to administer such funds in the efficient, wise and sympathetic manner which it has set itself as ideal." Because no comprehensive system of social insurance seemed likely soon, said the report, "the Commission respectfully recommends the immediate enactment into law of the principle of State aid to the dependent children of widowed mothers."[24]

In 1914, four states provided aid to either parent. In all the other states the parent had to be the mother, and in four states the mother had to have been widowed. Other states included mothers whose husbands were in state institutions or totally incapacitated. Only four states provided pensions for mothers where the father had deserted, for there was a fear that the laws might encourage irresponsible fathers to desert. In all states the home had to be "fit," which in a few states was defined as having a mother who did not have a job or had only a part-time job. Administration was by a court—sometimes juvenile, sometimes probate—or by commissioners of the poor. Only in Pennsylvania was a special commission established: five women for each county, unpaid and appointed by the governor. The amount of the pensions actually paid varied greatly: as of 1914 the range was from $9 to $15 a month for the first child, with smaller amounts for other children, and often the cost was not to exceed what institutional care would cost.[25]

Mother's pension laws were almost universally seen as a way to persuade people to be good. "If we grant the aid to any woman whose care of her children will just pass muster," said one advocate of pensions, "we throw away a chance to make these women improve." Yet in spite of the congruence in aim between the mother's pension advocates and the charity organization societies, many leaders of the latter opposed pensions. Particularly in the East, where there were well-developed nongovernmental charity organizations, the pensions were seen as the entering wedge for a cold, mechanical government bureaucracy and therefore as the end of the kind of individualized aid provided by the charity organization societies. Of course, one could argue that these organizations simply saw pensions as a threat to their own position.[26] In any comparative sense, mother's pensions should be regarded as little and late. They brought the various states up to the point where, for example, the Local Government Board in England had been for years: providing "outdoor relief" for women with children. Conceptually they posed no challenge to the most devoted exponent of the English law of 1834. Practically their effect was small.

One other social insurance program should theoretically have had more impact on social assumptions than mother's pensions, but it seems not to have. This was pensions for public school teachers. In most cases, the pensions were real compulsory social insurance, with premiums from employer and employee and a legal right to the pensions under certain conditions. Yet the issue was not much discussed outside educational circles. By 1916, thirty-three states had established some sort of pension for teachers. Most of the plans were established in the 1911–15 period and were thus congruent with mother's pensions. In twenty-one states, contributions came from the teachers and the state treasury, in eight states there was a noncontributory plan, and in five states the contributions came entirely from the teachers. Pensions were not discretionary. Teachers were entitled to them, but usually only after twenty-five or thirty years of teaching, most of it in the state. In some states, pensions were higher for men than for women. In several states the pension funds were administered by a board that included some elected members of the teachers themselves.[27]

Pensions for teachers appear to be a glaring exception to the generally cool reception for social insurance in the United States. Teachers studied the system in other countries (particularly Great Britain), agitated, organized, (often under female leadership), and achieved their goal. However, teachers pensions should probably be seen as a special program for a special group—women. Like children and idiots, it was regarded as permissible for the state to be particularly solicitous of women's welfare. In arguing in favor of teachers pensions, one woman wrote, "The nervous system of a woman is less strong than that of a man." Besides, there was no less stressful place for elderly teachers, as there might be in a railroad or other large firm. Thus pensions might enable a school board that hesitated to fire older teachers on humanitarian grounds to improve their system with younger, better, and cheaper teachers. Also, pensions might bring some stability—and some men—into a profession in which most members were women who stayed on the job only a few years.[28]

In practical terms, teachers pensions did not mean very much. Few teachers stayed for a full career to retirement age. Although there seem to be no follow-up figures, the total costs of the systems were very low, and may have been an actual saving because younger teachers could be hired at lower salaries. Teacher salaries were very low, and pensions might also be seen as a way to keep them down. In any case, the systems were for a small number of one segment of public employees. Not many people were involved. Pensions for teachers were not used as a precedent when pensions were considered for other groups.[29]

By 1920, then, there were three types of government income-maintenance programs in nearly all states and one in the federal government: workmen's compensation, mother's pensions, and retirement pensions for schoolteachers. During the progressive years, however, a broader attempt to create social security failed.

13

Progressive Reform
in the United States:
The Failure of Social Insurance

Workmen's compensation was a success for the reformers; but benefits were not as high as most advocates would have liked, some people wanted the right to sue as well as compensation, and there was a good deal of variation between states. Many flaws and shortcomings could be found, but on the whole the aims of those who wanted change had been achieved. Moreover, this success had been perceptible in the first few years after of 1910 and was clearly visible by about 1915.

Encouraged by this success, advocates of other kinds of social insurance believed that old-age and health insurance, especially health insurance, could also be inaugurated. Yet with the success of workmen's compensation before them and with a successful strategy to learn from, advocates of other forms of social insurance seemed blind to the tactical lessons that could be learned from the battle just won. One lesson could have been that a political program needs not merely good ideas but also some support from many groups. Another could have been that the reform should be worked out with some thought given to existing institutions and legal structures and not be cut from new cloth. Still another could have been that through the federal system different solutions could be tried—politically as well as substantively—and experience in one state could be a guide for other states. Yet it was as though advocates of health or old-age insurance had been sleeping through the whole previous battle. They drew no lessons whatsoever. No political program could have been better calculated to produce defeat.

Another implication that is important for this comparative study is that any attempt to graft programs from one set of political, economic, and social circumstances to another is futile. This is not to say that better political tactics would have produced success. In the first place, health insurance and old-age insurance were far different from accident insurance, and Samuel Gompers was quite correct when he insisted on the differences. Illness and old age were not traditionally anyone's liability; no powerful economic group was directly injured through either. There were no traditional institutions in the United States onto which a government insurance plan could be grafted. Most important, there was no pressing demand for either type of insurance. Employers, organized labor, and doctors asserted again and again that the United States was prosperous enough that poverty caused by old age or illness was rare and easily dealt with through voluntary efforts, that no coercive bureaucratic system was needed to do what American voluntarism was already doing adequately. Yet a proposal that produced opposition from employers, labor unions, insurance companies, and doctors could conceivably have been improved on.[1]

Social insurance was not a matter for serious discussion in the United States before the early years of the twentieth century. Before 1904 there were few articles on the subject in magazines of general circulation, and even journals aimed at people in charitable work did not pay much attention to the subject. At the 1904 World's Fair in St. Louis, however, there was a large exhibition of German accomplishments, especially Germany's progress in industry. For most observers it was this industrial portion of the exhibit that attracted the most notice, but for the members of the National Conference of Charities and Corrections, the part of the exhibit devoted to social insurance was the most interesting. The NCCC established a special committee to investigate the subject of social insurance and report in two years, with a preliminary report after a year.

The preliminary report was generally negative. The chairman of the special committee emphasized that the German system "must needs act as a tremendous handicap to the extension of German trade to other countries, especially to the United States." In fact, he suggested that the entire elaborate exhibit was probably designed to convince other countries to adopt a similar system and thus load Germany's competitors with the same sort of handicap. Another member of the committee, John Graham Brooks, who ten years earlier had written a report on the German system for the U.S. Department of Labor, pointed out that if social insurance was a handicap the rapid growth of German industry indicated that it was a bearable one. He praised the principle of insurance and said that it was bound to continue spreading to other countries but that the differences between Germany and the United States were so great that the German system was not applicable to America. He believed it was self-evident that the federal government could not run the system. The excellent German civil service could just barely manage, he said, whereas the American civil service "would wreck any conceivable scheme of . . . insurance in a year." Moreover, American workers would not be satisfied with the tiny pensions offered in Germany.

The discussion following the reports was even more negative. The president of the NCCC argued that any problem of poverty in the United States concerned the unskilled and that "for unskilled labor, where there is no permanent employment and no permanent receipts, the whole scheme of workingmen's insurance is utterly impossible." One discussant said that if anyone wanted to see the pernicious effects of pensions he only had to go to any village square and see the veterans receiving pensions and hanging around in indolence when they could and should be working.[2] The only clearly positive voice at the convention was the sharp sarcasm of Florence Kelley, who had been doing graduate work in Germany when the Bismarckean program was being inaugurated. Kelley pointed out that although the federal government was limited in its sphere, it had occasionally learned to do new things. "A government which finds it possible, for instance, to take care of the health of young lobsters on the coast of Maine, would seem to have ingenuity enough at a pinch to enable it to make some sort of provision for the orphan children of skilled and unskilled workers. It may take a long time. It has taken a long time to learn to take care of lobsters."[3]

This generally negative response was among the people one would have expected to be most sympathetic to the German laws. Most Americans simply ignored the social insurance aspects of the German pavilion. By the time of the final report of the special committee on social insurance, the NCCC had joined the general hostility or indifference. Discussion was almost entirely about various company insurance plans, particularly on the railroads. Discussing "insurance from the employer's standpoint," E. A. Vanderlip made no attempt to disguise why a pension at the end of thirty or thirty-five years of work in the same company was good for the company. "The pension attaches the employees to the service, and thus decreases the liability to strike," he argued, adding, "every employee in the service . . . will be under strong inducement for good behavior."[4]

As a part of this initial flurry of interest in German social insurance, Isaac M. Rubinow made his first appearance in a magazine with a wide circulation. Rubinow had been born in Russia in 1875, had an M.D. and a Ph.D., and had spent most of his career as a statistician and economist in various branches of the federal government. In 1904 he began his long fight for social insurance, which he would see become at least partially victorious more than three decades later. He argued forcefully that savings for hard times was not adequate protection for workers—after all, it was not adequate protection for businessmen who insured against fire—and that something like European insurance was the only logical solution. Whenever this was pointed out, he said, "The answer is invariably given that no matter how successful in Europe, with their strongly bureaucratic administration, State labor insurance is utterly at variance with the individualistic ideas of the American people." He directly challenged this individualism, which he said "has had its foundation very much weakened of late by the continuous attacks of perceptible social forces." By thus challenging the very ark of the covenant, he ensured his frustration. Yet when Social Security finally did pass, it would be at least partly because of his years of frustrated work and his persistence in the face of failure.[5]

There was another burst of interest in social insurance after 1909, when Lloyd George introduced his budget. The Russell Sage Foundation published *Workingmen's Insurance in Europe,* and although there were no explicit policy recommendations in the work, the implication was clear that social insurance was something the

United States should consider. In its twenty-fourth annual report, the Bureau of Labor published a large volume with the same title in 1909.[6]

When the insurance proposals in Great Britain were passed in 1911, interest in the United States intensified. Scores of articles appeared in American journals of all shades of political opinion. The writers in *Survey* (the new name for *Charities and the Commons*) were ecstatic. "If the United Kingdom succeeds in its bold efforts to round out its system of social insurance, the enlightenment of American public opinion cannot be long delayed" was only one of the excited comments.[7] And yet policy recommendations of the NCCC seemed to be turning in another direction. Instead of stressing social insurance, those who wanted reform stressed protective legislation. At the 1911 meeting, only the paper given by Louis D. Brandeis was on social insurance. All the others in the session, which was titled "Standards of Living and Labor," were on hours, wages, and working conditions or on the prevention of child labor. Brandeis made the case on grounds that were different from Rubinow's arguing that insurance would mean an increase in individual freedom, but even at the NCCC few seemed interested.[8]

Comment in more popular magazines was even more negative. "How long will it be," asked *The Nation,* "before the workingmen insist that their employer and the state pay the whole bill? . . . Excellent impulses often lead to dire consequences. . . . It is a vicious thing in a democracy to get into the heads of the people that, as Grover Cleveland said, they are not to support the government, but the government is to support them."[9]

The Bull Moose platform of 1912, drawing on NCCC influences, mentioned social insurance in vague terms, but everyone knew that platform had been drawn up even less as a plan for future action and more for the purpose of gathering groups of supporters than most other political platforms. The issue for the Bull Moose Party was first and last Theodore Roosevelt, and the platform was more irrelevant than usual.

A more important high point—perhaps intellectual rather than political—for social insurance was the appearance in 1913 of Isaac Rubinow's *Social Insurance.* Rubinow argued that such insurance was necessary in the United States, and he used examples and

171

statistics from other countries to buttress his case. It is significant that Rubinow felt he had to insist on two points that were much more a matter of course in Europe: that a high proportion of the population was and would remain wage-earners, and that many wage-earners earned too little to save for a rainy day. He spent a large portion of his book showing that the much vaunted steps that had been taken in the United States, such as mother's pensions and old-age pensions in private firms, were pitifully inadequate to meet the problem and that public compulsory insurance was the only solution.[10]

In the 1915–20 period the emphasis shifted so that without abandoning the idea of old-age pensions more effort was expended on health insurance. It was here that the proponents thought they had the greatest possibility of success, and here that the opposition successfully mobilized. In the course of those five years, about a dozen states established investigatory commissions or actually introduced bills for some form of compulsory medical insurance. The bill that came closest to passing was the 1920 proposal in New York. The chief force for the passage of medical insurance was the American Association for Labor Legislation (AALL) founded in 1906. In 1913 the AALL held the first Conference on Social Insurance on July 6 and 7 in Chicago. Beside health insurance, the discussions included accident and unemployment insurance and mother's pensions, but health insurance was the central issue.[11]

By 1916 the American Association for Labor Legislation had developed a model bill. There was no significant attempt to have health insurance passed at the federal level. Whether national health insurance would or would not have been desirable from the AALL point of view, such effort would have been a waste of energy. The model bill was intended to be the basis for bills in the individual states. The entire June issue of the *American Labor Legislation Review* was devoted to health insurance. The model bill was surrounded with blankets of argument and justification. Reading it in the 1980s, knowing that it would be half a century before any kind of medical insurance was enacted—and then on a very different basis—one is struck by the bill's lack of political realism: it was in fact more or less the German law, translated into English and slightly modified by British experience since 1911. Many in the American Association for Labor Legislation had written on German social insurance. They demonstrated that they knew a good deal about insurance but very little about the United States.[12] The model bill proposed compulsory insurance for anyone employed within the state in manual labor or for anyone whose wages did not exceed $100 a month, with the exception of public employees. Governance was to be like the regional sickness funds (*ortskrankenkassen*), as revised in 1911: a board of governors elected half by employers, half by employees. There was to be state supervision as well as a medical advisory board made up of physicians.[13]

The medical profession, as represented by the American Medical Association (AMA), had not yet established the firm position of opposition it was to adopt after 1920. The AMA appointed a Subcommittee on Social Insurance under their Council on Health and Public Instruction, which employed Rubinow as a consultant. In the June 17, 1916, issue of their journal, the council repeated a good deal of the information in the *American Labor Legislation Review* and without actually endorsing it also printed the model bill. The lengthy report showed slightly more concern than the AALL with the manner and level of physician compensation, but it emphasized as well the benefits of European plans and the inadequacy of health care for America's poorest inhabitants. Falling just short of outright approval of government insurance, the Subcommittee on Social Insurance made clear the "advantages of a governmental system."[14]

In April 1916, Samuel Gompers published an article in the *American Federationist* in which he detailed his opposition to compulsory state health insurance, putting his own emphasis at the same point where business opposition was strongest: compulsory insurance would interfere with individual freedom and would create an army of government bureaucrats.[15] In December 1916 a conference on the general subject of social insurance, including health insurance, was held in Washington, D.C. The conference was organized under the auspices of the International Association of Industrial Accident Boards, but it also discussed health insurance. Not quite an official conference of the U.S. government, its proceedings were nevertheless printed as a bulletin of the Department of Labor, and much of the arranging was done by Royal Meeker, commissioner of labor statistics, who also wrote the introduction to the report. While the conference did not pass any resolutions or come to any clear positions, it was evidently meant to "educate" public officials on issues of social insurance, which the arrangers of the conference clearly favored. John B. Andrews, of the American Association for Labor Legislation, and Florence Kelley (formerly at Hull House, now of the National Consumers League) were among the conference planners. At the conference itself, Andrews made a plea for compulsory health insurance and asserted that "probably each one of you realizes that workmen's health insurance is coming in your State."

The position taken by organized labor at the conference did not support Andrews' optimism. Grant Hamilton, speaking for the legislative committee of the AFL, was contemptuous of "social insurance enthusiasts who attempt to apply systems evolved in other countries" to the United States. His argument was direct, epigrammatic, and angry, asserting that American workers wanted freedom, not state compulsion, and that all the advances in the direction of freedom for workers had been made by the workers themselves, operating through trade unions and not by legislative remedies. Social insurance, Hamilton said, "provides for the division of society into classes, based on wages received. Those who receive less than a specified sum automatically come under Government supervision, upon the theory that they are unable to care for themselves." Hamilton went on to assert that "for the prevention of disease, there is no more effective remedy than higher wages." He praised insurance by unions or federations of unions. In a sense he was doing nothing more than protecting the AFL's own turf, but in fact more was involved. He expressed suspicion of well-to-do reformers and of government, and he rejected what was taken for granted in Europe: the existence of classes. He too was operating within the American ideology—or mythology, if one prefers—of a graduated society but not a stratified one, a society that needed to spread its prosperity through social justice, not subsidize injustice through insurance.[16]

By 1916, then, one could see that on a national level there was some support for some forms of social insurance, but the support was ill-formed. There was growing opposition from organized labor and insurance companies, and they were soon joined by doctors. From the point of view of insurance advocates, the situation was difficult but not hopeless. The political battles took place at the state level, as they had in the case of workmen's compensation. In New York,

Massachusetts, Wisconsin, California, and elsewhere, the political weakness of the whole subject, as well as the flawed tactics of its proponents, was revealed.

Massachusetts, the state with the longest history of industrialism in the country and in many ways the state with the most humane history of dealing with the poor, established a Commission on Old-Age Pensions, Annuities, and Insurance as early as 1907. While dealing with only one state, the final report of the commission in 1910 is probably an indication of a more widespread opinion of the knowledgeable, and not radical, observers. The basic conclusion of the report was that there was evidently small demand and little need for social insurance. No political group or coalition was demanding pensions, and the commission argued that the need was slight in relation to England, where old-age pensions had just been established. The commission found that the economy was abundant enough that through savings, company pension plans, and private charity old-age destitution could be dealt with adequately.

A brief pro-pension flurry in 1917–18 quickly evaporated. A new Special Commission on Social Insurance had recommended not only old-age pensions but also noncontributory pensions. The 1917 report quoted liberally from Lloyd George's 1908 statement that there could in reality be no such thing as noncontributory pensions. Like the Danes, Lloyd George argued that everyone had spent a lifetime paying taxes and contributing to the economy and had therefore earned a pension.

The issue of health insurance was dealt with more clearly by a special commission that issued its report in January 1918. The report revealed the political weakness of health insurance. Organized labor was divided on the principle of health insurance, but almost all organized labor opposed any compulsory and contributory plan. Employers were "practically unanimous in voicing opposition to the scheme." Doctors argued that because "the cost of medical care and attention is not beyond the means of the ordinary workingman" no insurance was necessary. There was vigorous and unanimous opposition from insurance companies. Absolutely alone in support of their own plan was the Massachusetts branch of the AALL. The commission rightly concluded: "The so-called compulsory contributory system of health insurance has few supporters."[17]

175

If not in Massachusetts, the proponents of social insurance might hope for success in one of the progressive states of the Midwest. The case of Wisconsin is a dramatic example of the progressive emphasis on seeking social justice rather than social security. For the entire period from 1901 to 1920, the La Follette progressives dominated the state, emphasizing public regulation of corporations and protective legislation of all varieties. Because of his opposition to American entry into the World War, Robert La Follette himself had fallen a bit from grace by the time health insurance was considered in the state, but his political organization was still strong.

A special joint committee of the Wisconsin state legislature was appointed in 1917 to consider social insurance and delivered its final report on January 1, 1919. Although called the Special Committee on Social Insurance, it really considered only health insurance, more specifically the model bill of the AALL. The committee asserted, rather than demonstrated, that the workers of Wisconsin were thrifty and foresighted. It estimated that the medical, sanitary, and housing needs of working people were at least as well provided for in Wisconsin as they were in other parts of the nation and that the cost of health insurance under the proposed model plan would exceed the entire state budget of 1919. In assessing the political pressure for health insurance, the committee noted the divided or vague views of organized labor and concluded that the "rank and file have not given the subject any serious attention" and that unorganized labor has "no knowledge or information on the subject." Employers were either hostile to the whole idea or regarded it as "still in its theoretical stages." Practicing physicians were overwhelmingly opposed.

The special committee concluded that there was no significant demand for the proposed legislation, and no particular need. Their recommendations were preventive measures, not insurance for the cost of curative ones. "The expenditure of $1,000 for preventive measures will serve the cause of public health more effectively," argued the committee, "than the expenditure of twenty times that sum in experimental curative schemes."[18]

If health insurance could not achieve a breakthrough in a state with a strong tradition of state intervention for the common good or in the strongly progressive state of Wisconsin, perhaps it could achieve its breakthrough in the state with the largest number of industrial workers and a very well organized labor movement—New York State. Health insurance came closer to enactment in New York than in any other state. Bills for health insurance were introduced into the New York legislature in 1916, 1917, and 1918, but did not get anywhere. In 1919, however, Al Smith, who had a reputation as a friend of government action for social ends, became governor. He immediately appointed Frances Perkins a member of the Industrial Commission, and the supporters of health insurance thought that with this help they might have a better chance. A bill based on the AALL model was again introduced in January 1919. The bill was endorsed by the governor, by a number of civic clubs, and by the New York Federation of Labor. Both houses of the New York state legislature were nominally controlled by the Republicans, but in the Senate the majority was so thin that when three senators bolted their party and supported health insurance—plus a minimum-wage bill and an eight-hour day for women and children—all three bills passed on April 10, 1919. In the state assembly the Republican majority was larger, and none of the social welfare bills were brought to the floor from the Rules Committee. Al Smith had to compromise, giving up the social welfare bills but gaining a graduated state income tax.[19]

If one were to judge solely from the hoopla in the *American Labor Legislation Review,* one would think that every leading newspaper and organization in New York was pushing the bill and that every leading politician in the state was working for it. Its defeat, according to the American Association for Labor Legislation, was due only to a few stubborn, self-interested businessmen and to the undemocratic machinations of the Speaker in the state assembly. In fact, there was less here than meets the eye. The coverage in the *New York Times* was about as extensive as coverage on a dog ordinance in Schenectady. The substance of the issue was not even mentioned. When workmen's compensation was at issue, the newspaper printed much of the text of the proposed law, the court decision, the constitutional amendment, and the revised law, but from the *Times* it would have been impossible to tell what the health insurance bill contained. What was important was the split in the Republican ranks and the politics of Al Smith. The bill was not followed in any national magazine except the *Survey,* and there was no mention of the

New York case at the National Conference of Charities and Corrections. Prominent progressive names were notable by their absence, and even Al Smith's endorsement was backing someone else's bill, a backing he was politically willing to abandon in return for an income tax. In any case, Smith's reputation came from his support for factory legislation and hours limitation—social justice—not from support for social insurance—social security.[20]

By 1920 the American Medical Association had become a clear opponent of health insurance. Articles in its journal agreed that medicine had a social responsibility, but that responsibility was to preventive medicine and public health. In order to practice their profession as they should, doctors "must have freedom," and state insurance would "dictate the terms" on which medicine was practiced. In 1921 the secretary of the same Council on Health and Public Instruction, a subcommittee of which had written in favor of government health insurance five years earlier, had nothing but scorn for the idea. He asserted that "arguments in favor of the plan rest on estimates and opinions and not on facts. . . . [They] are fragmentary, incomplete and unconvincing." This position of the American Medical Association would be unchanging for the next half-century, but that is not the primary reason that compulsory health insurance and old-age insurance failed in the United States.[21]

Old-age and health insurance failed in the United States essentially because, as the Massachusetts commission of 1918 concluded, they "had practically no support" or, as the spokesmen for private insurance companies had sneered, "a few college professors, social workers and doctors" favored them. The arguments that the idea was "made in Germany" or that it was "bolshevist" were sometimes convenient slogans but not of central importance. The somewhat broader argument that health and contributory old-age pensions were un-American was more frequently mentioned and had substance behind the words. People who used this argument were insisting that American values required that there be as little government compulsion as possible. Certain kinds of coercion were permissible for the general welfare—schooling was the most frequently mentioned—but if the country could get along without a particular form of compulsion, it should do so.

In Great Britain, leadership from Lloyd George, Winston Churchill, and William Beveridge was important in the success of the old-age pension and national insurance bills. The United States had a leader with a similar amount of energy, vision, and political shrewdness in Theodore Roosevelt. He showed himself willing to take the leadership on social issues, and not only after he was out of office. It is true that his 1912 platform endorsed social insurance, but neither before nor after did Roosevelt make the issue an important one. It was not a question behind which there was much pressure, and it was not one that offered a politician much mileage. Moreover, there was no traditional institution in America, like the *freie Kranken-kassen* (sickness funds) in Germany, the *sygekasser* (mutual-aid sickness societies) movement in Denmark, or the friendly societies in Great Britain onto which insurance could be grafted. There were a few programs in large corporations and a few in some craft unions, but the movement was too small to be a base for expansion.

It comes down to the fact that Americans did not have social insurance before 1935 because Americans did not want social insurance. Social insurance was not a historical imperative whose absence has to be explained by finding a conspiracy of self-interested doctors or a misconstructed civil service to explain. Later scholars may regret that absence, but it can be attributed to the workings of democracy.

PART FOUR

Convergence:
Between the Wars

14

From Socialism to Social Welfare in Germany

Between the two world wars there was a convergence of institutions among the four countries, but not necessarily a convergence of perceptions. In Germany and Denmark, the welfare state—which had been a subject of controversy before World War I—became a matter for broad consensus by World War II. Out of the chaos of the first world war, Germany emerged with the Social Democratic Party forming the government. Some movement toward socialism might be expected. The Social Democrats tried but failed. Having failed in its first aim, the party then turned to another aim—social welfare—of which it had previously been scornful. The Danish story is the same in outline, but with different motivations and perceptions. Britain seemed unable to react to the crisis of the Great Depression until the crisis of World War II. What is most surprising is that the United States made a sharp departure from its history to adopt its own version of the capitalist welfare state. The story in Germany, Denmark, and Great Britain can be seen as a continuity with past developments—there was change to be sure, but within an already existing perceptual context. The United States had to change its perceptions more than any of the other three countries under study here.

In Germany the last years of the *Kaiserreich* can be seen either as victorious years for the unions (they were recognized as equal partners in the economy) or as ultimate defeat for the unions (they served the national state rather than the working class). The Social Democrats themselves could not resolve this dilemma, so they split in two: the Majority Socialists supported the war effort, while the smaller Independent Socialists remained true to the international tenets of their party. This split was made worse by the Russian revolution, with Independents more likely to support a similar revolution in Germany, and Majority Socialists more likely to oppose it. Eventually, the more revolutionary Socialists formed the German Communist Party, and those among the Independents who would not go so far rejoined the Majority Socialists in 1922. In late 1918, hopes of preserving the monarchy dissolved, and on November 9, 1918, the Kaiser fled to Holland, leaving power in the hands of the new chancellor, Friedrich Ebert, of the Majority Socialists.

Ebert was faced by enemies on the political Right, but his most significant opposition at first came from two groups on the Left: (1) socialists who had not supported the war and (2) those who hoped that the German revolution could be a continuation of the Russian revolution. The former were a group trying to organize under the title "Independent Socialists," the latter were styling themselves the "Spartacists." Probably most of the popular councils that had been established in several cities were not Bolshevist, but Ebert did not want to play Kerensky to Rosa Luxemburg's Lenin. He aimed at socialism, but through democracy, and his devotion to democracy was no sham—it was a conviction in the service of which he was willing to use military force. Ebert accepted an offer from the military, and the army, which now consisted mostly of independent units organized on their own by returning officers (the *Freikorps*), put down the Spartacists with military might, including machineguns and flame-throwers. A republic had been established in Germany by default and secured at least temporarily with the help of the most reactionary elements in society—the officer corps. Even so, one should not assume that the republic was foredoomed to failure. There were choices to be made over the next years, and these choices were not always made in the worst possible way.

During World War I there was in Germany a great expansion of welfare provisions for the families of men called into the military. This was no great theoretical departure and was in fact based on a law passed in 1888. What was new was the scope of the commitment. The war, as a total war, sucked a greater proportion of the population into its service, and the categories of family members eligible for support were broadened. Such support did not have to be at a minimum level, yet these were emergency measures and did not necessarily signify a break with the past. They were, after all, carried out by the *Kaiserreich*.

In the interim between the abdication of the Kaiser and the formation of a new constitutional structure, Germany was governed by the Council of Representatives of the People (Rat der Volksbeauftragten), whose dominant figures were Ebert, head of the Social Democratic Party since August Bebel's death in 1913, and Gustav Noske, longtime Social Democratic Party representative in the Reichstag. The council had to deal with the allies, with a disorganized society at home, and with the misery caused by war, defeat, and the allied blockade that restricted the normal flow of foodstuff, even after the war was officially over. This government was given great powers under the demobilization law, and only four days after the abdication of the Kaiser in 1918 the council issued a decree on poverty, in effect disguised as a part of demobilization. The Social Democratic Party had for a long time rejected the whole idea of insurance as a way of dealing with social misery, and would again in the future. After all, insurance placed the burden on the victims. More equitable would be simply *Fürsorge*—that is, a responsibility of the collective society to meet the needs of its individual members with no premiums involved. The decree, called the Decree Concerning Relief for People without Jobs ("Verordnung über Erwerbslosenfürsorge," November 3, 1918), was, however, probably more a product of emergency desperation than of theoretical preference for *Fürsorge*.[1]

National government funds were made available to communities or associations of communities so that they could organize relief for the unemployed, which according to the decree they were required to do. Relief received under these arrangements would not have the force of poor-law relief—that is, recipients would retain all their civil rights, including the right to vote. Half the expenses of relief would come from the national treasury, and one-third would come from the individual states, but where localities could not meet the remaining one-sixth, national government funds might make up the difference. Paragraph 14 of the decree specified that labor organizations could distribute the aid as long as they did so in accordance with the decree, but they seem not to have done so. The entire program was to be supervised by public officials, and although it was originally to last one year it was extended several times until the passage of unemployment insurance in 1927.

This decree was an interesting combination that represented a continuation of traditional patterns, but with enough modification to make the content something new. The relief was actually "poor relief" for anyone who had worked in the past, because there was no attempt to define unemployment attributed to demobilization. This poor relief was to be administered by the communities under the supervision of the officialdom. The amount of relief was set in an interesting way. It was supposed to be (but not required to be) at least equal to the amount provided by the various insurance systems, though which system was not specified, and all kinds of other income, from whatever source, were to be taken into account to bring people up to this minimum. The crucial difference with traditional practice was that relief would not limit a person's civil rights and that decisions on relief would be made not by local volunteers, who traditionally did not come from the working class, but by a committee that by law was required to have representatives of the workers.

The new form of government, known as the Weimar Republic, was devised by a National Constituent Assembly elected under a new law of November 30, 1918, which defined the electorate as all German men and women over the age of twenty who were not under guardianship or who had not lost civil rights through conviction for a felony. Because receipt of poor-law support was not mentioned as a disqualifying factor, a person who received such support did not lose the franchise. The constitution for the Weimer Republic contained many clauses that indirectly affected relief and social insurance, but some were specifically directed at welfare arrangements. Article 161, the last clause of which was taken almost word for word from the Erfurt (1891) program of the Social Democratic Party, said:

> For the maintenance of health and the ability to work, for the protection of motherhood and for care in the case of economic conse-

quences of age, weakness and misfortunes of life, the nation will create a comprehensive insurance department with predominant participation of the insured.

Article 163 said:

> Every German shall be given the opportunity to support himself through profitable work. In the case that suitable work cannot be provided, the necessary maintenance will be provided. Further details will be provided by law.

The Weimar constitution was clearly influenced by the Majority Socialists and was pushing further than the *Kaiserreich* had gone, but within the same patterns. Insurance should be and was continued, but participation would be expanded rather than shrunk. The more radical portions of the constitution looked toward a gradual socialization of economic life that would presumably make welfare legislation less and less necessary. The constitution had clauses that prepared the way for land distribution, nationalization of economic enterprises and for a planned economy. Whether it succeeded depended on a host of factors, many of which no government could control—for example, the world economy, how the victorious powers treated Germany, and basic psychological and intellectual attitudes of the populace.

Since World War II it has been customary to see the Weimar period—indeed all of German history—backward, through the shadow of Hitler and Dachau and to look for continuities between the Germany of Bismarck and that of the Weimar Republic and Hitler. This is a necessary and fruitful endeavor, but history must also be seen forward, so that Weimar is not only seen as the gateway to Nazism but also evaluated in its own right. What constitution could have withstood the stresses of reparations, inflation, and the Great Depression (to mention only the economic)?[2]

As wrong as it is to assert an inevitable continuity from Bismarck's to Hitler's Reich, it is also wrong to posit too much historical or social discontinuity. For instance, the schools, as Gordon Craig says, "continued to be what they had been before the war, a buttress of the existing social order."[3] On another side of the political spectrum, those who were supposed to be in favor of democratic government were scornful of the Weimar example of it. Still another reaction was the privatism of a group of young aesthetes calling themselves "the birds of passage" (*Wandervogel*). Amid a crosscurrent of political murders, crisis, contempt, putsch and counterputsch, national humiliation, bankruptcy and corruption, flourishing anti-Semitism, vicious militarism, and pure confusion there occurred perhaps the most creative period of German culture, whether in the theater (Brecht), the practical arts (the Bauhaus), ironic comedy (*Weltbühne*), or painting (Max Beckmann) and the novel (Mann).[4]

Whatever dispute there might be among socialists on the meaning of socialism, it certainly implied public control over the means of production, which for the Germans meant nationalization. Right after World War I, German socialists might have thought that nationalization was soon to become reality. For example, even while the Weimar constitution was being debated, the *Reichstag,* which functioned throughout the war and the transition after the war, debated and passed a general nationalization law and a more specific law on nationalization of the coal industry.[5] In fact, nothing happened, and the socialists learned that socialism in Germany would not arrive through nationalization.

If there was no nationalization, perhaps industry could be "socialized" through workers councils in each firm, in accordance with article 165 of the constitution. The workers councils were a watered-down version of what the more revolutionary socialists wanted—soviets instead of parliamentary democracy. While the Weimar constitution chose the latter, it did envision regional workers councils (*Bezirkarbeiterräte*), which never became a reality, and a National Economic Council (Reichswirtschaftsrat), which did become a reality, although its function was only advisory and it never became politically important. The workers council law, passed during the brief period before June 1920 when the Majority Socialists controlled the Labor Ministry, created councils with economic and social responsibilities in most firms. Introducing the bill, Labor Minister F. E. Alexander Schlicke tried to sound radical by declaring, "The law before you is the first step toward a new social order," but at the same time he made it clear that it was not a new political or economic order: "The government rejects the idea of councils in political life. Beside a parliament chosen in a free election, we do not believe there can be created another, higher parliament." Schlicke also explicitly rejected the idea that the councils would lead to nationalization. Instead, he emphasized that they would work toward avoiding conflict between employees and employers and toward improving the poor state of the German economy. In practice, the councils became cockpits for considerable conflict between those who saw them simply as continuing wartime cooperation between workers and management and those who had more radical aims for them. The radicals were defeated, partly by the unions, and neither the great hopes of some workers nor the great fears of some employers were realized. The *Betriebsräte* (workers councils) became a relatively routine part of most larger concerns.[6] Socialists learned that just as socialism in Germany would not come through nationalization, it would also not come through "economic democracy"—that is, workers' influence in the workplace.

In the first months after the revolution and in the first months of the new republic, the Far Left had been defeated, partly by the military force against the Spartacists and partly by the adoption of parliamentary democracy instead of soviets. The next threat came from the Right when in March 1920 Wolfgang Kapp marched into Berlin with the support of a unit of *Freikorps* troops, declared himself Chancellor, and announced the end of the Weimar Republic. Kapp soon found he had very little support in the country, and the attempted putsch was put down, but notably less brutally than had been the case with the Spartacists in Munich.

One might think that, with the defeat of the extremes of Right and Left, the moderate center would prevail and the government would be able to concentrate on dealing with the victorious allies and reviving the German economy. This was the course recommended by the Majority Socialists. As a writer in the *Sozialistische Monatshefte* had said, a patient who is sick cannot stand a major operation. The Germany economy was terribly sick and must have a "turning back to the old basis of production."[7] Of course, one could also argue that the German economy was failing and needed a complete transformation, or that "Everything was better under the Kaiser." The latter two views seemed to prevail in the Reichstag election of June 6, 1920. The Majority Socialists lost about half their support (from 11.5 million votes to 5.5 million), while the Independents doubled theirs to almost 5 million and the Conservative parties together received 7.3 million. The Catholic Center Party received 3.5 million votes, and the Democrats received a bit over 2 million. If one added together the Center, the Democrats, and the Majority Socialists, there would be a plurality for the republic, but the Far Right and Far Left would be a constant threat.

The Siamese-twin crisis of reparations and inflation meant that the Weimar coalition of Majority Socialists, Democrats, and the Center had to concentrate on simply raising payments under existing social insurance and poor laws in a frenzied and ultimately losing race with the inflation, instead of revising social security systems in a way that would break with the past. At the beginning of October 1923, the jobless relief was about 6 million marks a week per worker; by the middle of the month it was several score million; and by the end of the month it was several hundred million marks a week.[8] These figures are an index to the inflation that meant in effect the complete collapse of the German economy.

Reactions were varied, inside and outside Germany. Earlier than anyone had thought, article 48 of the Weimar constitution was employed. Under it an empowering act (*Ermächtigungsgesetz*) was passed on October 13, 1923; this law set aside parliamentary powers for one year and gave the government power to take whatever measures were necessary without action by the legislature.[9] Externally, the result of the crisis was the Dawes Plan, which was accepted by Germany about a year later. The plan slowed down but did not cancel reparations, and it allowed the issuance of new currency and stabilized the economy by eliminating inflation. These actions, as well as the emergence of Gustav Stresemann as a dominant political figure, resulted in what has been called the "stabilization"—that is, for about five years it looked as though the Weimar constitution and the Republic might survive.

Unfortunately for historians, the new law on welfare was passed during the period when the Empowering Act of 1923 had put the Reichstag out of business, so there is no record of the debate. The law of February 13, 1924, on "relief duties," replaced at long last the 1870 poor law. It eliminated the need to become a "resident" of an area, but it did not eliminate ultimate local responsibility for relief. It still permitted a community to require that the able-bodied perform "suitable" (*angemessene*) work and that families support their needy members. This law was a change, but not a revolution. In spite of a revolution in 1918, there was much in the Weimar Republic that was not revolutionized.[10]

By the early 1920s the Social Democrats had learned that neither nationalization nor workers councils would bring socialism. As in Denmark, the Social Democrats found that the social welfare—and more particularly social insurance and reform of the poor law—was the direction in which they could move.[11] This change in the policy of the Social Democratic Party was due partly to the circumstances but also to the conscious attempt of women within the party to end the monopoly that the "bourgeoisie," particularly bourgeois women, had on charity. While many of the people involved in voluntary charity, especially in leadership positions, were men, there was traditionally some feeling in all social classes that charity had to do with qualities of womanhood. The word *Mütterlichkeit* ("motherliness" or, freely, "the nurturing functions of women") was frequently used to emphasize the natural affinity of women and charity. This seemed to apply, however, only to voluntary poor relief. Administrators of any of the insurance laws, even when elected by the insured, were men.

In the crisis of 1919 the Social Democrats formed a Standing Committee on Workers Welfare, which was closely tied to the women's movement in the party. The women's movement was by no means an expression of charitable influence and of bountiful ladies caring for the less fortunate. Far more important were things like equal pay for equal work, and influence within the party and in public administration generally. Poor relief, however, was an effort that had a far greater participation by women than other aspects of the party's policy. For many years, social workers (professionals, not unpaid workers for the local relief authorities) were always denoted with a feminine ending (*-arbeiterinnen*). Spokesmen (spokeswomen) for the standing committee were frequently women. When the committee began publishing a journal, *Arbeiterwohlfahrt,* the editor and many of the contributors were women. An argument that had been common in the United States in the first decade of the century appeared twenty years later in Germany. Marie Bock, writing in the women's journal of the Social Democratic Party, described the responsibilities of the women in the family and said, "The community budget has almost the same responsibilities as the family budget. The administration of finance must show . . . that it is being used for the interests of the common good. . . . Women can do this just as well if not better than men."[12] Here Bock was arguing that the quality of *Mütterlichkeit* should not be confined to voluntary efforts but should be made an essential part of public administration.

There were also some attempts, notably by the German social worker Alice Salomon, to introduce American methods of social casework into German poor relief. Salomon's *Soziale Diagnose* (1926) was not really a translation of the American pioneer social worker Mary Richmond's *Social Diagnosis* (1917), but it tried to introduce some of the same ideas. The administration of relief in the United States, which was often by party hacks, was universally scorned in Germany, but some professional social workers admired American casework and the schools of social work.[13]

Probably just because so much welfare work—proto-social-work like the settlement houses—was voluntary in the United States, whereas in Germany it was a function of officialdom, Americans had been forced to experiment and to develop techniques outside of government for dealing with poverty. Just as American social workers were trying to achieve the twin goals of professionalism and incorporation within public administration, German poor relief was trying to develop some of the freedoms that American social workers had had and were perhaps losing to bureaucratization. In the United States, however, social work began before women had the vote and was often seen as a substitute or base for political action. The professional social work movement began in Germany among women about the same time they got the vote and was simply one aspect among many others of the women's movement. Marie Juchacz, the first editor of *Arbeiterwohlfahrt,* often appeared in the pages of *Vorwärts* writing about issues that had nothing to do with poor relief.

Active women, conscious of their role as women, were one factor pushing the Social Democratic Party in Germany toward social welfare, but there was a drift of Social Democrat members of both genders into administering relief. Most of the actual administering of poor relief in Germany was done by unpaid workers, traditionally from the upper layers of society. During and immediately after the war, this changed as more and more industrial workers found themselves filling these "honorary offices" (*Ehrenämter*), as they were called. Rather than being mere recipients, they found that if they were both the administrators and recipients of relief the feeling of class solidarity could be augmented rather than diminished. "The working class has learned that relief work with their own participation can be something quite different from charity," wrote Meta Kraus-Fessel in *Sozialistische Monatshefte* in 1923.[14]

The adoption of social welfare by the Social Democratic Party can be seen clearly when the Committee on Workers Welfare began publishing its own journal in October 1926. The first article in the journal, written by Helene Simon, whose name was to appear frequently in *Arbeiterwohlfahrt*, was titled "Socialism and Poor Relief." In it Simon defined socialism as the "struggle toward an economic and social structure that guarantees all the members of the commonality (*Gemeinschaftsbildung*) equal opportunity for development of their talents and skills."[15] The next month the magazine argued, "Social Democrats must clearly understand that along with political activities . . . social welfare is necessary. . . . The increase in social welfare is for the Social Democratic Party part of the better organization of public life of the present day."[16]

The Social Democrats also moved toward social welfare politically. On the question of unemployment insurance, the socialist unions, the basis of the electorate of the Social Democratic Party, had for years favored a system of unemployment insurance known as the "Ghent System" that was local and run by the unions. It meant that public funds would be administered by one side in the economic conflict, a political impossibility in Germany. Yet the unions maintained their enthusiasm right up to 1914.

After the war, the "jobless relief" (*Erwerbslosenfürsorge*) was the answer of the Majority Socialists. However, this was altered radically when in 1923 and 1924—that is, during the inflation and Empowering Act—the government of Stresemann decreed in October 1923 that the only way the relief could possibly be financed was through contributions from employers and employees. Even that would cover only a part of the costs, the rest of which would come from the national treasury. Once these decrees were issued, "jobless relief" had, from the point of view of the Social Democrats, the worst aspects of welfare (a means test and no legal right to relief) and the worst aspects of insurance (the burden was put on the victims), for they regarded the so-called employer's contribution as in reality coming out of wages. For a while, however, the economic stabilization seemed to deal with the problem. Unemployment among industrial union members went down between the third quarter of 1924 and the corresponding quarter of 1925 from 10.5 percent to 4.5 percent. The numbers swelled in 1926 but then declined again in 1927. Apparently the problem could be considered in an atmosphere of concern, but not crisis. Mass unemployment was a constant threat, although no one predicted how bad it would get by the early years of the coming decade.

A bill on unemployment insurance was introduced in December 1926. The unions abandoned their devotion to the Ghent System and supported the law. The Social Democrats spoke and voted for it in the Reichstag.[17] Opposition came from the Communists and the Nazis. The Communists sneered at the Social Democrats for now supporting the policy of Bismarck.[18] The Nazis, who now had seven seats in the Reichstag, said that the only way out of the current crisis was not to give the unemployed a small dole but to create a public policy that increases the number of jobs available. Their spokesman was particularly critical of the benefit rates for the white-collar workers and insisted that solidarity of all workers was not inconsistent with greater differentiation of benefit levels to the advantage of the better paid: "The higher paid office worker has completely different expenses . . . than the lower paid." Thus, the Nazis tried to appeal to the workers, but seemed to be making more attempts to woo people who might regard themselves as being in a higher social class.[19]

The bill was finally passed on July 7, 1927, with only the Communists (26 votes), the Left Communists (8), and the Nazis (7) casting negative votes, against 355 in favor. Perhaps one could hope that for a large majority of Germans a general consensus at least on welfare policy and perhaps on the degree of centralization had at last been reached. Within a few years events in German society and the German economy would be such that the extremes would grow and overwhelm what in 1927 seemed to be a fairly broad-based consensus.[20] In fact, with this law on unemployment the pre-Hitler system of social welfare and social insurance reached its high point and completion. There were discussions about further systematizing social policy, about filling in holes where they appeared. But policy from 1927 was more defensive than anything else.

For the first few months, the unemployment insurance system seemed to be working, but by the winter of 1927 there was already a deficit in the accounts. There was improvement in the spring of 1928 because of the time of year, but not as much improvement as there should have been, and in December 1928 a special law had to be written so that seasonal work (e.g., bricklaying) would not fall under regular unemployment insurance. By October 1929 the Reichstag believed it needed to define more precisely, and more restrictively, the meaning of "unemployment" to make sure that marginal cases would not further burden the insurance.[21]

After 1927 the Social Democratic Party found itself in the unaccustomed position of defending not only the specifics of unemployment insurance but also the whole insurance system. As the Danish party would do one year later, the Social Democrats waged the election of 1928 largely on the basis of social policy—for example, protective legislation, such as the eight-hour day, but also social insurance and pure welfare. As the election approached, the Social Democratic Party increased its emphasis on social policy, and in April the left wing of the party asked for a "broadening of social insurance."[22] Ten days before the election—that is, on May 10, 1928—under the headline "Even More Social Policy," *Vorwärts* stated: "The Social Democrats are the only party that does not need any special justification for appearing with recommendations in the area of social policy. Our Party emphasizes social policy because—we are the Social Democratic Party. Social policy is for the Social Democratic Party a matter of course."[23]

The election was a success for the Social Democrats in that they could once again form a government with the office of the Chancellor (Hermann Müller) and four other cabinet posts, but it was again in coalition with nonsocialists. This did not mean they could express their newfound enthusiasm for social insurance by continuing to broaden the programs. They had to fight hard to slow down the pace at which payments were decreased. In fact, Müller could keep his majority for only twenty-one months. The worldwide depression overwhelmed any steps Germany could take. By March 1930, unemployment among union members was around 20 percent, and in July there was another "emergency decree" containing sharp cutbacks in the unemployment compensation provision and also in the benefits of the sickness funds.

It was clear to all sides that as part of the broader economic crisis the structure of German social policy was in crisis. The nature of that crisis was clear and simple for the employers. As the magazine *Arbeitgeber* (Employer) maintained over and over again, the benefits of social insurance cannot be decided independent of the performance of the national economy. The national economy in 1930 and thereafter was in terrible shape. "Both workers and employers have an interest in maintaining a healthy and solvent social insurance system," wrote one person, and the only way to do that is to decrease the benefits. The employers clearly accepted the system but objected to its level.[24]

As the two revolutionary parties of the Nazis and the Communists increased their strength sharply, the crisis for the Social Democrats was not nearly so simple. In a poignant *cri de couer,* in *Sozialistische Monatshefte,* Hermann Krangold listed all the gains workers had made in the Weimar years, and noted that social insurance and poor relief had meant a "huge transfer of income to the advantage of the workers." But the workers do not realize how enormous their gains—which Krangold called "an anticapitalist correction"—have been. The workers also now keep a much higher proportion of the social product than ever before because their wages are better. In addition, even though their influence in the system is greater than ever, they do not realize that to secure these gains there must be a solid political system and that by constantly belittling the gains, by drifting to radical parties, the political system is endangered. The workers "are sawing off the branch on which they themselves sit," Krangold said prophetically.[25] By the time he wrote—July 1932—it was too late.

Adolf Hitler's appointment as Chancellor on January 30, 1933, can be considered more or less legal, but the election of March 5, with its repression of the Social Democratic Party press and open violence, with the uses made of if not causing the Reichstag fire, with the Nazi monopolizing of the radio, can only be considered a sham election. The Enabling Act of March 21, giving Hitler dictatorial power presumably for four years, was clearly illegal. Thus, by March 1933, the Weimar Republic had ended. Hitler had ridden to power partly on the crisis of worldwide depression, and two days after being appointed Chancellor he had promised to eliminate unemployment within four years. He kept his promise, more or less, with a massive program of public works, as the Nazis had been proposing for years. But this program, along with other parts of the Nazi policy, were all aimed at power for the dictatorship. Unemployment insurance, the sickness funds, the press laws, a civil service law, and repression of political parties and labor unions—all these and many more made up the Nazi power structure. An analysis of that structure is out of place in this study. Suffice it to say that whereas social control had been one element in social policy up to 1933, it was the only element after 1933.

Although the Social Democratic Party had drastically changed its position on social welfare, the German social insurance system as an institution was characterized by continuity. By the 1930s social insurance was taken for granted by most sections of German society. It continued to exist under Hitler in some form,[26] and it exists in modified form in the German Federal Republic. What had started under the Kaiser grew out of German history and is still part of that history.

15

From Socialism to Social Welfare in Denmark

Like the German Social Democratic Party, the Danish Social Democrats in the course of the 1920s gave up any lingering
program in the direction of socialism and turned instead to the defense and enlargement of the capitalist welfare state as their major
policy. When World War I broke out, Denmark stayed neutral,
though it was not unaffected. Like other countries, both those directly involved and those less involved, Denmark was more or less
aware that the good old days were gone, never to return. Yet in
Denmark the world war was a more distant trauma than in Germany or Great Britain. The first volume of one of the most popular
novels about the era was titled *Thunder in the South*—that is, there
was a storm, its effects were discernible in Denmark, but it took
place somewhere over the horizon.[1]

During the war, Denmark managed to satisfy the regulations of
both sides, to continue to trade with both Germany and Great Britain,
and to create what came to be known as "gulasch barons," war profi-
teers who made a killing. As in other countries, the war meant a great
expansion of government power, with regulation of prices, production, working conditions, and the like. A major change was a new
constitution, written in 1915 but not put into effect until 1918. It
removed the undemocratic features of the previous constitution and
established what was virtually adult suffrage, including women, but

it retained the clause disfranchising anyone who had received help under the poor laws and had not repaid that help or had the debt forgiven. Another factor that affected Denmark at this time was the self-determination principle of the Treaty of Versailles, according to which a portion of Schleswig that had been taken from Denmark by Prussia in 1864 would revert to Denmark. In some of Schleswig a plebiscite was to be held in 1920 on the question of whether the people wanted to remain German, as they had been since 1864, or to become Danes, as they had been before that date. This question of reunification had consequences for welfare legislation.

Denmark was very proud of its social legislation, and believed it was showing the way for the world, but Germany had publicly subsidized disability insurance, and Denmark did not, and the German health insurance system was more comprehensive. In some respects, then, former German citizens would be worse off becoming Danes. During 1919 to 1921, the *Folketing* (the Danish lower house) was much taken up with the extension of Danish law to the territories that had been German. Disability insurance had been mentioned for years. In 1919 Social Democrat Thorvald Stauning, as a minority member of the wartime ministry that was still in power, introduced a bill for disability insurance. He wanted the income for the insurance fund to come entirely from employers because, he claimed, much disability was industrial illness. He emphasized that Germany had such insurance and that reunification made it imperative that Denmark have it too. He also wanted the insurance tied to membership in a sickness fund and to make payment of insurance dependent on two-thirds diminution in earnings ability—both provisions copied from the German law. The law was not passed in the form Stauning proposed, but the next year the new Left ministry introduced a similar bill with a somewhat different premium structure, which was passed.[2]

The law on disability insurance was in some ways a sharp break from past Danish social legislation. Previous laws had at least kept the fiction that the insurance was voluntary. This law of May 11, 1921, says in its first paragraph that anyone who is a full member of a recognized sickness fund, who is between eighteen and sixty-two years old, and who is a resident in Denmark is insured against disability and required to pay a premium, which varied according to wages. The law was also a sharp departure in that it was the first social legislation available to the well-off. If they had ceased to be needy or were never badly off, they could be insured against disability by paying a premium that was three times the premium for the poor (clauses 2 and 5). This was the first legislation to apply the idea that laws originally meant to help the poor, could, by simple extension, apply to other members of society as well. The aim in this case was not to transfer wealth from one class to another but to collectivize the risk with the help of the state. This new idea of making such social legislation available to the more well-off in addition to the poor became important after World War II.

The law was also a departure from precedent in that it set a definite sum of 800 kroner a year for a full disability payment, instead of leaving the amount up to local authorities. A person was to have that payment if his earning ability was, because of the disability, only one-third or less of what a person of similar training and ability could earn. The provisions for diminished earnings sounds very exact, but who was to say when earnings ability was no more than one-third of what it had been? The law established an *invalideret,* or disability court, which dealt with every single case on its merits and had the right of subpoena and whose decisions were final (secs. 12, 16).[3] Of course, this court was not really a court where a prosecutor and a defendant battled. People came to the court as supplicants, not as one party to a conflict, and the president of the court was not really a judge but an administrator. Expenditures under the law climbed until as part of the Left's "cutting back" (*nedskaering*) the individual pensions were reduced in 1928 and 1929. When the Social Democrats were in power after 1929, the portion of the total expenditures covered by premiums paid by the insured themselves in fact continually increased, while the proportion paid by the employer decreased. If this was the way to socialism, it was certainly a roundabout way of getting there.[4]

From 1921 on, the story of the welfare state is essentially a Social Democratic story. The legislation of the 1890s was passed by a coalition of Left and Right, and since that time legislation had been passed by the Left. From the Disability Insurance Act through World War II, welfare legislation would be a matter for the Social Democrats, in frequent coalition with the Radical Left Party. (The

Radical Left Party, formed in 1905, was neither radical nor left. It was made up of small farmers who felt excluded by the large farmers controlling the Left, plus urban intellectuals who were reform-minded but uncomfortable being Social Democrats.) It is striking that there was very little socialism—if we take that word to mean, as a minimum, public ownership of at least the basic means of production—in the Social Democratic Party after World War I.

In 1923 the Social Democratic party adopted a new election platform that showed how little any version of socialism influenced the public stance of the party, but one can also see that there was no decision on a substitute for socialism. Welfare legislation plays as small a role in this public stance as collective ownership of the means of production. The platform addressed itself to issues of concern at the moment: tariff reduction and regulation (not public ownership) of banks. Only one of the platform points was possibly socialist, and even that was worded ambiguously and came well down the list. It asked that "industries and import firms that tend toward monopolies should be taken over by the state or subjected to effective controls." The point also called for workers councils. Points 9 and 10 in the platform touched on social welfare, but asked only for slight revisions in the existing pension and child support laws.[5]

This moderation paid off at the polls in the election of 1924. The years since the war had been troubled ones for the Danish government, characterized by strikes, lockouts, a fall in the value of the krone, and a constitutional crisis that seemed to place parliamentary democracy itself in doubt for a while. Probably in 1924 any opposition party that was plausible could have been elected. In the election of April 11 the Social Democrats became the largest but not the majority party in the lower house. With the support of the Radical Left, Thorvald Stauning formed the first Danish Social Democratic government. During their thirty-one months in power, the Social Democrats learned exactly where the boundaries of success were. Where the reforms were mild and did not threaten the existing distribution of power or deference, they succeeded; where reforms were more thoroughgoing or did threaten power or deference, they failed.

If class conflict, revolution, and nationalization were not to be the definition of socialism, perhaps worker participation in management—co-determination, as it is now called—was a reasonable substitute. The idea for workers councils (*bedriftraad*) of some kind had been in the air for some time.[6] When F. J. Borgbjerg, the social minister, introduced legislation to create such workers councils in March 1924, he did not emphasize the gradual socialization of society, but rather the good old days of handicraft, where there was virtually no conflict, he said, between master and man. Modern industry had made this kind of relationship obsolete. He had to underscore again and again that the workers councils would not interfere with management's right to manage and were not intended to overturn society. With the memories of the soviets in Russia and similar proposals of the German left in the 1918–20 chaos in that country, the other parties would have nothing to do with the idea. The Left argued that such proposals were unnecessary in Denmark, where most industries were small and relationships between employer and employees were not distant. A workers council would more likely increase class conflict than decrease it. The Radicals, although they were supposedly part of the parliamentary majority, maintained that profit-sharing was a more logical and effective means for workers to share the fruits of industrialism.[7] The proposal was buried in committee, where Radical doubts ensured that it would not emerge. Thus the Social Democrats learned that there was no hope of socialization through workers' participation in private industry.

One might think that modifying class structure in Danish society might be a step toward democratic socialism. Leaders of the "workers movement" were now in power, and if not all of them were workers (the foreign minister was a count) they still might be expected to challenge the class structure. One institution that clearly maintained class difference was the school system, and one point in the new election program called for democratization of education. Nina Bang, widow of Gustav Bang, the major ideologist of the left wing of the Social Democratic Party, was minister of education. She had indicated that she agreed with her husband's indictments of Danish society, and she had written some telling essays on her own. Yet her proposals, while they created a good deal of passionate debate, were more important symbolically than they were in actuality, and there could even be a question as to what they were a symbol of. She was indeed limited by the coalition nature of the *Folketing* majority and the conservative majority in the *Landsting,* yet her proposals did not even point the way to the future. The reorganization she proposed would give a bit more autonomy to local communities and remove the parish minister (a civil servant) from ex officio membership on the local school board, though he still might be elected. It was this last proposal that caused such fierce controversy. It was viewed as a step toward socialist elimination of religion, an extension of democracy into areas where it did not belong, an attack on order. In the end, the proposal passed both houses more or less intact, but the class nature of the schools, including the university, was not altered. The Social Democrats learned that they could pass proposals that did not have much effect.[8]

The obvious and unavoidable aspect of social welfare facing the government in the 1920s was unemployment. High throughout the period, it increased from about 10 percent to about 20 percent between 1924 and 1926.[9] Neither the results achieved nor even the proposals of the Social Democrats pointed the way toward an expanding welfare state or any further socialization of society. Their proposals were no bolder than the timidity of the first brief Labour party government in London. A mild proposal to start public works that were already technically prepared was passed.[10] A somewhat more significant proposal to raise the amount by which the national treasury subsidized the unemployment insurance was passed in the lower house and defeated in the upper. In the course of the debate, the Social Democrats made their ritual bow to socialism by saying that of course unemployment could not really be solved under the capitalist mode of production, but that the problem should be dealt with as much as possible. The Conservatives picked up on this remark and accused the Social Democrats of contributing to class conflict, but the Social Democrats insisted that they were not a class party at all, that they represented the whole nation. They thus indicated again that the way to appeal to Danes was to assert consensus rather than accept conflict.[11] Quite against their principles, the Social Democrats then introduced a law subsidizing wages in particularly hard-hit industries, but even this failed to convince the opposition, which perhaps saw electoral victory in the near future. It too passed the lower house but failed in the upper.[12]

It would be misleading to argue that the Social Democrats had no ideas on the welfare state in general. After all, they had appointed one of their most prominent leaders to the post of social minister—F. J. Borgbjerg. His general remarks, set out in his discussion of the first budget (*finanslov*) ever introduced by a Social Democratic government, are worth analyzing, but it should always be remembered that welfare legislation was just one of many topics being discussed. Borgbjerg said, in October 1924:

> The major idea and purpose of social legislation is to maintain the physical, moral, and intellectual health of the lower class such that it can work and struggle and fight its way upward to a height where it can begin to reorder society in accordance with its own interests. And the interests of the deep layer of the people always is historically identical with the interests of the whole society, as the interests of the upper class never are.

If the Conservatives have their way, he contended, and social legislation is stopped or even rolled back, the result would not be the peaceful evolution that characterized Danish history, but revolution.[13] Borgbjerg thus found a way to unite his desire for social legislation here and now with a theoretical—or one might even say rhetorical—desire for socialism eventually. He also found a way to unite his theoretical desire that his party represent the working class with the demands of Danish politics that it not be a class party or promote class conflict. Only three years later his arguments would be subtly but significantly different.

The Social Democrats' concentration on welfare was pushed on them by the policies of the Left ministry, which took over as a result of the election of December 2, 1926. Unfortunately for his party, the new prime minister, Thomas Madsen-Mygdahl, was a man of consistency and principle. He believed that the way out of current economic difficulties was to reduce the cost of production, including wages, thereby making Danish goods more competitive in world markets. He had been saying this for years, so the party knew what it was getting when they chose him for their leader.[14] The Social Democrats had already staked out their position in opposition to Madsen-Mygdahl in a long speech that Borgbjerg had given as social minister in October in anticipation of the election a little over a month away. Borgbjerg first pointed out how much the lower classes themselves paid as insurance premiums and then asked what would happen if these programs were cut back or eliminated. Either people would be thrust back on the poor law—not a cheap alternative—or they might end the general calm that prevailed in the labor movement.[15]

Yet one of the chief accomplishments of the Left government between 1926 and 1929 was the cutting down on all national expenditures. The government insisted that times were not so hard, that benefit levels had been set when the krone was worth less, and that all "cutting down" really did was establish benefit levels at about their real value of a few years ago. In vain the Social Democrats argued that people had paid their premiums and were entitled to benefit levels prevailing at the time the premiums were paid.[16] Throughout 1927 the columns of the *Social-Demokraten* were filled with stories with such headlines as "Shall Thousands Be Driven Out of the Sickness Fund?" "Will the Left Destroy the Danish Sickness Fund Movement?" or "War of Starvation Against the Working Class."[17]

At the Social Democratic Party congress in 1927 the most important speech was given by Borgbjerg in defense of social legislation. The speech was ostensibly an attack on "cutting down" and did end with that, but it was mostly a historical and philosophical treatment of the place of social legislation in a society's development. The central point in the speech was that social legislation was actually a breaking out of the framework of capitalism, where the interests of the bourgeoisie were the only determinants. As welfare increases, capitalist society in fact dissolves, and the workers get more powerful both in the sense of determining their own destiny and in the sense of gaining real property rights because they can determine what happens to the fruits of property. Borgbjerg went on to say, "Through the sickness funds with state support, he [the worker] achieves security in the case of sickness; through accident insurance in the case of accidents . . . through social legislation he is assured a relatively high degree of freedom and security."

Claiming support from on high, Borgbjerg quoted Marx's approval of the ten-hour law in England in 1846, but he had clearly diverged from the master in important ways, and from his own position in 1924. No longer would limits on hours and wages, or on health, unemployment, and accident insurance, enable the proletariat to take the reins and bring about a socialized society. These laws themselves eroded capitalism and constituted a socialized society. Borgbjerg took the specific example of unemployment, which he termed a problem that can be cured by only a little tinkering with mere technicalities. Unemployment was no longer the basis of capitalism as a pool of surplus labor, not because unemployment had been ended but because the unemployed now had enough to eat because of their income through unemployment insurance. He took issue with those who would call social insurance laws mere "patching up" of capitalism, called such arguments "sectarian," and dismissed them as misguided. After this speech it was clear that the Social Democrats would claim that socialism would come not through crisis, not through co-determination in industry, not through a process of nationalization, even a gradual one, but through social legislation.[18]

All that was needed to bring the Social Democrats back to power was a split between the Left and the Conservatives, which occurred in 1929 over the issue of defense expenditures. The Social Democrats used whatever issues they could to attack the government, but their chief plank was opposition to "cutting down." The major election manifesto for the election that took place on April 24, 1929, claimed, in a strange twist for a presumably socialist party, "Never before has a Danish government waged class warfare like that of Madsen-Mygdahl." Clearly the Social Democrats were appealing to the Danish sense that a unified society must be protected from attacks from any one class. They turned such feelings to their advantage by claiming that they spoke for society as a whole while their opposition spoke for only a segment of it.[19] The election of 1929 was not an unalloyed triumph for the Social Democrats. They still needed the support of the Radicals to form a majority in the *Folketing,* and the major party of the opposition, the Left, almost maintained its strength. But the Social Democrats won eight more seats than they already had, and when that was taken in conjunction with the loss of six seats for the Conservatives and two for the Left, the result was that Stauning was prime minister again.

Welfare was by no means the only plank in the Social Democrats' platform, but it was the only one where a detailed program was already almost in existence in the form of K. K. Steincke's *Welfare for the Future.* The book had been written ten years earlier, when Steincke was the administrator of poor relief in Frederiksberg, a large district physically within but administratively distinct from Copenhagen. Now, with relatively few changes, it formed the basis for the proposals of the Social Democratic Party in what became known simply as "the social reform." In the new Social Democratic government of 1929, Steincke became social minister, and this made it possible for him to put into practice what he had been preaching for a decade.

Steincke himself was not a member of the proletarian class. He was university educated, a lawyer, had been a member of the *Landsting,* and was in fact a bit of a snob. Through his administrative experience and his writings he had become an expert on the Danish welfare system, its problems and virtues. In *Welfare for the Future,* Steincke made brief references to the Marxian tradition of socialism, but it was clear that his devotion to the tradition was perfunctory.[20] He described the lot of the poor Danish worker:

> In the endless rows of tenements, there is no possibility of feeling at home. What is left of well-being, calm, quiet, and human warmth, in those rooms filled with people, furniture, and all sorts of junk, in houses whose stairs, hallways, and doors are full of noise of factories, or arguments and gossip, or dust and stink? Where is any sense of good order, where the basis for fulfilling well-planned duties, where any regular pattern of life, in these alleys and corners where there is no definite place for anything, and where nothing is in its right place? (P. 7).

In other words, what the proletariat needed is not revolution but an old-fashioned, well-ordered Danish home, with a place for everything and everything in its place. Steincke—and by implication, his party—could not stop being Danes. Another Danish desideratum that Steincke emphasized was continuity. "One does not break continuity to try new and unproved ways," he said, "unless it is necessary or there are solid reasons for doing so" (p. 13). Clearly he did not see the necessity in 1919 or 1929.

Steincke also emphasized that the only requirement for receiving public help should be that the recipient is in need. There should be no other requirement—needs should be met—so there should be no moral distinction between "worthy" and "unworthy." Moreover, citizens have a right to receive relief: "As far as possible, help is granted as a right for the needy from the public, a definite, limited but legal right, enforceable at law, whose granting is dependent on the recipient fulfilling certain conditions, which have been specified beforehand, not from arbitrary estimation after the fact by some official" (p. 271). One senses that throughout the book Steincke is fighting not pure liberalism, to which only a fringe of Danish politics adhered, but the conservative argument that help from the public in whatever form should carry some sort of stigma. He believed it should not. Yet even as Steincke made these points he could not quite get away from treating the poor as though they were morally weak, rather than victims of society. He knew, for example, that the premiums paid by the sickness fund member did not pay for more than a portion of the benefits, but by paying this premium the man on the street *thinks* he is insuring himself and therefore gets the feeling of independence, if not the reality (p. 13). The aim of welfare was "to raise the needy and appeal to his sense of honor and independence" (p. 158).

Nowhere in the book does Steincke challenge the traditional Danish class system. He mentions "equality," but only in passing, and he was clearly and explicitly proposing a social minimum—nothing more disruptive than that, just a better administered minimum than existed at the time. Those who stood highest in the prestige hierarchy could support or at least acquiesce in the laws without endangering their social position. The system as it existed, Steincke claimed, could not be reformed. It was wrong in principle and must be replaced. The rest of his book is a description of what he proposed to put in its place—a system that was not discontinuous with past history but was still based on principles more consonant with modern social thinking—and he referred to English Fabians more than any other source.[21]

With all his talk of new principles and with all his social philosophy, one would expect Steincke to come up with entirely new programs, but what he came up with were more in the nature of amendments to the existing system. He was more or less in favor of the government bill for disability insurance, which was before the Rigsdag when he wrote the book (p. 326). He was more or less in favor of the government bill on old-age pensions, though he believed that all elements of estimate of need should be replaced by a fixed sum according to a sliding scale of need (p. 328). He would have liked a premiumless pension for all—no forced insurance, like the German law—but he realized that such a law was not economically possible at the moment. He wanted to keep the current sickness fund institution, but extend it so that the chronically ill were included (which was done in 1921). Steincke insisted that if all these changes were made—slight as they may seem—the whole tenor of public relief and popular attitudes toward it would change (p. 382). Public help would be seen as part of the machinery of a society trying to maintain itself, rather than charity for the weak or unworthy. The book ends with a couple of sentences repeating that the problem cannot really be solved with the current system of ownership and production but that his system is at least an improvement.

Because Steincke was the kind of person he was—scornful of those who disagreed with him, full of self-confidence, almost arrogance—and because his proposals are set in the context of trumpet fanfares announcing their own importance, most historians have tried to deflate him by concluding that his system was only old wine in new bottles. In a sense this is true, because one can talk about the "sickness fund," for example, in 1900, 1920, and 1960 and still be discussing a similar institution. And yet the changes Steincke proposed involved a fairly large step in the direction of a welfare *state,* as opposed to a *system* of welfare. He essentially wanted the system nationalized and he left local control only where he felt the forces of history were too great to overcome.

On December 12, 1929, Steincke introduced the laws with one of the longest speeches ever made in the Rigsdag. In the speech, he essentially repeated his arguments from *Welfare for the Future.*[22] In spite of Steincke's attempts to keep "the social reform" within traditional Danish patterns, to emphasize its conservative nature and how much it was merely a simplification and systematization of existing laws, it was seen by both those who opposed it and those who favored it as a departure from past practice, a summing up of Social Democratic welfare policies, and a portent for the future. It took some three-and-a-half years of parliamentary maneuvers to pass it, and then it was passed only by including it at the last moment in the famous Chancellor Street Compromise (*Kanslersgadeforlig*).

The proposals aroused great interest in the press and great discussion among the population. Employer groups led the opposition.

Their expenditures under the proposed system would go up, and they characterized it as "bread and circuses" for workers and more a product of the "party politician Steincke" than of the "expert in social administration Steincke." They argued that expenses for Denmark's social programs were "miles higher" even than Sweden's and Norway's and that the new proposals would increase expenses even more, in spite of the falling prices. The increased expenses would, they said, make it difficult for Danish industry to compete in world markets with other nations.[23]

The opposition of employer groups was relatively muted and pragmatic. More principled opposition, and a good deal more shrill opposition, came from the Danish Taxpayers Association (Dansk Skattebogerforening) and its journal *The Taxpayer* (*Skatteborgeren*). Over and over the Taxpayers Association argued that capitalism was good for society and that it must be defended more vigorously. Steincke was consciously aiming at a socialist society and must be stopped. Antitax parties are a fairly common phenomenon of the post–World War II period, but in the 1930s few people were principal supporters of this position. In fact, it had no significant influence on debates in the Rigsdag.[24]

The Left might permit itself an occasional defense of free competition in its condemnation of socialist oppression of individualism, but in general they were not principled nineteenth-century liberals. Niels Neergaard (an important Left politician for more than forty years and prime minister at times), as finance minister vigorously defended his party's record on social legislation, saying in 1929 that there was no reaction against it in his party. He said proudly, "No country in the world has better social legislation or even equal to ours."[25]

The debates in the Rigsdag were not crucial to the law that emerged or even to its passage. Yet the debates reveal a good deal about fundamental social attitudes. There was as little pure Manchester liberalism in the halls of the Rigsdag as in the press. "Danmarks Retsforbund," a minor party that often did not have enough votes even to have a representative in parliament, might praise freedom, condemn tendencies to socialism and get angry about compulsion in modern society, but almost everyone agreed at least with the position of C. J. F. Sven, which Sven delivered as spokesman for the Conservative Party, that in the case of misfortune, society (through government) must step in to help.[26] Members of the Left even condemned the "cutting down" policies of their own party so vigorously that Madsen-Mygdahl was forced to defend them as merely reflecting changes in the buying power of the krone, not an attempt to diminish social welfare.[27] The Social Democrats agreed that there should be poor laws and force at the bottom of the system, so they were willing to retain a distinction between the worthy poor and the unworthy poor in spite of Steincke's theoretical opposition.[28]

The "social reform" was not the only or even the chief issue before the Rigsdag, and its fate was ultimately determined by linking it to other issues. All these issues were in one way or another a product of the Great Depression. Farm foreclosures had forced auctions all over the country. Unemployment in the cities was massive, reaching as high as 50 percent at times and averaging 33 percent for all of 1932. When the British pound was devalued, a large part of Danish agriculture suffered, and in 1932 there was agitation for a decline in the value of the krone.

All these issues came to a head in 1933. In January many major contracts ran out. Noting the lower consumer prices, employers wanted lower wage rates. With large numbers of unemployed, labor unions were in a weak position to hold on to gains they had won. A lockout and strike were threatening. Thorvald Stauning was determined to propose a bill that would continue the current contracts for a year. Through complicated negotiations, the large and small landholders had agreed on a devalued krone. But what if England reacted with further devaluation? And how could employers be induced to support a continuation of existing contracts? Stauning would need support either from the Left or from the Conservatives to get his bill through the *Landsting*.

Final agreement on a program was reached the night of January 29, 1933, at Stauning's apartment on Chancellor Street and was hence called "the Chancellor Street Compromise." Representatives of the Left, the Radical Left, and the Social Democrats negotiated until four in the morning, finally agreeing on a legislated continuation of existing labor contracts and on a fall in the value of the krone in relation to the pound, as well as on various minor other points.

The labor unions, as well as the employers, therewith gave up their freedom of action temporarily. This loss of principles was made more palatable to the unions because wages were to continue at a higher level than they otherwise might and because the decision was made by a Social Democratic government. The Chancellor Street Compromise was another one of those great compromises that occur throughout modern Danish history. "We have sacrificed some principles," said Stauning the next day to the staff of the *Social-Demokraten,* "but we have saved the country." Then, in a typically Danish gesture, he bought everyone a beer.

The "social reform" was not included in the original compromise, and Steincke had not been present on January 29. The next day Steincke, Oluf Krag (the leader of the Left), and Stauning met, and Krag asked if Stauning was issuing an ultimatum that "the social reform" must be included in the compromise. "It sure as hell sounds like it," growled Stauning, (somewhat freely translated from "Ja, det lader s'gu til det")[29] and passage in the *Landsting* in May 1933 was ensured; the Conservatives voted no and the Left abstained.

Anyone reading the legislation of 1933 in conjunction with that of 1891 and 1892 cannot help but be struck by some contrasts. The legislation of the 1890s is short, uncomplicated, and leaves a great deal to the judgment of local officials. It is designed for a simple traditional society. The "social reform," while containing vestiges of these features, was obviously designed for a more bureaucratic, legalistic, and systematic society. Many more variations and instances were dealt with explicitly. The legislation of the 1890s contains virtually no numbers—no specifications of amounts of aid or of income limits. The legislation of the 1930s contains rules and regulations for determining how much a person will receive and rules for what happens if a recipient cheats. In the 1890s it was enough to allow local officials to police the poor.

The 1933 law providing general assistance was called the "Law on Public Welfare" (*offentlig forsorg*), no longer "the poor law." Gone were references to "forced work houses" and "poorhouses." Instead they were called "institutions" (*anstalter*), a category that included old-age homes, orphanages, and the like. No longer were the poor-law authorities authorized to punish people for up to six months. In fact, much of the law was not so much a welfare law as a law on children's welfare.

The law on social insurance was closest to Steincke's heart. The welfare laws were only to fill in gaps in the various kinds of insurance. The greatest departure was making disability insurance and old-age pensions dependent on whether a person had been a member of a sickness fund. Full membership in a sickness fund was still limited by income to "not-well-off members of the working class" (*ubemidlede personer af arbejderklassen*) and people on their economic level. Note that this definition of who was eligible was still based not on one's relationship to the means of production but on one's standard of living. The owner of a small factory, even an employer, who was poor might be eligible. Each year the social minister would specify the income limits that were to coincide with the income of the average skilled worker. Benefits under sickness insurance or old-age or disability insurance were specified and (with a few small exceptions) were not affected by the estimation of local authorities.

The "social reform" was clearly not like the American Social Security Act of 1935. The American law was much more nearly on an actuarial basis, its insurance features provided only old-age and unemployment insurance, and much of it was divided between state and federal governments. The Danish "social reform" more nearly resembled Great Britain's Beveridge Plan of 1943. Like that English reform, it got rid of most of the moral judgments involved in delivering relief and was more centralized. Unlike the Beveridge Plan, it did not provide a flat rate of benefit for a flat rate of contribution. The Danish system was income-related and had income limits, which the Beveridge Plan did not have. The "social reform" may have had something to do with the program of the Fabians in England, but basically it was a continuation of Danish institutions and Danish ways of thinking.

16

From Dead Center
to the Welfare State
in Great Britain

In Great Britain the impact of World War I was nearly as great as in Germany. The destruction and death were less than in Germany, there was no overt and violent revolution, the monarchy and the empire endured, and outwardly at least, most of the institutions endured. Yet the trauma was deep and permanent. It was not simply that war was no longer what it was supposed to be—Great Britain was no longer what it was supposed to be.[1]

Yet certain fundamental ways of thinking seemed to have remained similar. The formulations from 1834 had remained in place for seventy-five years. To some degree they had been given up in 1911, and in their turn the formulations from 1911 achieved a new rigidity. As these mechanisms proved inadequate in the 1920s, Great Britain seemed unable to move beyond them to deal with a new and more extreme set of problems. One principle had at least in part been given up; the idea that invariant principles could be found remained.

Through the welter of details, confusion, and shifting policies, one can discern three interlocking trends in income-maintenance policy in the two decades between the wars. First, the root of all the trends, was the apparently insoluble problem of unemployment and the struggle against it. The policies that tried and failed to deal with unemployment had the dual effects of decreasing both local power and judgmental power over the poor. As long as the poor were subject to the will of local Boards of Guardians, which functioned only with the loosest of guidelines, the Guardians had considerable control over the recipients. As more and more of the poor came within the purview of either the various unemployment schemes or the contributory insurance run by the central government, the local authorities lost their power to judge. Thus the second trend, the tendency toward national programs, was at the same time a tendency away from programs that involved making judgments about people's worthiness. The third trend was the growing interest in "all-in" insurance. This was the idea that everyone should be insured, for a premium, against all disruptions in income. The idea, which had many variants, got nowhere in the 1920s and 1930s, but its result was the Beveridge Report of 1942.

WE CAN CURE UNEMPLOYMENT! proclaimed an election pamphlet for the Liberals in 1929. But they could not. That could have been an election slogan for any party during any of the elections between 1921 and 1939. No one succeeded. The Labour Exchanges found they had nothing to exchange. The unemployment insurance proved hopelessly inadequate.

While trying to maintain a facade of continuity, the various governments abandoned the poor-law precepts of 1834 but had nothing to put in their place until the Beveridge Report of 1942. The permanent civil servants at the Treasury were adamantly opposed to deficit spending, convinced that a contraction of government expenditures was the way out of the depression.[2] The government—and it made little difference from which party or combinations of parties the government was made—staggered from one stopgap desperation step to another, each failing in its aims, only to be succeeded by another stopgap. What resulted was the "dole"—called by various names, such as "extended benefits" or "transitional payments," but the dole nonetheless. The word "dole" was spoken with scorn by those who received it, by those who gave it out, and by social analysts. It was a small payment, enough to keep a person alive, given grudgingly and not in return for any product, premium, or work.

It is only fair to say that there were many sides to Great Britain between the wars other than unemployment. Overall personal income increased. Studies of poverty found that, compared with Booth's and Rowntree's studies at the turn of the century, things had improved. Housing for the poorly paid working family got better. For much of the 1920s, the state of the economy of London and the home counties might be called a boom, and for a small part of the population one might even talk about a decade that roared.[3] The 1920s were also years of great and bitter strikes. There was the coal strike in 1921 and the "general strike" of 1926. There was revolution, civil war, and partition in Ireland. Unemployment and unemployment policies are only one aspect of the period, but it is the aspect that grew to be necessarily an unrelenting concern of policy-makers.

There was a brief period of prosperity right after World War I. A program of "Out-of-Work Donations" was passed in 1915 for servicemen who could not find work after discharge. In 1918 the program was expanded to civilians who were unemployed because of demobilization. The first payments under the plan were in 1918, and it ended in 1921. It was an emergency measure, not intended to deal with peacetime unemployment. In a sense the Old-Age Pension Act of 1919 was also an emergency measure in that it raised the pensions and allowed applicants to have more wealth and still be pensionable. However, it did something else. No one seemed to notice—or if they noticed, to care—that the last vestiges of a test of worthiness were removed as a criterion for old-age pensions. The act explicitly repealed the provisions in the 1908 law making "habitual failure to work," drunkenness, or a previous imprisonment, disqualifications for receiving pensions. The law passed through all its stages on the last day of the session with only superficial debate. No one was interested any longer in attempting to make judgments about the lives of the aged poor.[4]

Starting in 1920, unemployment became the central and necessary obsession of government. It leaped upward that year and the next and stayed in double digits except for one year (9.7 percent in 1927) until the war, with a high point of 22 percent average for 1932. The 1911 National Insurance Act had covered about 2.5 million people for unemployment. In 1916 this was increased to about 4.0 million. Unemployment had been very low during that period, and the system had accumulated a surplus of more than £22 million. Early in 1920 the coalition government proposed expanded coverage to some 12.0 million people, with agricultural workers and domestic servants the principal large groups still outside the system.[5]

By the fall of 1920 the Committee on Unemployment, established in August, reported to the Cabinet that there was "a serious state of unrest" in which "social disaster is not to be disregarded."[6] The sense of panic spread to the Ministry of Labour. The ministry had estimated an average of 9.5 percent unemployment, and the figure in May 1921 stood at 23.0%. The insurance was spending £2 million a week and taking only in one-sixth of that. Benefit rates had to be reduced, and premiums increased. By a law enacted in March 1921, the unemployment insurance program was authorized to borrow up to £10 million from the Treasury. In June the labour minister asked that his borrowing authority be increased to £20 million. By 1922 he said that "the relaxation of the ordinary rules of insurance has been inevitable" and asked that the borrowing authority again be increased, to £30 million. This borrowing to provide "extended benefits"—that is, beyond what the premiums would have produced—is the real beginning of the dole. It still applied, however, only to those who were in insured trades.

Ten years earlier, while national insurance was being debated, an optimistic member of Parliament had rejoiced that the old ideas from 1834 were ready for burial. He was wrong in 1911, but one can see that the burial had taken place by March 29, 1922. In debating the unemployment insurance bill of 1922, Baronet Frederick Bambury, whom the historian Charles Loch Mowat called "crustiest of the City Tories," invoked the workhouse, saying that if people were offered the workhouse they would "find work for themselves." "Where?" shouted several members. "The old line," said another, and there were several groans. The idea was simply swept aside, with no one even feeling the need to argue. What had survived for seventy-five years could not survive the war. There was no funeral.[7]

There was also no alternative. The Conservative prime minister, Stanley Baldwin, unexpectedly called an election for December 1923. The result was that no party had a majority. Because one reason for the election had been Baldwin's turn to protection, a Liberal-Conservative alliance was impossible, considering their fundamental differences on that issue. A Labour-Liberal alliance, with the Labour Party forming the government under Ramsay Mac-Donald, was the only solution. The *New Statesman* had been calling for "useful work" instead of "useless toil." Now the party of the working classes was in power. One could expect a reversal of previous policies, perhaps a program of nationalization or at least of massive relief works. Nationalization was not an issue, but with trade unionists in the government (although to a smaller degree than they thought they deserved), and with Sidney Webb at the Board of Trade and as head of the Committee on Unemployment, things could be expected to move. Things did not move. This was not simply a matter of a socialist or reformist party being frustrated by their coalition partner. Labour had no significant ideas to be frustrated. Labour was as afraid as anyone of the Treasury, and more important, it shared the Treasury's aversion to deficits.[8]

The Committee on Unemployment had been established by the coalition government in 1920. In 1921 the committee had condemned "mere measures of relief" as being "from every point of view, the least satisfactory," and relief works as "only slightly better." In the new Labour government the chief idea-man for the labor movement, Sidney Webb, was in charge of the committee. A month after Webb took over, he told the Cabinet in an "Interim Report on Unemployment" that because of the short time they had to prepare they could only recommend continuing the policies already in place. This meant work on the roads, forests, and other such projects— none of them major expenditures or of major use in finding work for the unemployed. In their "Second Interim Report," their last, the phrase "The Committee recommend that no change . . ." recurs like a refrain. Webb, along with the rest of the government, pinned his hopes on revival of trade, particularly foreign trade. As that did not seem to happen, the government had no further suggestions.[9]

One might expect more radical proposals from the more radical members of the party. After all, Philip Snowden was now Chancellor of the Exchequer. It was he who, the previous March, had engineered a debate in the House of Commons on a motion condemning capitalism. That was easy enough, with unemployment among insured workers at about 12 percent, but the debates resulted in little more than an hour or so of banalities from both sides of the house.[10] Now that Snowden was in power, he adopted all the caution of his predecessors and showed more timidity than even his Conservative successor. The best he could do was propose that a person could have a little more income or wealth and still be eligible for the old-age pension. He was made fun of by the Conservative opposition, which read some of the Labour Party campaign documents promising much more. Snowden, sounding a bit himself like a crusty Tory, based his argument not on humanity or justice but on the argument that the income limits were a disincentive to thrift, which he wanted to encourage.[11]

In Germany there was a clear division between committed socialists at the party level and moderate "bread-and-butter" trade unionists. The division was not as clear in Great Britain, but the most moderate were in the government, with one of their number as prime minister. There were radical socialists in the party hierarchy, but there were more among trade unionists—although in neither case did this mean sympathy with the Soviet Union.[12] The situation, while not entirely simple, was almost the reverse of the situation in Germany.

On issues quite unrelated to unemployment, the government fell after less than ten months in office, in October 1924. In the United States, Franklin Roosevelt in one hundred days would create more agencies and ideas than most people could keep track of. In almost three hundred days, about the only achievement of the Labour Party on the domestic front was a public housing program with no discernible effect on employment. The meager accomplishments of the first Labour government can be explained by Labour's short time in office, and that as a minority. Neither can explain their lack of vision and dearth of proposals. In Germany and Denmark the pressures of the depression pushed the Social Democrats from socialism toward social welfare, and when depression came to the United States, the Democrats, never having been socialists, adopted social welfare. In Great Britain the Labour Party, which had a somewhat divided tradition on a capitalist welfare state, moved neither toward socialism nor toward social welfare. At least as much was done by the Conservatives as by Labour.

Unemployment policy in Great Britain continued under the Conservatives about as before. An Unemployment Grants Committee continued to subsidize local projects, but these employed only a tiny fraction of the unemployed. The committee ceased to meet after 1925. Relief continued as before. Neville Chamberlain was minister of health in the new Conservative government. He came into office with a broader vision than anyone in the Labour Cabinet. His ideas included poor-law reform on roughly the lines advocated in the Minority Report of 1909, a consolidation of various health and medical programs, and a system of contributory pensions on top of the noncontributory pensions.

The latter appealed to Chancellor of the Exchequer Winston Churchill, who swept the idea into his own sphere, proceeded to work out the details, and pushed it through Parliament.[13] In his budget speech introducing the idea of widow's and old-age contributory pensions, Churchill said that Great Britain had moved from the old laissez-faire ideas to "scientific state organization." At the second reading Neville Chamberlain was interrupted from the Labour side with statements that the plan should be noncontributory, but he had the inestimable advantage that the Labour Party when in power had continued the contributory tradition, so he could read their own policies back at them. Labour had a difficult time making its objections sound plausible, and the bill passed its second reading without difficulty.[14]

The Widows, Orphans, and Old-Age Contributory Pensions Act in essence provided contributory old-age pensions between the ages of sixty-five and seventy to everyone insured under the National Health Insurance Act of 1911—that is, most employees in manual labor outside agriculture and domestic service. Again, women paid lower premiums and got lower benefits. Except for low-wage-earners, where the employer would pay more, the cost was split equally between employer and employee. The state paid no part of the premium, except in a few special occupations, but the state would pay pensions for all those who reached the age of sixty-five even if they had been fairly near that age when the act was passed. The act, although tied to the National Health Insurance Act, made no use of the friendly or approved societies. Thus the state was moving away not only from local authorities but also from indirect administration.[15]

At the same time, another idea was growing. It was not considered a serious possibility in 1924 and might still be regarded as a crank idea—except that it became reality almost twenty years later. This was the idea of "all-in" insurance. Although rejected by a parliamentary committee of inquiry, the idea was the subject of at least two academic works and two popular pamphlets. One of the pamphlets was a product of an informal group of Liberal and Conservative members of Parliament led by a man appropriately named Broad. Working spasmodically since 1921, the group produced the Broad Plan in 1924. This plan confronted the "four dreads" of all workers: sickness, unemployment, old age, and death of the breadwinner. It proposed covering all people who were gainfully employed for flat-rate premiums and flat-rate benefits, without income limit. Under this scheme "no worker, his wife or child, need ever seek Poor Law relief or go to a Workhouse."

William Beveridge's plan, set out in a pamphlet titled "Insurance for All and Everything," was more sober and less rapturous in tone. He did not propose any grand unified scheme, but rather a coordination of existing insurance. There would be two "insurance sections" only, one for the sick and injured, one for everything else: widowhood, unemployment, dependents. All would be covered by a contributory plan, with benefits and premiums lower than those T. T. Broad proposed. The idea of "all-in" aroused some interest and some comment in the press, but no one seemed prepared to go further with it at the moment.[16]

That the Labour Party would offer no more than the Conservatives was confirmed during the second Labour government, which Ramsay MacDonald formed in June 1929. Sir Oswald Mosley—formerly a Conservative member of Parliament, now a Labour member, and eventually the most outspoken leader of the British Fascists—proposed a program of increased pensions, tariffs, and import controls, much greater public control of industry and banking, and deficit financing. The proposal was shot down in the Cabinet, most particularly by Philip Snowden as Chancellor of the Exchequer. Whether such a program could have weathered Conservative and Liberal opposition is uncertain, but it was never given the chance to try.

There were minor changes in the unemployment compensation in the years between 1930 and 1934. The term "extended benefits" was replaced by "transitional benefits" for those otherwise ineligible for insurance. No longer was the applicant required to prove he was "genuinely seeking work" in order to receive benefits; instead, the official was required to prove that an applicant was *not* seeking work, in order to deny benefits. The "transition" was supposed to be to better times, which did not come. In fact, the transition was to the Unemployment Act of 1934.[17]

It was this Unemployment Act, in force for the remainder of the years between the wars, which finally abandoned any pretext that the system was basically an insurance system with some "unconvenanted," or "extended" or "transitional," supplements. The 1934 act established a regular insurance system for those able to pay premiums, and a national network of "Unemployment Assistance Boards" for those unable to pay premiums. These boards were to aid any previously employed person who might have used up insurance benefits, or anyone who had never been employed since reaching age sixteen but "who might reasonably have been so employed but for the industrial circumstances of the district in which he resides" and who is in need of an allowance. In other words, it provided an allowance to almost anyone who needed it and could not find a job. No other solution was found.[18]

It was not that no other solution was known. John Maynard Keynes had been pressing his expansionist views on various governments for years. Lloyd George and the Liberals had asked for a more active policy of public works, and there were the Mosely proposals. Also, in the 1930s the general idea of economic planning was more in the air than ever before. In addition, both the German and the American experiences were noted. All these policies were explicitly rejected.[19] The American solution when unemployment became acute in the 1930s—in the long run perhaps equally unsuccessful economically, but certainly better psychologically—was work relief. The Germans had no solution during the 1920s, but unemployment was eventually solved in the 1930s through massive public works financed by deficit spending, many of which had ultimately military goals. It was likewise expenditures on arms that eventually caused unemployment rates in Great Britain to fall toward the end of the 1930s, though unemployment was still about 14 percent at the beginning of 1939 and 9 percent by year's end.[20]

As unemployment insurance was being abandoned, the poor law was also broken up about as recommended by the Minority Report from 1909. In 1929 the Local Government Act replaced the Boards of

Guardians with Public Assistance Committees. The name change itself is significant; now there was at least verbal acknowledgment that the poor were not to be wards of anyone (although some subcommittees were still called Guardians). These Public Assistance Committees were made up of elected local officials plus some appointed members, at least one of whom had to be a woman. The new committees were to be financed by the central government based on need as calculated by the central government following a formula in the law. According to Bentley Gilbert, the Local Government Act was, among other things, an attempt to reassert central control over Boards of Guardians, who from the standpoint of the Conservatives had been too generous to "paupers." It was also, through the formula for calculating need, a clear abandonment of the "less eligibility" principle, which that central control had been initially designed to ensure ninety-five years previously. For what was called, even in the 1909 Minority Report, "the residuum" (e.g., a casual worker not covered by unemployment insurance) the status of "pauper" remained, and with it certain legal disabilities. Through the Local Government Act of 1929 and the various changes in the unemployment acts, that residuum was made very small, but it was not entirely eliminated.[21]

After the Unemployment Act of 1934, then, there was insurance for health, unemployment, and pensions for those between the ages of sixty-five and seventy; there was coverage for widows and orphans; there were war pensions and noncontributory old-age pensions; and there was aid under the Unemployment Assistance Boards and the Public Assistance Committees. There were specialized institutions for "lunatics," chronically ill with various diseases, and for people with specific other problems. The safety net was fairly complete. If it was not as tidy as one might like, it had few significant holes, and there were sound historical reasons for each development, so why go further?

Until Great Britain was involved in another world war, there was no more movement, but in the midst of the war for survival there was. The motivation was in part undoubtedly the war itself. After the war things were not to be allowed to go back to the way they had been in the 1930s. There were hopes for "a better Britain." The concern that led to the Beveridge Report seems to have started with dissatisfactions about health insurance and workmen's compensation. Benefits under the former were too low and under the latter too various. The Trades Union Congress was particularly pressing the former issue and the Ministry of Health (since 1929 the central authority for questions relating to poverty) was urging the latter. Between April and June 1941, the government, which had broadened its concerns to include the whole area of "social insurance and allied services," created a committee of inquiry and appointed William H. Beveridge as chairman.[22]

Beveridge was a logical choice for the job, but he had objectives far broader than the title of his report would indicate and broader than those of his 1924 pamphlet. His goal was nothing less than the elimination of poverty. In none of the other four countries under study was that the objective of any serious government official. In Germany, Hitler's goals had to do with other things. The Danish "social reform" assumed the continued existence of poverty, an assumption that was not challenged until well after World War II. In the United States, Franklin Roosevelt is supposed to have said that the Beveridge Report was really the Roosevelt Report, but programs in the United States did not really even declare war on poverty until 1964.[23]

In 1941, after more than two decades of depression and in the midst of war, William Beveridge proposed to eliminate poverty in Great Britain. It appears that he was quite serious. After all, there was nothing in the charge to the committee asking him to do more than reorganize the system that already existed. He was not the kind of person to make empty gestures to arouse enthusiasm for the war. He had first broached the idea of comprehensive insurance seventeen years earlier, when he endorsed the "all in" idea. He seized the opportunity that the Committee on Social Insurance and Allied Services furnished him. Beveridge pointed out many times that although only he signed the report it was in fact a collective decision, that he had consulted various interest groups. This was a sham. He knew what he wanted all along. By December 1941 Beveridge had already written a memo modestly titled "Basic Problems of Social Security with Heads of Schemes," which was actually a fairly complete picture of the proposals Beveridge would make almost a year later.[24]

224

Various interest groups appeared before the committee or sent written statements of opinion. Virtually no one opposed the idea of a general social insurance program. Even friendly societies and the charity organization societies had supportive things to say. The friendly societies spoke about a "national obligation" to see that everyone has enough to live on "even though he has made no provision for himself." The charity organization societies supported the principle of compulsory contributory insurance. Although the British Medical Association itself did not appear, the ophthalmologists and dentists spoke in favor of the program. The "relieving officers," and the approved societies saw no end of problems with the existing system. As one might expect, the most vigorous support came from the Trades Union Congress. To a degree one might call the Beveridge Report the Trades Union Congress Report. "Ours is the principle," TUC spokesmen said, "that for a certain sum of money [everyone] should be entitled to a certain sum in benefit—that is, a flat-rate benefit for a flat-rate contribution.[25] That was the basis for the committee's final report. Presumably there were people and groups in Great Britain who opposed such expansion of state power, who upheld the older values of thrift and self-help, who believed that such a program as Beveridge's would sap people's character, but they remained remarkably silent. If Beveridge was not forming a new consensus, he certainly gave that appearance.

There is no way to measure how much the acceptance of this new consensus was due to the war. The Battle of Britain, the "finest hour," the genuine fears of invasion, and the calls of Winston Churchill to fight on the beaches and from hedgerows if necessary made the older devotion to individualism seem almost quaint. It is always possible that the British saw the Beveridge Report as merely administrative detail and not as a new view of society, but Beveridge was quite explicit about formulating that new view. The term "social insurance," he wrote in the introduction to the report, implies that "men stand together with their fellows. . . . None should pay less because they are better situated, or receive more because they are used to earning more."[26] With regard to social insurance, Beveridge saw society as a collective and the state as the mechanism of that collective. The collective should guarantee to every one of its members a national minimum, sufficient to meet the need for a healthy and decent existence. That was the premise of the Beveridge Report, and once that was accepted all else was detail. There was no discussion of this basic premise; it was assumed from the start. The report attributed most poverty to "interruption or loss of earning power" (p. 7). The very wording indicates that this interruption or loss was an external intrusion, pressing on an individual from the outside. The individual was the victim, not the cause. Hence, the cure lay either in eliminating the cause, which the report mentioned briefly, or protecting the individual from the effects, which the proposals in the report aimed at doing.

Some poverty resulted from a "failure to relate income during earnings to the size of the family." This somewhat mysterious phrase is indicative of a whole philosophy and in a sense rediscovery of the Speenhamland principle of "relief in aid of wages." What the phrase referred to was family allowances. A person might have adequate earnings to support a single person, but that same salary might be inadequate if there were four children. Before 1834 there had been in some places an attempt to evaluate family needs, usually in relation to the price of bread, and then to supplement low earnings to reach that minimum. Germany had never abandoned that idea, and supplementing low wages with poor-law help was possible throughout the *Kaiserreich*. Such supplements were routine in Denmark. The whole nineteenth century in Great Britain had substituted the idea that income was in relation to the product, not to need. The Beveridge Report rejected that identity and in an astounding phrase wrote: "A national minimum . . . cannot be secured by a wage system" (p. 154), but no one seemed astounded.[27]

For poverty engendered by interruption of earning power, the Beveridge Report proposed comprehensive compulsory contributory social insurance: one payment and one benefit. The insurance should include a "comprehensive national health service [which] will ensure for every citizen there is available whatever medical treatment he requires, in whatever form he requires it," to be provided for a premium, but "where needed without contribution conditions in any individual case," for "restoration of a sick person to health is a duty of the State" (p. 158).

The report went on to say that the state should attempt to maintain full employment but that effort would have to be supplemented by unemployment insurance. Payment of benefits "on the most generous scale compatible with preservation of the mobility of labour and of the incentive to seek work and reject idleness will maintain the purchasing power of workpeople, if trade depression begins, and will thus mitigate the severity of the depression" (p. 164). There should also be retirement pensions, invalidity payments, training benefits for wives left widowed without children, and supplementary pensions for widows if there were children. Housewives should be in included in all branches of insurance.

Such provisions would make the need for direct assistance smaller, but some need would remain. "However comprehensive an insurance scheme, some, through physical infirmity, can never contribute at all and some will fall through the meshes of any insurance." Therefore national assistance "is an essential subsidiary method in the whole Plan for Social Security. . . . But the scope of the assistance will be narrowed" (p. 12). The whole plan, save national assistance, should be financed by contributions, because any alternative is "wrong in principle. . . . The insured person should not feel that income for idleness, however caused, can come from a bottomless purse. The Government should not feel that by paying doles it can avoid the major responsibility of seeing that unemployment and disease are reduced to a minimum" (p. 12). In other words, Beveridge was proposing a new view of poverty, a new view of the state, a new view of the relationships of individuals to one another, and a new view of the way the economy worked. These ideas were received with enthusiasm.

The narrowness of the views represented by witnesses appearing before the committee was repeated in the reaction to the report once it was published. Whatever there was of Far Right beliefs, whatever there was of revolutionary socialism, seemed to have been weak and silent. Beveridge had found a middle to which there was no extreme.

Prime Minister Winston Churchill thought that consideration of the report would have to wait until after the war, but others were more impatient. Within a year the government issued a parliamentary paper endorsing the Beveridge proposals in principle, and another specifically proposing a national health service along the lines described in the report. In fact, the war had ended and a new Labour Party government was elected before the National Insurance Act was passed in 1946. The details of that act and how it worked in practice are beyond the scope of this study. It is the Beveridge Report that ends this phase of the story and opens the next.[28]

In the worldwide movement in the direction of the welfare state, Great Britain had been laggard. Examples had been drawn from Germany, Denmark, New Zealand, and elsewhere. With the Beveridge Report and its acceptance by the country and the government, Britain had in one giant leap become a leader. Yet Britain needed the desperation of the war to stimulate it to this giant leap. The Great Depression alone had not been enough. The United States would not make the same leap, but it would make a leap as large as before the war began.

17

Holding Fast in the United States

In the United States, World War I was not so traumatic and not as dramatic a change as in the European countries. Some of the social reform issues, such as the battle over health insurance, went on relatively unaffected by the fighting. Yet World War I was also seen by Americans of the time and since as a major alteration both in American society and in America's place in the world.

When the decision to enter World War I was made, most Americans, of whatever political coloration, rallied to the cause. A few progressives dissented. Robert M. La Follette was the most prominent dissenter, and he was joined by a few "social progressives," particularly from the settlement houses. Most progressives were enthusiastic, however. Some saw in the mechanisms used to organize American society for war the culmination of what they had been working for. Military construction seemed to be an improvement over even the most far-reaching tenement house legislation; war industries limited child labor and women's work hours; prostitution and the sale of liquor were limited in the neighborhood of military bases. Most important, the country seemed to be finally using its democratic political system to organize its economy on a systematic basis. The doctrine of laissez-faire was finally seen for what, from the reformers' viewpoint, it had always been—an obsolete hindrance.[1]

But the end of the war was also the end—or almost the end—of progressive hopes. Not only were the central planning mechanisms dismantled and the doctrine of laissez-faire revived, but child labor laws that had been passed after great effort were overturned by court decision. Prohibition survived, an issue on which progressives, fundamentalist religions, and social conservatives could agree. Immigration was restricted, partly from a pro-labor point of view but more out of a confluence of interests than from any clearly progressive motivation. There was an attempt to maintain wartime nationalization of the railroads—which failed. There were attempts to make Muscle Shoals, later a part of the Tennessee Valley Authority, into a center of public electrical power—which failed. There was constant effort throughout the decade to do something to improve the income and the credit possibilities for farmers—which failed. The high point of an attempted revival of the progressive spirit was surely the third-party presidential run by Robert La Follette in 1924—which failed. Prohibition and immigration restriction were both in part "progressive" reforms, and some progressives backed them. They also had strong conservative backing, however, and of course neither had to do with income maintenance.[2]

One reform did not fail. This was an old-age pension system for civil servants, which finally became law in May 1920 after decades of agitation. People were entitled to this regardless of need or worthiness. Such pensions could be seen as a step on the road to general national old-age annuities. Yet such a view would be a misinterpretation. Retirement for civil servants was presented to the Congress not as part of "improving the lot of the working class" but as a way to improve the efficiency of the bureaucracy. The Pendleton Act in 1883, creating civil service rules, meant that a class of civil servants (the "classified" group) could not be dismissed except for cause determined after a hearing. This meant that very few were actually dismissed. The heads of federal departments testified that a significant portion of their departments were made up of "superannuated" employees—employees too old to do their job. Because the low salary of the average government employee did not permit savings, most had no source of livelihood outside their job. Of course, they could be dismissed for incompetence, but this would have meant a hearing in each individual case and then, in the phrase used in the debates, tossing a lot of old people "on the scrap heap"—that is, the poor-house. Out of both humanity and political self-interest, no adminis-tration was willing to do much of this.

Pensions were endorsed by both parties in the 1916 platforms, and they were backed by both parties in the House of Representatives. The major speech in favor of pensions was given by Representative John Nelson of Wisconsin, who brought in piles of affidavits from the executive branch, including one from Undersecretary of the Navy Franklin D. Roosevelt, saying that pensions would enable them to get rid of the most "inefficient" employees and thus to do more work at a lower cost. This would, claimed Nelson, put the government on a more "business like" footing. Several advocates in fact referred to the model of railroad pensions and other large em-ployers. The federal government, as the largest employer in the world, should be as good an employer as these corporations. Al-though a few opponents fumed against a paternalistic government that took care of some people at the expense of the many, the bill received overwhelming support, with passage in the House by more than 5 to 1. The law also included disability insurance—anyone totally disabled could, so long as the disability was not due to "vi-cious habits, intemperance or willful misconduct," receive the same pension he would have had he retired.

The old-age pension law received relatively little notice in the press—there were, after all, more important things going on. John R. Andrews of the American Association for Labor Legislation greeted the act in the pages of the *Survey* as "a long step ahead in farsighted care" for the elderly, but this was clearly wishful think-ing.[3] This law only put the United States on a par with an ancient practice in the other countries. For years before pensions were made available to the general public in Germany, Great Britain, and Den-mark, civil servants in those countries had had them. Indeed, this was one of the prestigious distinguishing marks of a civil servant. In the United States, though, it was something new.

Private charity continued. There were further attempts to orga-nize the process through community chests. Charity organization societies continued, generally renamed "family agencies." While in some respects the organizations maintained aspects of earlier atti-tudes, they became far more professional, often insisting that their employees have degrees from an accredited school of social work. Professionalism had its negative as well as its positive aspects. Much has been made, for instance, of withdrawal of the "social progressives" or social workers from general reform into increasing professionalism. The 1920s saw a decline in the influence of settlement house workers, for whom the whole urban environment had been the object, and a growth in influence of social casework—work with individuals to try to help them with their particular problems. Yet it was probably necessary for social work to develop its own rationale, its own schools, its own techniques. These aspects of professionalism may have their bureaucratic, exclusionary function, but they have other functions as well, such that people in other parts of the world found much to learn from the American version of the profession.[4]

The American Association for Labor Legislation continued to exist, but it paid less attention to social insurance and more to strikes, and particularly to safety legislation, industrial accidents, and sickness. In 1927 it was joined by the much weaker American Association for Old-Age Legislation, the guiding spirit of which was Abraham Epstein, whose *Facing Old Age* had appeared in 1922 and whose *Insecurity: A Challenge to America* would appear in 1933. Sometimes the two organizations seemed more bent on arguing with each other than on affecting social policy, but they did keep broader issues alive. For example, the number of states having some form of old-age assistance continued to expand. These laws were modeled on the widow's pension laws and thus were essentially slight modifications of the poor laws. The first law, that of the territory of Alaska, was passed in 1915, but ten other states passed some form of an old-age assistance law between 1923 and 1929. Of these, only California could be characterized as an industrial state. The laws, however, were in any real sense trivial, because as late as 1929 only about one thousand people in the whole country were receiving assistance under the laws. By the time of Franklin Roosevelt's inauguration, something like one hundred times that many people were nominally on the roles, but even that figure was tiny, and many programs were bankrupt.[5] Much the same thing can be said about the mother's pension laws, although they were already in effect well before the war. The Children's Bureau reported that as of 1931 some 36,000 families in cities across the country were receiving aid that varied in average monthly amount from $10 in Dallas to $73 in Boston, with the majority of cities providing between $30 and $50. Again, the number of people being helped was trivial.[6]

The only program of the federal government was the Sheppard-Towner Act of 1921, providing federal matching funds for states establishing maternal and well-baby clinics. Its supporters saw it as a beginning, but the appropriations were small and finally ended only eight years after they began. In the general area of income maintenance, the federal government took no part.

Even when there were economic crises at the end of the 1920s, attempts to deal with them were through traditional private and local mechanisms. Herbert Hoover had first come to public attention as administrator of relief to starving Europe in 1918–19. As secretary of commerce from 1921 to 1929, he was generally concerned with quite other matters.[7] His credentials as an efficient and humane relief administrator were renewed in 1927, however, when the Mississippi Valley was flooded. The secretary of commerce left Washington to go into the devastated area and organized efficient relief through the Red Cross and other voluntary and local agencies. It was a large operation embracing more than 170 counties and must be counted a success. People were helped over the emergency.

In the summer of 1930, though, a major drought hit the lower Mississippi Valley, extended north to the Ohio Valley, to the East Coast via the Upper South and Southern Midwest, and went as far west as Oklahoma and Texas. More than one thousand counties in twenty-one states eventually needed some form of relief. In August, now President Hoover established a Federal Drought Relief Committee, which included representatives of twenty states, the federal government and the Red Cross. The committee tried to assess needs all across the drought area, and it concluded that a loan program—not grants—of $60 million would be necessary. A bipartisan bill to this effect was introduced with—the members of Congress believed—the backing of the Hoover administration. This bill included food for the hungry as one of the approved objects for loans. Apparently without consulting anyone from Congress, however, Hoover proposed a substitute bill for

$25 million, to be limited to loans for animal feed, fertilizer, and fuel oil. As part of his relief package, the President also proposed speeding up construction of already approved public works.

Senators from the drought states tried to get loans for food included in the bill, arguing that if it was not a "dole" to feed mules it could not be a dole to feed children. When that move failed, the senators tried to appropriate $25 million to the Red Cross as a non-partisan way of distributing relief. The Red Cross itself declined to become that much of a government agency and instead launched a $10 million fund-raising drive, while assuring the country that it could handle the situation. Tempers flared both inside and outside of Congress as the relief bills were debated, and the short tempers were not over trivial issues. Republican Representative John Tilson, majority leader in the House, warned that "once . . . our local charities are paralyzed, as they will be when the federal government takes over responsibility for charitable relief, the appropriations that must follow . . . would now stagger belief." He was confident, he said, that the road the nation should follow was the road that had always been followed—a road "lined on both sides with ten thousand charitable agencies maintained by generous givers ready to minister to those in need."[8]

There was no detailed philosophy of government in the response, just a desperate need, but out of that need came an implicit philosophy. And that philosophy was radical. It might not be radical for Germany, Great Britain, or Denmark, but it was for the U.S. House of Representatives in 1931. "It is the duty of the government," said Representative Edward Eslik from Tennessee (and this Southern Democrat left no doubt that he meant the federal government), "to take care of its people and see that they do not starve or freeze."[9] Finally, in March 1931 the administration approved an appropriation of $45 million in loans for feed, fertilizer, and fuel, plus $20 million for "crop production and rehabilitation." Senator William Borah pressed the secretary of agriculture to state just what that phrase meant, and the secretary eventually admitted that the words could include food for people.[10]

The debate over drought relief took place in the context of worsening depression. Arguments made on the former issue clearly applied also to the latter. The depression was of a different order of magnitude than previous depressions, even the great sag in the 1890s. It called into question that most basic of all American beliefs—that the country offered a bountiful and ever-expanding prosperity. Instead of being dissipated by a return to boom, the depression got ever worse. Private charity, public relief, and national policy seemed unable to effect the slide downward, ever downward. President Hoover tried to retain old ways of thinking, but the country as a whole was developing new ways.

In Great Britain, people had two decades to develop new ways of thinking. In the United States, the drop from prosperity to depression was more sudden and shocking. Attempts to maintain continuity, while existing in both countries, were more quickly abandoned in the United States. President Hoover tried to maintain as much continuity as he could. In 1930 he revived the President's Emergency Committee on Employment, which with a slightly different name had been created during the depression of 1921, then lapsed. As the depression of the 1930s worsened, the committee changed its name to the President's Emergency Committee on Unemployment and finally to the President's Committee on Unemployment Relief. At first the committee simply tried to systematize and centralize traditional methods for dealing with unemployment. That alone constituted something of a change. However, staff members sent to survey the situation in the winter and spring of 1931 reported that unemployment was at crisis levels and that employers and local officials were near panic. Yet the committee continued to express satisfaction with the voluntary and local agencies: "The President's Committee is convinced that the most effective relief for unemployment distress can be accomplished through locally provided funds locally administered," they said in July 1931.[11]

Congress heard the cry for relief more distinctly than the executive branch did. In the winter of 1931–32, Robert La Follette held hearings ostensibly on a bill to create a National Economic Council. The hearings were a device for La Follette and others to make the point that local relief and private relief were being overwhelmed and that the federal government must act. The bills that La Follette and Senator Edward P. Costigan from Colorado introduced as a consequence of these hearings contained money for relief—some outright grants to the states and some federally financed work relief. None of the bills passed.[12]

Despite his devotion to a balanced budget, President Hoover might approve loans made through the Reconstruction Finance Corporation (RFC). The RFC had been created early in 1932 to make loans to businesses so they could maintain production and employment—but neither had been maintained. A bill increasing the appropriation to the RFC for loans for, in a mysterious phrase, "self-liquidating" public works, especially roads, was debated throughout the winter and spring of 1932. There was considerable feeling in the House that the bill did not go far enough. The main opposition argument was the traditional one—that such large appropriations ($132 million was proposed) would unbalance the federal budget and constitute a raid on the Treasury. Proponents replied that there was no way to aid the unemployed without spending money. The bill passed the House by a margin of better than 5 to 1 and the Senate by an unrecorded but large majority. Although he had already vetoed similar bills, President Hoover reluctantly signed this bill on July 21, 1932. Another veto at this point would probably have been overridden.[13] States and municipalities immediately flooded the RFC with applications for the "loans," which everyone knew would never be repaid. They were canceled by later legislation—that is, after only two years of depression the American political system had abandoned long-held views about public relief and even federal relief and had responded in an emergency way to a crises.

While members of both parties had stood on both sides of the issue, relief was more clearly identified with the Democrats, and resistance with the Republicans. The identification became more complete when President Hoover ordered the army to evict the "Bonus Army" from their shantytown on Anacostia Flats in Washington, D.C. The Bonus Army was a group of destitute war veterans, numbering as many as twenty thousand, some with wives and children, demanding that a bonus due to be paid in 1945 be granted immediately, in 1932. The President concluded that they were a mob of dangerous radicals, and General Douglas MacArthur, with the aid of tanks, routed the ragtag group.

President Hoover and the conservatives believed responsibility for relief lay with the states and localities. As the depression worsened, the states were beginning to act, first very cautiously, then with more urgency. Just as Hoover had a President's Emergency Committee on Employment, so Governor Franklin D. Roosevelt established a New York Committee on the Stabilization of Industry and for the Prevention of Unemployment. There were similar commissions in Ohio, Illinois, and Pennsylvania, but when New York's commission reported in December 1930, it was the first to do so. The recommendations, all of which could have been endorsed by any member of either party, proposed spreading the work and establishing a system of state employment offices.

Although almost all other industrial countries, certainly the four treated in this book, had unemployment insurance by this time, and although Franklin Roosevelt had endorsed unemployment insurance at the 1930 Governors Conference, the commission tiptoed gingerly around the question. Insurance in private firms was praised, but the report expressed doubt that such plans would be adequate. "We are aware that American opinion is by no means settled on the wisdom of such elaborate systems of unemployment insurance as have been adopted in England and European continental countries. . . . On the other hand, the public conscience is not comfortable when good men anxious to work are unable to find employment." But the report made clear that something must be done, because even after the depression "despite efforts to minimize it, some unemployment will remain."[14] Governor Franklin Roosevelt and Frances Perkins, chairman of the New York State Industrial Commission and later, as the first woman cabinet member, President Roosevelt's secretary of labor, tried to help "settle" American opinion with a conference of governors of six industrialized states (Ohio, New Jersey, Rhode Island, Connecticut, Massachusetts, and New York) in Albany in February 1931. The conference heard a number of papers advocating compulsory unemployment insurance.[15]

The governor of New York also acted a little more vigorously than most on the question of relief. On September 23, 1931, he signed into law an act creating the New York Temporary Emergency Relief Administration (TERA). The act declared that there was an emergency that threatened the "public health and safety" and that no local ordinances could nullify the act. The language was necessary to avoid New York City's ban on "outdoor relief," still extant from 1897. TERA is important in its own right, but more so because its administrator, its verbal caution, and its policy boldness were all direct models for the Federal Emergency Relief Administration begun when Franklin Roosevelt became President of the United States. The administrator was Harry L. Hopkins, an Iowan who had worked for a number of private agencies, including the Red Cross, before becoming TERA administrator. Later he was to run so many New Deal agencies that he would be known as the "minister of relief." In 1931, however, he was not known as a radical. He had, after all, worked for such traditional private charity organizations as the Association for Improving the Condition of the Poor.

The verbal caution is indicated in the first paragraph of the law creating TERA: "The duty of providing aid for those in need . . . is primarily an obligation of the municipalities." Because municipal expenses could be 40 percent reimbursed by TERA, most municipalities decided to cooperate, but they were not forced to and a few did not. In October 1932 a TERA report reiterated that the state would not supply administrators but would rely on local administration. The reality was a little less cautious. TERA soon found itself supplying if not "administrators" then people with the title "investigator," because many localities lacked trained personnel. These "investigators" were borrowed from private social work agencies, community chests, church charities, and the like, and in effect constituted a new and larger bureaucracy of public welfare.

The case with financing was similar. TERA started with $20 million out of current revenue, but Roosevelt soon proposed a $30 million bond issue, which he defended on emergency grounds: "I am well aware of the fact that this would be a departure from the pay-as-you-go policy; I am also aware of the fact, however, that conditions which now face us, in their gravity akin to war conditions, warrant deviation from that principle." The bond issue was approved in November 1930, and another $60 million would come in the same election that sent Roosevelt to the White House. During TERA's first two years of existence, $130 million was spent, about half for work relief (for which Hopkins had a theoretical preference) and half for what was called "home relief." There was a means test and an attempt on the part of the agency to determine a minimum necessary budget. At its height there were on TERA's roles some 400,000 "families," which term included unattached individuals. Thus while taking local and traditional sensibilities into account, Hopkins and Roosevelt simply went ahead and did what they believed needed to be done. Neither paid much attention to economic theories.[16]

New York was in the forefront on relief, but that was by no means the case with unemployment insurance. Here leadership came from Wisconsin and the close cooperation between academics at the University of Wisconsin and the state government. The Wisconsin act was an important influence on the way the Social Security Act was later written, and many of the people central to writing the Social Security Act came from Wisconsin. Some form of unemployment insurance bill had been introduced into the legislature every session since 1921, most of them written by John R. Commons at the university. None of them had gotten very far, in spite of endorsement from the Wisconsin Federation of Labor. In 1931 a new insurance bill appeared. Some of the larger employers in the country had set up reserve funds to take care of unemployed workers. The 1931 Groves Bill, named after its sponsor in the Wisconsin Assembly, made such a fund compulsory for Wisconsin employers. Organized labor and organized farmers favored the bill, while the Wisconsin Manufacturers Association favored a voluntary plan. The pro-insurance forces simply said that the compulsory feature would not apply to firms having voluntary plans as good as the compulsory one. As in Denmark with the "social reform," this amounted to compelling people to join a voluntary scheme. One author of the Wisconsin act was Paul A. Rauschenbusch, son-in-law of Justice Brandeis. He praised the plan of individual reserves as "the closest possible adaptation to actual business conditions and attitudes in this country." In other words, the aim of the act was not to introduce a new social philosophy, but to accomplish what needed to be accomplished while requiring as small a change in thinking as possible.[17]

By the time of the presidential election of 1932, there was considerable pressure and the beginning of achievement in most of the income-maintenance programs that would be inaugurated over the next few years. There were old-age pensions in several of the largest firms, pensions for many teachers, and some system of old-age assistance in many states. There were federal pensions for civil servants. There was, on paper, aid for dependent children in virtually all the states. Unemployment insurance was law in one state, as well as the rule in some large firms; it was being actively considered in several states. Relief was being centralized from local to state level and in the guise of loans was in fact being offered at the federal level. Work relief was favored, but opposition to "home relief" was weakening. Whereas Herbert Hoover had grudgingly acceded to some of these pressures, Franklin Roosevelt would encourage them—indeed, he was a part of them. The country, almost numbed by the shock of sudden depression, might have been willing to accept almost any change. Roosevelt, however, built on what already existed. Almost nothing he did was totally unprecedented. Yet the sum of these changes amounted to giving up long-held views. Representative Eslik's belief became national policy: it is the duty of the government to take care of its people and see that they do not starve or freeze.

18

The United States Adopts the Welfare State

There is some evidence that President Franklin D. Roosevelt may have had in mind something like the Beveridge Report for the United States, but nothing as far-reaching as that was accomplished during his administration, or indeed during subsequent administrations. Yet for the United States the New Deal was the great transformation. It brought the nation into the mainstream of welfare state developments from which it had consciously been standing aside up to then. The relief and social insurance reforms of the New Deal were rapid and sharp departures from what had existed. They took history into account, but they constituted a major movement within those historical constraints.[1]

All presidential candidates assert that the fate of the nation turns on the current election, but in 1932 there was more substance in the claim. The nation had seen how reluctant Hoover was to meet the needs of the depression. Although there was no very clear idea of what kind of alternative the governor of New York would come up with, at least he would not be more of the same. Probably general knowledge of Roosevelt's actions as governor were only dimly perceived outside his home state, although his relief program must have had some impact on the perceptions of the electorate.

Roosevelt sought to assure the business community that he would not be financially reckless, and in fact he attacked Hoover for unbalancing the budget. In the course of the campaign, Roosevelt spoke on almost every side of every issue. He was in favor of high tariffs and of low tariffs. He would cut government expenses, yet run a deficit in case of "dire necessity." Some scholars have found the shape of almost the entire New Deal in the campaign, which is possible, but there was so much else that no one could tell what Roosevelt favored. What Roosevelt said may have had little effect on how he was perceived. People knew two things about him: he was a "wet"—that is, against prohibition—and he was not Herbert Hoover. Probably a white rabbit—provided he was a wet Democratic rabbit—could have won against Hoover. Hoover accused Roosevelt of wanting to change the system, and this probably helped Roosevelt. A change was just what most people thought was needed, and what they voted for on Election Day.

For President Roosevelt, the most important part of his program was clearly the part aimed at recovery and prevention of other depressions. The National Industrial Recovery Administration was to stabilize wages, employment, production, and prices in industry. The Agricultural Adjustment Administration had the same purpose in agriculture. The Securities and Exchange Commission was to guard against some of the more flagrant abuses in the stock market. New banking regulations were meant to restore confidence in the credit structure.

While no one in Washington thought that relief could solve the problems of the depression, it was equally true that everyone knew that federal relief was needed, and promptly. Unemployment figures for the nation averaged about 24 percent at the height of the depression, but in some states it was closer to half the work force. Private charity, local welfare agencies, and state boards had long since reached the end of their possibilities, and only federal relief remained. On May 12, 1933, President Roosevelt created the Federal Emergency Relief Administration (FERA) with Harry Hopkins as administrator and an initial appropriation of $500 million.

Hopkins set to work with a zeal and vigor that made even other vigorous administrators in Washington look lazy. The contrast with the caution of Sidney Webb, as head of the Committee on Unemployment in London, is even more striking. At the outset Hopkins decided that public relief would be administered only by public agencies. In a sense this was creating difficulties for himself. There were hundreds of private groups—family agencies, church groups, settlement houses—willing and eager to administer relief if they had the money. Hopkins favored using the people in these organizations but hiring them as civil servants. As with the Temporary Emergency Relief Administration in New York State, private charity was eclipsed by public relief. There seems to have been no serious discussion of this decision, but its effect was to emphasize a sharp break with what Hoover called "the American System." Yet in another way, FERA maintained a tradition that would also reach into the Social Security Act—state administration. FERA would make grants to the states that would equal one-third of the relief spent by the state. If the states had no resources, there could be outright grants, with no state matching. The initial grants, made on a matching basis, were authorized less than two weeks after Roosevelt's executive order creating FERA, and the first nonmatching grant was made about a month later. The funds were to be administered by state emergency relief administrations.[2]

The authorized $500 million was granted in 1933, making up about 60 percent of the funds distributed by FERA (the remainder being state and local funds distributed through the FERA apparatus), but by the end of 1934 so many states had run out of funds that federal grants were more than 75 percent of the total. There were notable regional differences, however. In New England a large proportion of the money—roughly 40 percent—came from local sources, while in the Deep South almost none did. In October 1933 a bit more than 10 percent of the population was on relief.[3]

This regional variation leads naturally to the question of how blacks, still primarily in the South, fared under the relief program. Aware of the issue, the Washington office included specific studies of the race of relief recipients in its reports. In the nation as a whole, about twice as high a *percentage* of blacks as whites were on relief (18 percent vs. 9.5 percent) in October 1933. In some states, however, the proportion was lower, and because blacks were disproportionately poor, it should have been higher. In Washington itself the proportion was higher, with some 10 times as great a percentage of blacks on relief as whites. The most careful study of blacks and relief concludes that in general in northern cities blacks were treated reasonably fairly, in southern cities less fairly, and in southern rural areas very unfairly.[4]

Although Hopkins had administered "home relief" in New York, he came to adopt traditional American attitudes against giving something for nothing. The New Dealers in general explicitly disliked the British dole and preferred "work relief" even though it was more expensive. In the summer and fall of 1933, Hopkins persuaded President Roosevelt to inaugurate the Civil Works Administration (CWA) with Hopkins as administrator. The Federal Emergency Relief Administration continued to distribute direct relief, but the work relief was to be taken over and enlarged by the CWA. The executive order establishing the Civil Works Administration was issued on November 9, 1933, with Hopkins pledging to have 4 million people on the roles by the end of the year. He started with the 2 million already on FERA work relief, but doubling that figure was a huge challenge. He did not quite meet his goal, for it was not until the end of January that the Civil Works Administration reached 4 million people.

A crucial difference between the Civil Works Administration and the Federal Emergency Relief Administration was that under the new program people would receive "regular work for regular wages," as Hopkins telegrammed the state emergency relief administrators, who now also became the state civil works administrators. Work would still go to the unemployed, but once a person was in that category there would be no means test, work would not be given in relation to need, and wherever possible people would be employed in their own skill. The one attempt to spread the work was the limitation that in general the work week would be 30 hours (later reduced to 24 hours in cities and 15 hours in rural areas).

There was an explicit effort, pushed by Eleanor Roosevelt, to take special notice of the needs of women, who hitherto had been generally treated as dependents. Starting with a White House Conference on the Emergency Needs of Women on November 20, 1933—that is, less than two weeks after the Civil Works Administration was inaugurated—the CWA made special efforts to find work considered appropriate for women. Presumably many women could have done some of the labor usual in relief work—clearing paths in parks and the like—but the CWA established projects in specifically "female" occupations. Sewing employed the most women, with clerks, typists, and librarians next in order. Women worked as nurses, adult educators, and participants in a large study of children's health. Many CWA projects kept no records of the gender of the recipient, but from the records that do exist it appears that more than 300,000 women were employed.

Of the men, by far the largest number were employed on roads, but this did not mean simply pick-and-shovel work. Surveyors, draftsmen, engineers, and carpenters worked in their own trades. Large numbers worked on public buildings, such as sewage treatment stations, courthouses, and firehouses. Swamps were drained, sanitary privies were built, emergency airports were constructed. The most massive project was under the direction of Parks Commissioner Robert Moses of New York City, who alone put 63,000 men to work on every conceivable aspect of the city parks.

At the height of its popularity, the Civil Works Administration ran into predictable opposition. Many CWA projects—even traditional relief work like road repair—was in direct competition with private business. Even when that was not the case, workers might prefer the relative security of a CWA job to the uncertainties of private employment in a depression. In a purely financial sense, the Civil Works Administration became harder and harder to justify, with costs many times FERA costs for an equivalent number of people. In the middle of February 1934—only a little more than three months after it had begun—the CWA received its final money by executive order: $450 million to close down. All relief work relapsed into being a FERA responsibility. The Federal Emergency Relief Administration took over unfinished projects, but paid wages only in relation to need and then only "security wages" rather than regular wages.[5]

For about the next year, the Federal Emergency Relief Administration carried the major burden of relief, until May 1935, when the Works Progress Administration (WPA) was created. From 1935 until as late as 1941, the WPA was the largest civilian employer in the United States, having between about 1.5 million and 3 million people on its rolls at any one time. The Works Progress Administration was a combination of the philosophies of the Federal Emergency Relief Administration and work relief as pioneered by the Civil Works Administration.

The largest part of the accomplishments of the Works Progress Administration were in traditional areas of work relief. In the course of its six years of existence, the WPA constructed or repaired 600,000 miles of roads, built or rebuilt 116,000 bridges, and built or repaired 110,000 public buildings. Of the total cost of $11.4 billion, about half was spent on such work—far more than in any other category. But there were other types of work. WPA policy, only partly successful, was to preserve skills. This included not only skills in trades, but also skills in the professions and the arts. There was a theater project, eventually killed by Congress when they thought the plays became too left-wing politically. There was an arts project, which employed artists to paint, sometimes pursuing their own vision, sometimes murals on walls of public buildings. There was a writers project working on, among other things, detailed guides to the states. The National Youth Administration found jobs for young people, including college students. Wages were deliberately kept below those in private employment in hopes that people would move into the private sector as jobs became available.

There was a good deal of criticism and ridicule of the work of the Works Progress Administration. There were tales of ludicrous use of money, such as an allegation, which proved to be not true, that money for malaria control was being spent in New England. There were accusations of corruption, inefficiency, and workers being paid for useless work or for doing no work at all. The lazy worker, collecting pay for leaning on a shovel, has gone into American folklore in song and story. There is undoubtedly some truth in the collective memory, but most people approved of most WPA projects, and most of the projects were clearly useful or even necessary.

Other federal programs had relief as an effect—sometimes as a primary goal, sometimes as a secondary goal. There was the construction of large-scale public works, such as dams, under the Public Works Administration. The Civilian Conservation Corps brought young men from the city out to federal parks, where under semimilitary conditions they cleared brush, planted trees, built drainage ditches, and did similar conservation work.

It is difficult to arrive at any estimate of the total number of different people aided by one or another form of federal relief. The high point was in February 1934, when almost 8 million households with 28 million members were receiving home relief or work relief—that is, some 20 percent of the population were in households where there was some form of aid. The total number of people who between 1933 and 1941 received either home relief or work relief was substantially higher than that, but we do not know what number (because no records were compiled on how many people on the roles had received relief previously) except to say it was "a lot." One can say that these programs were a success in only a limited sense—people in need were helped. When the programs were decreased in 1937, the number of unemployed increased again, and the "pump-priming," at the level of New Deal expenditures, did not seem to get the economy moving again. Only the war did that.[6]

In a time that seemed naturally made for it, there was relatively little revolutionary radicalism. The Socialist Party, tiny except in a few localities, found itself helping the unemployed get relief and jobs under the federal programs and in fact the socialists became a part of the New Deal efforts. It became increasingly difficult to differentiate between them and the left wing of the Democratic Party. Although the Communist Party made small inroads, often serving immediate needs of the unemployed more than organizing revolution, there was surprisingly little radicalism in places where unemployment was worst. Many of the unemployed were either simply numb, regarding their plight as a time of terrible troubles, probably temporary, with no particularized cause. Many blamed themselves.[7]

Compared with Great Britain, Denmark, and Germany, the New Dealers showed remarkable inventiveness and freedom from the constraints of tradition, or rather a willingness to transform that tradition. A deeply held American value was that people should earn their living. All right, then, emphasize work relief! Another deeply held American value was that states should have some power. All right, then, work with state administrators of federal programs! Subsidize existing but bankrupt state programs! Businessmen, even in the depression, were believed to be able administrators. All right, then, use them to administer relief programs!

The relief efforts of the New Deal were in many ways the most dramatic of the laws and programs of the 1930s. They affected the most people, at least in the short run. Yet the only monuments they left behind were monuments—post offices, bridges, parks. In an institutional sense they left no permanent imprint. The FERA, the CWA, the WPA, and the PWA all vanished in the war, and though there has been some talk of reviving something like the Civilian Conservation Corps, there has been no serious talk of reviving the others. Relief was necessary, but social progressives within and outside the Roosevelt administration agreed that a broad program of social insurance was both necessary and a political possibility. According to Frances Perkins, Franklin Roosevelt agreed with this idea even before his inauguration, but of course he was a master at making people he spoke to believe that he agreed with them.[8]

Before the new President was sworn in, one of the major spokesmen for Roosevelt in the Senate, Robert F. Wagner of New York, began hearings on a program of retirement annuities for railroad workers. Many railroad companies already had pensions. On the one hand, this would mean that any federal legislation would not be introducing a new idea but on the other hand, it would allow the carriers to argue that there was no need for the federal laws because they were already acting voluntarily. Of course, the company pension plans were very restrictive in that they required long service for the same company (frequently thirty years), they were not uniform, and they provided no kind of vested rights in a pension. If it could be shown that even the most comprehensive private pension system was inadequate, the argument for some sort of public plan would be much strengthened.

When Senator Wagner introduced the Railroad Retirement Act in June 1934, it was not the peculiarities of the railroad business or federal jurisdiction that he emphasized. He stated clearly that this was the first step, a laboratory experiment. "I believe that a nationwide and general system of old-age protection should be devised speedily. Under the leadership of our socially minded President, such will undoubtedly be the case. But in the meantime, nothing could be more helpful than the establishment of a system . . . which will serve as a laboratory." The Railroad Retirement Act was passed on June 14 with not a single negative vote. Many of those not voting left word that they were in favor. It provided old-age pensions at age sixty-five with premiums to be paid one-third by the employees and two-thirds by the railroads. Participation was compulsory for all railroads subject to the Interstate Commerce Act, save street railways.[9]

Although the Railroad Retirement Act was declared unconstitutional in May 1935, it provided a legislative beginning for what would become a more comprehensive approach to social insurance. Harry Hopkins outlined the Roosevelt administration's overall plan for economic security to the National Conference of Social Work in May 1934. To be sure, he was talking to his old colleagues and could be expected to tell them what they wanted to hear, but he could expect the nation also to hear what so close a confidant of the President was saying. He assumed, he said, that even after the depression was over there would be a need for a considerable amount of what he called "outdoor relief" and that much of this relief would be public. In addition, however, there should be a comprehensive program to deal with the other hazards of economic life. This program should not be charity, but a combination of "pensions" and public works. This program should include old-age pensions and aid for dependent children (which at that point Hopkins was still calling widow's pensions). Both old-age and widow's pensions should be income-related. In addition, there should be unemployment insurance, which would last for a relatively short time—Hopkins suggested six to eight weeks—and a public works program that could shrink and expand with the need. He favored a program of health insurance, but one can almost see him tiptoeing on eggs as he proposed it. While saying this, he went out of his way to assure physicians that any program must protect the interests of doctors and that doctors must be central in its administration.[10]

Hopkins was not making up this program out of a combination of speculation and hope. Approximately one month later President Roosevelt established a Committee on Economic Security consisting of Secretary of Labor Frances Perkins, Secretary of Agriculture Henry A. Wallace, Secretary of the Treasury Henry Morgenthau, Attorney General Homer S. Cummings, and FERA administrator Harry L. Hopkins. Clearly Morgenthau was there to present an image of fiscal responsibility, and Cummings to indicate that someone was watching out for the constitutional questions. After all, Hopkins and Perkins might be considered social-minded progressives who would ignore fiscal and constitutional problems. In fact, an awareness of the constitutional issues hung like a threatening rain cloud over the deliberations, shaped the nature of the recommendations, and were always in the back of people's minds, even when the issues were not being explicitly discussed.

There were a few changes in the Social Security bill in Congress, but the major shape of the legislation was decided in the Committee on Economic Security working through its executive director, Edwin Witte. Witte was a part of La Follette progressivism in Wisconsin and had worked for the Wisconsin Industrial Commission and the Wisconsin Legislative Reference Library. He proved to be an excellent scholar-bureaucrat-politician. First he did a thorough job investigating the questions discussed by the Committee on Economic Security, then he skillfully wove his way among the conflicting technical reports, and finally he was an excellent witness in the congressional hearings on the bill. He was not alone, of course. He had the President and the Cabinet behind him, as well as powerful voices in Congress.[11] Beneath the Committee on Economic Security was a Technical Board of experts and an Advisory Council made up of lay people. The council included a number of sympathetic representatives of big business who turned out to be important in convincing conservative opinion that the Social Security Act would not be the entering wedge for Bolshevism.

The greatest controversy within the Committee on Economic Security was over unemployment insurance. Should the system be national, or state-run under federal guidelines? There was strong sentiment within the Technical Board, and some sentiment in Congress as well, for the former. The main reason it was rejected was probably the doubt about whether the U.S. Supreme Court would consider it constitutional. Clearly, however, state action would not come without some federal persuasion or coercion. The commerce clause seemed to be a weak reed, because the Supreme Court had already ruled that it could not be used to achieve social ends unconnected with commerce and would soon do so again. What was the federal carrot or stick to be?

A possible solution was suggested in one of those informal conversations so crucial to the way any large supposedly formal organization works. Sometime early in 1934, Frances Perkins and Justice

Harlan F. Stone were at a social occasion where Perkins had spoken of her hope of developing a broad social insurance program. She also mentioned her doubts, because the Supreme Court had been quite restrictive about "what the Constitution permits." Stone had answered, "The taxing power of the Federal Government, my dear; the taxing power is sufficient for everything you want and need." Perkins took the news directly to The Boss, and the taxing power became the device of choice for allowing federal action on social issues. Of course, Stone could not speak for all nine justices, so there was still doubt.[12]

The decision to reject a totally federal system was not made until November 9, 1934, so the rest of the work on unemployment compensation had to be done quickly. The federal government used the taxing power to levy a tax on every employer of eight or more. Some 90 percent of this tax would be refunded to any state that would use the refunded amount for an unemployment insurance law. The 10 percent would be for federal administration, because the actual money was to be kept in the federal Treasury. The whole elaborate mechanism was in a sense a subterfuge, a way to exercise federal leverage that would be allowed by the U.S. Supreme Court. The Republicans pointed this out during congressional debate, and they were clearly right. New Dealers, however, believed they were forced into the subterfuge by the restrictive social ideas of the justices.[13]

The other major area of concern for the Committee on Economic Security was old age. Without much controversy, the committee agreed that there should be a program of federal matching grants to aid the states. This provision, which Witte and the CES wrote with ease, turned out to be controversial in two ways. The first was the quite reasonable objection that in the poorest states—where the aid was most needed—matching the federal funds would be difficult. The other objection was simply unanticipated by Witte, who had lived his whole life in Wisconsin. Senator Harry Flood Byrd and others were afraid that the provisions of the Social Security bill might be taken as dictating to the states—that is, the Southern states—to whom they must give old-age assistance, including blacks on a nondiscriminatory basis. There seems to have been little inclination at any level of the administration to insist on standards of racial equality. The CES quickly concluded that if there was suspicion that the federal government was dictating to the states on the issue the bill would not pass, so the objectionable passages were rewritten.[14]

Although half a century later old-age assistance and the insurance aspects of the Social Security Act may seem to be quite unrelated programs, the two were viewed at the time as aspects of the same issue. Assistance was often referred to as the "noncontributory old-age program," the annuities as the "contributory" part of the program. This was partly because the annuity program would not benefit those near, at, or above retirement age, and Witte estimated that there were several million people in that category.

The old-age annuity program resorted to the same device the unemployment insurance program used, but this time it was entirely federal, instead of being a state-federal cooperative program. The Technical Board reported that no lifetime annuities could be run state by state, that people simply moved around too much. A tax was put on employers and employees as part of the taxing power. These funds were put in a reserve fund, and the federal government would pay pensions to retirees over the age of sixty-five who had been contributing to the fund. As Witte wrote, what the committee sought was "to get away from an insurance plan altogether, but to establish the equivalent of such a plan without resorting to definite insurance."[15] What they sought, in fact, was insurance that the Supreme Court would be willing to approve. The "aid to dependent children" aspects of the Social Security Act—essentially federal grants to the widow's pension programs in the states, became the largest welfare program in the United States. That was not foreseen at the time, and that portion of the bill was developed and passed with relatively little controversy.

As one could anticipate, the greatest amount of opposition the Committee on Economic Security encountered was over health insurance. There were objections from doctors about the people running the subcommittee on health, about representation on the medical advisory board, and about the subject as a whole. A long editorial in the *Journal of the American Medical Association* argued that the administration was trying to ram health insurance through without consulting the profession. Physician and social insurance proponent Isaac Rubinow remarked, "If we continue making progress, soon we may be where we were in 1916." Even that bitter remark was too optimistic. The records of the CES bulge with more correspondence on this subject than on any other. Not all the correpondence is hostile, for some doctors favored compulsory medical insurance, but the American Medical Association took an increasingly adamant position. Perkins and Hopkins favored making health insurance part of the Social Security bill, but Witte thought it would doom the whole bill. In December 1934, Witte could answer Arkansas Democratic Senator Joseph Robinson that the "committee does not expect to make any recommendations for health insurance legislation." The final decision not to include health insurance, even as a supplementary bill, was made by President Roosevelt sometime in the summer of 1935.[16]

No significant changes occurred during congressional hearings on the bill, but the views of various groups were heard. Many witnesses opposed any increase in federal spending, and the National Association of Manufacturers sent three spokesmen to argue against further increasing the national debt. They also opposed any bill that would "decrease individual energy and efficiency of individuals attempting to take care of themselves." The manufacturers also argued that the bill was clearly unconstitutional.

Paul Kellogg, speaking for leading social workers at the hearings, thought the bill should go much further. He regretted that a thoroughgoing federal system of social insurance had been rejected, but believed there should be more federal participation in the unemployment insurance and that there should be higher benefits paid for a longer time.

Charles H. Houston, for the National Association for the Advancement of Colored People (NAACP), spoke bitterly against the bill. The NAACP was struggling for national recognition, but it was uncompromising in its opposition. This uncompromising position was quite reasonable because the bill excluded domestics and agricultural workers and made no provisions for non-wage-earners, such as sharecroppers or tenant farmers. Houston estimated that, simply on its face, the bill excluded about three-fifths of the black population. In addition, the old-age assistance, child welfare, and unemployment insurance sections did not contain any nondiscrimination requirements. Moreover, many of the states that did not have any old-age assistance laws were in the South, where most blacks still lived, and there was no requirement that the states pass such laws.

Earl Browder of the Communist Party opposed the bill at the hearings as totally inadequate to protect the living standards of the masses. John B. Andrews of the American Association for Labor Legislation thought the bill was excellent. But the most amusing portion of the hearings came when Dr. F. E. Townsend of California was the witness. Townsend was the leader of a huge popular movement to give everyone over the age of sixty and retired $200 a month, provided it would all be spent within 30 days. There were "Townsend Clubs" all over the country, armies of supporters, a newspaper, and a fervor most appropriate to a revival meeting. There was even a bill in Congress aimed at putting his plan into effect. It would be fair to say that the Senate Committee on Finance made hash of Townsend and his plans at the hearings. His figures did not work out, he did not have adequate information or adequate arguments. After he left the stand, the Townsend (McGroarty) Bill in Congress was changed so that it was not that different from the old-age assistance portion of the Social Security bill. The Townsend movement lived on, but it had no further legislative reality.[17]

Articles in more-popular magazines reflected the views of the groups that had testified at the hearings, yet the business members of the Advisory Council acted as a counterweight to the arguments of the National Association of Manufacturers, which was mostly representative of smaller businesses.

In May 1935, while congress was in the midst of considering the Social Security bill, the Supreme Court made clear what could not be done. In a 5-to-4 decision the Court declared the Railroad Retirement Act unconstitutional. The act had established a pension system in accordance with the power to regulate interstate commerce, but the Supreme Court, in *Railroad Retirement Board et al. v. Alton Railroad Company et al.*,[18] declared that establishing a pension was "not in purpose or effect a regulation of interstate commerce within the meaning of the Constitution." "There is no limit," wrote Justice Owen Roberts in his opinion, under the theory he rejected, "to the field of so-called regulation." He then gave a series of horrible examples, such as free medical attention and housing for workers, and asked, "Is it not apparent that they are really and essentially related solely to the social welfare of the worker, and therefore remote from any regulation of commerce as such?" That said about as plainly as could be that the commerce clause could not be used for social purposes. The bill was almost immediately repassed in Congress, with the taxing power instead of the commerce clause as its legal basis. Ironically, by the time the principle of taxation for federal purposes got to the Supreme Court, Justice Roberts had decided to take a broader view of the meaning of commerce and of the powers of the federal government, so that even the previous method of financing and justifying federal intervention might have met with 5-to-4 approval.[19]

Besides the administration bill, there were two other bills in Congress on Social Security: the revised Townsend Bill and the Lundeen Bill, introduced by a representative from Minnesota and supported by the Socialist and Communist parties. The Lundeen Bill was a general compulsory social insurance bill for unemployment, old age, health, and disability and provided that the insured would receive "the prevailing local wage" in times of unemployment. Neither bill had much political backing, but their existence is an indication that the most telling political criticism of the Social Security bill was that it did not go far enough. The alternatives were easily defeated, and the Social Security Act passed both Houses by a margin of better than 10 to 1. It became law on August 14, 1935, a day that should be considered the moment at which the United States began to be a member of the Western world's capitalist welfare states.[20]

One can find all kinds of motives, pressure groups, and arguments to explain the passage of this act that seems to be such a departure from previous history. The experts believed they had great influence. Some historians see it as a triumph of long-term liberal pressures. Others consider support from large business and business precedents as decisive. Others see Social Security as a protective reaction against more radical solutions. All these views perceive a bit of the truth, yet the overwhelming driving force was surely the desperation of the depression. Aid to families with dependent children was by now an old tradition. Most state programs were bankrupt. Old-age assistance programs were widespread. Most state programs were bankrupt. Unemployment was such an obvious problem that no one needed to point to it. No matter how many experts, how much liberal pressure, how much business precedent, this step would not have been taken without the depression. The overwhelming majorities in Congress indicate that the step was not considered a radical one, for people with a very wide spectrum of political views voted for the act. Social Security was, in the words of Clarke Chambers, "the welfare consensus of the New Deal."[21]

It took almost two years for legal challenges to the Social Security Act to reach the Supreme Court, but in May 1937 the Court in two companion cases certified the constitutionality of the act. The decisions were as wide-ranging in their way as *Alton* had been in its way. In *Stewart Machine Co. v. Davis,* which had to do with the unemployment compensation section of the Social Security Act, the majority in the 5-to-4 decision argued that the tax-offset mechanism was a valid way for the nation to meet a national problem. After asserting that unemployment was a national problem as well as a local problem, the Court said, "There was need of help from the nation if the people were not to starve. It is too late today for the argument to be heard with tolerance that in a crisis so extreme the use of the moneys of the nation to relieve the unemployed and their dependents is a use for any purpose narrower than the promotion of the general welfare." One could hardly propose a sentence giving broader power over welfare to the federal government. *Helvering v. Davis* validated the old-age benefits in much the same terms, but in addition asserted that Congress could reasonably conclude that old-age pensions must be on a national rather than state level and that the states had to conform.[22]

By the time these cases were decided, all the states had passed unemployment compensation laws, and the Social Security Board was heavily involved in approving them or negotiating with states about aspects of the laws that the board disapproved of—for example paying the unemployment funds through state offices of "poor relief." Forty of the forty-eight states had some system of merit rating, so that firms with more stable records of employment paid lower premiums, and forty-four states had pooled funds. Many states insured employees at firms that were smaller than the Social Security Act required. In most states the premiums were paid entirely by the employer, but in eight states (Alabama, California, Indiana, Kentucky, Louisiana, Massachusetts, New Hampshire, and Rhode Island) the employee also contributed up to one-third. Benefits were usually half the normal wages, to a maximum of $15 a week, and the benefit period varied between twelve and twenty weeks. The U.S. Bureau of Labor Statistics estimated that some 25 million workers were covered, about half the labor force.[23]

All the states had programs for public health, for aid to dependent children, and for old-age assistance and programs of public assistance. The old-age annuity program was functioning. The system as a whole was functioning, and although continuously modified, it has been functioning ever since. Thirty years after the Social Security Act was first passed, a limited health insurance was added.

The law was certainly a cautious one, careful to offend as few centers of power as possible, particularly in the Congress. Southern whites would find no challenge to racism, doctors no challenge to their status or earning. Workers in small firms were not covered by the unemployment compensation, and states could have laws that were quite varied. Most blacks were not covered by the law, and there was not a single anti-racial-discrimination clause anywhere. The premiums for the old-age annuities—to use the real terms rather than the subterfuges—were regressive, and the pensions for most people would be very small. All the programs have needed modification, sometimes because of unforeseen problems, sometimes because American society changed.

Yet with all these limitations, with all this pandering to the various groups in the Congress and the nation, the law was a phenomenal new departure. Franklin Roosevelt, the Committee on Economic Security, and supporters in Congress, working within constraints imposed by the political, economic, and intellectual world of which they were a part, had made that world move. The central government of the United States was now involved in a fundamental way with the well-being of every citizen. Even where the involvement was not direct, the central government set up requirements that states had to meet in devising their own programs. Perhaps it was a small step, but it was probably the largest step that could have been taken at that time, and it was a step in a new direction. With the Social Security Act, the United States had begun.[24]

The Social Security Act provided what every industrial Western country had had, some for decades. The passage of the act signaled the recognition that in a wage economy, even that of the United States, interruptions in earnings could throw a family into destitution, and these interruptions could not all be guarded against by the prudent or saved for by the thrifty. The act also seemed to recognize that government was not necessarily a tyrant to be limited, but could be an expression of the society acting in common to spread risk. Yet the act was by no means simply a transformed German, British, or Danish social insurance act. It took into account state powers, trod carefully around constitutional issues, and tried hard to accommodate important pressure groups. It built on existing programs of old-age and mother's pensions. It even tried hard to accommodate strongly held ideas on what constituted businesslike insurance principles. And yet it was a greater transformation than Bismarck's reforms, the Danish social insurance laws, or national insurance in Great Britain. It required a greater change in thinking than any of them.

PART FIVE

Conclusion

19

Assumptions and Perceptions

A certain type of joke, currently in disrepute, begins "There was an American, a Dane, and a German who were . . ." and goes on to build on the presumed national characteristics of each. Scholarship is supposed to destroy such simple national stereotyping, for of course there is no typical Dane, German, or anything else. Yet these stereotypes are built on something other than nasty remarks made by disgruntled tourists or occupation armies. After living for a considerable time in all four countries under study in this book, I have come to the conclusion that there is something to these myths—not applying to any individual, and certainly not genetic, but with some social basis. In summing up the results of this study and trying to strain out the assumptions and perceptions in the four countries— some of the assumptions having to do directly with poverty and welfare, some more indirectly—I have to admit to strengthening some of the stereotypes. The German system was in fact heavily bureaucratized. The British were unbending. The Danes have a strong and sometimes oppressive sense of group. The Americans are individualistic, materialistic, and intellectually flexible. In this case, therefore, scholarship has not eliminated the stereotypes, but made them more complex, more nuanced.

The uniformities in this story either involve a distortion of history or are banal. All four countries were Western and resemble one another more than any resemble a hunting-gathering nomadic tribe. None of them had an urban-industrial welfare state until there were urban-industrial economies. Beyond these kinds of obvious remarks, uniformities that have so far been suggested simply do not work, even for these four countries and still less if one includes more countries. The degree of industrialization varied widely among the countries at the time their income-maintenance legislation was passed. Denmark was relatively slightly industrialized in the 1890s, and by the decade before World War I, Great Britain was heavily industrialized. The degree to which the labor movement was politically active varied widely and the extent of socialism within the labor movement does not seem to have been decisive. In some cases it appears that political democracy was influential, in other places it was not. The most recent survey of the history of social legislation in fifteen European countries during the last century, after a survey of the historical literature and the historical record, concludes that none of the generalizations scholars have proposed is borne out by the events.[1]

The conclusion we must make is in the sentence from Alexander von Humboldt quoted in the Introduction: "Whenever we offer philosophical or political reasons for political institutions, we will in actuality always find historical explanations." Germany reacted in a certain way to urban-industrial poverty because of what Germany was in the 1880s, and what Germany was in the 1880s was a product of German history. The same applies to the other countries. The United States did not follow the German, Danish, or British roads to social insurance because there were American traditions and perceptions that were unique to the United States. The history of each country was not isolated—leaders in each country were aware of what was happening in all the others—but each perceived their neighbors' actions in accordance with their own preconceptions. When enthusiasts for health insurance tried to graft the German system to the United States, the graft did not take. People in each country had different perceptions of crucial concepts in the sphere of welfare legislation, concepts represented by such words as "state," "class," "poverty," "private," and even "social welfare."

Sequence and Motive

The sequence in which the four countries passed the major income-maintenance programs was similar but not identical. Germany passed the sickness and accident insurance programs almost at the same time (1883–84), old-age and disability programs a few years later, and had no unemployment insurance for some forty years. In Denmark, sickness and old-age programs were passed almost simultaneously (1891–92), accident insurance a few years later, and unemployment insurance after another few years. In Great Britain, workmen's compensation was passed more than a decade before the old-age pensions of 1908, with sickness and unemployment insurance coming three years after old-age pensions. In the United States, only workmen's compensation existed by World War I, and old-age pensions and unemployment insurance were created in 1935. There was no national program of health insurance before the 1960s. This large variation in sequence is at least a hint that the various countries were responding to imperatives within their own society that must be understood in relation to that specific society.

The central imperatives that lay behind the developing welfare states were different in each of the four countries. In Germany the overwhelming need was to weld a unified nation-state out of a political and social system that offered many alternatives. The localities had to be welded into a *Reich,* and the workers had to be made less class-conscious and more nationalist. Protestant and Catholics had to be persuaded to cooperate. A long tradition (and not only in Prussia) of an interventionist public authority made state action seem the obvious way to proceed.

The Danish system grew out of no such imperatives. In fact, national unity had been welded more firmly by military defeat at the hands of the coalescing Reich when Denmark lost the war with the Prussia in 1864. There was no threat that Danish workers would be anything other than Danes. Almost everyone was of the same religion. A society based on maintaining a fragile consensus found a solution to growing political tensions in what everyone had always agreed on anyway—the collective responsibility for the welfare of the individual.

The British belief system was also based on an attempt to preserve continuity and consensus. Both are summed up in my phrase "the principles of 1834," which refers to the moral philosophy set out in the 1834 Poor Law Report. As in Denmark, holes were punched in the poor law of 1834, but there was a difference. The thrust in Denmark was to shrink the area in which the poor law was applicable; the poor law was being explicitly abandoned. In Great Britain, however, the exceptions to the poor law were spelled out, but always with the idea that the poor law itself was left intact—that is, until the years between the world wars, during which it was destroyed and a different formulation was devised.

Until the 1930s there was no imperative driving Americans toward a welfare state. For all but a few American reformers, even among those concerned primarily with the poor, income maintenance was simply not among the issues discussed. When it came to questions of "social security," the reformers lived in the same world—actual and conceptual—as the conservatives. Above all, the reformers, like the conservatives, were aware that they were living in "a prosperous community," an open and expanding economy. If certain barriers were eliminated, certain practices forbidden, the prosperity would flow into all corners of society. "Mankind are crowding upon each other in the centers, and struggling to keep each other out of the feast set by the new science," wrote Henry Demerest Lloyd.[2] He and others took for granted that the feast was there; it only remained to regulate the struggle so that all could partake.

Types of Intellectual Justification

The types of intellectual support regarded as persuasive for action were strikingly different in the four countries. German law was based heavily on rationality and statistics—on science. The bills were always accompanied and supported by detailed statistical supplements. Premiums and benefits were calculated on a statistically sound basis, and where there were no statistics there was no legislation. In Denmark, by contrast, statistical data was considered far less important. Legislation was enacted on political or moral grounds, with the idea that it could be altered as experience dictated. The

German conception of the world was more rationalistic, the Danish conception was more historical.

In Great Britain, statistical information was not nearly as detailed as on the European continent, and assertions that did not have any discernible basis were made. Great Britain was "scientific" in another sense. Once the principles of political economy were discovered, holding fast to these principles was believed to be the way to produce correct results. The British seemed to believe in what might be called "the principle of principles"—the idea that truths that can act as immutable guides to action can be found. The Americans hardly pretended. No one knew how many work-related accidents there were, or even how many employees and or how many firms; estimates on the number of aged persons were only guesses. Americans went ahead as best they could, perhaps on the basis of that national characteristic—optimism.

State and Society

One continuum on which the four countries differed strikingly was their conception of the relationship between "the state," on one hand, and "society," on the other hand. At one extreme is Denmark, at the other is the United States. The shape Danish welfare legislation took stemmed from a conception of the relationship between the apparatus of government, on one hand, and the society, on the other, that is notable for anyone who has studied cognate debates in the United States. During the entire period from the 1880s on, all sides of the debates used the terms "society" (*samfund*), "the public" (*det offentlig*), and "national and local government" (*staten og kommunerne*) as synonyms or near synonyms. Instead of seeing "government" (for which no precisely corresponding Danish word exists) as one of many institutions in society with important but limited spheres of activity, in Denmark government was society manifest. Because government was society, the distinction between government and society was not just unimportant—it did not exist. There was disagreement about exactly what government ought to do, but that was the same as the question of what society ought to do. If society had a responsibility to the sick, the old, the unemployed, that responsibility was expressed through government. And this was an assumption on which a social democrat would find himself in agreement with a classical conservative.

In Germany there is a clear distinction between "state" and "society," and the two distinct entities have a superior-inferior relationship. In Germany there is no question but that the state can command society. No matter what degree of democracy there might be, this is not altered. "The state" after 1870 included the Reichstag (not, it need hardly be said, in foreign policy). It was the German state, not the society, which provided for social insurance.

In Great Britain the state had potentially almost as much power, as well as ultimate responsibility, as in Germany, but whereas in Germany the state was an always available resource, the assumption in Britain was that this potential resource should be used as sparingly as possible. Winston Churchill might revel in state power, but for most people every extension of state power had to be justified.

In the United States, the "state" (here meaning the entire government apparatus) was a small part of society, with important, shifting, but strictly limited powers. The basic document of government (the U.S. Constitution) sets all kinds of limits on what "the state" may do. The relationship between the state, on one hand, and society, on the other, is vividly illustrated by legislative hearings in the United States. In contrast to other countries, most hearings in the United States were means for the "state" to find out what its masters— society—wanted. Where does organized labor stand? What do social workers think? What do employers or doctors or blacks see as in their interest? In the other countries, most hearings are to probe a subject, to gather information, or to give the investigating committee an opportunity to illustrate a particular point. There is that kind of hearing in the United States as well, but the hearings on the Social Security Act, for example, were clearly of the other type—that is, society is the master, and the state is the creature, not just in a theoretical sense but in a day-to-day political sense. In Denmark most legislation is submitted to "the interests"—the national labor organization, the organized employers—for their comments. There is subtle difference here from American hearings. Denmark is consciously a society made up of subsocieties, and it is believed that the subsocieties should be allowed to participate in the legislative process. In the United States, hearings are soundings into the demos.

The Bureaucracy

The apparatus of government—the bureaucracy, the civil servants—can be seen as the manifestation of the state, at least in peacetime. It is on this issue that Germany is at one extreme, with the United States at the other. According to Jürgen Kocka, perhaps the most insightful of German social historians, the German bureaucracy cannot be rightly understood as either a "class" or a *Stand* (estate); the bureaucracy is a group sui generis, and I use the term "caste," although not really correctly.[3] This quasi-caste regarded itself as rationally administering a rational system and as having the training and wisdom to do it correctly. It was they who had ultimate supervisory powers over all aspects of civilian life, including social insurance, and they who made ultimate detailed decisions on implementation. All German social insurance laws set up a massive complex administrative apparatus with provision for representatives of the interested parties to participate, but ultimate administrative supervision. Decisions in doubtful cases or in case of a tie were always in the hands of the *Beamtenschaft* (officials). The Social Democratic Party and the social democratic labor unions regarded these officials as representatives of the enemy, and the civil servants in the *Kaiserreich* regarded the Social Democrats as threats to order, but the *Beamtenschaft* kept its power through Weimar period and even through the Nazi period. The state manifest—the bureaucracy—was implicitly acknowledged as superior to other members of society. Within this strong state apparatus considerable freedom was possible. A person might fulfill his obligations under the sickness insurance laws in a variety of ways. Geographic mobility was protected in the old-age pensions. Freedom was within the system, not in the possibility of breaking out of it.

The Danish bureaucracy was in some ways similar to the German—for instance, its members received pensions at retirement well before there were pensions for the general population. Yet the position of the Danish bureaucracy in society was not quite the same. During the nearly two centuries of relatively enlightened and honest absolute monarchy before 1848, confidence in public officials had been built up. In those years, even though final authority rested with the monarch, councils of generally competent civil servants ran the day-to-day operations of the government. Also, increase in the power of the central government had meant, in general, a protection against local tyrannies and an increase in the fairness with which government policies (e.g., taxation) were administered. When democracy came, the same staff of civil servants who had served the absolute monarch continued to administer the new form of government as they had the old, without objection from any side. Although Danish government officials enjoyed high pay and prestige, they were not regarded as a class apart in quite the same way as in Germany. They had earned respect by serving well. Nor were they granted the kind of power that their German counterparts enjoyed. When it came to social welfare legislation, it is significant that the Danish laws were far less bureaucratic than the German welfare laws. The state in Denmark held a far lighter hand over its citizens than Germany.

Great Britain was ambivalent about the apparatus of government. On the one hand, Englishmen prided themselves on being a lightly governed people with a good deal of local autonomy; they sneered at the centralization in Germany and France. On the other hand, the central government established policies, such as the factory acts and the poor law, that demanded strong central control. One result was that the laws were ignored or defied. The inspectorate system set up by each of those acts had neither the personnel nor the means to do effectively the job it was expected to do. Between the ineffective policy of issuing writs and the blockbuster policy of calling in the army, inspectors had few tools to draw on. The other result was to try to work out mechanisms for enforcing central government policies that would not involve government civil servants, or not involve them very much. The "offer of the house" was supposed to be a perfect self-acting test to distinguish the destitute from others. Neither detailed investigation nor much bureaucracy would be necessary. The invention of approved societies in the 1911 Insurance Act meant that already existing organizations would simply be folded into the system, with only limited government supervision.[4]

In the United States, contempt for government employees was almost as traditional as respect for the *Beamtenschaft* was in Germany. The American bureaucracy before 1933 was small, ill-paid, ill-educated, and often appointed as a reward for political, not academic or administrative, achievement. The Pendleton Act of 1883 made only slight improvement in the reality and no change in the conception Americans had of public officials. The incompetence and venality of government employees were often used as arguments against any enlargement of government responsibilities, including an enlarged welfare state.

Reform from Above?

Does having a powerful state with a powerful bureaucracy mean that reform in Germany was, as various critics have maintained, from above instead of what is considered the normal course of events—having reform fought for by the people? This is part of a general controversy over whether Germany fits in with the normal course of Western development or must be seen as pursuing a *Sonderweg*—that is, its own "special way" into the modern world. In Germany, reform "from above" is undoubtedly the case in many spheres, and certainly includes social insurance. To what extent is it true in other countries?

In Denmark, the basic democratic reform—that is, the 1849 constitution—came on command from above. In relation to social insurance, old-age pensions were from above. The case of sickness insurance is ambiguous. The institution had grown from below, but the law was from above. All other laws grew out of the sickness insurance law, and when that was passed the Social Democrats (presumably speaking from "below") were not a significant political force. In fact, the reforms came at a time when democracy was at a low point in Danish history. Was reform from above or below? For Great Britain, it is also difficult to differentiate between forces from above and those from below. Certainly the lawmakers felt pressures from an increasingly broad electorate. Old-age pensions may have been a direct response to these pressures, but national health and unemployment insurance presents a more ambiguous picture.

In the United States there was certainly pressure for various forms of labor legislation and for workmen's compensation "from below," but the laws came into existence only after there was pressure from above, in the form of the National Association of Manufac-

269

turers and the National Civic Federation. Even the pressure from below came filtered through the voices of social investigators, not through direct pressure from the workers. As for the 1930s, it is difficult to hold that pressure from workers brought the Social Security legislation. Workers—organized and unorganized—certainly did vote for Franklin Roosevelt, but hardly for social insurance. The law was drawn up by social workers and bureaucrats and was actually opposed by significant segments of the people it ostensibly served (although supported by others). With regard to social insurance, the German story does not appear to be strikingly different from the other three countries.[5]

Welfare as Means or Ends?

The importance of welfare legislation in the hierarchy of public concerns also varied among the countries under study. In Germany and Denmark before World War I, social welfare policy must be seen as subsidiary—that is, the welfare of the poor was seen not as an end in itself but as a means of pursuing other objectives considered "larger." In Germany the larger objectives were centralization of the government and winning the inevitable class struggle. In Denmark the larger political (and the term "larger" was actually used) objectives were avoidance of conflict on the road to a more democratic political system, and amelioration of the regrettably unavoidable class conflict. One could say that in both Germany and Denmark welfare policy was a means for attaining national unity—or better, for avoiding disunity—but in the one case the means were winning a battle, and in the other case, avoiding battle if at all possible.

This is not to imply that the welfare of the poor was not a consideration in Germany and Denmark. After all, the larger political goals could have been pursued by other means, as they were in the United States and for a considerable period in Great Britain. The United States had a problem with federalism that was as severe as Germany's, but legislation was never thought of as a way to deal with it. Class antagonisms were severe in Britain, yet until the end of the nineteenth century, welfare legislation was not aimed either at ameliorating them or at winning the class war. In Germany and Denmark a large part of the influential portion of the population understood social welfare legislation, particularly social insurance, as a natural and historically legitimated function of government, and therefore saw it as a tool for achieving other objectives. In Great Britain, welfare legislation was understood this way in only a limited sense. In the United States it was not a legitimate tool at all, and not even under serious consideration, before the depression. Instead, social *justice* was the goal in the United States, and it was presumed that well-being would automatically be the product.

Class

Economic classes and class conflict exist in all four countries, yet the concept of "class" is understood differently in each, a difference that had a direct impact on welfare legislation. In Germany the social insurance laws were for employees and are normally listed in indexes and library catalogs under "workers insurance." The eligible class is defined in terms of their position in the economic scheme—that is, in relation to the means of production. Danish indexes list social insurance the same way, but the laws were not exclusively for employees. Those eligible were always defined in terms of what they had, not in terms of their position in relation to the means of production: "people of small means" or "low-paid workers and others on the same economic level," or similar categories. A shopkeeper with a small income and a large family was also eligible. The issue was simply whether a person was needy or not.

The laws in Great Britain were explicitly for employees, but British lawmakers saw many working *classes,* not just a single working class. Their view of class thus demanded a picture that was more complex than merely the relationship to the means of production. In the United States the uses of the word "class" are a whole genre in sociological scholarship. There is much question about whether there *are* classes, in what sense, how many of them, and so on. For instance, Samuel Gompers both was very class-conscious and rejected the idea of class in connection with welfare legislation. He occasionally used the term "working class," but his more common usage was "wage-earners," a more flexible or more ill-defined group.

Social insurance was originally written for employees, but it has been extended to the "self-employed," a word that is meaningless if taken literally. The German, Danish, and British views of the working class are not applicable to American self-perceptions.

There is another aspect of the European countries' class system, especially the German system, that sets that system off from the American system. In the European countries, the gap between classes was seen more as a cultural gap, almost like a gap between species, as well as an economic gap. The social struggle was a class and economic struggle, a quest for power and profits, but to see it as a struggle over these things exclusively is to oversimplify. Over and over again, representatives of the upper orders of society in Germany would say something like "I consider the social question to be basically a cultural question," and workers would be referred to as *ungebildete* (uneducated, uncultured), and all the social insurance laws were called "workers insurance"—that is, workers were seen as distinctly different creatures. One can see this in Gerhart Hauptmann's play *The Weavers*. Hauptmann's purpose is to express contempt for the attitudes of the upper orders, who cannot understand what the striking and starving weavers could possibly want and who fear them as one would fear wild beasts. But the play, performed first in 1892, expressed a reality. Workers were viewed as if they came from another culture, like people from Africa or Asia, for example. As a matter of fact, the phrases "inner colonization" and "inner mission"[6] were common, implying that dealing with workers was equivalent to dealing with foreigners.

The German workers too regarded themselves as a foreign country. The unions tried to be nearly total institutions, providing recreation, legal services, and so forth, for their members and their wives and children. Membership in the union meant far more than the rather limited bread-and-butter purposes of American unions. Workers developed a sense of self-identification—largely but not entirely as part of the Social Democratic Party—which set them off as a cultural group. The gap between this cultural group and the rest of the nation was very great, but there is no precise way to measure it. No matter how much one may find fault with the American myth of a "classless society" in the United States, the social distances across class boundaries in Germany were immeasurably greater.[7]

272

It also appears that the sense of class unity in Germany was strengthened by the fact that within the working class itself there was less differentiation than in some other countries. The definition of "skilled" seemed to go rather far down the ladder, so that one could identify oneself as a "book printer" even if one's daily task was an unskilled one. There were differences between *ungelernt, angelernt,* and *gelernt* (roughly: unskilled, semiskilled, and skilled), and there was a special union for the unskilled, but whereas in the United States for half a century the skilled unions would not include the unskilled, the "unorganizable," and would not bargain for them, that difference did not lead to as much antagonism in Germany. "German labor unions early organized the skilled and unskilled together and struggled for the advantage of all workers."[8]

This social gap between a "closed" working class and "non-workers" is only one cleft in a multilayered society, as illustrated by the special insurance law passed explicitly for "white-collar" workers (*Angestellte*) in 1911. There are distinct words for "white-collar worker" or "office worker" in German, but in American English one must rely on euphemisms (in Great Britain the term "salaried worker" is often used). It is always clear to a German whether one is an *Arbeiter* or an *Angestellte.* An older word for *Angestellte* is *Betriebsbeamte,* or *Privatbeamte,* and *Beamte* is the word for public offical or civil servant. Office workers, by describing themselves as "officials of the firm" or "private officials," made public officials into what had been called a "normative reference group"—that is, they were making clear to themselves and to society that they were not *Arbeiter.*[9]

It is also significant that in Germany the word "class"—except for someone like Marx, who wanted to use it in a special way—is used almost exclusively to define "the working class." Everyone else wants to be a *Stand,* which is more familiar in English as the word "estate" (from the French), but *Stand* really has no precise equivalent in English. It means something like social position or rank in society, but it is also applied to one's position in the economic order, as in the phrase "we do not want the profession of doctor to lose its place in society" or "farmers frequently act as a stand." The Prussian election system is frequently called a "three-class" system, whereas "three *Stände*" would be more accurate.

The German historian Jürgen Kocka set out the difference between *Stand* and class.

> Stand means a large social group which through a particular legal position, a particular participation in political control, a particular form of wealth production, a particular prestige position, is differentiated from other Stands . . . often in opposition to market mechanisms. Every Stand (for example, the Religious, Noble, Urban Bourgeois, Peasant) has normative rules to regulate the daily lives of its members, so that each individual carries on his life in a fashion which is conventional for that Stand. . . .
>
> A class, on the other hand, means a large social group whose membership is determined by similar interests on the basis of a similar position in the market.[10]

This distinction exists in all European societies, not just in Germany, but the *Stand* elements were probably particularly strong in relation to the "class" elements for a longer time in Germany than even in England, and certainly stronger than in the United States. In one way this made social welfare legislation easier in Germany, because merely transferring income did not transfer the kind of prestige and deference that went with a *Stand*. On the other hand, it may have made class conflict more intense, because the battle was across a huge social gulf, almost with foreigners.

In Great Britain too the workers tried to create a class society that was more or less exclusive and internally cohesive. The English historian E. P. Thompson argued that they succeeded. Whether or not one accepts the idea of a closed, self-conscious British proletariat, for the upper orders in Great Britain as well, the poor were regarded as strange, primitive, and foreign. Philanthropists like William Booth felt as if they were missionaries to foreign countries when they entered London's East End, but there is little evidence of this sort of thinking in Denmark or in the United States.

Class Conflict

The relationship between the classes in the four countries varied on two dimensions: the degree of social distance between the classes and the degree of antagonism between them. Although it is impossible to document, the social distance between classes may be equally great between workers and nonworkers in Great Britain and Germany, but the degree of antagonism across that gulf is greater in Germany. In Denmark, although the distance is still considerable, there is less social distance and less antagonism than in Great Britain. In the United States there is great antagonism and less social distance between classes, at least less acknowledged social distance.

The level of antagonism between labor and employer in Germany was intense. There were the socialist laws and, on the other side, suspicion of anything emanating from government. During the revolution of 1918, there was vicious warfare with machineguns and flame throwers—and this was at least partly class warfare. There was great bitterness before World War I, and even more for the entire between-the-wars period. The level of conflict across the social gulf was far angrier and far bloodier than in Great Britain. A feeling of solidarity on the part of the workers against the rest of society was more pronounced.

In Great Britain there were bitter strikes and bitter speeches—sometimes rocks or bricks were thrown—but pitched battles between classes did not occur. The dockers strike of 1894 was harsh and bitter, but not bloody. There was nothing like the oppression of the German socialist laws, and as a matter of fact the Taff Vale and Osborn court decisions, which virtually stripped unions of their right to strike or participate in politics, were undone by a Parliament made up largely of nonworkers. The fact that "the working classes" was almost invariably used in the plural may indicate that class consciousness in Great Britain was a consciousness of a multitude of gradations, not just two antagonistic groups. In Germany before World War I an alliance between the Social Democrats and the Liberals was unthinkable, and no alliance between the Center and the Social Democrats occurred, but "Lib-Lab" is a common term in British politics.

In Denmark, the highest purpose of society, and more particularly of welfare legislation, was to mollify or temper conflict. Between the skilled (*faglært*) and the unskilled there was and is a great gulf, between both of them and an office worker another gulf, and to the professional or manager there is still another. Under extreme provocation, the skilled and unskilled might band together and strike against the employer. They may even shout epithets or chant slogans, but class conflict will rarely go beyond that. Strikes in Denmark are regulated by a compromise worked out in 1899, modified but still basically the same. There are strict rules regulating strikes and lockouts, and a court to enforce the rules. To anyone used to American strikes, the Danish pattern looks like a ritualized imitation of class conflict, almost like a play where the two sides come out from opposite sides of the proscenium, shake their fists and shout slogans, then meet before the curtain to take a bow together. Sometimes on television they literally do take bows together. Violence is virtually unthinkable.

In the United States the level of violence was very great. Employer-employee conflicts from the Coeur d'Alene mining wars to the Homestead steel strike were more akin to war than to strikes. The American case is complicated by ethnic, racial, and national antagonisms being mixed with class ones. Yet it would be a mistake to make employee-employer warfare into *class* warfare. The workers at the Homestead steelworks wanted shorter hours and better wages. That they were fighting a war for the working class, or for a change in the economic system, is less clear. Gompers may have been class-conscious, but he could fight for workmen's compensation alongside the National Association of Manufacturers. Class conflict seemed so un-American to settlement house workers that ameliorating it, overcoming this unnatural phenemonon, was one of the main motives for founding settlement houses. The well-off could perhaps bring something of their education and culture to the poor. They would learn—and teach others—lessons in humanity, human diversity, and a more genuine morality from the poor. When the New Deal began to pass welfare measures, labor was supportive, and even the socialists found themselves absorbed by a political party dominated by nonworkers. In the United States, in spite of harsh conflict, workers and nonworkers believed they could work with each other.

The class divisions of society in both Denmark and Germany are explicitly recognized in their welfare laws. In both countries, representatives of employers and workers are seated on decision-making boards and are assumed to have conflicting interests. This is so in virtually all parts of the German system, a little less so in Denmark.

In Great Britain, appeals boards for workmen's compensation and unemployment insurance contained, by law, representatives of workers and of employers, but the issue was less important in Great Britain than in either of the other two continental countries. In the United States, class distinctions figured in welfare legislation in only a few places. In about half the workmen's compensation laws, disputes were left to the courts. In others there was a special appeals board on which employees, so defined, had to be members. In no other branch of social insurance was there a place reserved for workers. In some cases, boards had to have members of each political party. Perhaps it was assumed that democratic pluralism would ensure that workers could protect themselves.

Labor Support for Welfare Legislation

The degree of support from organized labor for income-maintenance programs varied with time and place. In Germany, organized labor, to the extent that it was represented by the Social Democratic Party, opposed government welfare plans before 1911 because they opposed the government and all its products. The Social Democrats believed that the laws had as one of their purposes weakening the Social Democratic Party, and that was correct. Yet the labor unions themselves were far less opposed to the laws in prospect and were fairly pleased as the laws became familiar and showed themselves to be beneficial. Although organized labor was not a significant political force when the Danish laws were passed, labor came to support them as labor became a political power. Eventually the Danish Social Democrats and the German Social Democrats came to think of welfare legislation as their main objective, even if it was within capitalism.

Labor in Great Britain was also divided, but along a somewhat different line than in Germany. Almost the whole movement favored noncontributory old-age pensions, although less-restrictive ones than those were passed. On social insurance, labor was of two minds. The more centrist elements, particularly those in Parliament, favored social insurance while the element further left, often in the trade unions, opposed it. The centrist elements dominated, and the Labour Party supported and extended the contributory insurance principle. In the United States, organized labor before the Great Depression opposed social insurance, but by no means for the same set of reasons as in Germany. Gompers too, in spite of having some strongly class-conscious ideas, did not want workers divided into those who needed government help and those who did not. Workers would solve their own problems, and American society was abundant enough to have that happen if labor got a fair share.

The perception of the possibility for social mobility—not its actuality, but its perceived possibility—influenced the nature of welfare legislation, but not labor support for it. The German laws assumed a higher degree of possibility for social mobility than the Danish laws. Some workers might move to a "higher" position. Before the twentieth century the Danes assumed a more static society. The British laws of social insurance all made provision for "voluntary contributors," who were above or who moved above the income limits set in the law but who might still be insured if they wanted to, for a higher premium. In the twentieth century Denmark adopted the same mechanism. For Americans, mobility was of central importance in their whole approach to social welfare. The society was thought to be so open that only a very limited welfare safety net would be necessary—or so it seemed until the 1930s. It was even debatable whether most "wage-earners," to use Gompers' term, would remain wage-earners. Terms like "proletariat" or "working class" had a somewhat radical ring.

The Worthy Poor and the Unworthy Poor

None of the four countries gave the poor any rights under the poor law. Even in Denmark, where the poor had a constitutional claim, they were simply the recipients and objects of other people's policies. In Denmark and Germany these other people had considerable nonappealable quasi-judicial power, including the power to imprison without trial. The poor in Great Britain had only the right to enter the poorhouse. This was not a prison—one could leave at any time—but inmates were subject to the regimen of the poorhouse. In the United States before the New Deal, recipients of welfare had no rights, even in jurisdictions where the authority was legally bound to supply relief.

Not providing any rights was not equivalent to treating "the poor" as an undifferentiated mass. In Germany the distinction between "worthy" and "unworthy" poor seems to have been important for only a few of the people administering aid, and in fact to have been explicitly rejected by most. In general, aid was to be given because it was absolutely necessary. For Danes the distinction was important. Both categories should receive aid, but there should be a difference, usually a legal one. The distinction has had decreasing force during the twentieth century, more so since the Danish "social reform" of 1933, but anecdotal evidence indicates that it persisted to some degree even after World War II. In Great Britain, worthiness was not important for the minimal aid—residence in a poorhouse. Both the drunkard and the honest laborer could get that minimum subsistence. Increasingly a problem was perceived when the worthy poor—say, the aged—entered the poorhouse. For the "unworthy," the poorhouse was to provide, in effect, punishment; for the "worthy" it was an asylum. Beyond that minimum, the idea of "worthiness" was significant for receiving "outdoor relief" and, after 1908, for old-age pensions. In no country was worthiness a criterion for receiving social insurance. Insurance was available to all who fulfilled the "statutory provisions" and paid premiums.

Worthiness was of central concern for the private charity of the charity organization societies both in the United States and in Great Britain. In some jurisdictions in the United States (e.g., Massachusetts) the authorities were required to give aid to anyone who was a legal resident, which took ten years. In many jurisdictions, decisions were left more to local authorities, who could use whatever criteria they chose. In the first broadly enacted public aid program in the United States—mother's pensions—the recipients had to be "fit" (or some synonym), with no further definition of the requirement.

Compulsion and Welfare

In emphasizing the contrast between Germans and Danes, the Danes speak continually about the compulsion in the German laws and the voluntary nature of the Danish laws. The distinction between compulsion in Germany and voluntarism in Denmark was more important in principle than in practice. The German laws were compulsory, but in the case of the law that touched the most people—sickness insurance—requirement could be met in a variety of ways. Danish insurance was indeed voluntary before 1933, but Danes were bribed (or perhaps it is more polite to say there were incentives) to join, and virtually everybody did. All the British laws were compulsory, but many contained provision for voluntary membership for those of higher income. This was also true in Denmark and Germany. In the United States the laws contained bits of voluntarism in some places for a short period. Some of the early workmen's compensation laws were voluntary, though they were soon made compulsory. Insurance under the Social Security Act was compulsory, although in the 1950s the self-employed could decide whether they wanted to join. Medicare has a voluntary feature. In general, however, social insurance is compulsory in the United States.

Welfare and Social Control

Was the social welfare legislation, as some have suggested, a way of disciplining the poor, a way of exercising a subtle or not so subtle control to make the poor accept the status of loyal subordinates whose social respect as well as self-respect was measured according to how hard they worked? Was social insurance designed to produced subordinates who would not disrupt the social order in a demand for more of the common product? The makers of public policy were not bothered by this kind of question. They had no doubt that their society, all societies, needed people with certain qualities: order, hard work, a sense of responsibility toward dependents. Whatever the organization of the economy—capitalist, mercantilist, or large agrarian estates—society would be constructed in a way that encouraged the desired values and discouraged their reverse.

Such words as "regulating" or disciplining" have a strongly negative air. One disciplines children or regulates subordinates, not colleagues or equals. A word that members of the Deutsche Verein used frequently was "education" (*Erziehung*), or "bringing up," and the charity organization societies in England and the United States used similar words—that is, members of the Verein or the charity organization societies or the poor-law authorities in Denmark believed that part of their responsibility was to train people to fit into their society to the extent that they would be more likely to be able to support themselves. To accuse them of being witting or unwitting tools of the ever more important capitalists is to oversimplify. Some of them were the capitalists and wanted to produce loyal workers. Some had a sense of Christian responsibility that had little to do with creating industrious workers. Most wanted to preserve order, perhaps more order than there had been in the early part of the century. Some were interested in a degree of social justice. Some of the people who wrote the welfare legislation were anticapitalists who wanted to limit the excesses of an overweening capitalism, which they believed was destroying the proper balance in their society.

Modern social science would use neither the negative term "disciplining" nor the positive ones "education" or "training," but would look for a more neutral one, such as "socialization." All societies socialize their members, whether the society is hunting-gathering, nomadic, warrior, or monastic. But they do not simply socialize their poor. For example, the discipline for a Prussian civil servant was extraordinary, beginning at home, carried further in school and gymnasium, and enforced through the examination system, with clear rewards for succeeding and punishments for failing. Discipline for the poor was sometimes harsh, but discipline in a gymnasium could also include considerable physical abuse. All societies try to discipline, to socialize, their members. That this was more so for the poor than for other social groups, or that it was in the service of the capitalists, is more difficult to maintain.[11] Threats to order, such as burning poorhouses or even nonviolently camping on unused grounds in Washington, D.C., were harshly put down, but threats to order anywhere in the social system would be put down harshly. There were no pretenders to the Hohenzollern throne, but can there be any doubt that a campaign against the royal family would have been put down as brutally as a bread riot?

To argue that the aim of poor relief was not relief but disciplining is to make a false dichotomy. There is no reason to place the two functions on opposite poles, and there is every reason to see them as compatible. People should be relieved and trained and socialized, and violence should be repressed. There is perhaps a bit of romanticism in the argument that poor relief was a form of discipline—

281

romanticism for the past and for the future. The vagabond or beggar or peasant or working-class member is presumed to be in a sense freer than the powerful classes want him to be, potentially a figure inherently critical of a capitalist means of production, perhaps in the future the foundation for a noncapitalist society, more cooperative then competitive, more social than individualistic.[12] Intellectuals making the oppressed into the group that will redeem the society through inherent virtues are repeatedly disillusioned.

Perhaps in a discussion of "social control" the emphasis should be on the first word rather than the second—that is, the control or disciplining is now social, coming from the society in general instead of from some other force, such as religion or the authority in an authoritarian system. This seems more plausible, but it raises further questions. In any kind of social system the controls always come via a portion of that society—a priesthood or officialdom. These controls are usually internalized so that at least to some degree they come from the controlled as well as from the controllers. In a welfare society the social control is also exercised not by some vague will of all but by the system: officials, forms, legislation. Also, a good deal of the discipline is internalized. It is questionable whether this kind of social control is really more social than previous types. In any case, at this level, the analysis has been reduced to saying little more than that society socializes its members.

The ultimate social control is the totalitarianism of the National-Socialist state in Germany between 1933 and 1945. Along with every other German institution, from orchestras to secret police, social welfare became a tool for social control. Social control may have been one of the factors behind welfare before 1933, but in the Nazi state it became the only factor. The motivations and structures of social policy during the Nazi period are too complex and multifarious to discuss here. Suffice it to say that although one can find many continuities with social policy before 1914, enough new elements or new emphases existed to make Nazi social policy, even for those who were included in it as other than victims, new and unique. When discussing Nazi social policy, one cannot exclude the death camps, and whatever strength anti-Semitism or militarism or authoritarianism may be said to have traditionally had in Germany, the *Vernichtungslager* were unprecedented.

To the Present

Two major conclusions come out of this sort of history, and in a way they lead in opposite directions. The first, and the one that emerges explicitly in the body of the book, is that of differentiation, of specificity. Charity organization societies in Great Britain and the United States had the same name and same motto, but even in such closely related countries they performed different roles. The words for the German and the Danish medical insurance programs, *Krankenkassen* and *sygekasser,* are directly translatable into each other, but they were understood in different ways. When Englishmen wanted to use the example of Denmark, they translated a Danish word into an English concept and used it in an English way. When Americans working for health insurance tried to transplant the German system too literally, they got nowhere. The words "state" and "class," with only trivial differences in spelling, are used in all four countries, but they have different meanings. Each country was influenced by others, yet each moved toward its version of the welfare state in its own way. It should be made clear that this does not mean one way was right and the others were deviant. The entire point of this book is that countries worked out their present in relation to their past and that what was right for one country was not necessarily relevant for another country. The most powerful influence on the shape of each version of the welfare state was the history, institutions, and perceptions within that country.

The other conclusion, which is obvious but less explicit, is that all four of these countries (and of course many other countries too) worked their way toward a more or less capitalist, more or less democratic, more or less welfare state. Most groups in these countries found that in one way or another, or in view of the defeat of alternatives or failures in the system without a welfare state, this solution worked reasonably well. Even the United States, though coming late to that conclusion, has finally embraced its own version of the capitalist welfare state. President Harry Truman, it is true, could not continue the process his predecessor had begun. Truman's "Fair Deal," most notably his program of national health insurance, proved to be politically impossible. Far more important for the continuation of the welfare state was what Dwight D. Eisenhower did *not* do. He did not dismantle anything. The changes Franklin Roosevelt brought to the American scene remained. In fact, during the Eisenhower years the sphere of the welfare state enlarged a bit. Another enormous expansion, conceptual as well as institutional, came with Lyndon B. Johnson's "War on Poverty." With a series of programs almost as numerous as the New Deal, Johnson sought to change the concept of the welfare state in two ways. Whereas Franklin Roosevelt's programs had aimed at aiding the economy or the poor in general, Johnson's were aimed at more-specific targets—an area, such as Appalachia, or a specific group, such as untrained teenagers. Johnson's measures were taken in the context of prosperity, not in response to an economic crisis. Again what is striking is that when the opposition party came to power it did not eliminate such basic parts of the Johnson expansion as health insurance. Richard Nixon even enlarged the food stamp program, essentially a limited negative income tax. It is difficult to know how serious Nixon was about expanding basic welfare through the Family Assistance Plan, but he certainly did not roll the clock back. What is the most convincing evidence for the permanence of the welfare state in the United States is that President Ronald Reagan did not roll the clock back very much either. His antigovernment, antiwelfare rhetoric was extraordinary. The 1984 inaugural contained language that is very reminiscent of the Poor Law Report of 1834. Yet a careful examination of the Reagan years reveals that the structure of institutions, and probably the structure of the ideas behind them, is now as firm a part of the social perceptions of the United States as it is in the other countries dealt with here.

In the Reagan years the "safety net" of programs for people whose earnings have been interrupted has been weakened, but not decimated, for the very poor. The working poor, those whose earnings were just above or just below the government-established poverty line, were the ones who suffered from the weakening safety net. The growth in the various income-maintenance programs slowed, but there was little rollback. These programs were larger in 1986 than they had been twenty years earlier. Over and over again it has been impossible for this most anti-welfare-minded president to alter the Social Security Act significantly. Also, most transfer programs for the poor have been protected either by Congress or by the courts.

The antiwelfare efforts and effects of the Reagan years have probably peaked as of this writing. As has been traditional in the United States, work opportunities and incentives are preferred over pure income transfers, but Americans show little enthusiasm for cutting program funding below the 1970 level, which is subtantially higher than it was before the War on Poverty.[13] During Ronald Reagan's first term, David Stockman was head of the Office of Management and Budget and a major ideologist for the administration. He has concluded regretfully that "the American electorate wants a moderate social democracy to shield it from capitalism's rougher edges."[14] Whether one regrets or applauds it, the conclusion seems correct.

Particularly since 1945, in all four countries' laws originally written for the "workers" or "people of small means" have expanded. Slowly, beginning in a small way even before World War I, increasing in the interwar years, and increasing rapidly since 1945, the middle class discovered that by simple extension it can benefit from the laws too. At the same time, workers have lost their character as a special class, both in life-style and in the way they are thought of and think of themselves. This process has been called the *embourgoisement* of the proletariat. The result has been a rough consensus on internal policy in all four countries. The Right has won in the sense that capitalism has been preserved. The Left has won in the sense that conditions of life and labor are much improved. There is now something approaching agreement on the issues that have created much bitterness over the past centuries. Domestic politics in all four countries may have become something of a bore, because the largest issue has simply melted away. This is a sign not of failure, but of success.

Notes

Introduction

1. A good introduction to problems of explanation in history are the chapters by C. G. Hempel and Michael Oakshott in William Dray (ed.), *Philosophical Analysis and History* (New York: Harper and Row, 1966). R. G. Collingwood discusses the same in various places in *The Idea of History* (New York: Oxford University Press, 1956). See also Arthur C. Danto, *Analytic Philosophy of History* (Cambridge: Cambridge University Press, 1968), esp. chap. 11, which is particularly useful on the relationship between explanation and narrative.

2. The whole problem of theory in social science and the false analogy with a false understanding of the physical sciences is explored more deeply in John G. Gunnell, *Philosophy, Science, and Political Inquiry* (Morristown, N.J.: General Learning Press, 1975), and idem, *Between Philosophy and Politics: The Alienation of Political Theory* (Amherst: University of Massachusetts Press, 1985), esp. chap. 2, "Theory and Science." See also my review of *Vom Armenhaus zum Wohlfahrtsstaat* by Jens Alber in *Comparative Studies in Society and History* 29 (October 1988):823–826.

3. The significance of these paintings is discussed in Leo Marx, *The Machine in the Garden* (New York: Oxford University Press, 1964).

4. Oddly enough, it is in a book devoted to economic history, that one finds a defense by March Bloch of this kind of comparative history, but the editors believed that a five-page introduction to Bloch's essay was necessary. See March Bloch, "Toward a Comparative History of European Societies," in Frederic C. Lane and Jelle C. Riemersma (eds.), *Enterprise and Secular Change: Readings in Economic History* (Homewood, Ill.: Irwin, 1953), 494–521. This is a translation of Bloch's 1928 article in *Revue de synthèse historique*. See also Carl Degler, "In Pursuit of American History," *American Historical Review* 92 (February 1987): 1–12.

5. This list is limited to works that focus on or have clear implications for developed, industrial nations in North America and Europe and for Japan. On state-building in general, see Stein Rokkan, "Dimensions of State Formation and Nation Building," in Charles Tilly (ed.), *The Formation of National States in Western Europe* (Princeton: Princeton University Press, 1974). Peter Flora and Jens Alber, "Modernization, Democratization, and the Development of the Welfare State," in Flora and Arnold Heidenheimer (eds.), *The Development of Welfare States in Europe and America* (New Brunswick, N.J.: Transaction, 1981). See also Peter Baldwin, "The Scandinavian Origins of the Social Interpretation of the Welfare State," *Comparative Studies in Society and History* (forthcoming).

6. See Harold L. Wilensky and Charles N. Lebaux, *Industrial Society and Social Welfare* (New York: Russell Sage Foundation, 1958); Harold L. Wilensky, *The Welfare State and Equality: Structural and Ideological Roots of Public Expenditures* (Berkeley and Los Angeles: The University of

California Press, 1975). The quotation is from the latter work, p. 47. Because the book deals only with the post–World War II period, Wilensky may have different views about the earlier founding of welfare programs. See also John Barnes and Talapady Srivenkataramana, "Ideology and the Welfare State: An Examination of Wilensky's Conclusions," *Social Service Review* 56 (June 1982): 230–245; Christoph Sachsse and Florian Tennstedt, *Geschichte der Armenfürsorge in Deutschland vom Spätmittelalter bis zum l. Weltkrieg* (Stuttgart: Kohlhammer, 1980), esp. 257–267; Gaston Rimlinger, *Welfare Policy and Industrialization in Europe, America, and Russia* (New York: Wiley, 1971); the quotation is from p. 35. Rimlinger and Gerhart A. Ritter made their points at a symposium in Berlin on the one hundredth anniversary of the Royal Message from the German Kaiser recommending what eventually came to be the German social insurance laws. The symposium's proceedings are in Peter A. Köhler, Hans F. Zacher, Martin Parrington (eds.), *Beiträge zur Geschichte und aktueller Situation der Sozialversicherung* (Berlin: Bunker and Humbolt, 1983); for Rimlinger, see esp. p. 122; for Ritter, see 106–108.

7. Flora and Heidenheimer, *Development of Welfare States,* the quotation is on p. 22, in a chapter the editors wrote. They do not reject the Marxian analysis; they believe it is compatible with their own. For Cutwright, see Phillips Cutwright, "Political Structure, Economic Development, and National Security Programs," *American Journal of Sociology* 70 (1965): 537–550. Cutwright's conclusion is at odds with the widely accepted views of David Collier and Richard Messick, "Prerequisites versus Diffusion: Testing Alternative Explanations of Social Security Adoption," *American Political Science Review* 69 (1975): 1299–1315, who find that the less-democratic regimes adopted welfare before more-democratic ones, but they have to make some controversial decisions to come to that conclusion. See also Kjeld Philip, *Staten og Fattigdom* (Copenhagen: Gjellerup, 1947); Hans Achinger, *Sozialpolitik als Gesellschaftspolitik* (Frankfurt a.m.: Ergen, 1971); Hugh Heclo, *Modern Social Politics in Britain and Sweden: From Relief to Income Maintenance* (New Haven: Yale University Press, 1974); Ann Shola Orloff and Theda Skocpol, "Why Not Equal Protection? Explaining the Politics of Social Welfare in Britain and the United States" (Paper delivered at the Annual Meeting of the American Sociological Association, Detroit, Michigan, September 2, 1983); Samuel Mencher, *From Poor Law to Poverty Program* (Pittsburgh: University of Pittsburgh, 1967). T. H. Marshall also belongs in this group; see his *Social Policy in the Twentieth Century* (London: Hutchinson, 1965). See also Peter Flora, *Modernizierung und die Entwicklung der Westeuropäischen Wohlfahrtsstaaten* (Mannheim: Habilitationsschrift, 1976). I take the description of Flora's work from Jens Alber, *Vom Armenhaus zum Wohlfahrtsstaat: Analysen zur Entwicklung der Sozialversicherung in Westeuropa* (New York: Campus, 1982), 84. Flora's suggestions are attractive, but I wonder how far they get us. Do they include so much variability that they

end by asserting simply that the story was different in different times and places? Size does not work as an explanation either. The only fixed point we have is that the United States was larger and later. But Germany was fairly large and was a federation in which an average farmer in the north had no common language with a farmer in the south. Denmark was tiny, England was fairly large. Nor is war any use as an explanation. Bismarck proposed the laws after a series of victories, Denmark after a defeat, England after she had in effect conquered most of the world.

8. See Val Lorwin, "Working-Class Politics and Economic Development: Western Europe," *American Historical Review* 63 (January 1958): 338–351; John D. Stephens, *The Transition from Capitalism to Socialism* (London: Macmillan, 1979), 89; David Cameron, "The Expansion of the Public Economy," *American Political Science Review* 72 (1978): 1243–1261; Walter Korpi, *The Working Class in Welfare Capitalism: Work, Unions, and Politics in Sweden* (London: Routledge and Kegan Paul, 1978); Francis G. Castles, *The Social Democratic Image of Society* (London: Routledge and Kegan Paul, 1978); Iver Hornemann Møller, *Klassekamp og Sociallovgivning, 1850–1970* (Copenhagen: Socialstiske Økonomers Forlag, 1981); Gösta Esping-Andersen, *Social Class, Social Democracy, and State Policy: Party Policy and Party Decomposition in Denmark and Sweden* (Copenhagen: Institute of Organization and Industrial Sociology, 1980); Ian Gough, *The Political Economy of the Welfare State* (New York: Macmillan, 1979); Frances Fox Piven and Richard A. Cloward, *Regulating the Poor: The Functions of Social Welfare* (New York: Pantheon, 1971).

9. Daniel Levine, "Socialism, Social Democrats, and Social Welfare: Denmark and Germany, 1918–1933," *Comparative Social Research* 6 (Greenwich, Conn.: JAI Press, 1983), 67–86.

10. These conclusions are reported in Alber, *Vom Armenhaus zum Wohlfahrtsstaat.*

11. Alexander von Humboldt, quoted in George C. Iggers, *The German Tradition of History: The National Tradition of Historical Thought from Herder to the Present* (Middletown, Conn.: Wesleyan University Press, 1968), 51.

Chapter 1. England's Poor Law Report and the United States

1. American workers do seem to have received higher real wages, but even more important was the constancy of the wages and demand for labor, which also seems to have been greater. See E. H. Phelps Brown with Margaret H. Browne, *A Century of Pay: The Course of Pay and Production in France, Germany, Sweden, the United Kingdom, and the United States of America, 1860–1960* (London: Macmillan, 1968). See also David Potter, *People of Plenty* (Chicago: University of Chicago Press, 1958).

2. Martin Anderson, *Welfare: The Political Economy of Welfare Reform in the United States* (Stanford, Calif.: Hoover Institute, 1978).

3. *NCCC 1881–1882,* 157.

4. Ibid., 115–116. This view is also reflected in an official report titled "The Causes of Poverty," submitted in 1875 by Dr. Charles Hoyt, first secretary of the New York Board of State Commissioners of Public Charities. See David M. Schneider and Albert Deutsch, *The History of Public Welfare in New York State, 1867–1940* (Chicago: University of Chicago Press, 1941), 2:27–28.

5. Josephine Shaw Lowell, *Public Relief and Private Charity* (New York, 1884), 8. The Charter of New York City, 1897, prohibited "outdoor relief" for everyone but the blind (Schneider and Deutsch, *History,* 2:181).

6. Mark Blaug, "The Myth of the Old Poor Law and the Making of the New," *Journal of Economic History* 23 (1963): 151–184; idem, "The Poor Law Reexamined," ibid., 24 (1964): 229–243. James Stephan Taylor, "The Mythology of the Old Poor Law," ibid., 29 (1969): 292–297, says he disagrees with Blaug, but he actually only says that Blaug's evidence was inadequate, not that his conclusions were wrong.

7. The law itself is 4 & 5 Will. 4, c. 76. The quotation and page references are to S. G. Checkland and E. O. A. Checkland (eds.), *The Poor Law Report of 1834* (Harmondsworth, Middlesex, Eng.: Pelican, 1974), 169–170. Gertrude Himmelfarb goes to considerable logical lengths to assert that Oliver Twist "affirmed and validated one of the principles that inspired the law. The law was meant to separate the pauper from the independent poor" (*The Idea of Poverty* [New York: Vintage, 1984], 460).

8. See M. A. Crowther, *The Workhouse System, 1834–1929: The History of an English Social Institution* (London: Methuen, 1981); I use the 1983 paperback edition. Crowther on p. 60 (1983 ed.) estimates that about 0.5 percent of the English population was in poorhouses or workhouses. Surprisingly, this is about the same as the figure estimated for Denmark in Ingeborg Christmas-Møller, *På Fattighuset* (Copenhagen: Nationalmuseet, 1978), 14. The law in Denmark did not prohibit outdoor relief, and these figures might be a further clue that the law was not strictly administered in England. It is logically possible that practice against outdoor relief was stricter in Denmark than the law required, but certainly there is not even anecdotal evidence of this.

On enforcement of the law, see Nicholas C. Edsall, *The Anti-Poor Law Movement* (Manchester: Manchester University Press, 1971); William Apfel and Peter Dunkley, "English Rural Society and the New Poor Law: Bedfordshire, 1834–1847," *Social History* 10 (January 1985): 37–69. Michael E. Rose, "The Allowance System under the New Poor Law," *Economic History Review,* 2d ser., 19 (1966): 607–620; David Roberts, "Dealing with the Poor in Victorian England," *Rice University Studies* 67 (1981): 57–74.

David Roberts, "How Cruel Was the Victorian Poor Law?" *Historical*

Journal 6 (1963): 97–107, argues that tales of cruelty were greatly exaggerated or that the acts were done in violation of the law. This last point seems forced, because the law created the circumstances under which the cruelty occurred. Ursula Henriques, "How Cruel Was the Victorian Poor Law?" ibid. 11 (1968): 365–371, agrees that some of the stories of cruelty were greatly exaggerated but that real cruelty was there. Without offering any evidence, Henriques argues that it was "the terror induced in the gentry of the southern counties by the risings of 1830" which was the real cause of the law. Peter Dunkley, "The Hungry Forties and the New Poor Law: A Case Study," ibid., 17 (1974): 329–346, claims that in Durham at least, during the 1840s, the central authority acted as a limit on local "cheese paring." The reverse seems to have been more general, at least after mid-century. We cannot tell whether the law was a deterrent to seeking aid. Administration was so local that no overall figures are available.

9. James Leiby, *Charity and Correction in New Jersey: A History of State Welfare Institutions* (New Brunswick, N.J.: Rutgers University Press, 1967), esp. 165–180; Schneider and Deutsch, *History,* esp. 2:125–138. Charles Loring Brace, *The Dangerous Classes of New York and Twenty Years Work among Them* (New York: 1872), 284–285, indicates that about half the budget of the Children's Aid Society came from public sources.

10. William R. Brock, *Investigation and Responsibility: Public Responsibility in the United States, 1865–1900* (Cambridge: Cambridge University Press, 1984), argues that the public authorities were active in welfare, but as Robert H. Bremner wrote in his review (*Journal of American History* 72 [September 1985]: 420–421), what Brock describes is actually a "record of good intentions." For the influence of the English poor law and Poor Law Report, see Glenn C. Altschuler and Jan M. Saltzgaber, "Clearinghouse for Paupers: The Poorfarm of Seneca County, New York, 1830–1860," *Journal of Social History* 17 (Summer 1984): 573–600, esp. n. 6, p. 592.

Chapter 2. The Charity Organization Societies in Great Britain and the United States

1. Josephine Shaw Lowell, *Public Relief and Private Charity* (New York, 1884), 8.

2. See F. K. Prochaska, *Women and Philanthropy in Nineteenth-Century England* (Oxford: Oxford University Press, 1980); Anne Summers, "A Home from Home: Women's Philanthropic Work in the Nineteenth Century," in Anne Summers and Sandra Burman (eds.), *Fit Work for Women* (New York: St. Martin's Press, 1979), 33–63. Summers emphasizes the continuity between COS visiting and early types, that the Christian impulse was of central importance in all visiting, and that visiting was not just a pastime, but serious work.

3. For more on the London COS, see Charles L. Mowat, *The Charity*

Organisation Society 1869–1913: Its Ideas and Work (London: Methuen, 1961). Madeline Rooff, *Voluntary Societies and Social Policy* (London: Routledge and Kegan Paul, 1957) is not specifically about the COS, but it shows how slow any change was before World War I. Her *Hundred Years of Family Welfare: A Study of the Family Welfare Association (formerly Charity Organisation Society), 1869–1969* (London: Michael Joseph, 1972) is more of an overview. Michael J. Moore, "Social Work and Social Welfare: The Organization of Philanthropic Resources in Britain, 1900–1914," *Journal of British Studies* 16 (1977): 85–104, asserts that other private philanthropic organizations, particularly the Guilds of Help, were more flexible and as important as the charity organization societies; on the first point he is certainly right. Alan J. Kidd, "Charity Organisation and the Unemployed in Manchester, c. 1870–1914," *Social History* 9 (January 1984): 45–66, illustrates how the ideas of the London COS were not confined to the capital city. The same point is made by Ruth Hutchinson Crocker, "The Victorian Poor Law in Crisis and Change: Southhampton, 1870–1895," *Albion* 19 (Spring 1987): 19–44.

4. David Roberts, "Tory Paternalism and Social Reform in Early Victorial England," *American Historical Review* 63 (1958): 323–337, shows how Tories deplored all sorts of inhumanities in the industrial system but consistently voted against laws that might improve things.

5. The quotations are from Octavia Hill, "Organized Work Among the Poor," *Macmillan's Magazine* 20 (October 1869): 219–226. For a more sympathetic view, emphasizing Hill's contribution to housing reform, see Robert H. Bremner, " 'An Iron Sceptre Twined with Roses': The Octavia Hill System of Housing Management," *Social Service Review* 39 (1965): 222–231.

6. For one clear statement of fundamental beliefs, see COS, *The Best Means of Dealing with Exceptional Distress* (London, 1886); see also COS *Annual Report 1888.*

7. Octavia Hill, "The Charity Organisation Society," in COS, *Occasional Papers 1896,* 15, 17. It is not entirely clear to me whom Hill meant by "we." Partly she means the "better" classes, partly the charitable, and when she talks about feeding children she means the state, through its program of school meals. See also Thomas Mackay, "Old-Age Pensions and the State," in ibid.; "Winter Distress," in ibid., 53, 229–232; "Relief and Charity Organisation," in ibid., *1905,* 8, 55–56. In "The Science of Charity," ibid., *1896,* 19, 33–36; the Archbishop of Canterbury makes a lengthy parallel to the methods of Isaac Newton; and "Relief and Charity Organisation," ibid., *1905,* 8, 55–56, from 1902, is one of many instances detailing the direct relief provided by the COS.

8. Earlier forms of "visiting" and their connection with newer forms are explored in Bernd Weisbrod, " 'Visiting' and 'Social Control': Statistische Gesellschaften und Stadtmissionen im Viktorianischen England," in Christoph Sachsse and Florian Tennstedt (eds.), *Soziale Sicherheit und soziale Disziplinierung. Beiträge zu einer historischen Theorie der Sozialpolitik* (Frankfurt a.M.: Suhrkamp, 1986), 181–206.

9. José Harris, *Unemployment and Politics* (Oxford: Oxford University Press, 1972), 147, reports how the London COS, especially after 1900, followed a deliberate policy of trying to get COS members elected to the Board of Guardians in order to uphold traditional principles.

10. See A. W. Vincent, "The Poor Law Reports of 1909 and the Social Theory of the Charity Organization Society," *Victorian Studies* 27 (Spring 1984): 343–363.

11. Charles S. Loch, "The State and Unemployment," COS, *Occasional Papers 1900,* 253–360: COS, *Annual Report 1899,* 1–3; ibid., *1904,* 10–12.

12. Among historians of the last quarter-century, the American COS has had a fairly bad press. It has been contrasted unfavorably with the settlement houses, a contrast drawn in no uncertain terms by the settlement people themselves. The American COS has been harshly criticized by those scornful of its elements of "social control," which in fact were very evident but perhaps not deserving of all the scorn. The COS care in investigating each case has been ridiculed by, among others, "Boss" Plunkett, the archetypical "pol" from Tammany Hall. The bad press is particularly evident in Robert H. Bremner, *From the Depths: The Discovery of Poverty in the United States* (New York: New York University Press, 1956), 50–57; Walter I. Trattner, *From Poor Law to Welfare State,* 2d ed. (New York: Free Press, 1979), 80–85; Allen F. Davis, *Spearheads for Reform: The Social Settlements and the Progressive Movement, 1890–1914* (New York: Oxford University Press, 1967), 18–19; Michael B. Katz, *In the Shadow of the Poor House* (New York: Basic Books 1986), 66–85. Marvin Gettelman, in his "Charity and Social Class in the United States, 1874–1900," *American Journal of Economics and Sociology* 22 (July 1983): 313–329, 417–426, is scornful of the "social control" aspects of all charitable efforts, including those of the COS. Verl S. Lewis has a more favorable attitude in "The Development of the Charity Organization Movement in the United States, 1875–1900" (diss., Case Western Reserve, 1954). Robert H. Bremner, "Scientific Philanthropy, 1873–1893," *Social Service Review* 30 (June 1956): 169–173, is too short to be more than suggestive. The standard survey is Frank D. Watson, *The Charity Organization Movement in the United States: A Study in American Philanthropy* (New York: Macmillan, 1922), which is celebratory and written from the COS point of view. There are several studies of individual charity organization societies. One such, with perhaps wider implications, is Kenneth L. Kusmer, "The Functions of Organized Charity in the Progressive Era: Chicago as a Case Study," *Journal of American History* 60 (December 1973): 657–678. John A. Mayer, "Private Charities in Chicago, 1871–1913" (diss., University of Minnesota, 1978) is particularly interesting for what it says about social control and about the functions that charities served for the people engaged in them. There are a number of articles by the settlement workers critical of "friendly visiting," the urtype of which is Jane Addams, "Charity Visitor's Perplexities," *Outlook* 61 (March 1899): 598–600.

13. One example of this argument is in the COS of Buffalo, *Annual Report 1902,* 113.

14. COS of Baltimore, *Annual Report 1902,* 15.

15. W. J. Breed, "The Obligation of Personal Work and the Aid to Right Structure of Character," *NCCC 1892,* 460. The handbook is COS of the City of New York, *Handbook for Friendly Visitors among the Poor* (New York, 1883). See also Lowell, *Public Relief,* 90.

16. See Lowell, *Public Relief,* 85.

17. See, e.g., Mrs. C. R. Lowell, "Considerations upon a Better System of Public Charities and Corrections for Cities," *NCCC 1881–1882,* 169–185.

18. *Associated Charities of Boston Annual Report 1889,* 41.

19. Ibid.

20. Phillip Jackson, "Black Charity in Progressive Era Chicago," *Social Service Review* 52 (1978): 400–417; Alvin B. Kogut, "The Negro and the Charity Organization Society in the Progressive Era," ibid., 44 (1970): 11–21.

21. COS of Buffalo, *Annual Report 1881,* 5.

22. The quotation is from Amos G. Warner, *American Charities* (New York, 1894), 116. For a different emphasis, see James Leiby, "Amos Warner's *American Charities,*" *Social Service Review* 37 (December 1962): 441–445.

23. See David P. Thelen, "Social Tensions and the Origins of Progressivism," *Journal of American History* 56 (1969): 323–341.

24. Douglas W. Steeples, "Five Troubled Years: A History of the Depression of 1893–97" (diss., University of North Carolina, 1961).

25. R. D. M'Gonnigle, "The Winter in Pittsburgh," in *NCCC 1894,* 36–42; Charles D. Kellogg, "Charity Organization," in ibid., 55.

26. COS of Cincinnati, *Annual Report 1895–1896,* 7; COS of Buffalo, *Annual Report 1889, 1901, 1902;* Associated Charities of Boston, *Annual Report 1895,* 12; *NCCC 1896,* 241.

27. COS of the City of New York, *Annual Report 1896;* ibid., *1897,* 13.

28. *A Handbook on the Prevention of Tuberculosis,* being the 1st Annual Report of the Committee on the Prevention of Tuberculosis of the Charity Organization Society of the City of New York (1903), 34, 107–108, 113.

29. Mary E. Richmond, *Friendly Visiting Among the Poor* (New York: Macmillan, 1897).

30. See Zilpha D. Smith, "Report of the Committee on the Organization of Charity," *NCCC 1888,* 120; Associated Charities of Boston, *Report of the Committee on Industrial Training,* Publication 24 (Boston, 1881).

31. *NCCC 1912,* 377–395. Committee reports were not considered by the full gathering, so there is no way to assess the opinion of charity workers in general.

Chapter 3. The Poor Law as a Unifying Force in Germany

1. On the literature about pauperism, see Liselotte Dilcher, *Der deutsche Pauperismus und seine Literatur* (diss., University of Frankfurt, 1957).

2. *RV,* February 25, 1870, 87.

3. The entire law, "Gesetz über Unterstützungswohnsitz vom 6. Juni 1870," is *RGBl,* 1870, 360. It did not apply to Bavaria, which had its own poor law, or to Alsace-Lorraine, which maintained its French law, but it did include by far the majority of Germans and all the important industrial areas. The nature of German administrative courts is explained clearly in Frieda Wunderlich, *German Labor Courts* (Chapel Hill: University of North Carolina, 1946), esp. the introduction. The Prussian law is "Das Preussische Gesetz betreffend der Ausführung des Reichs-Gesetzes über den Unterstützungswohnsitz," March 1871. The Bavarian law is "Gesetz, die öffentliche Armen- und Krankenpflege betreffend," April 29, 1869. For the rights of the poor-law authorities over the family life of the recipients, see Christoph Sachsse and Florian Tennstedt, "Fürsorge, Wohlfahrtspflege, Sozialarbeit," in Christa Berg and Detlev K. Müller (eds.), *Handbuch der Bildungsgeschichte,* vol. 4 (Munich: Charles Beck, 1988), and in Christoph Sachsse and Florian Tennstedt, "Familienpolitik durch Gesetzgebung. Die juristische Regulierung der Familie," in Franz X. Kaufmann (ed.), *Staatliche Sozialpolitik und Familie* (Munich and Vienna: Oldenbourg, 1982).

4. The Elberfeld System is discussed in Christoph Sachsse and Florian Tennstedt, *Geschichte der Armenfürsorge in Deutschland vom Spätmittelalter bis zum 1. Weltkrieg* (Stuttgart: Kohlhammer, 1980), 214–222; the texts of the city ordinances are on pp. 286–289.

5. For the founding of the Verein, see DV, *Beiträge zur Entwicklung der Deutschen Fürsorge* (Cologne: DV, 1955), 156–157.

6. The amount of relief is compiled from "Art und Höhe der Unterstützungen," *Schriften* 19 (1894). One of many places in which there is explicit opposition to the English system is ibid., 9 (1890): 10.

7. The English figures are from *P.P.* 1913 (Cd. 6890), Forty-second Annual Report of the Local Government Board, p. vii. These figures, which cover 1890–1913, show no sudden change, while a graph between pp. 12 and 13 in ibid. shows a sharp decline after the pension and social insurance laws were passed in 1908 and 1911. I cannot explain the discrepancy. For the purposes of comparison with Germany, it is unfortunate that figures for individual cities other than London are not reported. London usually had a rate of about 3 percent.

8. DV, *Schriften,* vol. 16 (1892). Rüdiger vom Bruch (ed.), *"Weder Kommunismus noch Kapitalismus." Bürgerliche Sozialreform in Deutschland vom Vormärz bis zur Ära Adenauer* (Munich: Beck, 1985).

Chapter 4. Social Insurance in Germany in the Context of Conflict

1. For Prussian regulations before 1850, see Albin Gladen, *Geschichte der Sozialpolitik in Deutschland* (Steiner: Wiesbaden, 1974), 20–27. See also Georg Krichhoff, *Die Staatliche Sozialpolitik im Ruhrbergbau, 1871–1914*

(Cologne: Westdeutscher Verlag, 1958), esp. 9–18; Walter Vogel, *Bismarcks Arbeiterversicherung* (Braunschweig: Westerman, 1951), 29; Reinhart Koselleck, "Staat und Gesellschaft in Preussen, 1815–1848," in Hans-Ulrich Wehler (ed.), *Moderne deutsche Sozialgeschichte* (Cologne: Kiepenheuer and Witsch, 1976).

2. See Siegfried Eichler, "Die Behandlung der Lage der Industriearbeiter im Verein für Sozialpolitik im Laufe Seiner Geschichte" (diss. University of Cologne, 1949), esp. 94–99; Marie-Louise Plessen, *Die Wirksamkeit des Vereins für Socialpolitic von 1873–1890: Studien zum Katheder- und Staatssozialismus* [sic] (Berlin: Dunker and Humbolt, 1975). Plessen puts particular emphasis on the Verein as a conservative force. The most detailed history, emphasizing internal and generational conflicts, is Dieter Lindenlaub, *Richtungskämpfe im Verein für Sozialpolitik. Wissenschaft und Sozialpolitik im Kaiserreich, vornehmlich vom Beginn der "Neuen Kurs" bis zum Ausbruch des Ersten Weltkriegs (1890–1914)* (Wiesbaden: F. Steiner, 1967). Lindenlaub maintains that although the Verein had very few members of the Social Democratic Party, it became less antisocialist as time went on. It was interested in genuine reforms within capitalism. The chronology of the Verein is told in its autobiography; see Franz Boese, *Geschichte des Vereins für Sozialpolitik, 1872–1932*, Schriften des Vereins 188 (Berlin: Verein für Sozialpolitik, 1939). See also Rüdiger vom Bruch (ed.), "Weder Kommunismus noch Kapitalismus": Bürgerliche Sozialreform in Deutschland vom Vormäz bis zur Ära Adenauer (Munich: Beck, 1985).

3. On the conference, see Verein für Sozialpolitik, *Schriften*, vol. 5 (Leipzig, 1874).; ibid., vol. 21 (1882). In 1901 Hans Herman Berlepsch, who in the course of his life held many important government positions, and others founded the Gesellschaft für Soziale Reform (GSR), which was more political than the Verein für Sozialpolitik. See Rüdiger vom Bruch, "Bürgerliche Sozialreform und Gewerkschaften im späten Deutschen Kaiserreich. Die Gesellschaft für Soziale Reform, 1901–1914," *Internationale Wissenschaftliche Korrespondenz zur Geschichte der deutschen Arbeiterbewegung* 15 (1979): 581–610; and Ursula Ratz, *Sozialreform und Arbeiterschaft. Die 'Gesellschaft für Soziale Reform' und die sozialdemokratische Arbeiterbewegung von der Jahrhundertwende bis zum Ausbruch des Ersten Weltkrieges* (Berlin: Colloquium, 1980). The GSR was especially interested in *Angestellte* insurance. The labor members were originally from the nonsocialist unions, but the GSR got closer to the *"Freie"* (socialist) unions in later years.

4. Stumm's early activities are sketched in Vogel, *Bismarcks Arbeiterversicherung*, 37–38. Business and industry in general are dealt with in Herbert Buren, "Arbeitgeber und Sozialpolitik" (diss., University of Cologne, 1934); and Hans-Peter Ullman, "German Employers and Bismarcks Social Legislation," in W. J. Momsen (ed.), *The Emergence of the Welfare State in Britain and Germany, 1850–1950* (London: Croom Helm, 1981), 133–149. See also Hartmut Kaelbe, *Industrielle Interessenpolitik in der Wilhelminischen Gesellschaft. Centralverband Deutscher Industrieller 1895–*

1914 (Berlin: de Gruyter, 1967). On large firms organizing their own insurance systems, see E. H. McCreary, "Social Welfare and Business: The Krupp Welfare Program, 1860–1914," *Business History Review* 42 (1968): 24–49. See also Hans-Peter Ullman, *Der Bund der Industriellen Organisation. Einfluss und Politik klein- und mittelbetrieblicher Industrieller im Deutschen Kaiserreich, 1895–1915* (Göttingen: Vandenhoeck and Ruprecht, 1978). The smaller firms had little interest in social policy, and more in such bread-and-butter issues as tariffs or the labor policy of the government. They were, however, very involved in trying to get a special insurance for white-collar workers, not simply in raising the income level of "workers" insurance. A surprisingly good source for the industrialists, because it contains the texts of many documents, is H. Axel Bueck, *Centralverband deutscher Industrieller,* 3 vol. (Berlin: CDI, 1905); vol. 2 is relevant for the early stages of social policy. Thomas Nipperdey, "Interessenverbände und Partein in Deutschland vor dem Ersten Weltkrieg," in Hans-Ulrich Wehler (ed.), *Moderne deutsche Sozialgeschichte* (Berlin: Kiepenheuer and Witsch, 1966), 369–388, tries to generalize so much that most specifics are lost, but his general conclusion is that the political parties and the state apparatus were increasingly powerful in relation to interest groups. Nipperdey mentions the Social Democratic Party but concentrates on business interest groups.

5. H. A. Bueck, "Kathedersozialismus," in Centralverband deutscher Industrieller, *Verhandlung, Mitteilungen, und Berichte,* vol. 104 (1904).

6. Shearer Davis Bowman, "Antebellum Planters and *Vormärz* Junkers in Comparative Perspective," *American Historical Review* 85 (October 1980): 787–790, discusses whether the term is appropriate even for the East Elbe region. See also Robert M. Berdahl, "Paternalism, Serfdom, and Emancipation in Prussia," in Erich Angerman and Marie-Luise Frings (eds.), *Oceans Apart? Comparing Germany and the United States, Studies in Commemoration of the 150th Anniversary of the Birth of Carl Schurz* (Cologne: Klett-Cotta, 1982), 29–46. Berlepsch's comments on paternalism are in his memoirs, *Sozialpolitische Erfahrungen und Erinnerungen* (Gladbach: Volks Verein, 1925), 19–30. Hartmut Kaelbe, *Industrielle Interessenpolitik in der Wilhelminischen Gesellschaft. Centralverband Deutscher Industrieller, 1895–1914* (Berlin: de Gruyter, 1967), 54, suggests that paternalism was an important part of the self-definition of the industrialists. Peter Domann, *Sozialdemokratie und Kaisertum unter Wilhelm II. Die Auseinandersetzung der Partei mit dem monarchistischen System, seinen gesellschafts- und verfassungspolitischen Voraussetzungen* (Wiesbaden: Steiner, 1974), discusses how the new Kaiser talked about the need for the workers to be convinced that they were a "gleichberechtigter Stand," and even Bebel had hopes for a "sozialdemokratischer Kaiser" in 1889. These hopes lasted about three years, but many Social Democrats thought they

had more to hope for from a monarchy than from a republic, which would necessarily be dominated by the bourgeoisie.

7. On Ketteler, see Vogel, *Bismarcks Arbeiterversicherung*, 60. See also Maria Moenig, "Die Stellung der deutschen katholischen Sozialpolitik des 19. Jahrhunderts zur 'Staatsintervention' in den sozialen Fragen" (diss., University of Münster, 1927), 51–56. In praise of Ketteler, see Joseph Höffner, *Wilhelm Emmanuel V. Ketteler und katholische Sozialbewegung im 19. Jahrhundert* (Wiesbaden: F. Steiner, 1962). For Ketteler's own words, see Wilhelm Emmanuel Ketteler, *Die grossen socialen Fragen der Gegenwart* (Mainz: F. Kircheim, 1978).

8. The literature on the churches' reactions and influence on social policy is enormous. An excellent starting point is E. I. Kouri, *Der Deutsche Protestantismus und die soziale Frage, 1870–1919* (Berlin: de Gruyter, 1984). In spite of its title, the book contains a good deal on both Catholicism and Protestantism.

9. On Bismarck here, see Hans Rothfels, *Theodor Lohman und die Kampfjahre der staatlichen Sozialpolitik, 1871–1905* (Berlin: C. S. Mittler, 1927), 9–55.

10. On the Catholic argument, see *Kölnische Volks Zeitung*, November 21, 1881, 2.

11. See Fritz Stern, *Gold and Iron: Bismarck, Bleichröder, and the Building of the German Empire* (New York: Knopf, 1977), for Bismarck's anti-Semitism and its limits. See also, on Bismarck's social ideas in general, Hans Rothfels, *Prinzipienfrage der Bismarckschen Sozialpolitik* (Königsberg: Gräf and Imger, 1929); Leonard Krieger, *The German Idea of Freedom: History of a Political Tradition* (Boston: Beacon Press, 1957), 22–26, 182–183. Some Conservatives united in support for social insurance with strong anti-Semitism. The most prominent of these was the court chaplain, Adolf Stöcker. On Stöcker, see Walter Frank, *Hofprediger Adolf Stöcker und die christlich-soziale Bewegung* (Berlin: R. Hobbing, 1928); and Karl Kupish, *Adolf Stöcker, Hofprediger und Volkstribun. Ein historisches Porträt* (Berlin: Haude and Spener, 1970). Stöcker was extremely conservative in every way and was close to the Kaiser.

12. *RV*, February 15, 1881, 1–2. Florian Tennstedt, "Vorgeschichte und Entstehung der Kaiserlichen Botschaft vom 17. November 1881," *Zeitschrift für Sozialreform* 27 (November–December 1881): 663–711 (the whole issue is on the anniversary of the message).

13. "Begründung" (Justification) to the first accident insurance bill, *RV Anlagen*, 1881, Aktenstück 41, p. 228.

14. *NPZ* January 5, 1882, p. 1 of Beilage; see also January 6 and 8, 1882, p. 1 of Beilage. When Karl Marx died, on the Ides of March 1883, he received a long obituary in the *Neue Preussische (Kreuz) Zeitung*. The obituary condemned the revolutionary activities of Marx, but not at all his economic

analysis. Marx, like the conservatives, was critical of capitalism, and conservatives found his labor theory of value and theory of surplus value especially convincing. He, like they, decried the degradation of labor into simply an item on the balance sheet whose value was determined by supply and demand. See *NPZ*, March 21, 1883.

15. *NTL-ZTG*, April 14, 1883. The early history of the *Krankenkasse* is from Friedrich Syrup (with Otto Neuloh), *Hundert Jahre Staatliche Sozialpolitik, 1839–1939* (Stuttgart: Kohlhammer, 1957), 123.

16. On the leader of the "consistent liberals," see Ina Susanne Lorenz, *Eugen Richter: Der entschiedene Liberalismus in wilhelminischer Zeit, 1871 bis 1906*, Historische Studien 433 (Husum: Mathiesen, 1981).

17. *RV*, April 20, 1883, 1995–1998; *Vorwärts*, March 26 and May 10, 1883.

18. See *RV*, April 19, 1883, 1977, 1983 (Zentrum), 1979–1980 (Buhl).

19. On whether the law should include agricultural workers, see *RV Anlagen*, 1881–1883, Aktenstück 14, "Begründung," 142–143; the law is *RGBl*, 1883, 73. The laws of Germany, France, Great Britain, Austria, and Switzerland are covered in considerable detail from the point of view of legal scholars in Peter A. Köhler and Hans F. Zacher (eds.), *The Evolution of Social Insurance, 1881–1981: Studies of Germany, France, Great Britain, Austria, and Switzerland* (New York: St. Martin's Press; London: Frances Pinter, 1982).

20. The provision that employees pay two-thirds of the premium and have two-thirds representation became controversial for members of labor unions almost immediately and has been controversial among historians since. Because the funds established by the 1883 law received income at least in part from employers, they could more easily pay the benefits required by the law. The so-called independent (*Freie*) aid funds could pay the minimum benefits only by charging higher premiums, and most of them quickly had to cease operation. One can see that this was a result of government attempts to repress independent workers organizations, which were a proletarian political force and in effect a proletarian culture. Indeed, there could have been a way, as demonstrated in Denmark, to subsidize independent organizations while at the same time requiring minimum standards for benefits. And yet it is probably imputing too much conspiratorial cleverness to Bismarck to see the sickness funds as a means of subverting independent funds. The law of April 7, 1876, encouraging these funds, was a first attempt, and its failure was frequently mentioned in the debates in the 1880s. The Sickness Fund Law of 1883 was a second attempt, and one that succeeded.

21. *RV*, March 14, 1884, 50 (von Botticher). Horst Kohl (ed.), *Die Reden des Ministerpräsidenten und Reichskanzlers Fürsten von Bismarck* (1884; reprint, Aalen: Scientia, 1970), 40–68.

22. *Socialdemokrat*, July 28, 1888, 1. Klaus Witte, *Bismarcks Sozialver-*

sicherung und die Entwicklung eines marxistischen Reformverständnisses in der deutschen Sozialdemokratie (Cologne: Pahl-Rugenstein, 1980), claims that opposition to Bismarck's "state socialism" drove the Social Democrats into the Marxian position. Witte argues an oversimplified "Zuckerbrot und Peitsche" view of the relationship. Vernon L. Lidtke, "German Social Democracy and German State Socialism, 1876–1884," *International Review of Social History* 9 (1964): 202–225, is far more nuanced and shows continuous tensions within the party, with August Bebel (for many years the party leader) being an extreme voice. Bebel's view disguised a considerable degree of attraction to state socialism, however defined, on the part of other Social Democrats. The Social Democratic Party's position on the laws in general is summed up in A. Bebel, "Das Gesetz über Invaliditäts- und Altersversicherung im Deutschen Reich," *Die Neue Zeit* (1889): 385–400.

23. E.g., *NPZ*, April 20, 23, and 30, 1889. See also *RV*, May 24, 1889, 203.

24. For a discussion of the effects of the laws, see Gerhard A. Ritter, *Staat, Arbeiterschaft und Arbeiterbewegung in Deutschland vom Vormärz bis zum Ende der Weimarer Republik* (Berlin: Dietz, 1980), 49–56. Figures for the coverage of the social insurance laws are from Karl E. Born, Hansjoachim Henning, and Manfred Schick, *Quellensammlung zur Geschichte der Deutschen Sozialpolitik, 1867 bis 1911* (Wiesbaden: F. Steiner, 1966).

Chapter 5. Changes in German Social Insurance

1. Robert Schmidt, "Die Privatversicherung," *SM*, November 18, 1909, 1495–1499. See also remarks about *Arbeitsekretariate* in "Rundschau," *SM*, July 15, 1909, 923, Herman Mücke, "Die Versicherungspflicht nach dem Entwurf der Reichsversicherungsordnung," *SM*, July 1, 1909, 821–824; idem, "Die Leistungen der Arbeiterversicherung nach dem Entwurf der Reichsversicherungsordnung," *SM*, September 8, 1910, 907–910; Julius Frässdorf, "Verbesserungen und Verschlechterungen der Krankenversicherung durch den Entwurf der Reichsversicherungordnung," *SM*, September 8, 1910, 1260–1266; Friedrich Kleeis, "Zum Projekt der Witwen- und Waisenfürsorge," *SM*, October 3, 1909, 1288–1293; idem, "Der Entwicklung des Versicherungsgedankens," *SM*, December 16, 1909, 821–824; Herman Mücke, "Versicherungsträger nach dem Entwurf der Reichsversicherungsordnung," *SM*, July 29, 1909, 967–973.

2. See Guenther Roth, *The Social Democrats in Imperial Germany: A Study in Working-Class Isolation and National Integration* (Totowa, N.J.: Bedminster, 1963); Vernon L. Lidtke, *The Alternative Culture: Socialist Labor in Imperial Germany* (New York: Oxford University Press, 1985).

3. See Centralverband Deutscher Industrieller, *Verhandlung, Mitteilung und Berichte*, vol. 82 (1899); Robert Schmidt, "Die Reform unseres Krankenkassenversicherungsgesetzes," *SM*, August 8, 1900, 475–460;

Zentralblatt christlicher Gerwerkschaften, September 29, 1913, 224, and October 13, 1913, 323–335. Bergitte Emig, *Die Veredelung der Arbeiter, Sozialdemokratie als Kulturbewegung* (New York and Frankfurt: Campus, 1980), discusses ways in which the Social Democratic Party wanted to become more than a political party, how they disagreed with what they took to be a bourgeois definition of *Kultur,* and how they wanted to replace it with one of their own—that is, dominance of the *Ortskrankenkasse* was part of a larger Social Democratic Party impulse.

4. *RV Anlagen,* 1911, 340, 119–121.

5. *RV,* May 11, 1911, 6568–6570.

6. Ibid., 6576; the speech itself continues to 6594.

7. The law restoring the two-thirds is "Verordnung über die Wahl des Vorstandsvorsitzenden der Ortskrankenkassen und über die Kassenangestellten," February 5, 1919, *RGBl,* 1919, 187.

8. *RV Anlagen,* 1911, 1035, pp. 63, 68.

9. *RV,* 1911, 7432–7435. The smaller and middle-sized firms lobbied heavily to have the insurance especially for *Angestellte,* not just an extended "workers" insurance. See Hans-Peter Ullman, *Der Bund der Industriellen Organisation. Einfluss und Politik klein- und mittelbetrieblicher Industrieller im Deutschen Kaiserreich, 1895–1915* (Göttingen: Vandenhoeck and Ruprecht, 1978), esp. 217.

10. See *RV,* October 20, 1911, 7477 (Zentrum), 7439 (Conservatives), 7445 (Social Democrats); The index reports that the vote was unanimous.

Chapter 6. Denmark and the Poor Law in the Context of Consensus

1. For the texts of the various constitutions, see S. Viskinge, *Vor Forfatnings Historie Gennem Tiderne,* 5th ed. (Copenhagen: n.p., 1928).

2. Vagn Dybdahl, *De Nye Klasser, 1870–1913,* vol. 12 of Politiken's *Danmarks Historie* (Copenhagen: Politiken, 1971), 176.

3. For a more detailed treatment of the politics of these years, see Per Salomonsson (ed.), *Den Politiske Magtkamp, 1866–1901* (Copenhagen: J. Paludan, 1968), esp. chaps. 6 and 7. See also Frede Bojsen (with Kristian Hvidt), *Frede Bojsens Politiske Erindringer* (Copenhagen: G. E. C. Gad, 1963).

4. On the history of the poor laws in Denmark, see Harald Jørgensen, *Studier over det Offentlige Fattigvæsens Historiske Udvikling i Danmark i det 19. Aarhundrede* (Copenhagen: Gyldendal, 1940), 5.

5. Ibid., 10–35.

6. See *Husmandsvennen,* 1889, passim; *Højskolebladet,* 1892, passim.

7. On the relationship between class and party, see Gösta Esping-Andersen, *Social Class, Social Democracy, and State Policy* Copenhagen: *New Social Science Monographs,* 1980), esp. 65–78 (this is probably easier

to obtain as a dissertation: University of Wisconsin, 1978). See also Peter Baldwin, "The Scandinavian Origins of the Social Interpretation of the Welfare State," *Comparative Studies in Society and History* (forthcoming).

8. The quotation is in *Social-Demokraten,* August 17, 1880, See also ibid., February 8, 1880, against taxing beer and snaps to pay for sickness insurance; June 11, 1880, arguing that the state should assume the cost of industrial accidents; and September 7, 1890, in praise of P. Knudsen and his study of sickness insurance for workers. See also *Social-Demokraten,* March 11, 1891, on old-age insurance; March 13, 1891, on sickness insurance; and March 29, 1891, on old-age pensions.

9. Niels Finn Christiansen, "Reformism within the Danish Social Democracy until the Nineteen-Thirties," *Journal of Scandinavian History* 3 (1978): 297–322. See also idem, "Den borgerlige politiske økonomi og marxism i Danmark, 1870–1900" (unpublished paper in author's possession, [1977?]). He sees conflict as a more important element in Danish society than I do.

10. *FT,* January 21, 1889, 2596.

11. *FT,* November 7, 1889, 826–827 (Holm); January 26, 1891, 2885–2886 (Hørup); January 22, 1891, 2648–2649 (Jensen).

12. *FT,* November 7, 1889, 822.

13. All citations are to the law of April 9, 1891, "Det Offentlige Fattigvæsen."

14. Jørgensen, *Studier,* gives details about how the laws were administered before 1890. Up to 1870, most aid was in kind, but after that year most was in money, in greatly varying amounts. Poorhouses were common, but "outdoor relief" was also provided. Local administration after 1890 has not been investigated.

15. *FT,* November 5, 1889, 722–734, and November 7, 1889, 865–866; January 24, 1891, 2841; January 24, 1891, 2853–2854.

16. *FT,* December 12, 1890, 1783.

17. All references are to the law of April 15, 1891, "Alderdomsunderstøttelse til Værdige Trængende udenfor Fattigvæsnet."

18. *FT,* December 20, 1890, 1771, 1773.

19. Ibid., 1757.

Chapter 7. Social Insurance in Denmark in the Context of Consensus

1. *LT,* October 13, 1888, 69–70. Note that Reedtz-Thott condemns socialism because it is "chaotic," not for other plausible reasons, such as that it was unchristian or threatened private property, arguments that might have appeal in a country with many small landholders. In Denmark, chaos was the most undesirable value one could evoke.

2. See Sven Christiansen, "Sygekasselov of 1892, Forudsætninger og

Tilblivelse," in *Fra Laugssygekasser til Folkeforsikring* (Copenhagen: n.p., 1942), 15–16; H. Daniel, *Danmarks Sygekassevæsen Gennem Aarhundreder* (Copenhagen: Videnskab og Kultur, 1937), 22–25.

3. Betænkning, *Undersøgels af Arbejderspørgsmaal, Danmark* (1878), xiii.

4. *Betænkning afgiven af den af Indenrigsministeriet til Overvejelse af Spørgsmaalene om Sygekassernes Ordning og om Arbejdernes Sikring mod Følgerne af Ulykkestilfælde under Arbejdet nedsatte Kommission* (Copenhagen, 1887), 19–22; Landsting, *Betænkning* (1881), 1–2.

5. P. Knudsen, *Sygeforsikring og Alderdomsforsørgelse, afgiven af det paa det københavnske og fredriksbergske sygekassers Fællesmøde den 29de* or *30te August, 1883, nedsatte udvalg* (1888), 209, 245–249.

6. *LT,* November 2, 1889, 239 (T. Nielsen); *FT,* February 19, 1890, 252.

7. All references are to the "Lov om anerkendte Sygekasser," April 12, 1892.

8. "Lov om Arbejders Forsikring mod Følger af Ulykkestilfælde i visse Virksomheder," January 7, 1898. See also A. Birkemose, *Ulykkesforsikringsloven. En håndbog i den danske ulykkesforsikringslovgivning gennem 50 år* (Copenhagen: Danske Ulykkesforsikringsselskaber, [1948?]).

9. On unemployment insurance, see Aage Vater, *Arbejdsløshedslovgivningen i Danmark Gennem 25 Aar 1907–1932* (Copenhagen: n.p., 1932), 10. See also Jesper Due and Jørgen Steen Madsen, *Kampen om Arbejdsløshedlovgivning* (Copenhagen: University of Copenhagen, 1978).

10. *RT,* 1906–1907 Tillaeg A, 2767 and 2785, where the virtues of trying hard are explicated.

11. *FT,* December 4, 1906, 2330, 2406, 2408 (Larsen); December 7, 1906, 2270 (Neergaard).

12. All references below are to the "Lov om anerkendte Arbejdsløshedskasser," May 1, 1907.

Chapter 8. Perfecting the Perfect System: Social Welfare within the Poor Law of 1834

1. For poor law medical services to 1868, see M. W. Flinn, "Medical Services under the New Poor Law," in Derek Fraser (ed.), *The New Poor Law in the Nineteenth Century* (New York: St. Martin's Press, 1976), 45–66. From the very first official policy had recognized that sickness would be an exception to the prohibition on "outdoor relief." For example, an "Out-door Relief Prohibitory Order," dated December 21, 1844, and issued by the poor-law commissioners, made an exception for people who "require relief on account of any sickness, accident, or bodily or mental infirmity" (in William C. Glen and Reginald C. Glen, *The General Orders of the Poor Law Commissioners, the Poor Law Board, and the Local Government Board Relating to the Poor Law* (London: Knight, 1887), 268.

2. H. of C. *Debates,* III:185, February 8, 1867, 157–158, 160–162 (Hardy); ibid., February 21, 1867, 753 (Verney).

3. Ibid., III:299, July 21, 1885, 1415 (Chadwick); July 16, 1885, 965–968 (no distinction could or should be made), 982–990; and July 21, 1885, 1456–1460 (Balfour). Chadwick may have opposed removal of the medical disqualification, but he had long been active in public health, particularly in sanitation and drainage.

4. See ibid., III:166, May 9, 1862, 1495–1505, where the president of the Poor Law Board asserts that the local resources are adequate. Michael E. Rose, "Rochdale Man and the Stalybridge Riot: The Relief and Control of the Unemployed during the Lancashire Cotton Famine," in A. P. Donajgrodski (ed.), *Social Control in Nineteenth-Century Britain* (London: Croom Helm, 1977), shows how the only unrest in the district was a riot against the private relief committee, which was far more rigid than the Guardians in upholding the principles of the new poor law.

5. Villiers speech is H. of C. *Debates,* III:171, June 18, 1863, 1050–1063. The most vehement speech against the manufacturers is by Mr. Ferrand, ibid., III:170, April 27, 1863, 775. For the extent of the distress and the results of the act, see *P.P.* 1864 (607), lii, "Distress in the Cotton Manufacturing Districts"; *P.P.* 1868–1869 (6), liii, "Public Works Executed in Cotton Manufacturing Districts and the Employment of Operatives." Sidney Webb and Beatrice Webb *English Poor Law History,* vol. 2 [1929; reprint, London: Archon, 1963], 657), deprecate the whole effort, partly because it was so small in scale but more because it was what they considered a palliative and did not try to prevent unemployment from occurring in the first place. They were so opposed to a capitalist welfare state that in spite of their massive and accurate scholarship their values did not allow them to see virtues in what they opposed.

6. E.g., "The Cotton Famine and the Lancashire Districts," *North British Review* 39 (1863): 126–137 (American edition; the pagination is different from the British edition); "Lancashire," *Westminster Review* 80 (1863): 85–98 (Am. ed.). Both are reviews of John William Maclure, *Return from the Relief Committees* (Manchester, 1863). See also "Lessons from the Cotton Famine," *British Quarterly* 41 (1865): 358–380.

7. The circular was titled "Report of the Local Government Board 1886–1887," Circular Letter No. 4, March 15, 1886. Note that the "working classes" are referred to in the plural, a common practice. Evidently such loans were made. See *Local Government Board and Official Gazette* 37 (October 31, 1908); 1917. Historians disagree about the circular's importance. See Webb and Webb, *History,* 2:645–647; and José Harris, *Unemployment and Politics: A Study in English Social Policy, 1886–1914* (Oxford: Oxford University Press, 1972), 76. The Webbs see the "principles of 1834" as being a matter of law, and so they are quite right in regarding the 1886 circular as a considerable alteration. Harris judges it by its effects, which were small. I

have been treating the 1834 report as an essay in moral philosophy and am impressed by the survival of that moral philosophy and its use in an economic world very different from that for which it was devised.

8. In the fifteen years or so before the "Unemployed Circular," the poor law was evidently more rigorously enforced than previously. The overall figures do not seem to have been greatly affected, but there was apparently considerable impact in some places. See Webb and Webb, *History,* esp. 435–446; *P.P.* 1878 (382), lxv, "Poor Law (Out Relief)"; Ruth Hutchinson Crocker, "The Victorian Poor Law in Crisis and Change: Southampton, 1870–1895," *Albion* 19 (Spring 1897): 19–44. For overall figures, see Karel Williams, *From Pauperism to Poverty* (London: Routledge and Kegan Paul, 1981), 158–160.

9. H. of C. *Debates,* IV:8, February 20, 1893, 1943–1961 (Asquith); ibid., 1961–1971 (Chamberlain); ibid., IV:9, March 24, 1893, 1059–1063 (Woods). In ibid., 1058, Bousfield reports that various resolutions of the TUC and labor unions oppose Chamberlain's amendment; in ibid., 1074, Balfour says the bill was written by the TUC, and Asquith does not deny it, or seem to feel the point needs defending. David Powell, "The Liberal Ministries and Labour, 1892–1895," *History* 68 (October 1983): 408–426, shows how during these years the influence of organized labor increased in the Liberal Party, thus pointing the way toward the "new" liberalism of Lloyd George and away from Gladstone's versions of liberalism. By contrast, D. J. Dutton, "The Unionist Party and Social Policy, 1906–1914," *Historical Journal* 24 (December 1981): 871–884, shows that except for Joseph Chamberlain the Unionist Party was not attuned to the social demands of politically active workers and therefore suffered a fatal decline.

10. Joseph Chamberlain, "The Labour Question," *The Nineteenth Century* 189 (November 1892): 676–710; on workmen's compensation, see 693–696.

11. For Home Secretary Sir Mathew White Ridley introducing the bill, see H. of C. *Debates,* IV:48, May 3, 1897, 1421–1434. Ridley takes the opportunity to sneer at the "elaborate system" in Germany, which is utterly foreign to Englishmen. For Asquith, supporting the bill with some regret that his 1893 bill is not part of the program, see ibid. IV:48, May 3, 1897, 1434–1442, and IV:49, May 18, 1897, 747–756. Labour expressing support is in ibid., IV:49, May 17, 1897, 668 (Broadhurst), 670 (Strauss). For employers expressing support, see ibid., IV:48, May 3, 1897, 1486 (Wolff); IV:49, May 18, 1897, 763 (Brunner) and 778 (Hickman). Sentiment opposing lawyers is expressed many places, among them ibid., IV:49, 743 (Provand) and 773 (Richardson). The bill passed the second reading without a division; see ibid., IV:49, May 18, 1897, 813.

12. *P.P.* 1904 (Cd. 2208), lxxxviii, gives a synopsis of the dispute. See also David G. Hanes, *The First British Workmen's Compensation Act, 1897* (New Haven: Yale University Press, 1968), esp. 70–71, where the letters to Asquith from businessmen are mentioned. See also *Journal of the London*

Chamber of Commerce, March Supplement 1897, p. 17, reporting the annual meeting of the national organization. For a general expression of views on the burden of the act, see ibid., August 1897, 165–168. The TUC approved of the act while recognizing its limitations (Trades Union Congress, *Report of the Annual Congress 1898,* 30–31). It is at least possible that British businessmen did not like to think of themselves as an interest group, that they fled even from seeing themselves as businessmen. The degree to which they were able to become landed gentlemen is disputable, but their lack of political activity, as businessmen, is added evidence that perhaps they wanted to become gentry. Martin Wiener finds considerable evidence that businessmen felt less than proud about being "in trade," were not eager to embrace the entrepreneurial spirit, and aspired to the land; see, e.g., Martin J. Wiener, *English Culture and the Decline of the Industrial Spirit, 1850–1980* (Cambridge: Cambridge University Press, 1980), esp. chap. 2. Roy Hay, "The British Business Community, Social Insurance, and the German Example," in W. J. Momsen (ed.), *The Emergence of the Welfare State in Britain and Germany, 1850–1950* (London: Croom Helm, 1981), claims that businessmen were politically active, but he judges the whole from one part—Birmingham. Lawrence Stone and Jeanne C. Fawter, *An Open Elite? England 1540–1880* (Oxford: Clarendon Press, 1984), find that great estates did not change hands often enough to allow businessmen to become landed. They do not address the issue of businessmen's aspirations or deal with the possibility that absorption could have occurred when smaller estates were involved.

13. The standard work is David G. Hanes, *The First British Workmen's Compensation Act, 1897* (New Haven: Yale University Press, 1968). Asquith barely mentions the act in his diary (see Herbert H. Asquith, *Fifty Years of British Parliament,* 2 vols. [Boston: Little, Brown, 1926], 1:276). J. L. Garvin and Julian Amery, *The Life of Joseph Chamberlain,* 6 vols. (London: Macmillan, 1932–1964), devote a few pages to the issue, but they concentrate on the skill with which Chamberlain managed the bill more than on the substance of the act. Even such a specific work as Elsie E. Gulley, *Joseph Chamberlain and English Social Politics* (New York: Columbia University Press, 1926), devotes little more than a page. Roy Jenkins, *Asquith: Portrait of a Man and an Era* (New York: Dutton, 1966), barely mentions workmen's compensation.

14. See Charles S. Loch, "Manufacturing a New Pauperism," *Nineteenth Century* 37 (April 1895): 697–708; John Burns, "Labour Leaders on the Labour Question," ibid., 32 (December 1892): 845–863. Other expressions of opinion are Samuel A. Barnett, "The Unemployed," *Fortnightly Review* 60 (December 1893): 741–749; Arnold White, "The Unemployed," ibid., 60 (October 1893): 454–462; J. Tyrrel Baylee, "The Problems of Pauperism: The Unemployed," *Westminster Review* 147 (March 1897): 274–285; James Mavor, "Setting the Poor on Work," *Nineteenth Century* 34 (October 1893):

523–532. Mavor's work is an interesting historical review of attempts to found labor colonies under the old poor law; he concludes that labor colonies had not done much good and probably never would. A. Dunn-Gardner, "The Drift to Socialism," *Contemporary Review* 65 (January 1894): 110–113, is almost as extreme as Loch, but Dunn-Gardner puts his emphasis not on the creation of more poverty but on the unscrupulous politicians—and he means particularly John Burns—who try to exploit the issue for their own gain.

15. Samuel A. Barnett and Sidney Webb, "Draft Report of the Toynbee Hall 'Unemployed' Committee," 1892, in the British Library, cataloged under "Toynbee Hall."

16. *P.P.* 1893 (C. 7182), lxxxii, "Report on Agencies and Methods for Dealing with the Unemployed"; ibid., 1895 (365), ix, "Report of Select Committee on Distress from Want of Employment" (Charles Booth's testimony is 412–429). The preliminary report of the committee is in ibid. (111), viii. The Labour Commission met from 1892 to 1894; its final report is in ibid., 1894 (C. 7421), xxxv. See also G. Stedman Jones, *Outcast London: A Study in the Relationship between the Classes in Victorian Society* (Oxford: Claredon Press, 1971). As Sean Glynn and Alan Booth point out in "Unemployment in Interwar Britain: A Case for Relearning the Lessons of the 1930s," *Economic History Review* 36 (August 1983): 332, the only figures on the years prior to 1914 are those compiled by the trade unions and applying only to their own members. While Glynn and Booth guess that the overall figure was higher, there is really no way to tell whether the issue disappeared because unemployment was actually getting less or because there was less concern about the problem, but the problem remained. See Harris, *Unemployment and Politics*, 151–152.

17. The apocalyptic alarms from the Conservative side are in H. of C. *Debates*, IV:147 (1905), 1128–1142, 1165–1170; for labor, see Keir Hardie, ibid., 1170–1180. The Unemployed Workmen Act is 5 Edw. 7, c. 18.

18. Joseph Chamberlain, "Old-Age Pensions," *National Review* 18 (February 1892): 734–744. Several plans for pensions are conveniently summarized in "State Pensions for Old Age," *Quarterly Review* 174 (1892): 505–533.

19. Charles Booth, *Pauperism, a Picture; and The Endowment of Old Age, an Argument* (London: Macmillan, 1892); idem, *Old-Age Pensions and the Aged Poor* (London: Macmillan, 1899); idem, *The Aged Poor: A Proposal* (London: Macmillan, 1907).

20. *P.P.* 1895 (C. 7684), xiv. The quotations from the majority are in ibid., lxxxiii–lxxxvii; Broadhurst's dissent is in ibid., xcvii–ciii; Marshall's testimony is in ibid., 529–550; for Octavia Hill's, see 550–567.

21. Ibid., 1898 (C. 8911), xlv.

22. Ibid., 1874 (C. 961), xxii. See also "Three Friendly Societies," in COS, *Occasional Papers 1896*, 25, 66–70; Patricia Mary Williams, "The Development of Old-Age Pensions in Great Britain, 1878–1925" diss., University of London, 1970), 11–14; Robert W. Moffrey, *A Century of Oddfellowship* (Man-

chester: The G[rand] M[aster] and Board of Directors, 1910). P.H.J.H. Gosden, *The Friendly Societies in England, 1815–1875* (Manchester: University Press, 1961). Bently B. Gilbert, *The Evolution of National Insurance in Great Britain* (London: Joseph, 1966), makes the "friendly societies" into the villains of the story, but he is clearly wrong. They came to support pensions as well as national social insurance at about the same pace as the rest of the nation. See also Joseph H. Treble, "The Attitudes of Friendly Societies toward the Movement in Great Britain for State Pensions, 1878–1908," *International Review of Social History* 15 (1970): 266–299.

23. The review of Booth's pamphlet is in *Odd Fellows Magazine* 20 (August 1894): 242–243; the denunciation of state aid is in ibid., 25 (December 1894): 4. Letters to the Rothschild Committee are in ibid., 28 (July 1897): 239–240; and (October 1897): 298–299. My evidence for the resolution in favor of state aid is the testimony of Past Grand Master Claverhouse Graham in 1899 saying it was passed (ibid., 30 [September 1899]: 267). The account of the "Bristol A.M.C." does not say anything about such a resolution, but in summarizing the year the magazine refers to the "complete *volte face*" made on the question. The Grand Master favoring pensions is in ibid., 31 (July 1900): 211–212. Information on the Druids is from Williams, "Development of Old-Age Pensions," 97. The Rothschild Committee report is *P.P.* 1898 (C. 8911), xlv; for the past director, see ibid., 64; for the current director, ibid., 29–33; for conclusions, ibid., 1–16.

24. See Arthur Marwick, "The Labour Party and the Welfare State, 1900–1948," *American Historical Review* 73 (1967): 380–403. Henry Pelling, "La Classe ouvrier Anglaise et les origines de la legislation sociale," *Mouvement Social* 65 (1968): 39–54. Marwick shows that the Labour Party had clear ideas about the kind of welfare state they wanted; Pelling that the working class opposed most extensions of state power and often supported the Conservatives. The two articles do not quite meet each other's points, but on the question of old-age pensions, Labour was clearly more pro than con. A very thorough examination of the whole subject is Pat Thane, "The Working Class and State 'Welfare' in Britain, 1880–1914," *Historical Journal* 27 (December 1984): 877–900.

25. TUC, *Report of Annual Congress, 1899,* 26; George Turner, *The Case for State Pensions in Old Age,* Fabian Tract 73 (London, 1897).

26. In the literature the National Pensions Committee is variously called the National Committee of Organized Labour (or NCOL), the National Committee, or the National Pensions Committee (NPC), which is the designation I use. That was what Francis Herbert Stead, its longtime honorary secretary, organizer, and major activist, called it in his *How Old-Age Pensions Began to Be* (London: Methuen, 1909).

27. The text of the opinion issued by the NPC is in ibid., 81–82. for a chatty account of the NPC, see Frederick Rogers, *Labour, Life, and Literature: Some Memories of Sixty Years* (London: Smith, Elder 1913); I used the

edition edited by David Rubenstein (Brighton, Sussex: Harvester Press, 1973). For many years Rogers was the operating head of the NPC.

28. *P.P.* 1899 (296), viii. J. S. Davy, the man whom the Chaplin Committee sent to Denmark, is discussed in Webb and Webb, *History,* 500, 547, among other places.

29. Public Record Office (PRO) CAB 37/51 (87), November 15, 1899 (Balfour); ibid. (88), November 17, 1899 (Joseph Chamberlain); ibid. (89), November 20, 1899 (HIcks-Beach, Chancellor of the Exchequer). See also Williams, "Development of Old-Age Pensions," 133–139.

30. PRO CAB 37/49 (12), February 10, 1899. Local Government Board, *Annual Report 1900–1901,* 18–20.

Chapter 9. Voices for Change in Great Britain and the United States

1. See *P.P.* 1895 (365), ix, Select Committee on Distress from Want of Employment; Charles Booth's testimony is in ibid., 412–429. See also Beatrice Webb, *My Apprenticeship* (New York: Longmans, Green, 1926), 210. The quotation from Booth is also in Webb (ibid.), 216, quoting Booth's *Condition and Occupations of the People of the Tower Hamlets, 1886–1887* (London, 1887), 7. See also Charles Booth, *Life and Labour of the People in London* (London: Macmillan, 1889).

2. *Spectator* 79 (July 24, 1894): 116–117. Ashley's reviews are in *Political Science Quarterly* 5 (1890): 507–519; 7 (1892): 149–153; 12 (1905): 719–723 (the quotations are from the first of the reviews). Ashley's connection with the German historical school is detailed in Günter Hollenberg, *Englisches Interesse am Kaiserreich: Die Attraktivität Preussen-Deutschlands für konservative and liberale Kreise in Grossbritanien, 1860–1914* (Wiesbaden: F. Steiner, 1974), 229–231.

3. Benjamin Seebohm Rowntree, *Poverty: A Study of Town Life* (London: Macmillan, 1902).

4. Helen Bosanquet of the COS published a devastating review of Booth and Rowntree showing how their determination of a "poverty line," while seemingly scientific, is purely impressionistic. The same criticism is directed at Rowntree's attempts to determine an adequate wage. Bosanquet says that Rowntree may not make explicit policy recommendations, but that he clearly had them in mind and a reader could gather what they are. Although she was right in her criticisms, one need not agree with her policies. Her views are in "The 'Poverty Line,'" COS, *Occasional Papers 1905,* 11, 221–235. There is no date on the paper itself, but 1904 would be a reasonable guess.

5. See Andrew Mearns, *The Bitter Cry of Outcast London* (New York: Humanities Press, 1970), a reprint of the 1883 original edition, with a full introduction by Anthony Wohl and some related articles. There was a dis-

pute between Mearns and William Preston, who also worked on the book, over who should get credit for authorship, and Preston is sometimes listed as the author. Not all the critical notes were sounded by religious figures. In 1890 a radical politician, D. Bicker-Caarten, published a series called "The Bitter Cry of Outcast Southampton" in the *Southampton Times*. See Ruth Hutchinson Crocker, "The Victorian Poor Law in Crisis and Change: Southampton, 1870–1895," *Albion* 19 (Spring 1987): 1944.

6. William Booth, *In Darkest England and the Way Out* (New York: Garrett Press, 1970), a photographic reprint of the first edition of 1890; the quotation is on p. 45. For an enthusiastic contemporary account of the Salvation Army's work with the poor, see Walter Besant, "The Farm and the City," *Contemporary Review* 72 (December 1897): 792–807. Victor Bailey, " 'In Darkest England and the Way Out': The Salvation Army, Social Reform, and the Labour Movement," *International Review of Social History* 29, pt. 2 (1984): 133–171, emphasizes links with socialists and the Labour Party.

7. Booth's views are confirmed for the Church of England by G. Kitson Clark, *Churchmen and the Condition of England, 1832–1885* (London: Methuen, 1973).

8. The quotations are from Samuel and Henrietta Barnett, *Practicable Socialism: Essays on Social Reform* (1888; reprint, Salem, N.H.: Ayer, 1972), 235, 245. The first quotation was originally from an article written in 1886, and the second was written in 1883, actually before Toynbee Hall was founded and very early to be talking about pensions under the poor law. A recent and rather critical view is Emily K. Able, "Toynbee Hall," *Social Service Review* 53 (1979): 606–632. See also Loretta Mae Lagana, "Toynbee Hall" (Diss., Columbia University, 1981). For Toynbee Hall's support of state action, see *Toynbee Record* 21 (March 1908): 73–75; GDM, "The Social Welfare Movement," ibid., 23 (December 1910): 43–47; Quintillius, "Insurance against Unemployment," ibid. (February 1911): 68–71; L. J. Stein, "East London and the National Health Insurance," ibid. (June 1911); 129–135. The standard work on the subject is David Owen, *English Philanthropy, 1660–1960* (Cambridge, Mass.: Belknap Press, 1964). Asa Briggs and Anne Macartney, *Toynbee Hall: The First One Hundred Years* (Boston and London: Routledge and Kegan Paul, 1984), is a celebratory anniversary study that touches on political participation (pp. 68–70), but it illustrates how really small a part political action played in the life of the settlement. Robert C. Reinders, "Toynbee Hall and the American Settlement Movement," *Social Service Review* 56 (March 1982): 39–54, claims great political involvement for Toynbee Hall; I see the settlement's other activities as far more important. My view is supported by Standish Meacham, *Toynbee Hall and Social Reform, 1880–1914: The Search for Community* (New Haven: Yale University Press, 1988).

9. Robert Dare, "Instinct and Organization: Intellectuals and British

Labour after 1931," *Historical Journal* 26 (September 1983): 677–697, has many points that are pertinent well before the period he treats. For Beatrice Webb's views on national insurance, particularly health insurance, see Norman MacKenzie and Jeanne MacKenzie (eds.), *The Diary of Beatrice Webb* (London: London School of Economics, 1982), 3:158, May 13, 1911.

10. Jane Addams to Mary Linn, March 13, 1889, Jane Addams Papers, Swarthmore College, Swarthmore, Pa. For the settlement movement generally, see also Judith Ann Trolander, *Professionalism and Social Change: From the Settlement House Movement to Neighborhood Centers, 1886 to the Present* (New York: Columbia University Press, 1987).

11. See "The Most Useful Americans," *Independent* (May 1913): 958. Allen F. Davis, *Spearheads for Reform: The Social Settlements and the Progressive Movement, 1890–1914* (New York: Oxford University Press, 1967), 29.

12. Jane Addams (ed.), *Hull House Maps and Papers* (Chicago, 1895).

13. Daniel Levine, *Jane Addams and the Liberal Tradition* (Madison, Wis.: State Historical Society, 1971), 89–179.

14. *NCCC 1896*, 254.

15. See Raymond Mohl and Neil Betten, "Paternalism and Pluralism: Immigrants and Social Welfare in Gary, Indiana, 1906–1940," *American Studies* 15 (Spring 1974): 5–30. COS of Buffalo, *Annual Report 1902*, 21, states that most settlement houses in Buffalo were church-affiliated.

16. Hartmut Diessenbacher, "Altruismus als Abenteuer: Vier biographische Skizzen zu bürgerlichen Altruisten des 19. Jahrhunderts," in Christoph Sachsse und Florian Tennstedt (eds.), *Jahrbuch der Sozialarbeit 4: Geschichte und Geschichten* (Reinbeck bei Hamburg: Rowohlt, 1981), 272–298.

17. See Albion W. Small, *The Significance of Sociology for Ethics* (Chicago, [1902?]), 113 (the first page of the offprint I saw); idem, "Scholarship and Social Agitation," *American Journal of Sociology* 1 (1895): 564–582; Vernon K. Dibble, *The Legacy of Albion W. Small* (Chicago: University of Chicago Press, 1975).

18. Robert Hunter, *Poverty* (New York: Macmillan, 1904), p. 339.

19. For reactions to the book, see Winthrop More Daniels, "Significant Books on Politics and Economics," *Atlantic* 95 (April 1905): 555; Florence Kelley, "Poverty," *American Journal of Sociology* 10 (January 1905): 555–556; Mary E. Richmond, "Poverty," *International Journal of Ethics* 15 (July 1905): 506. There were many other reviews.

20. See Clarke A. Chambers, *Paul U. Kellogg and the Survey* (Minneapolis: University of Minnesota Press, 1971); Steven Roy Cohen, "Reconciling Industrial Conflict and Democracy: The Pittsburgh Survey and the Growth of Social Research" (diss., Columbia University, 1981).

21. Crystal Eastman, *Work Accidents and the Law* (Pittsburgh: Charities Publication Committee, 1910). See also below, Chapter 12.

Chapter 10. Early Liberal Reforms: Toward Continental Solutions within British Assumptions

1. See Edith Sellers, *Foreign Solutions of Poor Law Problems* (London: Marshall and Sons, [1900]); idem, *The Danish Poor Relief System: An Example for England* (London: P. S. King, 1904). See the favorable review of the second edition of Sellers' *Foreign Solutions* in *Labour Leader,* May 29, 1908, 339. Some of Sellers' articles are: "Danish and Russian Old-Age Homes," *Nineteenth Century* 52 (October 1902): 643–645; "Old-Age Homes in Denmark," *Contemporary Review* 78 (September 1900): 430–441; and "Foreign Remedies of English Poor Law Defects," *Century* 62 (November 1907): 770–896. Sellers' testimony before the select committee is in *P.P.* 1903 (276), v, esp. p. 7. There is a Danish expression for the "unworthy poor" (*uværdige trængende*) that has about the same meaning as the English. In neither language, however, is it synonymous with "pauper." It is unclear to me whether or how well Sellers knew Danish. See Daniel Levine, "The Danish Connection": A Note on the Making of British Old-Age Pensions," *Albion* 17 (Summer 1985): 181–185.

2. See Sidney Webb, *Paupers and Old-Age Pensions,* Fabian Tract 135 (1907). Webb basically supported the Asquith proposals, but asked that they begin at age sixty-five rather than seventy and that the "pauper exclusion" be eliminated. He also wanted widows with children to be included, whatever their age.

3. Asquith's speech is in H. of C. *Debates,* IV:188, May 7, 1908, 463–477. For Lloyd George, see ibid., IV:190, June 16, 1908, esp. 731–734. Challenge to Lloyd George's idea of the belief that noncontributory pensions were not possible is in H. of Lords *Debates,* IV:192, July 20, 1908, 370–379. See also Stephen Koss, *Asquith* (London: A. Lane, 1976), 103–105.

4. H. of C. *Debates,* IV:188, June 16, 1908, 828 (Asquith) and 804–812 (Barnes). Asa Briggs' essay "The Language of Class," in his *Essays in Labour History* (London: Macmillan, 1960), 43–73, shows how Englishmen of at least the upper social orders believed their society was one in which social mobility was relatively easy and class lines were indistinct. All this was again very much like the idea Americans had of their own society, which Americans contrasted with the British society.

5. For example, at the annual conference of the Labour Party a resolution favoring universal noncontributory pensions passed unanimously (Labour Party, *Report of the Annual Conference, Belfast 1907,* 67). J. R. MacDonald, "The Budget and Old-Age Pensions," *Labour Leader,* May 15, 1908, 313, points out the inadequacies of the bill. Once again employers were passive. The London Chamber of Commerce (*Journal 1908*) simply reported that the bill passed; ibid. 72, 130, 225, 252.

6. H. of C. *Debates* IV:190, June 15, 1908, 563. Within three years it cost

twice that, as Lloyd George admitted in the debates on national insurance. See ibid., V:25, March 4, 1911, 619.

7. Ibid., IV:192, July 20, 1908, 1346–1350.

8. "Endowment of the Thriftless," *Blackwoods Magazine* 183 (June 1908): 881–883; "Socialism in the House of Commons," *Edinburgh Review* 204 (October 1906): 288–293. Supporters also had their say in print—for one example, see Harold Spender, "Government Old-Age Pensions," *Contemporary Review* 93 (January 1908): 94–107. Spender was close to Lloyd George and a member of the Fabian Society. He accompanied Lloyd George to Germany in 1909.

9. *Hearts of Oak Gazette,* no. 32 (January 1904): 5; ibid., no. 34 (September 1906): 79. *National Conference of Friendly Societies 1908,* 2. For the self-image of the largest "friendly society," see R[obert] W. Moffrey, *A Century of Oddfellowship* (Manchester: The [Grand] M[aster] and Board of Directors, 1910).

10. H. of C. *Debates,* IV:190, June 16, 1908, 831–835; H. of Lords *Debates,* IV:192, July 20, 1908, 1431–1432; the law is 8 Edw. 7, c. 40, August 1, 1908. The most significant difference from the original bill was that pensions were to be on a sliding scale, so that even people earning £31 a year could get a pension of one shilling a week. Hugh Heclo, *Modern Social Politics in Britain and Sweden: From Relief to Income Maintenance* (New Haven: Yale University Press, 1974), emphasizes the importance of experts and deemphasizes (more than I think is justified) political pressure from recently enfranchised or activated groups.

11. Sidney Webb and Beatrice Webb, *English Poor Law History* (1929; reprint, London: Archon, 1963), claim that the "principles of 1834" were abandoned by the Poor Law Commission of 1906–9 in both the Majority Report and the Minority Report, but this is mostly wishful thinking. What the majority tried to do—in fact, what they strained and struggled to do—was to hold on as tightly as they could to the 1834 report in greatly altered circumstances. The majority suggested some significant alterations but left much of the moral tone of the 1834 report untouched. The minority, with Beatrice Webb dominant, entitled their report *The Break-up of the Poor Law* (London: Longmans, Green, 1909) and did in fact reject the 1834 report and endorse contrasting fundamental attitudes—but a bit of the spirit of 1834 can still be discerned. Even though the Minority Report has received the most attention since 1909, it was the Majority Report that was the basis of subsequent policy. See A. W. Vincent, "The Poor Law Reports of 1909 and the Social Theory of the Charity Organization Society," *Victorian Studies* 27 (Spring 1984): 343–363, which emphasizes how the two reports, majority and minority, were not as far apart as the Webbs claimed.

12. Six members of the 1906–9 commission were COS members. See Charles Loch Mowat, *The Charity Organisation Society, 1869–1913: Its*

Ideas and Work (London: Metheun, 1961), 160–161. The report is in is *P.P.* 1909 (Cd. 4499), xxxvii. The Webbs' *History* is cited in the preceding note.

13. Beatrice Webb, *The Break-up of the Poor Law* (London: Longman, Green, 1909), 544.

14. Beatrice Webb wrote about national health insurance in her diary (October 11, 1912): "The fact that [the money] will be wastefully collected and wastefully spent may condemn it to the thoughtful Socialist or the economical-minded citizen—but to the ordinary elector it makes no difference since he is too dull witted to understand that it will be so." She thought that perhaps it was right for the Labour Party to go along, "especially since they had not the wit to offer an alternative." (*Beatrice Webb's Diaries, 1912–1924,* ed. Margaret Cole [London: Longman, 1954], 1:8).

Chapter 11. Liberal Reform in Great Britain: The Quest for Social Security

1. The first quotation is PRO CAB 37/98, item 40, Asquith to Cabinet, March 2, 1909, p. 41. The second quotation is PRO CAB 37/97, item 20, Asquith to Cabinet, February 2, 1909, p. 9.

2. Bentley B. Gilbert, "David Lloyd George: Land, the Budget, and Social Reform," *American Historical Review* 81 (1976): 1058–1066, argues that the National Health Insurance Act was a byway on Lloyd George's major interest—land reform. Whether or not national health insurance was close to his heart does not matter here. What is important is that he accomplished it.

3. Labour Party, *Annual Conference 1908,* appendix 1, 83–97 (the term "culpable unemployed" is on p. 85). Labour Party, *Annual Conference 1909,* appendix 1, pp. 91–101 (the cautious endorsement of insurance is on p. 93).

4. Beatrice Webb, *Our Partnership* (London: Longmans, Green, 1948), 404. See also Winston Churchill, *Liberalism and the Social Problem* (London: Hodder and Stoughton, 1909), a collection of Churchill's speeches on social issues since 1906. L. G. Chiozza Money, a Liberal member of Parliament, achieved great popularity with his *Riches and Poverty* (London: Methuen, 1905), which by 1911 was already in its tenth edition. See also José Harris, *Unemployment and Politics* (Oxford: Oxford University Press, 1972).

5. Harold Spender, "Unemployment Insurance," *Contemporary Review* 95 (January 1909): 25. For a description of Lloyd George's actions, see John Grigg, *Lloyd George: The People's Champion, 1902–1911* (Berkeley and Los Angeles: University of California Press, 1978), 313–351. Unfortunately, Bentley B. Gilbert, *Lloyd George: A Political Life* (Columbus: Ohio State University Press, 1987), appeared too late for me to make use of it. E. P. Hennock, "The Origins of British National Insurance and the German Precedent, 1880–1914," in W. J. Momsen (ed.), *The Emergence of the Welfare*

State in Britain and Germany, 1850–1950, (London: Croom Helm, 1981), 84–106, points out that insurance is for the low-paid worker while the poor law was for the unworthy. This is correct, but it does not recognize factors on both sides that blur the distinction. In Germany there was not quite the moral judgment involved in public relief that there was in Great Britain, so the distinction was not as clear. In Britain a series of exceptions were made so that people could be treated under the poor laws without having it be a judgment on their character (See Chapter 8). E. P. Hennock, *British Social Reform and German Precedents: The Case of Social Insurance, 1880–1914* (New York: Oxford University Press, 1987), also appeared too late for me to make use of it. For a more general view, see Günter Hollenberg, *Englisches Interesse am Kaiserreich: Die Attraktivität Preussen-Deutschlands für konservative und liberale Kreise in Grossbritannien* (Wiesbaden: F. Steiner, 1974), esp. 227–237. See also Peter Hennock, "Arbeiterunfallschädigung und Arbeiterunfallversicherung. Die britische Sozialreform und das Beispiel Bismarcks," *Geschichte und Gesellschaft* 11 (1985): 19–36.

6. *National Conference of Friendly Societies 1909,* 11–12.

7. G. N. Barnes, Arthur Henderson, et al., *Life and Labour in Germany* (Woolwich: Labour Representative Newspaper Printing and Publishing Co., 1910).

8. Winston Churchill to Arthur Wilson Fox, January 4, 1980 in Randolph Churchill, *Winston S. Churchill* (London: Heineman, 1969), companion vol. 2, pt. 2, 759. See also PRO CAB 37/97 (17), Churchill to Cabinet, January 17, 1909, "Memorandum on Labour Exchanges," saying that "the expansion of industry on the whole keeps pace with the expansion of the population" and that if the labor market were better organized nationally there would not have to be the waste of maintaining a large reserve of labor.

9. See Sir Henry N. Bunbury (ed.), *Lloyd George's Ambulance Wagon, Being the Memoirs of William J. Braithwaite, 1911–1912* (London: Methuen, 1957), 67–68.

10. Bentley B. Gilbert, "David Lloyd George: Land, the Budget, and Social Reform," *American Historical Review* 81 (1976): 1058–1066, sneers at Lloyd George's tendency to mention widows and orphans in his speeches but makes no attempt to justify this tone. See also Pat Thane, "The Working Class and State 'Welfare' in Britain, 1880–1914," *Historical Journal* 27 (December 1984): 877–900.

11. H. of C. *Debates,* V:25, May 4, 1911, 609–643.

12. *Hearts of Oak Journal* 4 (November 1909), 123; ibid., 5 (November 1910), 101; ibid., 6 (November 1911), 165–169.

13. H. of C. *Debates,* 5, May 4, 1911, 654. TUC Parliamentary Committee, *Quarterly Report, March 1911,* 74; TUC Annual Congress, *Report 1911,* 204–297.

14. On working women in Germany, see Jean H. Quataert, *Reluctant Feminists in German Social Democracy, 1885–1917* (Princeton: Princeton Univer-

sity Press, 1979). Meredith Tax, *The Rising of the Women: Feminist Solidarity and Class Conflict, 1880–1917* (New York: Monthly Review Press, 1980), explores some of the problems in the United States from a Marxist point of view, but her insistence on interpreting everything through Marxist theories throws doubt on her perceptions.

15. *P.P.* 1911 (Cd. 5869), lxxiii, 12–15. See also Mary MacArthur, "Women and State Insurance: A Criticism and Some Constructive Suggestions," *Labour Leader,* May 4, 1911, 310, "The Insurance Bill: Labour Conference and the Contributory Scheme," ibid., June 23, 1911, 396; "Women Workers and the Insurance Bill," ibid., July 21, 1911, 461.

16. The Snowden-MacDonald name-calling can be followed in *Labour Leader,* July 7, 1911, 422, and July 14, 1911, 438. In 1912 the Labour Party supported Snowden's position and censured the parliamentary party, but this was meaningless because the bill had already become law. On the Fabians, see Fabian Society, *The Insurance Bill and the Workers* (June 1911) (a pamphlet, but apparently not a Fabian Tract). Bentley B. Gilbert, "Winston Churchill versus the Webbs: The Origins of British Unemployment Insurance," *American Historical Review* 71 (1966): 846–862, details the Webbs' didactic intent. Beatrice Webb asked the party to accept the idea of contributory insurance at the annual convention in 1913, but her motion lost in favor of one asking for noncontributory insurance (Labour Party, *Report of Annual Convention 1913,* 104–106). Peter Wittig, *Der englische Weg zum Sozialismus. Die Fabier und ihre Bedeutung für die Labour Party und die englische Politik* (Berlin: Duncker and Humbolt, 1982), calls the Webbs basically totalitarian. That may be going too far, but devoted democrats they certainly were not; they were contemptuous of most of the population. See also A. Chamberlain, *Politics from the Inside: An Epistolary Chronicle, 1906–1914* (New Haven: Yale University Press, 1937).

17. "Special Representative Meeting," *British Medical Journal,* June 3, 1911, 352–361; "National Insurance," ibid., June 10, 1911, 403, 424.

18. *P.P.* 1911 (Cd. 5869), lxxiii, 26–29, 36–44. The Employers Parliamentary Council (which I have never seen referred to before or since) took place on June 26; the Association of Chambers of Commerce was on June 30. The deputation to the Chancellor is also described in London Chamber of Commerce, *Journal,* supplement, October 1911, 4–6.

19. *P.P.* 1911 (Cd. 5991), lxxiii; ibid. (Cd. 5995), lxiii, Explanatory Memorandum; ibid., (Cd. 5679), lxxiii, memorandum from Germany.

20. The original failure of the Labour Party amendment on married women is in H. of C. *Debates,* V:27, July 5, 1911, 1196–1214. Lloyd George's own amendment on the subject is in ibid., V:30, November 2, 1911, 1076–1090. The amendment was agreed to without division.

21. The statement about old ideas being buried is in ibid., V:26, May 24, 1911, 299–300.

22. Second reading vote is in ibid., V:27, May 29, 1911, 830; the third

reading is in V:32, December 6, 1911, 1528. The National Insurance Act is 12 Geo. 5, c. 55.

23. Gilbert, "Winston Churchill versus the Webbs," emphasizes the importance and daring of Churchill but assumes that social insurance has no "social control" elements. The Webbs were far more explicit than Churchill about their desire for control.

Chapter 12. Progressive Reform in the United States: The Search for Social Justice

1. See, e.g., "Employers Liability," *Annals of the American Academy of Political and Social Science* 15 (May 1900): 487–491.

2. Adna F. Weber, "Employers Liability and Accident Insurance," *Political Science Quarterly* 17 (June 1902): 256–283.

3. Frank A. Vanderlip, "Insurance for Working-men," *North American Review* 181 (December 1905): 921–932. The text of the British law is in *Bulletin of Labor Statistics* 70 (May 1907). Two articles on the law are Arthur B. Reeve, "Is Workmen's Compensation Practicable?" *Outlook* 85 (March 2, 1907): 508–511; and Maurice Low, "Shifting the Burden: Compensation for Injuries," *North American Review* 185 (July 1907): 651–660.

4. *CR,* 59-1, April 2, 1905, 4601–4608; ibid., June 1, 1906, 7696.

5. The cases are known collectively as "the Employer Liability Cases" (207 U.S. 463) and were decided on January 6, 1908. The revised law is in *U.S. Statutes,* chap. 149, p. 65.

6. CR, January 31, 1908, 1347–1349.

7. Ibid., May 16, 1908, 6412–6417 (House); May 30, 1908, 7266 (Senate). The law is in *U.S. Statutes,* May 30, 1908, chap. 236, p. 556.

8. Crystal Eastman, *Work-Accidents and the Law* (Pittsburgh: Charities Publication Committee, 1910). See also above, Chapter 9.

9. See Ferdinand C. Schwedtman and James A. Emery, *Accident Prevention and Relief* (New York: National Association of Manufacturers, 1911); the recommendations are on pp. 259–269.

10. AFL, *Convention Proceedings 1909,* 27, 314–315. See also "Industrial Insurance and Compensation in Germany and Elsewhere," *American Federationist* 17 (July 1, 1910): 595–596. See also Samuel Gompers, "Talks on Labor," ibid., 17 (January 1, 1910): 54.

11. See New York State Employer Liability Commission, *Report, 1910.*

12. For labor opposition, see *New York Times (NYT),* May 26, 1910, 3; For NCF support, see *NYT,* March 12, 1910, 8; See also Arthur B. Reeve, "Capital and Labor Agree on Workmen's Compensation," *Survey* 23 (December 4, 1909): 336–340. Enormously helpful for the intricacies of New York and other state politics is the detailed study by Robert Asher, "Workmen's Compensation in the United States, 1880–1935" (Diss., University of Minnesota, 1971). See also Robert Asher, "The 1911 Wisconsin Workmen's Com-

pensation Law: A Study in Conservative Labor Reform," *Wisconsin Magazine of History* 57 (1973–74): 123–140, and "Radicalism and Reform: State Insurance of Workmen's Compensation in Minnesota, 1910–1933," *Labor History* 14 (1973): 19–41.

13. *Laws of the State of New York, 1910,* chap. 674.

14. See *NYT,* March 25, 1911, 3, for the text of most of the decision.

15. *NYT,* October 26, 1913, 8, contains the full text of the amendment.

16. See *NYT,* March 12, March 22, and May 26, 1910; ibid., January 18, February 18, May 1, 1913. See also Irwin Yellowitz, *Labor and the Progressive Movement in New York* (Ithaca, N.Y.: Cornell University Press, 1965), 117–118; Asher, "Workmen's Compensation," 559–603.

17. On Ohio, see Hoyt L. Warner, *Progressivism in Ohio, 1897–1917* (Columbus, Ohio: State University Press, 1964). The act is House Bill No. 398. No hearings have been preserved.

18. See U.S. Bureau of Labor Statistics, *Bulletin 126* (1913); idem, *Bulletin 185* (1915).

19. *New York Central v. White; Hawkins v. Bleakely; Mountain States Timber Company v. State of Washington,* 243 U.S. 188 (1917).

20. Robert H. Wiebe characterizes the years 1890–1920 with the words "search for order." See Wiebe, *The Search for Order, 1877–1920* (New York: Hill and Wang, 1967).

21. *Illinois Laws,* 1913, 127–130.

22. State of Massachusetts, *Report of the Commission on the Support of Dependent Minor Children of Widowed Mothers* (Boston, 1913), 170–175, gives the practical results of the Illinois law.

23. See ibid., 9–35. *Massachusetts Laws,* 1913, chap. 763.

24. State of New York, *Report of the State Commission on Relief for Widowed Mothers* (Albany, 1914). See also *Laws of New York,* 1915, chap. 228.

25. See Children's Bureau, *Laws Relating to "Mother's Pensions" in the United States, Denmark, and New Zealand,* Publication 7 (Washington, D.C., 1914).

26. The quotation is from Ada E. Sheffield, "The Administration of the Mother's Aid Laws in Massachusetts," *Survey* 31 (February 21, 1914): 644–645. See also Robert Hebbert, "Relief to Needy Mothers in New York," *NCCC 1914,* 450–452. The anonymous article "Widow's Pension Bill for New York State," *Survey* 31 (March 28, 1914): 791, emphasizes COS opposition to the New York bill. See also L. A. Halbert, "The Widow's Allowance Act in Kansas City," ibid., 31 (February 28, 1914): 675–676. Mrs. John Glenn, "Relief for Needy Mothers in New York City," *NCCC 1914,* 452, argues that private charity does a better job. Stanley Howe, "Adequate Relief to Needy Mothers in Pennsylvania," ibid., 447–450, argues in favor of pensions in the broadest terms of society's responsibility, but these responsibilities are seen in terms of relief to the needy. There are many more articles in *Survey* and in *NCCC* indicating the controversy between the desirability

of public versus private relief. See also Robert H. Bremner et al., *Children and Youth in America: A Documentary History* (Cambridge, Mass.: Harvard University Press, 1970), 2:369–397; Mark H. Leff, "Consensus for Reform: The Mother's Pension Movement in the Progressive Era," *Social Service Review* 47 (1973): 397–418.

27. The laws are summarized and the laws of Massachusetts, Minnesota, and New Hampshire are quoted by W. Carson Ryan, Jr., and Roberta King, *State Pension Systems for Public-School Teachers* Department of the Interior, Bureau of Education, Bulletin 14 (Washington, D.C., 1916). The movement in general is discussed in William Graebner, *A History of Retirement: The Making and Functioning of an American Institution, 1885–1978* (New Haven: Yale University Press, 1980), 88–120, but Graebner is so concerned with his thesis that the laws were to promote efficiency and social control that he never actually says what the laws contained. He does not understand the meaning of "efficiency" as it was used in those years.

28. The quotation on the nervous system of women is from Lillian C. Flint, "Pensions for Women Teachers," *Century Magazine* 79 (February 1910): 618.

29. Figures on average length of service for teachers do not exist, but the impression that it was short was widespread. Some indication is in Henry S. Pritchett, "Pension System for Public Schools," *Independent* 74 (March 20, 1913): 617–619. Pritchett reports that only 5 percent of the male teachers and 16 percent of the female teachers in the Virginia system were sixty years old or older.

Chapter 13. Progressive Reform in the United States: The Failure of Social Insurance

1. On the AMA and health insurance, see James G. Burrow, *AMA Voice of American Medicine* (Baltimore: Johns Hopkins University Press, 1963), 151; Forest A. Walker, "Compulsory Health Insurance: 'The Next Great Step' in Social Legislation," *Journal of American History* 56 (1969): 290–304; Arthur J. Visalter, "Compulsory Health Insurance in California, 1918–1920," *Journal of the History of Medicine* 24 (April 1969): 151–182. See also Paul Starr, *The Social Transformation of American Medicine* (New York: Basic Books, 1982), esp. 243–257. Roy Lubove, *The Struggle for Social Security* (Cambridge, Mass.: Harvard University Press, 1982), 67–89, tends to put the blame mostly on physicians.

2. *NCCC 1905,* 455–457.

3. Ibid., 576–579.

4. *NCCC 1906,* 457–463.

5. Isaac M. Rubinow, "Compulsory State Insurance for Working-men," *Annals of the American Academy of Political and Social Sciences* 24 (September 1904): 331–342.

6. Lee K. Frankel and Miles M. Dawson, *Workingmen's Insurance in Europe* (New York: Russell Sage Foundation, 1910). For the foundation itself, see John M. Glenn, Lillian Brandt, and F. Emerson Andrews, *The Russell Sage Foundation,* 2 vols. (New York: Russell Sage Foundation, 1947).

7. The quotation is from H. R. Seager, "British National Insurance Bill," *Survey* 26 (September 23, 1911): 882.

8. Louis D. Brandeis, "Workingmen's Insurance: The Road to Social Efficiency," *NCCC 1911,* 156–162.

9. The quotation is from "England's Great Experiment," *Nation* 92 (May 11, 1911): 463–464.

10. Isaac M. Rubinow, *Social Insurance* (New York: H. Holt, 1913).

11. See I. M. Rubinow, "First American Conference on Social Insurance," *Survey* 30 (1913): 478–480.

12. See *American Labor Legislation Review* 6 (June 1916): 121–122.

13. The text of the model bill is in ibid., 239–268.

14. *Journal of the American Medical Association* 66 (June 1916): 1975–1977. See also Forest A. Walker, "Compulsory Health Insurance: 'The Next Great Step in Social Legislation,'" *Journal of American History* 56 (1969): 297.

15. Samuel Gompers, "Labor vs. Its Barnacles," *American Federationist* 23 (April 1916): 268–274.

16. Bureau of Labor Statistics, *Proceedings of the Conference on Social Insurance,* Bulletin 212 (Washington, D.C., 1917).

17. Massachusetts, House of Representatives, Commission on Old-Age Pensions, Annuities, and Insurance, *Report,* no. 1450, 1910; Massachusetts, House of Representatives, *Report,* no. 1850, 1917; Massachusetts Senate, Commission on Social Insurance, *Report,* no. 244, 1918.

18. State of Wisconsin, Special Committee on Social Insurance, *Report* (Madison, Wis., 1919).

19. The text of the bill is in *American Labor Legislation Review* 9 (June 1919): 211–214; Senator Davenport's speech introducing the bill is in ibid., 239—249. See also *New York Times,* March 17 and 20, and April 2, 11, and 18, 1919.

20. In 1919 an Illinois Commission recommended against health insurance, with Dr. Alice Hamilton of Hull House one of two dissenters (*Journal of the American Medical Association* 73 [August 30, 1919]: 703). A Connecticut commission did the same (ibid., 73 [October 4, 1919]: 1082–1083). The story in California can be followed in Arthur J. Visalter, "Compulsory Health Insurance in California, 1918–1920," *Journal of the History of Medicine* 24 (1969): 151–182. A referendum on the issue in that state lost by about 2 to 1.

21. See M. L. Harris, "Compulsory Health Insurance," *Journal of the American Medical Association* 74 (March 27, 1920): 907–908, continued in

ibid., 74 (April 1920): 1041–1042. See also Frederick R. Green, "The Social Responsibility of Modern Medicine," ibid., 76 (May 28, 1921): 1477–1480.

Chapter 14. From Socialism to Social Welfare in Germany

1. All references are to the decree on *Erwerbslosenfürsorge, RGBl*, 1918, 1305.

2. Until recently, much of the literature on the Weimar period has naturally had an "if only" quality, dominated by impending horrors. Nazism did come after Weimar, but to draw a direct line from the second to the third Reich and to accuse the republic of not doing enough to break this continuity is to ignore the fact that what seems inevitable now because it has already happened was actually only one of many alternatives from the point of view of the 1920s. The newer trend, which sees the struggle of the republic in its own right, not through the shadow of Hitler, is in Susanne Miller, *Die Bürde der Macht: Die deutsche Socialdemokratie, 1918–1920* (Düsseldorf: Droste, 1978), which while highly critical of sins of omission also recognizes "die überwältigenden Probleme, vor denen sie stand und für die niemand die richtigen Lösungen wusste" (p. 451). The historiography of the Social Democratic Party during this period is very large and in recent years has centered on the concept of "negative integration" dealing with the question of the degree to which the party was a participant in the political process before 1918 and what effect this integration, or lack of it, had on the 1920s. A useful review of this literature is in Richard Breitman, "Negative Integration and Parliamentary Politics: Literature on German Social Democracy, 1890–1933," *Central European History* 13 (June 1980): 175–195.

3. Gordon A. Craig, *Germany* (New York: Oxford University Press, 1978), 421.

4. See Peter Gay, *Weimar Culture: The Outsider as Insider* (New York: Harper and Row, 1968). See also the catalog *Tendenzen der Zwanziger Jahre* (Berlin: Council of Europe, 1977).

5. Law on Nationalization, 1919, *RGBl*, 341. Ludwig Preller, in *Sozialpolitik in der Weimarer Republik* (Düsseldorf: Anthenum, 1978), 241, says the attempts "ran out in the sands of inflation." Whether that is the correct causation, the temporal conjunction is certainly there. Debates on the law are in *RV*, March 8, 1919, 541–610.

6. The law itself is in *RGBl*, 1920, 147; the speech introducing it is in *RV*, August 21, 1919, 2721–2740. See Friedrich Syrup (with Otto Neuloh), *Hundert Jahre Staatliche Sozialpolitik, 1839–1939* (Stuttgart: Kohlhammer, 1957), 249; Julius Kaliski, "Der Rätegedanke beim Neuaufbau Deutschlands," *SM* 25 (March 24, 1919): 229–236.

7. Max Schippel, "Politische Unwälzung, Industrie, and Landwirtschaft," *SM* 24 (November 26, 1918): 1045–1050. Debates on the law are in *RV*, March 8, 1919, 541–610.

8. The figures in detail are given in *Vorwärts,* October 5, 15, and 20, 1923.

9. Ermächtigungsgesetz, *RGBl,* 1923, 943.

10. Verordnung über Fürsorgungspflicht, *RGBl,* 1924, 1:100.

11. See Edmund Fischer, "Armenwesen," *SM* 15 (June 29, 1911): 841–848.

12. Marie Bock, "Frau und Gemeinde," *Die Genossin,* September 12, 1928, 3–5.

13. On Salomon, see Monika Simmel, "Alice Salomon. Vom Dienst der bürgerlichen Tochter am Volksganzen," in Christoph Sachsse and Florian Tennstedt (eds.), *Jahrbuch der Sozialarbeit 4: Geschichte und Geschichten* (Rowohlt: Reinbeck bei Hamburg, 1981), 363–403. Christoph Sachsse, *Mütterlichkeit als Beruf: Sozialarbeit, Sozialreform und Frauenbewegung, 1871–1929* (Frankfurt a.M.: Suhrkamp, 1986), goes into the development of professional social work, esp. in chap. 7. See also "Was können wir von Amerika lernen?" *Vorwärts,* January 5, 1925; Joacham Wieler, *Erinnerung eines zerstörten Lebensabends. Alice Salomon während der NS-Zeit (1933–1937) und im Exil (1937–1948)* (Darmstadt: Lingbach, 1986).

14. Meta Kraus-Fessel, "Fürsorgewesen und Arbeiterklasse," *SM* 29 (November 27, 1923): 671–675; Gottlieb Binder, "Ehrenamtliche Mitarbeit der Arbeiterschaft in der Wohlfahrtspflege," *AW* 1 (November 15, 1926): 107–113; "Die Wohlfahrtskonferenz," *Vorwärts,* June 17, 1927, 3.

15. Helene Simon, "Sozialismus und Wohlfahrtspflege," *AW* 1 (October 1, 1926): 3–9.

16. Hedwig Wachenheim, "Der Vorrang der öffentlichen Wohlfahrtspflege," *AW* 1 (November 1, 1926): 65–72. See also Paul Gerlach, "Ueberorganisation der Wohlfahrtspflege," *AW* 2 (January 15, 1927): 33.

17. See *RV Anlagen,* December 16, 1926, 2885, 22–43. See also Allegemeiner deutscher Gewerkschaftsbund, *Jahrbuch 1926,* 53; Louise Schroeder, "Reichsgesetzliche Aenderungen der Sozialversicherung," *AW* 3 (July 1, 1928): 385; idem, "Umwandlung der Arbeitslosenfürsorge in Arbeitslosenversicherung," *AW* 2 (May 1, 1927): 133–136. A detailed history of unemployment insurance is in Michael T. Wermel and Roswetha Urban, *Arbeitslosenfürsorge und Arbeitslosenversicherung in Deutschland,* 3 parts (Munich: Pflaum, 1949).

18. See *RV,* July 5, 1927, 11268–11275.

19. Ibid., 11282.

20. Arbeitsvermittlung und Arbeitslosenversicherung, *RGBl,* 1927, 1:187.

21. See Wermel and Urban, *Arbeitslosenfürsorge und Arbeitslosenversicherung,* 2:5–15.

22. Ehrenfried Manning, "Die SPD und die Sozialversicherung von 1918 bis 1933" (diss., Marburg, 1956), 252–253.

23. *Vorwärts,* May 10, 1928.

24. Hans Braetsch, "Die Krise der deutschen Sozialversicherung," *Der Arbeitgeber,* July 15, 1931, 350–354; August 1, 1931, 386–391.

25. Hermann Krangold, "Die Krise der Sozialversicherung und der Wohlfahrtspflege," *SM* 38 (July 29, 1932): 675–682. Henning Köhler, "Sozialpolitik von Brüning bis Schleicher," *Vierteljahresschrift für Zeitgeschichte* 21 (1973): 146–150, claims that Brüning's thinking was not running toward solving unemployment but toward creating barter-based subsistence farming systems instead.

26. Christine Böhm, "Zur Entwicklung der Arbeitlosigkeit und zur Lage der Notstandsarbeiter im faschistischen Deutschland 1933 bis 1934," *Wissenschaftliche Zeitschrift der Humbolt Universität zu Berlin. Gesellschafts- und Sprachwissenschaftliche Reihe* 22 (1973): 65–79, discusses how the Nazi government employed hundreds of thousands of people at low wages essentially for military mobilization. Thomas E. J. DeWitt, "The Economics and Politics of Welfare in the Third Reich," *Central European History* 11 (1978): 256–278, and Aryeh L. Unger, "Propaganda and Welfare in Nazi Germany," *Journal of Social History* 4 (1970): 125–140, both stress the ways in which welfare policy became a tool of Nazi state- and party-building. Volker Hentschel, "Das System der sozialen Sicherung in historischer Sicht 1880 bis 1975," *Archiv für Sozialgeschichte* 18 (1978): 307–352, is a swift overview, but it deals with the Nazi period on pp. 323–324. Hentschel stresses the continuity of the system. This view is possible only if one focuses exclusively on the structures of the insurance systems and not on the reality that this legalistic approach might conceal.

Chapter 15. From Socialism to Social Welfare in Denmark

1. Jacob Paludan, *Jørgen Stein,* 2 vols. (Copenhagen: Hasselbalch, 1933). The first volume is titled *Thunder in the South.*

2. See *FT,* December 4, 1919, 1908–1911. Jørgen Dich, "Kompendium" (Århus, 1968, Mimeographed), says the law was independent of German influence, but this is clearly not true. See, e.g., K. K. Steincke, *Fra Hele Valpladsen* (Copenhagen: Fremad, 1946), 70–77; Kjeld Philip, *Staten og Fattigdom* (Copenhagen: Gjellerup, 1947), 76–77.

3. All references are to the "Lov om Invalidforsikring," May 6, 1921.

4. G. Dam, "Invalidforsikring, 1921–1942," in Sygekassevæsnet (ed.), *Fra Laugssygekasser til Fokleforsikring* (Copenhagen: n.p., 1942), 186–190.

5. The complete platform is in Arbejderbevægelsens Bibliotek og Arkiv, Copenhagen.

6. Niels Finn Christiansen, "Reformism within Danish Social Democracy until the Nineteen-Thirties," *Scandinavian Journal of History* 3 (1978): 297–322.

7. Borgbjerg's introduction of the bill is in *FT,* March 12, 1924, 1613–

2623; objections from the Left are in *FT,* March 13, 1925, 6015; Radical views are in *FT,* March 3, 1925, 5954. The Social Democrats were still proposing various forms of co-determination in the 1970s and getting nowhere with them.

8. The proposed law is in *RT,* Tillæg A, October 9, 1925, 2687–2726; the fierce debate is in ibid., March 27, 1925, 6554–6699.

9. See *Socialt Tidsskrift,* January 1929, Afdeling A, 127. The Social Democrats' policy of trying to increase the value of the krone against other currencies was partly to blame.

10. The position of the Social Democrats is in *FT,* October 13, 1925, 174–181; of the Left, 354–360; of the Conservatives, 362–371.

11. The proposal of the law is in *FT,* December 15, 1925, 3289–3295; Support from the Social Democrats is in ibid., 3382–3387; Conservative criticism is in ibid., 3401. The proposed law itself is *RT,* Tillæg A, 3789–3791.

12. Reluctance in setting forth the proposal is in Borgbjerg's speech, in *FT,* October 14, 1925, 178; see also *FT* January 14, 1926, 3936–3937, 3958–3967. Stauning's position can be seen in ibid., 3985. The debate and defeat in the *Landsting* is in *LT,* March 29, 1926, 1777–1794.

13. *FT,* October 29, 1924, 884–885.

14. *FT,* December 17, 1926, 1512–1514.

15. *FT,* October 28, 1926, 1017–1030.

16. Left arguments defending "cutting down" are in *FT,* February 2, 1927, 2365–2367; Social Democrat protests are in ibid., March 3, 1927, 2920–2926.

17. *Social-Demokraten,* January 27, 1927, and March 6, 1927.

18. Ibid., June 14, 1927.

19. See the election material for 1929 in Arbejderbevægelsens Bibliotek og Arkiv, Copenhagen.

20. Page references in the text below are to K. K. Steincke, *Fremtidens Forsørgelsesvæsen* (Welfare for the Future) (Copenhagen: Indenrigsministeriet, 1920).

21. Steincke argued that this social minimum should be guaranteed to all but should not include the right to reproduce if one had an inheritable disease, including the disease of being antisocial. Steincke cited the Dugdale study of the Jukes to prove his eugenic point (p. 235). Steincke's ideas for "improving the race" would be important for a study of Steincke, but they had no discernible effect on Danish social legislation.

22. *FT,* December 12, 1929, 3402–2454.

23. *Arbejdsgiveren,* February 13, 1931, 54; *Tidsskrift for Industri,* February 15, 1931, 37; *Arbejdsgiveren,* July 1, 1932, 220–224.

24. *Skatteborgeren* can be cited passim, but see, e.g., January 1930, 875.

25. *Frederiksborgs Amts Avis,* January 11, 1929, January 11, 1930, September 19, 1930, October 28, 1930 (p. 3 in all cases).

26. *FT,* January 17, 1930, 4187; October 10, 1929, 123–124.

27. *FT,* January 17, 1930, 4173–4175 (Left), 4147–4149, 4201; December 30, 1930, 2618–2642 (Conservative).

28. *FT,* January 16, 1930, 4107; December 3, 1930, 2518, 2530–2534.

29. K. K. Steincke, *Det Trækker Op* (Copenhagen: Fremad, 1947), 27.

Chapter 16. From Dead Center to the Welfare State in Great Britain

1. For an assessment of the impact of World War I on Great Britain, see Arthur Marwick, *The Deluge: British Society and the First World War* (London: Bodley Head, 1965).

2. G. C. Peden, "The 'Treasury View' on Public Works and Employment in the Interwar Period," *Economic History Review,* 2d ser., 37 (May 1984): 167–181, argues the reasonableness of the Treasury in the context of knowledge then available and what has been found since about shortcomings of Keynesianism. Sean Glynn and Alan Booth, "Unemployment in Interwar Britain: A Case for Relearning the Lessons of the 1930s," ibid., 36 (August 1983): 329–348, also argue that there was and is no guarantee that "Keynesian" ideas would have worked.

3. Benjamin Seebohm Rowntree, *Poverty and Progress: A Second Social Survey of York* (London: Longman, 1941), found considerable improvement over conditions at the turn of the century.

4. The law is 9 & 10, Geo. 5, c. 102; clause 3 eliminates the moral disqualifications.

5. H. of C. *Debates,* V:125, February 25, 1920, 1739–1755 (Sir Robert Horne, minister of labour introducing the bill; the figures are from his speech). See ibid., 1758–1762, for Labour Party objections. In 1921, dependents of insured workers were included, and premiums were raised to cover the additional cost.

6. PRO CAB 27/190, CP 1907, "Unemployment Committee Report to the Cabinet," October 6, 1920.

7. See H. of C. *Debates,* V:152, March 29, 1922, 1375–1380, (introduction of the bill); ibid., 1398–1399 (rejection of the workhouse test). See also Charles L. Mowat, *Britain between the Wars* (Chicago: University of Chicago Press, 1955), 155.

8. Ralph Hayburn, "The Unemployed Workers' Movement, 1921–1936: A Reappraisal," *International Review of Social History* 28 (1983): 279–295, argues that the Labour Party's views were so conventional and ineffective that the Unemployed Workers Movement was driven toward the Communist Party of Great Britain, though in many ways it was independent of that party.

9. PRO CAB 27/190, CP 3371, Report of a Meeting, October 6, 1921, of

the Cabinet Committee on Unemployment; ibid., CP 83 (24), "Interim Report on Unemployment," February 7, 1924; ibid., CP 143 (24), "Second Interim Report on Unemployment," February 29, 1924.

10. H. of C. *Debates,* V:161, March 20, 1923, 2472–2511.

11. Ibid., 175, June 25, 1924, 469–535. All the fun comes near the beginning.

12. Daniel F. Calhoun, *The United Front: The TUC and the Russians* (Cambridge: Cambridge University Press, 1976).

13. For Chamberlain's plans as he took office, see David Dilks, *Neville Chamberlain* (Cambridge: Cambridge University Press, 1984), vol. 1, esp. 426–427; Keith Feiling, *The Life of Neville Chamberlain* (London: Macmillan, 1946), appendix, 459–460. See also Churchill to Stanley Baldwin, November 28, 1924, and to Neville Chamberlain, March 20, 1925, among many others. The text is in Martin Gilbert (ed.), *Winston S. Churchill* (London: Heineman, 1979), vol. 5, Companion p. 1, 271–273, 439–442.

14. The Budget speech is in H. of C. *Debates,* V:183, April 28, 1925, 71–83; the second reading debates are in ibid., 184, May 18, 1925, 73–193, and May 19, 1925, 267–390. Speeches setting forth the larger views of the parties are in ibid., 73–121.

15. The act is 15 & 16 Geo. 5, c. 70. A minority of 4 out of 13 members of the Committee on Enquiry believed there should be health coverage available beyond strict insurance limits—for example, to dependents, and as long as necessary in the case of chronic illness. See *P.P.* 1926 (Cmd. 2596), xiv, "National Health Insurance," 327–329.

16. See T. T. Broad, *An All-in Insurance Scheme: Security for All Workers and Their Families* (London, 1924); William H. Beveridge, *Insurance for All and Everything,* (London, 1924); Williams, "The Development of Old-Age Pensions in Great Britain, 1878–1925" (Diss., University of London, 1970), 384, 396–397, 414.

17. The full details of all the various insurance acts and orders are in Eveline M. Burns, *British Unemployment Programs, 1920–1938* (Washington, D.C.: Social Science Research Council, 1941). Bentley B. Gilbert, *British Social Policy, 1914–1939* (Ithaca, N.Y.: Cornell University Press, 1970), is very detailed on the Cabinet politics of these and all other acts in this period; he is less interested in what the politics may reveal about social philosophy. Charles Webster, "Health, Welfare, and Unemployment during the Depression," *Past and Present* 109 (November 1985): 204–230, argues that all plans were inadequate.

18. The Unemployment Act is 24 & 25, Geo. 5, c. 29.

19. Keynes urging his views is in PRO CAB 58/150–151. Keeping track of the situation in Germany and the United States respectively are PRO R3899 and PRO R3900.

20. Mark Thomas, "Rearmament and Economic Recovery in the Late

1930s," *Economic History Review* 36 (1983): 552–559, tries to determine how much of a factor rearmament actually was. It was surely great, and he implies that large public spending before 1937 also might have led to recovery.

21. The act is 19-20 Geo. v, c. 17, Local Government Act, 1929. See also Gilbert, *British Social Policy,* 219–235. Gilbert is loose in his use of the word "pauper."

22. See PRO PIN 8/85, Arthur Greenwood to Ernest Brown, April 10, 1941, suggesting that health insurance and workmen's compensation need looking into; Brown to Greenwood, April 18, 1941, agreeing; April 19, 1941, memo of R. Hamilton Garner recommending a broader survey; and notes of a meeting at the Department of Health, April 24, 1941, agreeing, but only to the cash portion of social insurance and not to including unemployment insurance. On May 16, 1941, there was a meeting with representatives of the Treasury, the Ministries of Health and Labour, and the Home Office, plus two representatives from "friendly societies" agreeing to an all-inclusive survey. See also George Chrystal to Sir John Maude, June 6, 1941, saying that he (Chrystal) has established the interdepartmental committee under Beveridge, with only civil servants, not the "friendly society" representatives, as members.

23. In a stimulating few words, José Harris suggests that Beveridge had broader aims still. See José Harris, "Some Aspects of Social Policy in Britain during the Second World War," in W. J. Momsen (ed.), *The Emergence of the Welfare State in Britain and Germany, 1850–1950* (London: Croom Helm, 1981), 247–263. This article is also an excellent summary of the literature and the issue of how far the Beveridge Report was made possible by the war. Harris concludes that the war is far from a complete explanation, but she offers no other.

24. See PRO CAB 87/76, Minutes of the Social Insurance Committee, October 15, 1941; ibid., Beveridge to the Committee, November 15, 1941.

25. In chronological order, the views of the various interest groups are all in PRO: CAB 87/76, Association of Approved Societies, November 26, 1941; CAB 87/79, British Dental Association, December 1941 (no more precise date given); CAB 87/77, TUC, January 14, 1942; CAB 87/79, National Association of Relieving Officers, January 17, 1942; CAB 87/79, Charity Organization Society, January 28, 1942; CAB 87/77, National Conference of Friendly Societies, February 25, 1942. Neither the Chambers of Commerce of the United Kingdom nor the Federation of British Industries offered evidence, although the British Employers Confederation did. Beveridge's own account is singularly uninformative; see William H. Beveridge, *Power and Influence* (London: Hodder and Stoughton, 1953), 296–334. José Harris, *William Beveridge: A Biography* (Oxford: Oxford University Press, 1977), is a superb job of scholarship and much more helpful; pp. 378–451 have to do with the report.

26. William H. Beveridge, *Inter-departmental Committee on Social Insur-*

ance and Allied Services (New York: Macmillan, 1942). This is a photocopy of the original and what I used; the original is *P.P.* 1942 (Cmd. 6404), vi. Page numbers in the text are for the original.

27. For the background on family allowances, see Jon Macnicol, *The Movement for Family Allowances, 1918–1945: A Study in Social Policy Development* (London: Heinemann, 1980). For a new positive view of Speenhamland, see Milton D. Speizman, "Speenhamland: An Experiment in Guaranteed Income," *Social Service Review* 40 (1966): 44–55.

28. *P.P.* 1943–44 (Cmd. 6550), viii, is the government supporting the Beveridge proposals in principle. *P.P.* 1943–44 (Cmd. 6502), viii, is proposing the National Health Service, saying that the care of personal health should be "made available to everybody as a publicly sponsored service . . . divorced from ability to pay" (6–8).

Chapter 17. Holding Fast in the United States

1. On some of the impact of World War I, see Allen Davis, "Welfare, Reform, and World War One," *American Quarterly* 19 (1967): 516–533; Daniel Levine, "John Dewey, Randolph Bourne, and Legacy of Liberalism," *Antoich Review* 29 (Summer 1969): 234–244; Neva R. Deardorff, "The Demise of a Highly Respected Doctrine," *Survey* 39 (1918): 416–418.

2. As long ago as 1959, scholars saw a continuation of the progressive impulse into the 1920s. The start was Arthur S. Link, "What Happened to the Progressive Movement in the 1920s?" *American Historical Review* 64 (July 1959): 833–851. The issue, however, is still in question.

3. The major debate is *CR* 66-2, April 29, 1920, 6284–6326. The law is in *U.S. Statutes,* 66-2, chap. 195 (Public Law 215), 614–620. It is summarized in *Labor Legislation Review* 10 (June 1920): 1490–1492. See also John B. Andrews, "Old-Age Pensions for Federal Employees," *Survey* 44 (May 22, 1920): 271.

4. See Roy Lubove, *The Professional Altruist: The Emergence of Social Work as a Career, 1880–1930* (New York: Atheneum, 1969).

5. The laws before 1930 are summarized in detail in New York State, Commission on Old-Age Assistance, *Report* (Albany, 1930). The figures on the number of recipients are from Clarke A. Chambers, *Seedtime of Reform* (Minneapolis: University of Minnesota Press, 1963), 167.

6. Children's Bureau, *Mothers Aid 1931,* Publication 220 (Washington, D.C., 1933). In the same report the Children's Bureau, without emphasizing the issue, provided the race of the recipient family where such records existed. In some cities, mostly the larger ones, the percentage of "Negro" families receiving aid was larger than the percentage of blacks in the population. Washington, D.C., did the best in this respect. In most jurisdictions the percentage of families receiving aid was smaller than the percentage of the population, and in some cities black families received no aid. These results

are not remarkable, but it is worth noting that the Children's Bureau recorded such information.

7. Edward D. Berkowitz and Kim McQuaid, "Bureaucrats as 'Social Engineers': Federal Welfare Programs in Herbert Hoover's America," *American Journal of Economics and Sociology* 39 (1980): 321–335.

8. Quoted in Paul Kellogg, "Drought and the Red Cross," *Survey* 65 (February 15, 1931): 576.

9. *CR*, 71-3, January 30, 1931, 3664.

10. See "Relief Controversy at Washington," *Survey* 65 (March 15, 1931): 645; "Backstage in Washington, *Outlook* 157 (February 18, 1931): 251; "The Row over Feeding Our Hungry Farmers," *Literary Digest* 108 (January 31, 1931): 8; "Country Crying for Relief from the Relief Fight," ibid., 108 (February 14, 1931): 9. Clear statements in opposition to the "dole" are *CR*, 71-3, December 18, 1930, 1052ff. The whole matter is covered in detail in David Hamilton, "Herbert Hoover and the Great Drought of 1930," *Journal of American History* 68 (March 1982): 850–874.

11. J. C. Lawrence to Lawrence B. Dunham, November 22, 1930; Willars E. Hotchkiss to Colonel Arthur Woods, chairman of the committee, April 21, 1931; Pierce Williams to Fred C. Croxton, April 24, 1931; Fred C. Croxton, statement of July 31, 1931. The Dewey and Wise statement and all the above are in Box 41, Harry Hopkins Papers, Franklin D. Roosevelt Library, Hyde Park, New York.

12. Subcommittee of the Committee on Manufacturers, *Hearings on a bill (S. 6255) to Establish a National Economic Council;* Subcommittee of the Committee on Manufactures, *Hearings on S. 174, S. 262 (Relief), and S. 3045* (known as the Costigan–LaFollette Bill), 72d Cong., 1st sess., 1931–32.

13. The debates involving the largest questions of principle are *CR*, 72-1, 4850–4893. The House vote on the bill is in ibid., 15492. The act itself, called the Emergency Relief and Construction Act, is *U.S. Statutes*, 1932, chap. 520, 709–724. This and related issues are covered in Edward Ainsworth Williams, *Federal Aid for Relief* (New York: Columbia University Press, 1939), although by neglecting the drought, Williams finds that the RFC bill was the first entrance of the federal government into relief. See also Jordan A. Schwartz, *The Interregnum of Despair: Hoover, Congress, and the Depression* (Urbana: University of Illinois, 1970).

14. The report is printed in full in *Survey* 65 (December 1, 1930): 257–260, 290, 292.

15. *Survey* 65 (February 15, 1931).

16. The law is in *Laws of the State of New York, 1931,* chap. 798, 2399–2408. The reports of TERA are in *New York State Legislative Documents 1932,* no. 53 (January 12, 1932); ibid., no. 97 (February 23, 1932); ibid., no. 98 (March 10, 1932). See also ibid., 59 (March 1, 1934). The TERA report of

October 15, 1932, was issued as a separate publication. There is a statistical summary in TERA, *The State in Unemployment Relief,* New York Legislative Documents 59 (1934). See also Emma Octavia Lundberg, "The New York State Temporary Emergency Relief Administration," *Social Service Review* 6 (December 1932): 545–566. Lundberg worked for TERA.

17. Paul A. Rauschenbusch, "The Wisconsin Unemployment Compensation Law," *National Conference on Social Work, 1932,* 275–284. The law is in State of Wisconsin, *Laws of the Special Session, 1931,* chap. 201. The text is also printed in *CR* 72-1, 3653–3658. Unemployment insurance was being considered in other states as well, but no law had been passed by November 1932.

Chapter 18. The United States Adopts the Welfare State

1. See Keith Olsen, "The American Beveridge Plan," *Mid-America* 65 (April–July 1983): 87–99.

2. The decision against private agencies is in *FERA Rules and Regulations No. 1,* June 23, 1933. The chronology of the first grants is in Doris Carothers, *Chronology of the Federal Emergency Relief Administrations, May 12, 1933, to December 31, 1935,* WPA Research Monograph 6 (Washington, D.C.: WPA, 1937), 3–5.

3. See FERA, *Unemployment Relief Census* (Washington, D.C., 1936), 4–5. FERA, *Monthly Report, December 1 to December 31, 1935* (Washington, D.C., 1936), 40. FERA, Division of Research, Statistics, and Records, as reproduced in Edward Ainsworth Williams, *Federal Aid for Relief* (New York: Columbia University Press, 1939), 85.

4. For statistics on blacks, see FERA, *Unemployment Relief Census,* 7. On blacks in the relief program in general, see Richard Sterner (with Lenore A. Epstein and Ellen Winston et al.), *The Negro's Share* (New York: Harper and Row, 1943), 218–230. Warren C. Whately, "Labor for the Picking: The New Deal in the South," *Journal of Economic History* 43 (December 1983): 905–929, is not only concerned with blacks, but also shows how the AAA displaced tenant farmers, many of whom were black. See also Christopher Wye, "The New Deal and the Negro Community: Toward a Broader Conceptualization," *Journal of American History* 59 (1972): 621–693; Marie W. Kruman, "Quotas for Blacks: The Public Works Administration and the Black Construction Worker," *Labor History* 16 (1975): 37–51; Henry P. Guzda, "Francis Perkins' Interest in a New Deal for Blacks," *Monthly Labor Review* 103 (1980): 31–35; Harvard Sitkoff, *A New Deal for Blacks: The Emergence of Civil Rights as a National Issue* (New York: Oxford University Press, 1980).

5. This account of the CWA is largely based on Bonnie Fox Schwartz, *The Civil Works Administration: The Business of Emergency Employment in*

the New Deal (Princeton: Princeton University Press, 1984). In her superb study, Fox stresses the extent to which businessmen became more important than social workers as administrators in the CWA. This point seems more important to her than it does to me, but the amount of material Fox organized is most impressive. See also Doris Carothers, *Chronology of the Federal Emergency Relief Administration,* WPA Research Monograph 11 (Washington, D.C.: WPA, 1938), 27–49.

6. On the whole federal relief effort, see Donald S. Howard, *The WPA and Federal Relief Policy* (New York: Russell Sage Foundation, 1943); Arthur W. McMahon, John D. Millett, and Gladys Ogdon, *The Administration of Federal Work Relief* (Chicago: Chicago Public Administration Service, 1941); Anne E. Geddes, *Trends in Relief Expenditures, 1910–1935,* WPA Division of Social Research Monograph 10 (Washington, D.C.: WPA, 1937); Williams, *Federal Aid for Relief;* George McJimsey, *Harry Hopkins: Ally of the Poor and Defender of Democracy* (Cambridge, Mass.: Harvard University Press, 1987); Paul A. Kurzman, *Harry Hopkins and the New Deal* (Fair Lawn, N.J.: Burdick, 1974); Harry Hopkins, *Spending to Save: The Complete Story of Relief* (New York: Norton, 1936); Searle F. Charles, *Minister of Relief: Harry Hopkins and the Depression* (Syracuse, N.Y.: Syracuse University Press, 1963).

7. On the lack of revolutionary sentiment among the unemployed, see Roy Rosenzweig, " 'Socialism in Our Time': The Socialist Party and the Unemployed," *Labor History* 20 (1979): 485–509; Bernard Sternsher, "Victims of the Great Depression: Self-Blame/Non-Self Blame, Radicalism, and Pre-1929 Experiences," *Social Science History* 1 (Winter 1977): 137–177; Thomas H. Coode and John F. Bauman, " 'Dear Mr. Hopkins': A New Dealer Reports from Eastern Kentucky," *Register of the Kentucky Historical Society* 78 (1980): 55–63.

8. Frances Perkins, *The Roosevelt I Knew* (New York: Viking, 1946), 279.

9. The debate in the Senate is in *CR,* 73-2, June 12 and 14, 1934, 11482–11489. The Railroad Retirement Act is in *U.S. Statutes 1934,* 1283–1289. The Senate hearings on the bill are summarized in *New York Times,* January 12, 1934, 25; January 14, 1934, 21; January 17, 1934, 27; January 18, 1934, 34; January 19, 1934, 25; January 20, 1934, 26.

10. See Harry L. Hopkins, "Social Planning for the Future," in *National Conference of Social Work 1934,* 69–79.

11. See Joseph C. Dougherty, Jr., "The Genesis of the Social Security Act of 1935" (diss., Georgetown University, 1955).

12. See Perkins, *Roosevelt I Knew,* 286.

13. The November 9 date is in Edwin E. Witte, *The Development of the Social Security Act: A Memorandum on the History of the Committee on Economic Security and Drafting and Legislative History of the Social Security Act* (Madison: University of Wisconsin Press, 1963). The book was actu-

ally written in 1963, but it was based on diaries Witte kept while he was executive director of the CES.

14. The Byrd objections are in Witte, ibid., 143–144. Objections that the poor states cannot meet matching requirements are in House Committee on Ways and Means, *Hearings,* February 7, 1935, 1084 (Representative Colmer of Mississippi).

15. Witte, *Development of the Social Security Act,* 147.

16. On the CES and health insurance, see esp. CES Papers, National Archives, Box 40; Witte to Robinson, December 8, 1934 (telegram), in ibid. The story is told in some detail in Witte, *Development of the Social Security Act,* 173–189. See also Arthur J. Altmeyer, *The Formative Years of Social Security* (Madison: University of Wisconsin Press, 1966), 57–58; I. M. Rubinow, "Health Insurance," *National Conference of Social Work 1934,* 376–389 (the quotation is on p. 376).

17. On the Social Security bill, see Senate Finance Committee (74-1), *Hearings on S. 1130,* 921–940 (NAM); ibid., 900–906 (Kellog); 640–646 (Houston); 439 (Andrews); 1217–1219 (Browder); 1015–1051 (Townsend). There were also hearings before the House Committee on Ways and Means and the House Committee on Labor. In its revised form the Townsend bill, known as the "McGroarty bill" (H.R. 7154), was based on a much ridiculed "transaction tax." This tax was not very different from what has been used by several countries since World War II and called "value-added tax." See also Abraham Holtzman, *The Townsend Movement: A Political Study* (New York: Bookman, 1963).

18. 295 U.S. 330 (1935).

19. The second version of the act is *Public Laws 1935,* chap. 811, 967–974. The taxing provisions were formally another law, chap. 813, 974–977.

20. The votes are recorded in *CR,* 74-1, H.R. 6070 and S. 9650.

21. See Clarke A. Chambers, "Social Security: The Welfare Consensus of the New Deal," in Wilbur J. Cohen (ed.), *The Roosevelt New Deal: A Program Assessment Fifty Years After* (Austin: Lyndon B. Johnson School of Public Affairs, 1986), 145–159. The law is in *Public Laws 1935,* chap. 531.

22. *Stewart Machine Co. v. Davis,* 301 U.S. 548 (1937), 502; *Helvering v. Davis,* 301 U.S. 619 (1937), 503.

23. See *Labor Laws and Their Administration, 1937,* Bureau of Labor Statistics Bulletin 653 (Washington, D.C., 1938), 7–12.

24. See also Arthur J. Altmeyer, *The Formative Years of Social Security* (Madison: University of Wisconsin Press, 1966); Social Security Board, *Social Security in America: The Factual Background of the Social Security Act as Summarized from Staff Reports to the Committee on Economic Security* (Washington, D.C., 1937); Theron F. Schlabach, *Edwin E. Witte: Cautious Reformer* (Madison, Wis.: State Historical Society, 1969); Edward D. Berkowitz and Kim McQuaid, *Creating the Welfare State: The Political Economy of Twentieth-Century Reform* (New York: Praeger, 1980).

Chapter 19. Assumptions and Perceptions

1. See Jens Alber, *Vom Armenhaus zum Wohlfahrtstaan: Analysen zur Entwicklung der Sozialversicherung in Westeuropa* (Frankfurt a.M. and New York: Campus, 1982).

2. Henry Demerest Lloyd, *Wealth against Commonwealth* (New York, 1894), 2.

3. Jürgen Kocka, *Angestellte zwischen Faschismus und Demokratie* (Göttingen: Vandenhoeck and Ruprecht, 1977), 174–175.

4. P. W. J. Barstrip, "State Intervention in Mid-Nineteenth-Century Britain: Fact or Fiction?" *Journal of British Studies* 23 (Fall 1983): 63–83, details the ineffectiveness of the inspectorate system.

5. In considering more broadly this question of whether Germany deviated from historical developments in other Western European countries or whether Germany followed a *Sonderweg*, it seems clear that the latter viewpoint assumes that Great Britain is politically normative. This is particularly true for "liberal" or "whiggish" historians. At the same time, economic or class developments in Germany are regarded as normative, particularly by Marxist or leftist historians. "Warum gibt es in den Vereinigten Staaten Kein Sozialismus?" asked Werner Sombart in 1906. Sombart assumed that a lack in the United States of something that existed in Germany needed explanation. A great number of historians have tried to answer his question on the assumption that the growth of socialism among factory workers is natural and that a lack of socialism must be due to some interfering factor. On the other hand, scholars ask about a *Sonderweg* in Germany on the assumption that Great Britain or France provides the *Normaleweg*. Again, the deviation from the "normal" defines the factor that needs explanation. Why make these normative assumptions about "workers" or "the democratic tradition"? My point throughout this book is that of course Germany followed a *Sonderweg*—but so did everyone else. For a brief introduction to how the controversy stood in 1984, see Robert J. Moeller, "The Kaiserreich Recast? Continuity and Change in Modern German Historiography," *Journal of Social History* 17 (Summer 1984): 655–683. A full summary of the *Sonderweg* controversy would be out of place here. A good brief historiographic survey is in David Blackbourn and Geoff Eley, *The Peculiarities of German History: Bourgeois Society and Politics in Nineteenth-Century Germany* (Oxford and New York: Oxford University Press, 1984), 10–14. The whole book is really about the controversy and whether Great Britain constitutes the kind of model from which Germany is supposed to have diverged. Blackbourn and Eley's point of view (among others) is put into historiographical context by Wolfgang Mock, " 'Manipulation von oben' oder Selbstorganisation an der Basis? Einige neure Ansätze in der englischen Historiographie zur Geschichte des deutschen Kaiserreichs," *Historiche Zeitschrift* 232 (1981): 358–375.

6. The "Inner Mission" in Denmark was something different. It was a special kind of religious fundamentalism and puritanism, not service in a foreignlike region of the country.

7. The creation by the Social Democratic Party of a world beyond politics, a complete worker culture, almost a closed and self-sufficient world, is dealt with in May Nolan, *Social Democracy and Society: Working-Class Radicalism in Düsseldorf, 1890–1920* (Cambridge: Cambridge University Press, 1981), 135–145; and by Wilholm L. Guttsman, *The German Social Democratic Party from Ghetto to Government* (London: Allen and Unwin, 1981), 194–200. See also Peter N. Stearns, "The Unskilled and Industrialization: A Transformation of Consciousness," *Archiv für Sozialgeschichte* 16 (1976): 249–282. Glenn R. McDougall's "Franz Mehring and the Problem of Liberal Social Reform in Bismarckian Germany, 1884–1890: The Origins of Radical Marxism," *Central European History* 16 (September 1983): 225–255, is a provocative article that shows how difficult it was to attempt any nonsocialist reforms. McDougall finds class divisions too bitter and the Social Democratic Party too isolated for any attempts at a bourgeois-worker alliance. Carl Zengerl's "Modern Germany (1800–1945): The Workingclass Experience," *Trends in History* 1 (1979): 66–74, is a review article, some of which is relevant. An insightful recent discussion is in Vernon L. Lidtke, *The Alternative Culture: Socialist Labor in Imperial Germany* (New York and Oxford: Oxford University Press, 1985). E. P. Thompson, *The Making of the English Working Class* (New York: Vintage, 1962), asserts the same thing for England. Birgitte Emig, *Die Veredelung des Arbeiters: Sozialdemokratie as Kulturbewegung* (Frankfurt a.M. and New York: Campus, 1980), is a complex nuanced study.

8. Jürgen Kocka, *White Collar Workers in America, 1890–1940: A Social Political History in International Perspective* (Beverly Hills, Calif.: Sage Publications, 1980), 255, 265. The statement is not quite true because household servants and agricultural workers were not included.

9. Ibid., 309.

10. Jürgen Kocka, "Stand-Klasse-Organisation. Strukturen sozialer Ungleicheit in Deutschland vom späten 18. is zum frühen 20. Jahrhundert im Afriss," in *Klassen in der europäischen Sozialgeschichte* (Göttingen: Vandenhoeck and Ruprecht, 1979), 137–165 (the quotations are on pp. 138–139).

11. Frances Fox Piven and Richard A. Cloward, *Regulating the Poor* (New York: Pantheon, 1971), is an extreme example of this view in relation to Great Britain and the United States.

12. Some German analysts argue that the various social insurance schemes were meant as an alternative to the *Freie Hilfskassen* and were a subtle way of repressing a worker-controlled institution, perhaps the seed for a different kind of development than what actually occurred in Germany. Some employers preferred to have their workers remain in the *Hilfskassen,* to which employers did not have to contribute. In any case,

there is no indication in any of the debates that destroying the *Hilfskassen* was the intent of the lawmakers. F. M. L. Thompson, "Social Control in Victorian Britain," *Economic History Review,* 2d ser., 34 (1981): 189–208, and Martin K. Wiener's review of A. P. Donajgrodski, "Social Control in Nineteenth-Century Britain," in the *Journal of Social History* 12 (1978–79): 313–320, are good discussions of the whole issue.

13. On welfare in the Reagan years, see Peter Gottschalk, "Retrenchment in Antipoverty Programs in the U.S.: Lessons for the Future" (photocopied typescript in author's possession, 1987). See also *New York Times,* March 6, 1988, on recent expansion in the Medicare program.

14. David Stockman, *The Triumph of Politics: How the Reagan Revolution Failed* (New York: Harper and Row, 1986), 394.

Index

Abardare Commission (1895) (G.B.),
110, 111
accident insurance, 92, 93, 151, 155–
156, 162, 306n11. *See also individual
countries*
Accident Prevention and Relief
(Schwedtman and Emery), 155
Achinger, Hans, 8
Addams, Jane, 120, 122, 123, 124, 125,
294n12
aged, the, in poorhouses and workhouses (G.B.), 104, 133, 114. *See also*
old-age pensions
Agricultural Adjustment Administration (U.S.), 242
agricultural workers excluded from insurance coverage, 91, 161, 217, 220,
253, 335n8
agriculture during the Great Depression, 211, 230
aid to dependent children (U.S.): federal
249, 252; state, 233, 240, 251, 257. *See
also* mother's pension laws
aid funds (*Hilfskassen*) (Ger.), 57, 64,
300n20, 335–336n12
Alabama, 256
Alaska, 232
Alber, Jens, 7
all-in insurance, 215, 220–221, 224
allowance system (Speenhamland System) (G.B.), 19, 21, 22, 43

Alsace-Lorraine, 41, 296n3
American Association for Labor Legislation (AALL), 36, 152–153, 157, 231,
254; Conference on Social Insurance
(1913), 172; joined by American Association for Old-Age Legislation (1927),
232; and health insurance bill (1916),
145, 172–173, 174, 175, 176, 177
American Association for Old-Age Legislation, 232
American Charities (Warner), 32
American Economic Association (AEA),
48
American Federation of Labor (AFL),
156, 157, 174
American Federationist, 173
American Journal of Sociology, 126
American Labor Legislation Review,
172, 173, 177
American Medical Association (AMA),
173, 178, 252–253
Ancient Order of Foresters (G.B.), 105,
142
Anderson, Martin, 15
Andrews, John B., 36, 174, 231, 254
angelernt (semiskilled) labor (Ger.), 273
angemessene (suitable work) (Ger.), 191
Angestellte, unselbständige (dependent
salaried employees/white-collar workers) (Ger.), 3, 66–67, 68, 273, 297nn3
and 4, 302n9